'We all want happier, healthier and more productive working lives and two-way flexibility is a key part of the answer. A driving force in this book is the compelling argument around how we make flexible working work to give workers more control over where and how they work. This is essential reading for anyone who wants to build better, fairer and more humane workplaces.'

—*Frances O'Grady, General Secretary, Trades
Union Congress (TUC), UK*

'Disruptive changes in the nature of work and of working life have far-reaching implications for human and economic health and wellbeing across society. This book provides essential foundations for wise and well-informed discussions to guide the actions now necessary.'

—*Professor Dame Carol Black, Advisor on Health and
Work to Public Health England and UK National
Health Service Improvement*

I0130831

Flexible Work

Flexible Work: Designing Our Healthier Future Lives examines flexible working through the lens of social science, in particular using psychological perspectives to address not only what forms of flexible working there are and how they are evolving but also their prospect in the future of work. Bringing together views from thought-leaders and underpinned by research evidence, this book addresses two of the most fundamental business challenges for large and medium organisations – mental health and productivity – calling for the bridging of science and policy to design flexible working for our future healthier lives.

Growing from these foundations, this book explains the latest landscape in flexible working, looking at employee psychological health and productivity, including showing up for work sick. Perspectives are provided from around the world on leadership, line management, 'over attachment' with technology, commuting, skill-based inequality and control over working time. Readers are offered insights into the relevance of flexible working for a diverse workforce – invisible disabilities, disabilities, older workers and blended families. Throughout, the book offers suggestions for shaping future policy, practice and research.

Each chapter concludes with recommendations, making this essential reading for students, academics, human resource practitioners, policy-influencers, policymakers and professionals interested in flexible work.

Dr Sarah H. Norgate was formerly a Reader in Applied Developmental Psychology at the University of Salford, UK, and is a popular science author. Since completing her PhD at the University of Warwick, UK, she has widely published in both academic and practitioner journals and has enjoyed collaborating with diverse stakeholders on award-winning research. Sarah is also a fellow for life with the Winston Churchill Memorial Trust.

Sir Cary L. Cooper is the 50th Anniversary Professor of Organizational Psychology and Health at the ALLIANCE Manchester Business School, University of Manchester, UK, President of the CIPD and Co-Chair of the National Forum for Health and Wellbeing at Work.

Current Issues in Work and Organizational Psychology
Series Editor: Cary Cooper

Current Issues in Work and Organizational Psychology is a series of edited books that reflect the state-of-the-art areas of current and emerging interest in the psychological study of employees, workplaces and organizations.

Each volume is tightly focused on a particular topic and consists of seven to ten chapters contributed by international experts. The editors of individual volumes are leading figures in their areas and provide an introductory overview.

Example topics include: digital media at work, work and the family, work-aholism, modern job design, positive occupational health and individualised deals.

Flexible Work
Designing Our Healthier Future Lives
Edited by Sarah H. Norgate & Cary L. Cooper

Current Issues in Work and Organizational Psychology
Edited by Cary Cooper

Organizational Change
Psychological Effects and Strategies for Coping
Edited by Maria Vakola and Paraskevas Petrou

The Psychology of Humor at Work
Edited by Christopher Robert

Time and Work, Volume 1
How Time Impacts Individuals
Edited by Abbie J. Shipp and Yitzhak Fried

Time and Work, Volume 2
How Time Impacts Groups, Organizations and Methodological Choices
Edited by Abbie J. Shipp and Yitzhak Fried

For more information about this series, please visit: https://www.routledge.com/Current-Issues-in-Work-and-Organizational-Psychology/book-series/CURRENTISSUES

Flexible Work

Designing Our Healthier Future Lives

Edited by
Sarah H. Norgate and
Cary L. Cooper

Routledge
Taylor & Francis Group

LONDON AND NEW YORK

First published 2020
by Routledge
2 Park Square, Milton Park, Abingdon, Oxon OX14 4RN

and by Routledge
52 Vanderbilt Avenue, New York, NY 10017

Routledge is an imprint of the Taylor & Francis Group, an informa business

British Library Cataloguing-in-Publication Data
A catalogue record for this book is available from the British Library

Library of Congress Cataloging-in-Publication Data
A catalog record has been requested for this book

ISBN: 978-0-367-20845-5 (hbk)
ISBN: 978-0-367-34566-2 (pbk)
ISBN: 978-0-429-32658-5 (ebk)

Typeset in Bembo
by codeMantra

Contents

Figures

Tables

Contributors

Carol Atkinson is Professor of Human Resource Management, based in Manchester Metropolitan University Business School's Centre for Decent Work and Productivity, UK. She teaches Human Resource Management (HRM) to undergraduate and postgraduate students and her research interests include: intersections of gender, age and careers, focusing on gender pay gaps, older workers and flexibility, older women's careers and the menopause in the workplace; employment in adult social care, exploring employment practice and its implications for recruitment, retention and care quality; employment in small and medium-sized firms. Carol is on the Editorial Board of Work, Employment and Society and member of a number of learned societies.

Julian Barling FRSC is author of *The Science of Leadership: Lessons from Research for Organizational Leaders* (Oxford University Press, 2014). His research focuses primarily on the development of leadership. Julian has authored over 200 research articles, book chapters and several books, and he has served as editor of the *Journal of Occupational Health Psychology*. Julian is a fellow for the Royal Society of Canada and several other international organisations. He has received 'Distinguished Contribution' awards for this research from several organizations, including the European Association for Occupational Health Psychology and the C–SIOP Division of the Canadian Psychological Association. Julian has received several teaching awards, including the Award for Excellence in Graduate Student Supervision from Queen's University, Ontario.

Kate Bell is Head of the Rights, International, Social and Economics department at the TUC, UK. The TUC exists to make the working world a better place for everyone. We bring together more than 5.5 million working people who make up our 48 member unions.

Duygu Biricik Gulseren holds an MA degree in Social and Organizational Psychology. She is currently a PhD student in Industrial/Organizational Psychology at Saint Mary's University, Nova Scotia. Her research interests include leading healthy workplaces, chronic pain at work and the work-family interface.

Paula Brough is Professor of Organisational Psychology in the School of Applied Psychology at Griffith University in Brisbane, Australia, and Leader of the Occupational Health Psychology Research Lab. Paula's primary research areas are occupational stress and coping, employee mental health and wellbeing, work engagement, work-life balance, workplace conflict (bullying, harassment, toxic leadership) and the psychosocial work environment. Paula assesses how work environments can be improved via job redesign, supportive leadership practices, and enhanced equity to improve employee health, work commitment, and productivity. Paula works with a variety of organisations to reduce their employee's experiences of stress and burnout, and to improve employees' wellbeing, mental health and work-life balance. Paula has authored over 60 industry reports, over 100 journal articles and book chapters, and has authored six scholarly books based on her research.

Xi Wen (Carys) Chan is Lecturer in Management at the School of Management, College of Business, RMIT University in Melbourne, Australia. She graduated with BCom (Hons) in 2013 and PhD (Organisational Behaviour & Human Resources) in 2018 from the Australian National University. Her research interests are in the work-life interface, specifically exploring the link between personal resources (e.g., self-efficacy) and various work- and non-work-related demands, resources and outcomes. She is also working on projects on patient mistreatment victimisation, the boundaryless work-life interface, and the effects of personal and organisational humour on employees' work-life conflict. Her work has been published in the *International Journal of Human Resource Management*, *British Journal of Social Work*, *Personnel Review*, *International Journal of Manpower* and *Frontiers in Psychology*. Carys is also a regular employment relations and work-life contributor to Channel NewsAsia; she has also been featured in media outlets such as Business Insider Australia, HR Daily and CNA938.

Peter Cheese is the chief executive of the CIPD, the professional body for human resources (HR) and people development, with a membership of more than 155,000 HR and people development professionals around the world. He writes and speaks widely on the development of HR, the future of work, and the key issues of leadership, culture and organisation, people and skills. He has been recognised with three honorary doctorates, and is a fellow of the CIPD, AHRI (the Australian HR Institute) and the Academy of Social Sciences. He's also a companion of the Institute of Leadership and Management, the Chartered Management Institute and the British Academy of Management.

Sharon Clarke PhD is full Professor of Organizational Psychology at Alliance Manchester Business School, University of Manchester, UK. She has research interests in leadership, health and well-being and workplace safety. Her work has been widely published in leading academic and practitioner journals,. She has also co-authored books, including *Human Safety and Risk Management* now in its third edition (CRC Press, 2015). She is currently editor-in-chief for the *Journal of Occupational and Organizational Psychology* and associate editor for the *Journal of Occupational Health Psychology*.

Anika Cloutier is a PhD candidate studying in Organizational Behaviour at the Smith School of Business, Ontario. Her research focuses primarily on the antecedents of leadership, the work-family interface and occupational health. Anika has presented her research findings at international conferences and has published several articles. She has received numerous research talent awards, including the junior PhD research award at Queen's University, Ontario.

Cary L. Cooper is the 50th Anniversary Professor of Organizational Psychology & Health at the ALLIANCE Manchester Business School, University of Manchester, UK. He is President of the CIPD, Immediate Past President of the British Academy of Management, President of the Institute of Welfare and Co-Chair of the National Forum for Health and Wellbeing at Work (an employer's forum of 38 global companies and public sector bodies). He was awarded a knighthood by the Queen in 2014 for his contributions to the social sciences.

Anna Mary Cooper-Ryan is a Lecturer in Public Health at the University of Salford, UK, having completed a first degree in Psychology with Neuropsychology, a Master's in Counselling Psychology Studies and a PhD in Public Health. Anna has carried out a number of research projects for local community organisations and councils to evaluate their services and explore the current evidence base around a number of services. Anna's research focuses on behaviour change interventions, with a particular interest in the use of digital data collection tools within interventions and when evaluating interventions.

Alexandra Duval holds an MSc in Applied Psychology focusing on Industrial/Organizational Psychology. She is currently a commissioned officer in the Canadian Armed Forces, serving in the Personnel Selection Officer's Branch. Her research interests include fatigue at work, work-life balance, flexible work arrangements and employee selection.

Aristides I. Ferreira is an Assistant Professor at ISCTE – Lisbon University Institute, Portugal. He is also a researcher at the Business Research Unit in the same institute. He has more than 60 papers published in impact factor journals such as the *Journal of Organizational Behavior*, the *British Journal of Management*, the *Journal of Business Research*, the *International Journal of Project Management* and the *International Journal of Human Resource Management*. He has six books published and one computerised battery to assess human memory that will be published soon by Hogrefe.

Caroline Gatrell joined Liverpool University, UK, in 2016 as Professor of Organization Studies within the Management School. Her research centres on work, family and health. From a socio-cultural perspective, she examines how working parents manage the boundaries between paid work and their everyday lives. In so doing, Caroline explores the relationships between gender, bodies and employment, including development of the concept 'Maternal Body Work'. This construct describes how pregnant women, and/or mothers of infant children try to meet social expectations of 'good' mothering while also seeking to present themselves at work as committed employees. Following the award of a Leverhulme Fellowship in 2018, Caroline has been seeking to understand more about how fathers of dependent children reconcile masculine images of men as 'ideal workers' with notions of involved fatherhood.

Abolanle Gbadamosi is a PhD student at the University of Salford, UK, with a first degree in Microbiology and a Master's in Public Health. Abolanle's research focuses on the impact of commuting moderate-to-vigorous physical activity on metabolic markers. Abolanle's research interests also focuses on the objective measurement of physical activity, particularly with the use of the activPAL and other accelerometer-based devices.

Eleftherios Giovanis studied Economics at the University of Thessaly, Greece. He completed his MSc in Applied Economics and Finance at the University of Macedonia, Greece, and his MSc in Quality Assurance at the Hellenic Open University, Greece, in 2009. He completed his PhD in Economics at Royal Holloway University of London, UK. He was awarded the Marie Sklodowska-Curie Research Individual Fellowship at the University of Verona, Italy, in 2015 and he worked as Assistant Professor in Economics at Adnan Menderes University, Turkey, in 2017. He is currently Senior Lecturer in Economics at Manchester Metropolitan University, UK, and Marie Sklodowska-Curie fellow at Adnan Menderes University.

Sarah Jackson OBE is a leading expert on work-life issues in the UK. She led the work-life charity Working Families for 24 years and was appointed OBE for services to quality-of-life issues in 2007. She is Visiting Professor at Cranfield University School of Management, UK, and Chair of the industry campaign Parents and Carers in Performing Arts. Sarah has been instrumental in shaping family-friendly policy, legislation and public attitudes in the UK for over two decades. Her work with Jonathan Swan has included the development of the annual Working Families/Bright Horizons *Modern Families Index*.

E. Kevin Kelloway is the Canada Research Chair in Occupational Health Psychology and Professor of Psychology at Saint Mary's University, Nova Scotia. His research focuses on organisational and occupational health psychology including the study of occupational stress, safety, leadership and well-being.

Bernice Kotey is Professor of Entrepreneurship and Small & Medium Enterprise (SME) Development at the University of New England, Australia. She has published on a range of management issues affecting SMEs and the impact of the macro-environment on their operations. Her current focus is on human resource (HR) practices of SMEs, in particular, how SMEs are affected by and manage the flexible work needs of their employees. In relation to context, her research examines SMEs in local, regional, developing and developed economies. Bernice is a Certified Practicing Accountant (Australia) and completed the Education Management Program in Harvard in 2010.

Sara L. Lopes is a PhD student in Management at ISCTE-IUL – Lisbon University Institute, Portugal. She is also a researcher at the Business Research Unit in the same university. She received a BSc in Psychology and an MSc in Social Organizational Psychology from ISCTE-IUL. Her main research areas are presenteeism and leadership. In 2019 she started to develop teaching activities as an Invited Assistant Professor at ISCTE-IUL.

Nicola J. Millard in her long and varied career at British Telecommunications (BT), has done numerous jobs, including futurology, research, usability, customer service, marketing and business consulting. She was involved with a number of BT firsts, including the first application of artificial intelligence into BT's call centres and BT's initial experiments with home working. Her current areas of specialism are customer experience and the future of work. Nicola got her PhD in Computer Science from Lancaster University, UK, in 2005, and published her first book in 2009. She is an award-winning presenter, with two TED talks and hundreds of conference sessions under her belt.

Sarah H. Norgate PhD was formerly Reader in Applied Developmental Psychology at the University of Salford, UK, and is a popular science author (*Beyond 9 to 5: Your Life in Time*, Weidenfeld and Nicolson, 2006). She has research interests in people's health, well-being and digital environments. Her research has been widely published in academic and practitioner journals, and she is a fellow for life with the Winston Churchill Memorial Trust. Since completing her PhD at the University of Warwick, UK, she has directed and/or mentored award-winning research funded by research councils and charities and supervised to completion five PhD students.

Oznur Ozdamar is Associate Professor of Economics and Head of the Department of Econometrics in the Faculty of Economics at Adnan Menderes University, Turkey. She received her PhD from the IMT Institute for

Advanced Studies in Italy. During her PhD degree, she was research fellow at Northwestern University in the US. She was postdoctoral research fellow at the Department of Economics, University of Bologna, Italy. Her research interests include economics of health, environment, labour, gender and the evaluation of the impact of social welfare policies.

Laura Radcliffe joined Liverpool University Management School, UK, in 2014 and is currently Director of the Master of Research Programme. Her research centres on the intersection of work and family, with a particular focus on daily work-family practices, routines and decision-making. In exploring these practices, she also examines the influence of gendered norms and the impact on organisational diversity and inclusivity. To explore these issues, she draws on methodological approaches that have the ability to capture rich insights into peoples lived, daily experiences, with a particular interest in qualitative diary methods. Her research has been published in journals such as *Human Relations* and the *Journal of Occupational and Organisational Psychology*.

Egidio Riva is Associate Professor of Economic Sociology in the Department of Sociology and Social Research at the University of Milano-Bicocca, Italy. His research currently focuses on work-family policies and practices, the relationship between job quality, health and well-being, and ethnic entrepreneurship. His work has appeared in journals such as *Community, Work and Family, Employee Relations, Industrial Relations Journal, International Journal of Sociology and Social Policy, Journal of Ethnic and Migration Studies, Quality and Quantity* and *Social Indicators Research*.

Marcello Russo is Associate Professor of Organizational Behaviour and Human Resource Management at the University of Bologna, Italy. He is also Director of the Global MBA at Bologna Business School, Italy. He is an expert on work-life balance, with a focus on what individual strategies and organisational factors can help individuals accomplish their ideal model of work-life balance. His work has been published in *Harvard Business Review, Journal of Management, Journal of Vocational Behavior, Human Resource Management Review* and *Human Resource Management Journal*.

Anneke Schaefer is a PhD candidate in Organisational Behaviour at the University of Liverpool Management School, UK. Her research interests include contemporary fatherhood, non-traditional parenthood, how family transitions unfold over time and how this interacts with people's experiences managing their work and family commitments. Her PhD investigates the impacts of relationship transitions on parents' work-family experiences and their evolving self-concepts. Furthermore, she is currently working on a research project with the theme 'fathering in the absence of mothers', exploring how gay and/or lone fathers navigate employment and intensive caregiving.

Charlotte Stonier achieved a first-class degree in Psychology and Coun-selling at the University of Salford, where she now teaches Biological and Cognitive Psychology. Having also worked in psychiatric care with personality disorder and eating disorder patients, Charlotte intends to further her knowledge and experience of psychology with a three year Clinical Doctorate. This will secure her career as a Clinical Psychologist and enable further progression in the field of mental health. Charlotte is particularly interested in the relationship between neurochemical behav-iour and emotion dysregulation and hopes to integrate neurobiology into her person-centred approach to therapeutic practice. Charlotte's research interests also include investigating the structural brain changes linked to psychological trauma.

Jonathan Swan is Head of Research at Working Families. He has researched and written on work life issues for over 18 years. His work covers flexi-ble working, organisational culture and the changing role of fathers. He has collaborated on a number of influential research projects, including the experience of fathers combining work and family, and work-life bal-ance post-austerity. He is responsible for the annual *Modern Families Index*, which places family-friendly working debates within current policy con-texts. He has acted as adviser to the European Institute of Gender Equality on good working practices for women in STEM sectors.

Carolyn Timms is Lecturer in Psychology at James Cook University in Cairns, Australia. Her passion for researching antecedents of workers' psy-chological health and ill-health stemmed originally from personal experi-ence in her previous career as a high school teacher and has expanded since she embarked on an academic career in 2005. Carolyn's research interests encompass job burnout and engagement, career motivation, work-life bal-ance, and organisational culture. Carolyn's focus has been on examining aspects of the work environment that inspire or impede the full expression of workers' creative, ingenious and resourceful contributions to organisa-tional productivity and prosperity.

Stuart Wark is Associate Professor with the School of Rural Medicine at the University of New England, Australia. He has a 25-year working history in the community and public health sectors, and his specific research foci include intellectual disability, ageing, end-of-life care, mental health and rurality. He has worked extensively with unpaid carers, with a particular focus on determining how health services can better support individuals to continue to provide care for disadvantaged or at-risk groups.

Part I

Introduction

1 Designing our healthier future lives: Bridging science and policy for flexible work

The pervasion of 'cog in the wheel' workplaces across time

Sarah H. Norgate and Cary L. Cooper

Most of us, at one time or another, in our working lives have experienced disillusionment at the feeling of being a cog in our organizational wheel, enslaved by the pressing number of demands, low control, the sense of being unrecognized and readily disposable. Alongside our own subjective reflections, social scientists have also grappled to increase understanding of the nature of workers' negative perceptions of their relationship between themselves and their organizations. For instance, *'All they lack is a chain'* was originally a remark made by Braverman (as cited in Carter et al. 2011) while observing keypunch operators at work at an insurance company in the 1970s. Yet four decades later, similar observations persist in the twenty first century. The example of work conditions in call centres (e.g. Kim & Choo, 2017) and Amazon warehouses (Briken & Taylor, 2018) are already well publicized in the media. In addition, researchers have identified problematic cases like working in the hospitality industry services (Walker, 2017), doing public sector office clerical work (Carter et al., 2011), or working in a large hierarchy *per se* (Searle, 2019).

As we move into the fourth industrial revolution, the advent of automation and robots push into the foreground the need to redefine relationships between workers and employers. Yet within the context of manufacturing industries, where growth would be expected to be fastest, the greatest uptake of industrial robot workers only hovers around 710 and 658 robots per 10,000 employees in South Korea and Singapore, respectively (Statista, 2019). In the event of any future reports showing a slow use of robots by key adopters, then there seems a case to prioritize the design of jobs and work environments with and for humans in ways that prevent work related stress and add healthy value to our lives. And in the event of the converse scenario, where robot workers turn out to be more diffuse within and across sectors, then the challenge will shift toward the creation of new occupations.

As this brief historical take has shown, 'cog in the wheel' workplaces in industrialized societies are readily identified by researchers. The next step is to chart the health, psychological, and economic consequences of stressful workplaces, which in turn will enable us to focus on the purpose of this book, the quest to design our future healthier working lives.

The health, psychological, and economic costs of work-related stress

Whilst some degree of stress in our lives enhances performance (e.g. Kirby et al., 2013), psychological stress has a detrimental impact on health (Blanc-Lapierre *et al.,* 2017). At a day-to-day level, indicators of working in stressful workplaces include those where workers lack a sense of control over work (Liu, McGonagle & Fisher, 2018), demands are high (Maslach & Leiter, 2017), workers are not involved in setting the pace or volume, and do not participate in decision making about when to take a break or how, and where and when their work is undertaken (for review, see Cooper & Quick, 2017). Psychologically, there is agreement that work characteristics (e.g. job control) and worker attributes (e.g. locus of control) both contribute negatively to workers' mental health and work performance (Bond & Bunce, 2003) with research associating work stressors to poor mental health (cardiovascular disease (Schnall, Dobson & Landsbergid, 2017), cancer (Blanc-Lapierre et al., 2017) and lifestyle – for instance, alcohol consumption (Kouvonen et al., 2008).

Significantly, burnout is now recognized as an occupational phenomenon arising from chronic workplace stress and characterized by exhaustion, increased mental distance from job and reduced professional efficacy (International Classification Disease (ICD), 2019). Further, the World Health Organization (WHO, 2019) estimate that depression and anxiety cost the global economy US$1 trillion in lost productivity. Estimates of the costs pan-Europe uncovered the financial burden estimated between US$221 to $187 million (Hassard, Teoh, Visockaite et al., 2018). Nationally, estimates of mental health problems at work cost the UK economy £34.9 billion (Centre for Mental Health, 2018), with the largest proportion of the business cost attributed to reduced productivity in the form of presenteeism, where people turn up at work but are unwell. The Chartered Institute of Personnel and Development's (CIPD, 2018) report showed that more than 1,000 people responded to the survey and 86% of them said they had observed presenteeism over the course of 12 months. On the ground, one in six people experience mental health issues in the workplace and 12% of all sickness absence in the UK is attributed to mental health conditions (Centre for Mental Health, 2018).

Given these twin challenges of health and productivity, the next step is to bridge science and policy to enable scope to design future healthier lives at work.

Bridging science and policy to design healthier future lives at work: A flexible working future

The purpose of the book is to harness research evidence from social science, together with views from thought leaders to inform policy creation around the big challenges in productivity and mental health to impact positively on the future of healthy work, and specifically to make flexible working work. Although legislation (e.g. The Australian Fair Work Act, 2009; the US Telework Enhancement Act, 2010; the UK Flexible Working Regulations, 2014; Netherlands Flexible Working Act, 2016; Finnish Government Working Hours Act, 2019 etc.) has been passed in a number of countries to enable organizations to offer flexible work arrangements (FWAs) – either temporally based (e.g. reduced hours, compressed hours, part-time) or spatial (e.g. remote-working) to enable employees to balance their competing life responsibilities – on the ground, as we shall see, there have been barriers to implementation.

After introducing the key concepts in flexible working, this book's focus is initially on the twin challenges of psychological health and productivity, before considering what makes flexible working work and the considerations needed for different types of workers. Each chapter closes with a set of recommendations for use in policy, research, or practice. Taking together the relevant evidence, together with insights from thought-leaders, there is scope to drive policy-making forwards. While the Finnish Parliament is already trailblazing change in the workplace and gender equality having introduced the Working Hours Act 2020, which will mean working hours do not need to be tied to a specific place of work, and therefore is expected to smooth the navigation of agreements around work done from home.

Collectively, the contributors to this book have made a number of suggestions to inform future policy, practice, and research. To offer a flavour, highlights are offered below under each respective book section, with more detail found within each chapter.

Book structure

Part I – Introduction

- To implement legislation and grow workplace cultures that are pro-flexible working (in particular, remote/virtual), to enhance mental health, productivity, and economies.
- Make the case for flexible working with evidence of how it is working today, where the barriers are, and the difference it can make to individual and organizational outcomes in your own organizational context.
- To really embed flexible working effectively, take a holistic approach looking at culture, management, job design, workspace design, and people management and HR practices.

Part II – The impact of flexible working on health and productivity

- Organization-wide education to promote pro-flexible working cultures and to reduce the flexibility stigma.
- To reduce presenteeism, encourage time off from work when needed.
- Develop public policy which supports the equalization of caring.

Part III – What makes flexible working work?

- Encourage HR trainers to engage leaders in developing relevant behaviours (e.g. to see that leaders personally make use of flexible work opportunities).
- Build a positive and supportive culture, which will help to mitigate challenges associated with flexible working.
- For future research, consider the concept of productivity in the digital workplace, and how it could be redefined.
- To be ambitious about enabling remote or virtual working to enhance mental and physical health, and in tandem, reduce the need for commuting.
- To take account of commute duration in relevant level policies.
- To unlink the provision of FWA from employee skill level.
- To encourage the commitment of flexible workers to develop greater awareness of their own connectivity behaviours and to identify strategies to reduce work intensification.
- To enable workers to have more control over when they work, get rid of zero-hour contracts.
- To create shorter working weeks as a way of sharing time wealth generated by technological innovation.

Part IV – Flexible working for particular groups of workers

- To identify the barriers to implementing FWAs.
- To enable those with invisible disabilities to benefit from access to a range of FWA so they could craft work experience to fit their health status.
- To make FWA available to all employees.
- To commission new research which involves non-stable family forms.
- To increase dependable care facilities.
- For older workers, undertake mid-life reviews.

References

Australian Fair Work Act (2009). Retrieved from https://www.alrc.gov.au/publication/grey-areas-age-barriers-to-work-in-commonwealth-laws-dp-78/2-recruitment-and-employment-law/the-fair-work-act-2009-cth

Blanc-Lapierre, A., Rousseau, M.C., Weiss, D., El-Zein, M., Siemiatycki, J., & Parent, M.E. (2017). Lifetime report of perceived stress at work and cancer among men: A case-control study in Montreal, Canada. *Preventive Medicine, 96*, 28–35.

Bond, F.W. & Bunce, D. (2003). The role of acceptance and job control in mental health, job satisfaction, and work performance. *Journal of Applied Psychology, 88*(6), 1057–1067.

Briken, K. & Taylor, P. (2018). Fulfilling the 'British way': Beyond constrained choice – Amazon workers' lived experiences of workfare. *Industrial Relations Journal, 49*(5–6), 438–458.

Carter, B., Danford, A., Howcrofy, D., Richardson, H., Smith, A., & Taylor, P. (2011). 'All they lack is a chain': Lean and the new performance management in the British civil service. *New Technology, Work and Employment, 26*(2), 83–97.

Centre for Mental Health (2018). Mental health problems at work cost the UK economy £34.9 bn, says Centre for Mental Health. Retrieved from https://www.centreformentalhealth.org.uk/news/mental-health-problems-work-cost-uk-economy-ps349bn-last-year-says-centre-mental-health

Chartered Institute of Personnel and Development (CIPD) (2018). Retrieved from https://www.cipd.co.uk/about/media/press/020518-health-wellbeing-survey

Cooper, C.L. & Quick, J.C. (2017). *The Handbook of Stress and Health*. Chichester, UK: Wiley Blackwell.

Finnish Government Working Hours Act (2019). Retrieved from https://valtioneuvosto.fi/en/article/-/asset_publisher/1410877/tyoaikalaki-uudistuu

Flexible Working Act (Netherlands) (2016). Retrieved from http://wetten.overheid.nl/BWBR0011173/2016-01-01

Flexible Working Regulations (UK) (2014). Retrieved from http://www.legislation.gov.uk/uksi/2014/1398/pdfs/uksi_20141398_en.pdf

Hassard, J., Teoh, K., Visockaite, G., Dewe, P., & Cox, T. (2018). The cost of work-related stress to society: A systematic review. *Journal of Occupational Health Psychology, 23*(1), 1–17.

International Classification Disease (ICD) (2019). Burn out an occupational phenomenon. Retrieved from https://www.who.int/mental_health/evidence/burn-out/en/

Kim, H.J. & Choo, J. (2017). Emotional labor: Links to depression and work-related musculoskeletal disorders in call center workers. *Workplace Health and Safety, 65*(8), 346–354.

Kirby, E.D., Muroy, S.E., Sun, W.G., Covarrubias, D., Leong, M.J., & Barchas, L.A. et al. (2013). Acute stress enhances adult rat hippocampal neurogenesis and activation of newborn neurons via secreted astrocytic FGF2. Retrieved from https://elifesciences.org/articles/00362 (eLife 2013;2:e00362 DOI: 10.7554/eLife.00362).

Kouvonen, A., Kivimäki, M., Elovainio, M., Väänänen, A., De Vogli, R., & Heponiemi, T. et al. (2008). Low organisational justice and heavy drinking: A prospective cohort study. *Occupational and Environmental Medicine, 65*, 44–50.

Liu, M., McGonagle, A.K., & Fisher, G.G. (2018). Sense of control, job stressors, and well-being: Inter-relations and reciprocal effects among older U.S. workers. *Work, Aging and Retirement, 4*(1), January, 96–107. Retrieved from https://doi.org/10.1093/workar/waw035

Maslach C. & Leiter, M.P. (2017). Understanding burnout: New models. In C.L. Cooper & J.C. Quick (eds), *The Handbook of Stress and Health*. Chichester, UK: Wiley Blackwell, pp. 36–570.

Schnall, P.L., Dobson, M., & Landsbergid, P. (2017). Work, stress and cardiovascular disease. In C.L. Cooper & J.C. Quick (eds), *The Handbook of Stress and Health*. Chichester, UK: Wiley Blackwell, pp. 99–125.

Searle, R. (2019, October). The human underpinning workplace resource. *The Psychologist*. Leicester, UK: The British Psychological Society, pp. 42–43.

Statista.com (2019, 29 April) The countries with the highest density of robot workers. Retrieved from https://www.statista.com/chart/13645/the-countries-with-the-highest-density-of-robot-workers

Telework Enhancement Act (US) (2010). Retrieved from: https://www.telework. gov/guidance-legislation/telework-legislation/telework-enhancement-act

Walker, M. (2017). Parallel narratives: Resistance strategies of low-wage female hospitality workers and nineteenth-century black enslaved females. *Labor History*, *58*(3), 372–395.

World Health Organization (WHO) (2019). Mental health in the workplace. Retrieved from https://www.who.int/mental_health/in_the_workplace/en

2 A flexible working future – the opportunities and challenges

Peter Cheese

Our working lives and the future of work

We are in times of significant change, living in a context that has been described as volatile, uncertain, complex and ambiguous. The drivers of change in work today certainly include the extraordinary developments of artificial intelligence, technology and automation, but we are also seeing significant political, social and demographic change impacting our workforces and workplaces.

Organisations and even whole industry sectors are having to rapidly adapt. New competitors and new business models are emerging, consumers' demands and expectations are rising, but so are societal expectations for responsible and more transparent businesses. Our workforces are increasingly diverse, with many different needs and demands. People expect to be treated respectfully and fairly, to have choice and for their voices to be heard, and to work for managers and organisations that care about them.

Technology is enabling so much more choice and options in where and how we work, and how we can work smarter and be more productive. But the hours and demands of work and the challenges of balancing work with the rest of our lives are contributing more and more to the growing levels of stress, and the huge societal issues of mental health and poor wellbeing. For a number of years now surveys such as those by the Chartered Institute of Personnel and Development (CIPD) have shown how stress has become the biggest source of long term absenteeism from work,[1] and workload or volume of work is the most frequently cited cause.

Yet our working patterns and norms, which have governed our ways of working for many decades, remain very familiar. The standard five day working week is deeply embedded in our cultures and define our rhythm of life. We all know songs that describe it – Dolly Parton's 1980 hit '9 to 5', or Sheena Easton's 1981 hit 'Morning Train (Nine to Five)' being catchy examples. Across all of the more developed nations in the Organisation for Economic Co-operation and Development (OECD), only around 17% of the workforce works other than what is usually described as a 'standard' full time job.[2]

Rather than reducing our hours of work, in more recent years the phenomenon of presenteeism where employees still come to work even when not fully well appears to be growing. As technology allows us to keep connected to work more of the time, the idea of presenteeism is extending to also mean working more hours than needed to fulfil work commitments. In all these cases, employees are prioritising being present over their health and wellbeing, driven by employees worrying about the security of their employment or feeling they have to prove their commitment to work. The CIPD and Simplyhealth's regular survey on health and wellbeing at work in 2018 reported that presenteeism had more than tripled since 2010.[3]

The case for more flexible working

Not only are these working hours and pressures not good for our overall wellbeing, they also impact productivity – an issue at the heart of a lot of economic debate and a key business imperative. Higher productivity is an outcome of positive physical and mental wellbeing. Something that Henry Ford understood, and demonstrated, when in 1926 he reduced working hours to eight hours per day and five days a week and increased basic pay at the Ford Motor Company. This became one of the pivotal points in the institutionalisation of the five-day, eight-hours-a-day working week.

Better wellbeing itself should be a compelling reason for us all to look at more flexible and balanced ways of working. But another critical driver is to support the increasingly diverse workforce that every business needs to attract and retain. So many groups are not fairly represented in work because they can't or don't want to work a full working week but can't find the opportunities or support to work the hours that they can – people with caring or other responsibilities in their lives, or with disabilities, or older workers, or those who simply want the choice.

It is evident that younger people will look for more flexibility at work, and whilst this will be driven by obvious lifestyle needs such as caring for young children, it may also be a shifting expectation of how they expect to be able to work. According to a 2013 survey by Deloitte,[4] over 90% of the millennial generation say that flexibility is a top priority. With increasing female participation in the workforce, the current generation of women are combining child care and work, with research from the UK Office for National Statistics (ONS) showing that 'the employment rate for mothers in the UK was 74.0% in April to June 2018, which has increased from 68.9% in 2013 and from 61.9% in 1996'.[5] Evidence from the British Social Attitudes Survey showed that there has been a decline in the view that women should stay at home if they have a child under school age – from 64% in 1989, to 33% now'.[6] A preference for flexible working is more than just an attitude, it's an economic necessity.

Other surveys around the world have shown that more people would trade longer time off work for pay. A survey by Samsung in 2014 reported that some 27% of their interviewees would trade flexible working over a pay rise.[7]

Underlying much of this thinking is the desire or need for people to have more control and choice over their lives and not just be driven by rules or routines controlled by others. Autonomy is a major driver of engagement as Dan Pink highlighted in his popular book *Drive*.[8] It is good to observe modern work practices and cultures shifting from the rule-bound command and control philosophies of the past, recognising the whole person and the positive drivers of behaviour and output. Supporting flexible working is very much part of this more enlightened future of work.

For employers therefore, the business case should be clear. Almost every business today talks of their challenges in accessing and retaining the workers and skills they need, and as the nature of work and required skills changes, this will be one of the most important strategic issues for any organisation. Providing more flexible working opportunities for people therefore becomes a business imperative and competitive advantage in accessing and retaining all the talent and skills they need, and to properly support diverse and inclusive workplaces.

This all sets a context for us that we need to understand to drive the case for change. To help create a world where good work and opportunities are available for all – something that has been called out as one of the United Nations 17 global sustainable development goals for 2030 and is seen as a vital political and economic outcome. Good work or jobs includes areas like fair pay and terms and conditions, and how people's skills are used, opportunity for progression, and having their voice heard. But it also has as a central theme, support for work-life balance and wellbeing.

Patterns of work and the standard working week

In 1930, in an essay entitled 'Economic Possibilities for our Grandchildren', the famous economist John Maynard Keynes predicted that by now we would all be working around 15-hour or three-day weeks. He based this on what he saw as the improvements in work organisation and technology to allow people to be much more productive thereby enabling significant economic growth and individual earnings allowing us all to work less and the opportunity for more leisure time.

Since then, there have been many other sociologists, economists and even politicians who have projected great reductions in working time and increase in leisure time in the succeeding decades. But as we all know, the standard 5-day working week is still the working norm and many might reflect they are working closer to 15-hour days. The irony of working hours today is that more income tends to correlate with working longer hours, and at the same time there are many on low incomes who seek longer hours to sustain reasonable income levels.

Perhaps we will have the opportunity or need to distribute work more, to balance hours worked across the working populations, and reduce overall working hours to offset some of the fears about displacement or reduction in jobs in the future. This would also require us to address the issues of rising income inequalities and the sharing of wealth. Big debates for the future of work.

On average across most developed economies we have settled to around about 37.5 hours for full-time workers, having decreased from Keynes' time when it was closer to 50 hours. The International Labour Organisation laid out working time standards as long ago as 1935, but they estimate that about 22% of the workers in the world are still working more than 48 hours per week.[9]

This full-time working takes at least a third of our waking hours, and for the generations now coming in to work who are contemplating even longer working lives, it's not surprising that they are increasingly concerned about work-life balance. Nobody died wishing they had spent more time at the office.

There is variation across countries however, with the higher income economies generally having higher proportions of the workforce working part time versus emerging economies less so, for example in Eastern European countries. The UK has amongst the highest levels of part time working at around 25% as shown in Figure 2.1.

The US Labor Department has been collecting data on trends in working hours since 1968, a time when only 13.5% of US employees were part-timers. That number peaked at 20.1% in January 2010 largely in response to the global financial crisis, but since then it has reduced back down to 17% in 2019.

It is important to note how little these rates have changed over the last 20 years. The changes that are visible up and down these lines generally happen as economies strengthen and weaken, just as the US data shows. As economies weaken there is a drop off in full time jobs, and in times of economic growth and high employment, fewer part time jobs seem to become available.

In recessions there tends to be an increase in the number of 'involuntary' part-time workers, as the data on over- and underemployment shows.[10] More adverse economic conditions may also discourage employers from offering, or employees from asking for, shorter working hours.

High female participation rates in the workforce coincide with higher rates of part-time working. This results in significant gender differences in how many people work non-standard hours. Despite the push in many countries to shift long standing societal expectations or norms (including shared parental leave), many more women work part time, balancing caring responsibilities with work.

The Netherlands is the stand-out example where more than three-fifths of employed women work part-time hours. Trends for the UK as an example are shown in Figure 2.2 below.

Going back to Keynes, whilst we are unlikely to arrive at 15-hour weeks as the norm, the idea of 4-day working weeks is being actively explored in growing numbers of organisations and countries such as Finland, Sweden, New Zealand and Canada. Unions and the political left are also becoming more vocal on this idea as a longer-term goal utilising the benefits and opportunities from increasing automation. But whilst some organisations may be able to make reduced working weeks apply for all work, we still would have a very long way to go to make this more systemic and widespread.

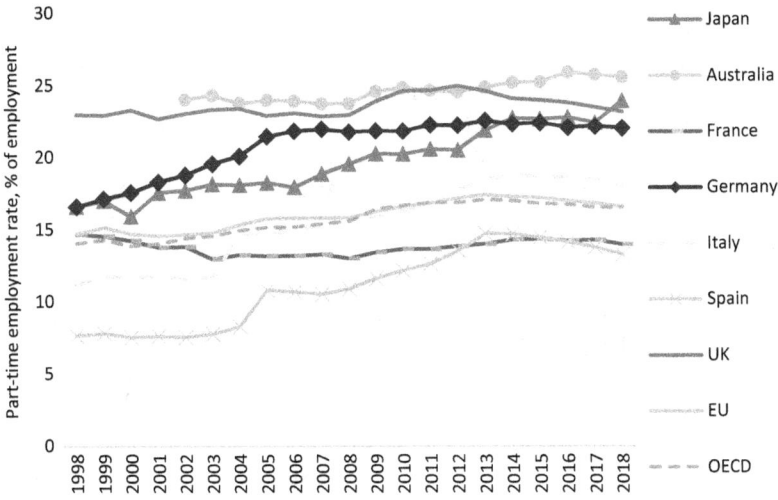

Figure 2.1 Part time working trends internationally.
Source: OECD data 2018.[11]

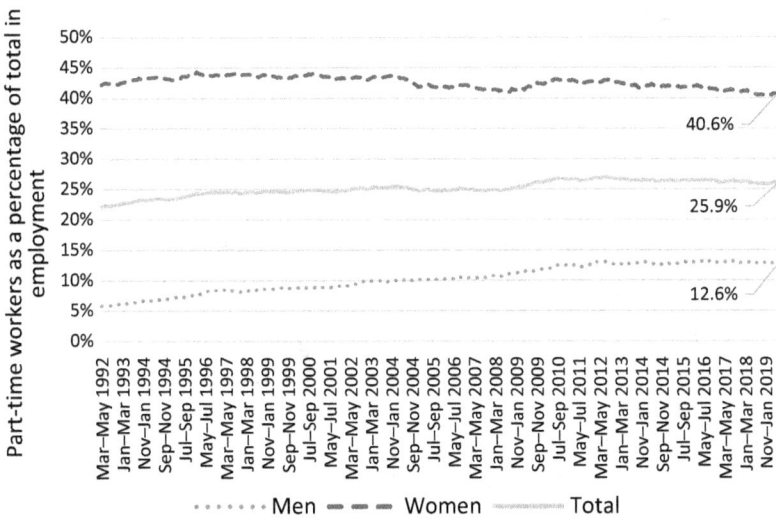

Figure 2.2 UK part-time workers as a percentage of all total employment, by gender, 1992–2019.
Source ONS.[12]

Definitions of flexible working

Part-time working, although the most widespread and visible practice, is far from the only dimension of flexible working. Whilst flexible working has generally meant working different hours from the 'standard' full-time working hours, it also encompasses choices in where people work, away from the normal office environment, such as from home or whilst travelling.

In more recent years, the construct of agile working has entered the lexicon. Whilst there are not absolute distinctions or definitions, the idea of agile working is to give workers more autonomy in choosing their patterns of work whilst fulfilling their required working hours and obligations across the week. The Nordic countries are generally leading the way, particularly Finland where the 1996 Working Hours Act gave employees the right to choose their patterns of work – for example flexing their start and finish times to suit their needs.

The terminology of flexible or agile working tends now to be used interchangeably, and for the purposes of this discussion we will talk about flexible working as including all the ways in which we can vary working hours, location, and patterns of work. Clearly not all jobs can be flexed in all these ways, and of course there are many jobs that require working shifts and very different working patterns. But even these should not be constraints to our ability to design working practices that enable more flexibility. For example, giving shift workers the opportunity to shift swap with colleagues gives them a greater sense of control and is being used in increasing numbers of organisations.

Across all the forms of flexible working, there has been more recent evidence pointing to some progress in part-time or flexible hours being offered, particularly for higher-paid jobs, most likely in response to demand in meeting skills shortages. Timewise, a UK based flexible working consultancy, found that over the last four years there had been a trebling in jobs paying over £80,000 advertised as flexible or part-time, and this had increased from 9% last year to now 16%, at the time of writing. The research revealed that 15.3% of all advertised jobs offered some form of flexible working, up from 12.5% in a similar study last year.

The CIPD's most recent survey of working lives in the UK[13] found that 54% of UK workers say they are able to work flexibly in some way, particularly those in higher-level occupations. However, among employees who have no access to flexible working, 78% would like it, and more than half the workforce (55%) would like to work flexibly in at least one form that is not currently available to them.

Legislation and policy

Flexible working came more into the language and thinking of work over the last 20–30 years. For example, legislation giving eligible employees the right to request flexible working in the UK was implemented and progressively extended between 2003 and 2014. Legislation in other countries varies considerably. Most European countries have some forms of legislation but are mostly linked to parental leave. Across Europe, according to Eurofound 2016, 'the working time setting regimes in the EU have remained essentially unchanged for the past 15 years'. The US also has limited general legislation, but there is growing pressure from both employers and workers to review.

The Nordic countries have the most forward-thinking legislation. Following their 1996 Working Hours Act, by 2011 Finland had the most flexible working practices anywhere. According to work by Grant Thornton, 92% of organisations in Finland allowed their workers to adapt their working hours versus 76% in the UK and US, 50% in Russia, and only 18% in Japan. Finland is taking this further with their new Working Hours Act, which comes in to effect in 2020 allowing workers to determine when and where they work for at least half their contracted working hours.

Early in 2019 the European Commission adopted the Directive on Work-Life Balance, which includes the extension of the right to request flexible working arrangements for all working parents and carers with dependent relatives. EU member countries will need to implement this over the next three years.

Use of different forms of flexible working

Heejung Chung of Kent University and Tanja van der Lippe of the University of Utrecht have done extensive research of surveys and reports on flexible working practices across Europe.[14] They make a useful distinction between schedule control where workers can adapt their working hours within certain limits (flexitime) and those with working time autonomy where their working hours can be self-determined.

Their review using data from Eurofound's European Working Conditions Survey of 2015 (EWCS, 2015) shows that roughly a quarter of employees had access to flexible schedules across 30 European countries, and about 12% did paid work from home several times a month in the past year. There is considerable variance from the Nordic countries, which show around 50% of employees saying they had access to flexible schedules, to some of the Eastern European countries in particular at the other end of the spectrum where the figure is closer to 10%.

Similar patterns showed up in the proportion of people who said they were able to work for some time from home. Nordic countries again are leading on the support for people working from home, but in the lower end of the spectrum it is surprising to see countries like Germany, despite overall having higher levels of flexible working than the average. Figure 2.3 summarises these variations for a selected group of countries.

A 2014 Eurofound survey asked a very general question about provision of flexible working.[15] Whereas over 80% of Danish employees said such arrangements were offered by their employers, in Cyprus the proportion was under 20%. The UK, like Belgium, had both a high rate of availability and a high proportion

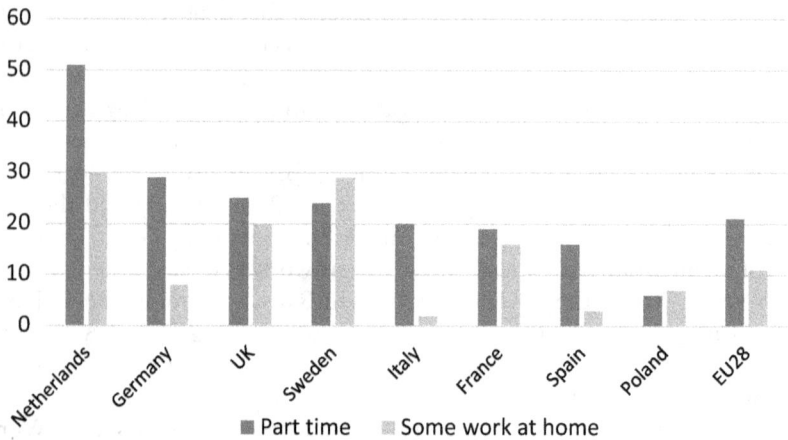

Figure 2.3 Selected country comparisons in proportions of people working part time and working from home.
Source: CIPD analysis from Eurostat data 2017.

of employees who said they didn't use these arrangements personally, which may have been because they were only available to some employees at their workplace.

Some of the variance may also be explained by high proportions of independent traders and small businesses, where people will often report working very long hours to earn enough money or to keep their businesses going. Typically they won't be recording the hours that they work, and managing and supporting this part of our economies is much more challenging. However, it's also true that for many small businesses, people do work flexibly partly because the demands for their particular skills are more variable, and they are often much less tied up in the formal working bureaucracies, which we have created over the decades to manage larger more complex organisations.

There is also variation of working hour practices and cultures across sectors. The UK Labour Force Survey[16] shows significant variances but this may be more due to the composition of the workforce and proportions working full time versus part time. Social care for example has a high proportion of women and with often flexible and part time ways of working. Public sector shows a notably higher incidence of flexible working than private sector and offers a greater range of flexible working practices and options.

The structural nature of employment and flexible working

The picture of employment is not complete without some understanding of the trends in so-called non-standard forms of employment, particularly the self-employed and contract or temporary employment workers. Many people choose these forms of working as it provides more autonomy and opportunity to work in different ways, but there are also those who find themselves in these forms of work involuntarily.

Data across the European Union as reported by Eurofound[17] has shown there were significant increases in the temporary employment rate across most countries during the 1980s and 1990s, but in the last decade and since the financial crisis and recession in 2008 this has slowed and the overall percentage of the workforce working in these ways has stabilised at just under 15%. In that time there has been the emergence of work mediated by digital platforms and the so called 'gig' economy, that is, trade in one-off exchanges of work for payment. The Eurofound report estimated that despite widespread publicity, the extent of such work accounts for no more than 0.5% of all employment in Europe. This tallied also with a more detailed survey in the US in 2015, based on a random sample of the population, where it was estimated also to be 0.5% of all employment.

The US has long been seen as a culture of hard work driving opportunity and success. But they are also seeing growth in many forms of flexible working and contingent working arrangements. In the US the Bureau of Labor Statistics (BLS) survey in 2017 found 10.6 million or around 7% of the workforce were working as independent contractors, 2.6 million or 1.7% were classified as 'on-call' workers, 1.4 million or 1% were temporary help agency workers, and about 1 million were provided via contracting agencies.

Data from the ONS shows the same overall patterns in the UK.[18] Most of the workforce still consists of formal or 'standard' employment, now at just under 85% in 2018 compared with just under 87% in 1998. The share of full-time employees has also fallen slightly, from just under 65% to just over 63%. The percentages of the workforce working in these different ways in the UK is shown in Figure 2.4 below.

However, almost half the growth in women in the workforce since 2008 in the UK are as contractors or self-employed (ONS data). And according to the Bank of England, half the increase in self-employed between 2004 and 2014 was linked to the ageing workforce. Most of the self-employed have a greater feeling of control over their working lives than employees. Indeed, this is one of the main reasons why many become self-employed in the first place.

For employers, utilising non-standard workers is mostly driven by the need to access particular skills for specific periods of time. Some sectors have long operated extensively with contract and contingent workers, such as construction, agriculture, media or the technology sector where workforce and skill demands can vary significantly over time. Google's workforce of temporary, vendor and contract workers (TVCs) exceeded that of its 'full time' or employed staff in 2018. Other sectors such as healthcare, which has such challenges in fulfilling their recruitment needs, have come to rely heavily on agencies that can source and provide contract workers to them, but at a cost.

So for some parts of the labour markets, these forms of working arrangements are fairly standard practice. But there is some evidence of increasing numbers who are making an active choice to work as contractors rather than

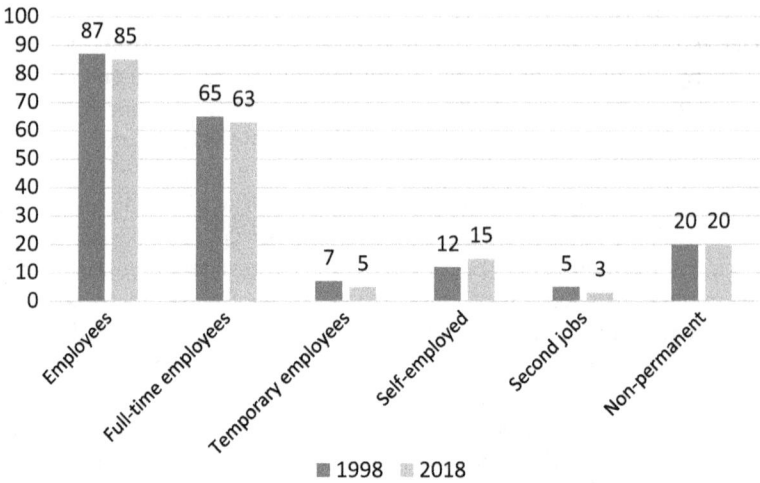

Figure 2.4 Structural trends in UK employment 1998 to 2018.
Source: Seasonally adjusted from ONS data. Contains public sector information licensed under the Open Government Licence v3.0.

employees. A report from the Recruitment and Employment Confederation in 2014 concluded that more than one in three people (36%) in the UK have worked as a contractor, freelancer or agency worker at some point in their career, and 41% are considering working that way in the future.[19]

One of the major differences for the worker in these forms of working arrangements is that they will have less job security, and they will have to be concerned with how they market themselves to ensure their own earnings and career progress. The highly skilled minority can have considerable bargaining power, but many contingent workers with lower skills will not, which can leave them more exposed to employers' changes in demand. Individuals are also likely to have the responsibility for their own training and development, healthcare and pensions and may not have other rights such as holiday or sick pay, which normally come with employment status.

Organisations may not see that they have the same duty of care, morally or legally, to contract or contingent workers who, for low skill work, are particularly vulnerable to automation or outsourcing.

These are important policy issues where clearer legal definitions, tax, benefits and other rights for the status of employees, workers and contractors or self-employed are now being more actively debated. Gig economy organisations such as Uber and Deliveroo are being challenged, with the starting point being the degree to which they exert control over what the contract worker does.

These concerns have been consistently highlighted by unions amongst others, where these changes in working patterns are described as shifts to more insecure work and calls for more control over these forms of working.[20]

All these different forms of work are part of the general picture of the many different ways and choices that people have in how they work, and of how they themselves can create more flexible ways of working. Flexible working practices can apply across all forms of work, but they tend to be discussed in the context of more formally organised workplaces, and where work is managed and allocated against employment hours, which are formally contracted for.

So let's review in more detail all the various different forms of flexible working in employment.

The variety of ways of working flexibly

As previously described, flexible working includes the dimensions of hours worked, location and patterns of work.

Over recent years with the advent of technology and communications, there are many more choices in where, when and how people work, and these are all part of the emerging modern working cultures and practices.

Typical constructs of flexible working include the following:

- Part-time working: work is generally considered part-time when employees are contracted to work anything less than standard full-time hours.
- Term-time working: a worker remains on a permanent contract but can take paid/unpaid leave during school holidays.
- Job-sharing: a form of part-time working where two (or occasionally more) people share the responsibility for a job between them.
- Flexitime: allows employees to choose, within certain set limits, when to begin and end work.
- Compressed hours: compressed working weeks (or fortnights) don't necessarily involve a reduction in total paid hours or any extension in individual choice over which hours are worked. The central feature is reallocation of work into fewer and longer blocks during the week.
- Annual, monthly, fortnightly hours: the total number of hours to be worked over a period is fixed but there can be variation during the period in the length of the working day and week. Employees may or may not have an element of choice over working patterns.
- Working from home on a regular basis: workers regularly spend time working from home.
- Mobile working/teleworking: this permits employees to work all or part of their working week at a location remote from the employer's workplace.
- Career breaks: career breaks, or sabbaticals, are extended periods of leave, normally unpaid, which may vary from weeks to months or even years.
- Commissioned outcomes: there are no fixed hours, but only an output target that an individual is working towards.

- Zero-hours contracts: an individual has no guarantee of a minimum number of working hours, so they can be called upon as and when required and paid just for the hours they work.

Whilst the list shows many different ways of flexible working, it isn't exhaustive. Flexible working can include other practices, for example employee self-rostering, shift-swapping or taking time off for training. Indeed, the list cannot be exhaustive. A flexible working arrangement is characterised as much by what it is not (full-time hours or regular, fixed hours or at a fixed workplace), as by what it is.

Many flexible working arrangements therefore require a significant degree of trust between employer and employee and may need to balance or compromise on the needs of both. Whether a particular working practice is judged as 'good' flexibility (mainly in the interests of employees?) or 'bad' flexibility (mainly in the interests of employers?) depends on who is making the judgement and on how the arrangement works in practice. We will come back to these points in the discussion about implementing flexible working practices.

For flexibility in working hours, the most common form is part-time working. In terms of flexible working arrangements, the most commonly provided and exercised is around more flexible start and finish times for work, as shown in Figure 2.5 below for UK data.

As already noted, working reduced hours has seen little change in either availability or take-up during the last decade. In 2017 in the UK, 27% of employees

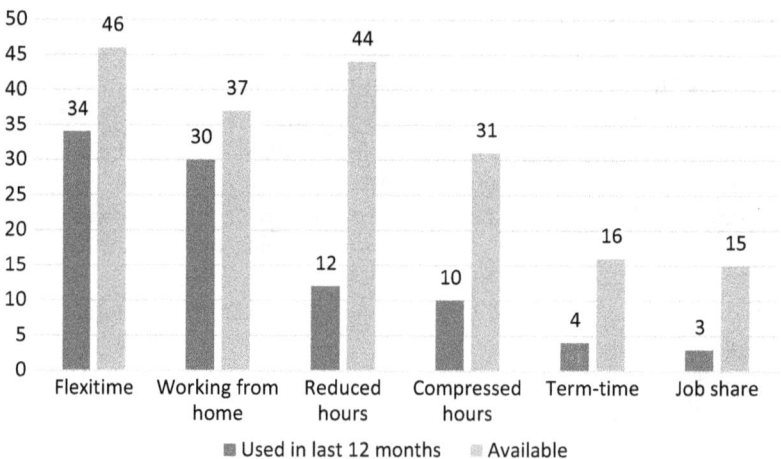

Figure 2.5 Percentage use and availability of different forms of part-time working in the UK proportion of categories of flexible working.
Source: CIPD UK Working Lives survey 2019.

had one of a set of specified flexible working arrangements (as defined in the Labour Force Survey), and 18% of employees worked part-time without one of these flexible working arrangements. In 2012, the comparable figures were 23% and 21% respectively. Some flexible working arrangements, such as job-sharing, seem to have become less widely used since the last recession.

However, given that many of the forms of flexible working do not require contractual change or formal reporting by employers it is hard to get an accurate picture. Most anecdotal evidence suggests that many employees make use of informal arrangements to work flexibly, either alongside or instead of more formal arrangements. The UK Labour Force Survey indicates a slow but steady increase over time in the proportion of employees who say they work mainly at or from home, from around 4.5% in 2002 to 5.6% in 2017. The majority of these said they work in different places, using home as a base.

Barriers to flexible working

Aviva research[21] across 500 private employers suggested that 65% of businesses think their workforce will work more flexibly in five years' time. But they also found 34% of businesses not offering flexible working as a standard and that one in five in the workforce 'dare not ask for flexible working' presumably because they worry it will be taken negatively and impact their prospects.

The reality is that there are still some significant cultural and other barriers to more widespread use of the many different forms of flexible working.

Mindsets and cultures

For generations who have lived with the long-standing working traditions of full-time work or standard working weeks throughout their careers, it can be hard to understand or accept very different working arrangements.

There is a pervasive 'work commitment' bias at work, where managers are biased towards positively evaluating people on what they see as effort and commitment. This may be quite conscious and explicit, and is almost celebrated in many professional services, finance, legal, media and advertising sectors where 'commitment' or 'ambition' is often read as working long hours. As a result, those working part time or even away from the office and eyes of their managers can find themselves at a disadvantage. In many other working cultures it may be much less explicit, but the reality is that there is a common tendency to bias our evaluations of performance on perceived input versus understanding output and outcomes.

Perception and reality of disadvantage

Given the challenges of many long-established cultures and mindsets about what a 'proper' job entails, it's not surprising to see that those who work part-time and flexibly can be disadvantaged in terms of their career progression.

A 2018 survey[22] by Deloitte with Timewise of 1,800 UK professionals (78% of whom said 'their current or most recent employer offered flexible working') found that 30% of flexible workers felt they were regarded as less important, and 25% said they were given fewer opportunities than colleagues who worked conventional hours. A quarter also believed they had missed out on promotion.

Part-time employees were less likely to think their job made use of their skills and experience or helped them to develop their career. Findings from a 2018 CIPD survey of several thousand workers across the UK[23] showed that whereas 26% of full-time employees thought they were overqualified in their current job, the proportion was 45% for part-time employees. Similarly, 35% of full-time employees and 45% of part-time employees thought they had the skills to cope with more demanding duties. The same survey in 2019 also showed how full- and part-time employees viewed their prospects, with a fairly clear difference in perceptions as shown in Figure 2.6 below.

Whether these are perceptions or realities, the outcome will be the same. If an organisation is perceived to have a bias against part-time working or the nature and the quality of the job is less, it will restrict people from requesting, as the Aviva study highlighted.

Involuntary flexible working and underemployment

Too often the only 'flexible' and part-time jobs available are low paid. Some estimates suggest a very large part-time pay penalty of up to 30%, and there may be as many as 1.5 million people in the UK workforce who are trapped in jobs like these, working below their skill level because they can't find better-paid jobs with the working patterns they need.

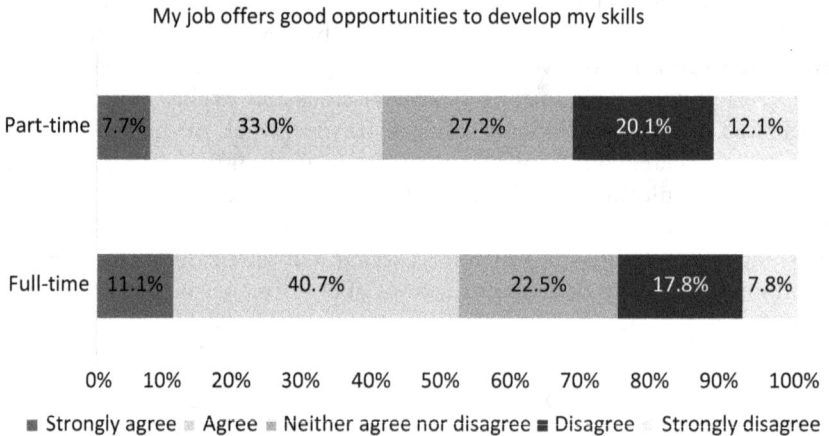

My job offers good opportunities to develop my skills

Part-time: 7.7% | 33.0% | 27.2% | 20.1% | 12.1%

Full-time: 11.1% | 40.7% | 22.5% | 17.8% | 7.8%

■ Strongly agree ▪ Agree ▪ Neither agree nor disagree ■ Disagree Strongly disagree

Figure 2.6 Skill and career development perceptions.
Source: CIPD UK Working Lives survey 2019.

According to the Eurofound 2017 survey, involuntary part-time work increased from 22.4% of all part-time work to 29.1% between 2007 and 2015 across Europe. They reported this change as correlated with the change in unemployment rates in some EU countries, with strong increases in Cyprus, Greece and Spain. By contrast, Germany showed the sharpest decline in both unemployment and involuntary part-time work.

This group of workers also contribute to the underemployed, where they may be working part-time but want to work longer hours. This affects women more than men. According to Working Families, almost twice the number of mothers than fathers are on a zero-hours contract or take on casual work. Their research showed that more than one in ten (11%) of parents have turned down a new job or promotion in favour of preserving their work-life balance, suggesting that once working parents have managed to obtain the flexibility they need, they feel unable to move on. Nearly two-thirds (65%) of mothers and half of fathers agree or strongly agree with the statement: 'I will stay in my job because I won't be able to get the flexibility I have now elsewhere'.

Hours versus wage rate

There has been a long-standing 'part-time pay penalty' that applies even when correcting for hours worked (and despite legislation prohibiting pay discrimination against part-time employees since 2000). This is because part-time work is less common in highly paid jobs and management roles.[24]

However, according to recent CIPD research, part-time employees are *more* likely to agree they are paid fairly than full-time employees.[25] Employees working part-time hours, however, appeared to attach less weight to their pay than full-time employees, instead being more likely to regard convenient hours as important or essential. And it seems part-time employees have found jobs for themselves that mean they are more satisfied than full-time employees with their working hours and with workplace relationships.

Hours worked in relation to overall pay have received little attention by policy makers, but that might be starting to change. Policies like minimum wage are widespread internationally, and the UK's Living Wage Foundation's Real Living Wage campaign are now putting more attention on hours worked as well as the hourly rate. The Resolution Foundation noted that whilst hourly pay at the bottom of the distribution has increased (because of the national minimum wage), weekly wages decreased because people were working fewer hours.[26]

This could be due to changes in the composition of the workforce and the choices workers are making, or it could be because large increases in the national living wage are prompting employers to cut back hours. The Resolution Foundation suggested that 'it may be that increasing the hours of those already in work offers one of the best options for boosting living standards over the course of 2018'.

Social attitudes and norms

Support for women and those with caring responsibilities actively working varies across countries and societies. As already noted, the Nordic countries have higher proportions of women working and working part time and this is partly due to different social attitudes. Norms or attitudes of this nature tend to change slowly, being transmitted from one generation to another.

However, there does appear to be growing support among employees in the UK for the idea that employers have some degree of responsibility for supporting people with their life outside work. In 2012/2013, 69% of male employees and 73% of female employees agreed, or strongly agreed, that 'employers should help mothers combine jobs and childcare'.[27]

Similarly, 60% of employees in workplaces with five or more employees agreed that 'managers here understand about employees having to meet responsibilities outside work'.[28] Just 15% of employees disagreed with this statement. Nevertheless, unsupportive or inflexible managers remain a big barrier, and we need to do more to train and encourage them to think differently.

Issues of remote working

A 2016 study from Lancaster University in the UK found that people valued mobile working (ability to work anywhere), noting how it enabled them to get more done (54%); made them feel trusted (49%); improved work-life balance (46%); made them feel empowered (41%); and reduced their travel time (37%).[29]

However the report also found that around a quarter of those surveyed claimed that all the work in their organisation was currently carried out on site. Furthermore, almost half of managers (45%) said that mobile working made them work longer hours, and a quarter (24%) said that it made them feel disconnected from their team. Organisational culture is clearly vital in addressing the barriers.

Flexible working office environments

Many places of work are being adapted to provide for different ways and styles of working. However, the trend for hot desking and open plan offices, which may have benefits in space utilisation and cost savings, is not always well supported by evidence that it works well for employees. Many employees dislike these practices, valuing their own workspaces, resenting bland and often inhuman hot desking environments, and will resent being forced to work from home when they can see the real driver is cost of office space. Some research has even shown that open plan offices can reduce levels of collaboration, which they were supposedly promoting.[30]

In providing for flexible working arrangements, it is very important to provide people with choice and not force them to work in specific ways that can undermine the benefits of providing the flexible working arrangements in the first place.

The business case for flexible working

As with any changes in working practices and policies, they are only sustainable if there is a positive business rationale. Given the various barriers described above, having a good evidence base for the benefits of flexible working is essential.

The key benefits were previously outlined, but they are worth exploring in more detail.

Attraction of talent

Most organisations today, particularly as we are seeing record high levels of employment currently, are finding it harder to access and recruit the skills they need. There is a strong unmet demand for more flexible jobs, which will open up new supplies of talent.

Timewise have used the research evidence that 87% of people want to work flexibly, but only 11% of jobs are advertised as being flexible, although as noted, this is on the increase.[31] This is especially true for roles with skill shortages and hard-to-fill vacancies.[32] Their research also showed that today only just over 10% of jobs at £20k full-time equivalent are advertised as being open to flexible working. A vital step in showing how the organisation is taking flexible working seriously and seeking to attract more diverse talent, is to advertise jobs as being open to flexible working.

In the UK, there is an initiative supported by the UK Flexible Working Taskforce (jointly chaired by the CIPD and Department for Business) to use a tagline on job adverts first promoted by Working Families of 'Happy to Talk Flexible' working. More and more organisations are using this but there is still a long way to go.

Improved engagement, job satisfaction and loyalty

Staff are more likely to recommend their employer, stay loyal to their organisation, and go the extra mile if their employer offers flexible working. Flexible workers have a higher level of job satisfaction, commitment, and are more likely to increase discretionary effort compared to those who do not work flexibly.[33] Engagement in these terms can yield significant advantages for employers – potentially generating 43% more revenue and improving performance by 20%, compared to disengaged employees.[34]

Reduced absenteeism and improved wellbeing

Flexible working can reduce absence rate[35] as it allows employees to manage disability and long-term health conditions as well as supporting their mental health and stress.[36] From all the characteristics that have been studied of what a good job looks like and how people feel about their work, improving or sustaining their wellbeing is for most the most significant determinant of their engagement and their productivity.[37]

Parents and carers (especially those on low incomes) benefit the most. They tend to have increased wellbeing and are less troubled by stress when given access to flexible work.[38]

Employee retention and progression

Flexible working practices are a key reason for staff at all career stages being satisfied with their work and staying with their employer. Access to flexible working allows people to continue working as their life circumstances change and therefore can reduce staff turnover. For example, in the USA, work re-design initiatives in retail have shown a positive link between working-time flexibility and reduced voluntary turnover as reported by Timewise in their 2018 research paper on flexible working in retail. The US technology products retailer Best Buy trialled giving employees flexibility over working time and measured productivity in the trial teams. Voluntary turnover rates reduced by 90% and productivity increased by 41%. People were happier and healthier too and more motivated to stay.[39]

For senior and managerial staff, flexible working arrangements are pivotal for being able to continue to work and develop as professionals, particularly if they become parents.[40] For entry-level employees, flexible working reduces job-life spillover, which in turn improves retention and commitment.[41]

Productivity

Employees and managers agree that flexible working increases individual performance and can be more motivating than a bonus or extra pay. A 2017 study by HSBC found that nine in ten employees consider flexible working to be a key motivator to their productivity at work (89% – even more than financial incentives at 77%).[42] Of those who have access to remote working, 81% believe it increases their productivity. Managers and co-workers also report a positive or neutral impact on individual performance in terms of quality and quantity of work when flexible working practices are adopted.[43]

When it comes to working with others, flexible work schedules help employees balance their work and life responsibilities and boost performance,[44] increasing average labour productivity for large and small businesses.

Improving workforce gender diversity

By providing more opportunities for women with children to return to work, the normalisation and support of flexible working arrangements can help businesses to reduce their gender pay gap.[45] Flexible working supports more diverse talent pipelines within organisations and helps improve board level diversity. As some global analysis shows, companies with diverse boards outperform their rivals and have an opportunity cost equivalent to around 3% of UK GDP.[46] Well-publicised research by McKinsey has shown how gender diverse leadership teams also deliver an 18% return on equity premium, which they estimated could add £150 billion a year to the UK economy by 2025.[47]

Engaging and retaining older workers

Flexible working is also important for many workers as they get older. Their need and ability to work changes, and some flexibility in work is often critical to attracting and retaining them.

In almost all of the more developed nations in the world, populations and workforces are ageing, so providing the flexibility for older workers to continue to engage is an important economic and social imperative. Europe, the US, Russia, Japan and Korea all have significantly ageing populations. As an example, in the UK a third of workers will be over 50 by 2020, and within 20 years, nearly a quarter of the UK population will be aged 65 or over. Japan has already reached these kinds of statistics, driving a lot of change in the workplace to support and sustain the older workforce. The US Bureau of Labor Statistics reported that by 2024, 25% of the US workforce will be composed of workers over the age of 55, and a third of those workers will be older than 65.

Labour market participation for the over 50 age groups are therefore of necessity increasing, particularly among women. In the UK the percentage of workers aged 65 and over has doubled in the last decade.[48] This potentially marks a reversal of the trend towards early retirement observed in the last quarter of the 20th century. But still participation rate in the UK is lower at 11% than the G7 average of 15%.

Agility and responsiveness to market change

Flexible working allows companies to adapt to fluctuating market demand to boost responsiveness and competitiveness. The Confederation for British Industry (CBI) Employment Trends survey 2017 found that 99% of all businesses surveyed believes that a flexible workforce is vital or important to competitiveness and the prospects for business investment and job creation.[49]

Tesco, Lloyds Banking Group and the Ford Motor Company are three examples of organisations using flexible working to increase responsiveness to customer demand:

- A Tesco superstore uses part-time working and multi-skilling practices to meet customer demand more effectively, generating value equivalent to approximately 13% of total workforce costs.
- A head office function of Lloyds Banking Group generates value equivalent to 7% of total workforce costs through using freelancers to meet seasonal demand and locating staff across multiple sites to lower the costs of their premises.
- A Ford Motor Company Ltd manufacturing plant saves the equivalent of about 3% of total plant costs by using outsourcing, flexible absence cover and alternative maintenance shifts to achieve cover in line with plant needs.[50]

Recommendations and conclusion

As has been discussed, we are at a time of significant change and perhaps re-evaluation of our long-standing working norms and practices in a future of work that in many ways will be different from the past.

The case for organisations providing the opportunities for more flexible working in all its forms has many different dimensions. The need to access and retain all the skills and talents businesses need and to create inclusive and diverse organisations, and working practices, and how we can support positive wellbeing in our workforces. Perhaps most importantly, providing flexible work is a key part of enabling productive and good work opportunities for all, driving both social and economic benefits. It doesn't seem unreasonable to believe in a future where work will be much more flexible, meeting all our different needs as individuals and businesses.

We all have agency in helping to create this future. Whether we are business leaders, human resource (HR) practitioners, regulators and policy makers, or individuals who want or need to work more flexibly.

There are now many sources of practical advice and guidance for employers on how to embed more flexible working practices and cultures. In the UK, organisations like Acas, CIPD and CBI all provide good guidance, as do specialist organisations like Timewise, Working Families and others.

Key ideas and recommendations:

- Make the case for flexible working with evidence of how it is working today, where the barriers are, and the difference it can make to individual and organisational outcomes in your own organisational context.
- To really embed flexible working effectively, take a holistic approach looking at culture, management, job design, workspace design and people management and HR practices.

- Start with reviewing how the options to work flexibly are presented externally to all potential recruits. Are jobs advertised as being open to work flexibly, or is the language just about full-time standard jobs?
- Focus on the development and training of managers at all levels so that they are properly equipped to understand how to manage and engage with employees or workers who are working flexibly.
- Create the supporting work environments for flexible working, including the right tools and technologies, highlighting benefits but also providing the support channels for individuals where they are finding it difficult or feeling they are being compromised in their progress.
- Challenge job design and where roles could be designed to work on different schedules, even where this may require job share or splitting the existing job to have some of the tasks picked up through another role.
- Be transparent on how the organisation is progressing and be prepared to report on for example how many employees or workers are working flexibly and how you are championing flexible working. Make the links to outcomes, such as employee retention and wellbeing, a part of creating a more agile and responsive business for the future.

Our goals for the future of work really should be about achieving good work for all and sustaining positive wellbeing. Flexible working has a big role to play.

References

1 CIPD (2019). *Health and well-being at work* [online]. London: CIPD. [Viewed 8 October 2019]. Available from: https://www.cipd.co.uk/Images/health-and-well-being-at-work-2019.v1_tcm18-55881.pdf
2 OECD (2019). *OECD employment outlook 2019* [online]. Paris: OECD. [Viewed 8 October 2019]. Available from: https://www.oecd-ilibrary.org/sites/9ee00155-en/index.html?itemId=/content/publication/9ee00155-en
3 CIPD (2018). *Health and well-being at work* [online]. London: CIPD. [Viewed 8 October 2019]. Available from: https://www.cipd.co.uk/Images/health-and-well-being-at-work_tcm18-40863.pdf
4 Deloitte (2013). *The Millennial Survey 2013* [online]. London: Deloitte. [Viewed 8 October 2019]. Available from: https://www2.deloitte.com/ke/en/pages/about-deloitte/articles/millennial-survey-positive-impact.html
5 Carter, T. (2018). *Families and the labour market, England: 2018* [online]. ONS. [Viewed 11 October 2019]. Available from: https://www.ons.gov.uk/employmentandlabourmarket/peopleinwork/employmentandemployeetypes/articles/familiesandthelabourmarketengland/2018
6 NatCen (2018). *British social attitudes 35* [online]. London: NatCen. [Viewed 11 October 2019]. Available from: https://www.bsa.natcen.ac.uk/media/39284/bsa35_full-report.pdf
7 Samsung (2015). *Research from Samsung reveals that a quarter of employees would give up a pay rise for flexible working* [online]. Samsung. [Viewed 28 October 2015]. Available from: http://www.samsung.com/uk/news/local/research-from-samsung-reveals-that-a-quarter-of-employees-would-give-up-a- pay-rise-for-flexible-working

8   Pink, D. H. (2009). *Drive: The Surprising Truth About What Motivates Us.* New York: Riverhead Books.

9   Lee, S., McCann, D. and Messenger, J.C. (2007). *Working time around the world – Trends in working hours, laws and policies in a global comparative perspective* [online]. Routledge. [Viewed 8 October 2018]. Available from: https://www.ilo.org/wcmsp5/groups/public/@dgreports/@dcomm/@publ/documents/publication/wcms_104895.pdf

10 ONS (2019). *EMP16: Underemployment and overemployment labour force survey* [Data set]. ONS. [Accessed 4 October 2019]. Available from: https://www.ons.gov.uk/employmentandlabourmarket/peopleinwork/employmentandemployeetypes/datasets/underemploymentandoveremploymentemp16

11 OECD (2019) *Part-time employment rate.* OECD (2019), Part-time employment rate (indicator). doi: 10.1787/f2ad596c-en, OECD. [Accessed 29 October 2019]. Available from: https://data.oecd.org/emp/part-time-employment-rate.htm

12 ONS (2019). *EMP01 SA: Full-time, part-time and temporary workers (seasonally adjusted)* [Dataset]. ONS. [Accessed 8 October 2019]. Available from: https://www.ons.gov.uk/employmentandlabourmarket/peopleinwork/employmentandemployeetypes/datasets/fulltimeparttimeandtemporaryworkersseasonallyadjustedemp01sa

13 CIPD (2019). *Survey report 2019: UK working lives* [online]. London: CIPD. [Viewed 8 October 2019]. Available from: https://www.cipd.co.uk/Images/uk-working-lives-2019-v1_tcm18-58585.pdf

14 Chung, H. and Van Der Lippe, T. (2018). Flexible working, work–life balance, and gender equality: Introduction. *Social Indicators Research* [online]. Available from https://doi.org/10.1007/s11205-018-2025-x

15 Eurofound (2005). *European survey on working time and work-life balance (ESWT)* [online]. Eurofound. [Viewed 8 October 2019]. Available from: https://www.eurofound.europa.eu/surveys/european-company-surveys/european-survey-on-working-time-and-work-life-balance-eswt

16 ONS (2019). *HOUR03: Average hours worked by industry* [Data set]. ONS. [Accessed 8 October 2019]. Available from: https://www.ons.gov.uk/employmentandlabourmarket/peopleinwork/earningsandworkinghours/datasets/averagehoursworkedbyindustryhour03

17 Eurofound (2017). *Non-standard forms of employment: Recent trends and future prospects* [online]. Dublin: Eurofound. [Viewed 8 October 2019]. Available from: https://www.eurofound.europa.eu/sites/default/files/ef_publication/field_ef_document/ef1746en.pdf

18 ONS (2019). *EMP01 SA: Full-time, part-time and temporary workers (seasonally adjusted)* [Dataset]. ONS. [Accessed 8 October 2019]. Available from: https://www.ons.gov.uk/employmentandlabourmarket/peopleinwork/employmentandemployeetypes/datasets/fulltimeparttimeandtemporaryworkersseasonallyadjustedemp01sa

19 Recruitment and Employment Confederation (2014). *Flex appeal: Why freelancers, contractors and agency workers choose to work this way* [online]. London: Recruitment and Employment Confederation. [Viewed 8 October 2019]. Available from: https://www.rec.uk.com/__data/assets/pdf_file/0006/155562/Flex-Appeal-2014.pdf

20 TUC (2019) *Insecure work* [online]. London: TUC. [Viewed 8 October 2019]. Available from: https://www.tuc.org.uk/research-analysis/reports/insecure-work

21 Aviva (2017). *Working lives report 2017* [online]. York: Aviva. [Viewed 8 October 2019]. Available from: https://www.aviva.co.uk/adviser/documents/view/workinglivesreport2017.pdf

22 Timewise (2018). *A manifesto for change: A modern workplace for a flexible workforce* [online]. Timewise. [Viewed 8 October 2019]. Available from: https://timewise.co.uk/wp-content/uploads/2018/05/Manifesto-for-change.pdf

23 CIPD (2018). *Survey report 2018: UK working lives* [online]. London: CIPD. [Viewed 8 October 2019]. Available from: https://www.cipd.co.uk/Images/UK-working-lives-2_tcm18-40225.pdf

24 Manning, A. and Petrongolo, B. (2006). *The part-time pay penalty for women in Britain* [online]. SSRN. [Viewed 8 October 2019]. Available from: https://papers.ssrn.com/sol3/papers.cfm?abstract_id=947068

25 CIPD (2018). *Survey report 2018: UK working lives* [online]. London: CIPD. [Viewed 8 October 2019]. Available from: https://www.cipd.co.uk/Images/UK-working-lives-2_tcm18-40225.pdf

26 Cominetti, N. (2019). *Low pay Britain 2019* [online]. London: Resolution Foundation. [Viewed 8 October 2019]. Available from: https://www.resolutionfoundation.org/publications/low-pay-britain-2019

27 Understanding Society (2013). *Wave 4* [Data set]. Essex: Institute for Social and Economic Research. [Viewed 8 October 2019]. Available from: https://www.understandingsociety.ac.uk/2014/11/19/wave-4-data-release-available

28 Department for Business, Innovation & Skills (2013). *The 2011 workplace employment relations study* [online]. London: Department for Business, Innovation & Skills. [Viewed 8 October 2019]. Available from: https://assets.publishing.service.gov.uk/government/uploads/system/uploads/attachment_data/file/336651/bis-14-1008-WERS-first-findings-report-fourth-edition-july-2014.pdf

29 The Work Foundation (2016). *Working anywhere* [online]. Lancaster: The Work Foundation. [Viewed 8 October 2019]. Available from: http://www.theworkfoundation.com/wp-content/uploads/2016/02/398_Working-Anywhere.pdf

30 Bernstein, E. S. and Turban, S. (2018). *The impact of the 'open' workspace on human collaboration* [online]. Royal Society Publishing. [Viewed 8 October 2019]. Available from: https://royalsocietypublishing.org/doi/pdf/10.1098/rstb.2017.0239

31 Timewise (2018). *Flexible jobs index* [online]. Timewise. [Viewed 8 October 2019]. Available from: https://timewise.co.uk/wp-content/uploads/2018/07/Timewise_Flexible_Jobs_-Index_2018.pdf

32 Joseph Rowntree Foundation (2016). *How flexible hiring could improve business performance and living standards* [online]. York: Joseph Rowntree Foundation. [Viewed 8 October 2019]. Available from: https://www.jrf.org.uk/report/how-flexible-hiring-could-improve-business-performance-and-living-standards

33 Working Families and Bright Horizons (2018). *Modern families index* [online]. Working Families. [Viewed 8 October 2019]. Available from: https://www.workingfamilies.org.uk/wp-content/uploads/2018/01/UK_MFI_2018_Long_Report_A4_UK.pdf

34 Tamkin, P., Cowling, M. and Hunt. C. (2018). *People and the bottom line* [online]. Sussex: Institute for Employment Studies. [Viewed 8 October 2019]. Available from: https://www.employment-studies.co.uk/system/files/resources/files/448.pdf

35 Giardini, G. and Kabst, R. (2008). Effects of work-family human resource practices: a longitudinal perspective. *The International Journal of Human Resource Management* [online], *19*(11), 2079–2094. [Viewed 8 October 2019]. Available from: https://doi.org/10.1080/09585190802404312

36 CIPD (2018). *Health and well-being at work* [online]. London: CIPD. [Viewed 8 October 2019]. Available from: https://www.cipd.co.uk/Images/health-and-well-being-at-work_tcm18-40863.pdf

37 CIPD (2018). *Survey report 2018: UK working lives* [online]. London: CIPD. [Viewed 8 October 2019]. Available from: https://www.cipd.co.uk/Images/UK-working-lives-2_tcm18-40225.pdf

38 Family Friendly Working Scotland (2016). *Family friendly working and low income families* [online]. Scotland: Family Friendly Working Scotland. [Viewed

9 October 2019]. Available from: https://www.familyfriendlyworkingscotland. org.uk/resources/35222FFWSPolicyBriefing-online.pdf

39   Timewise (2018). *Moving up in retail: An employer's guide to enabling talent progression through flexible working* [online]. London: Timewise. [Viewed 9 October 2019]. Available from: https://timewise.co.uk/wp-content/uploads/2018/02/ 1880-Timewise-Retail-Flexible-working-report-10.pdf

40   Working Families (2007). *Hours to suit: Working flexibly at senior and managerial levels* [online]. London: Working Families. [Viewed 9 October 2019]. Available from: https://www.workingfamilies.org.uk/wp-content/uploads/2014/09/Hours-To-Suit.pdf

41   Bond, J.T. and Galinsky, E. (2006). *How can employers increase the productivity and retention of entry-level, hourly employees?* [online]. Families and Work Institute. [Viewed 9 October 2019]. Available from: https://familiesandwork.org/ downloads/IncreaseProductivityandRetentionEntryLevelHourly-Brief2.pdf

42   HSBC (2017). *News release: Nine out of ten (89%) employees believe flexible working is key to boosting productivity levels* [online]. HSBC Commercial Banking. [Viewed 9 October 2019]. Available from: https://www.about.hsbc.co.uk/-/media/uk/ en/news-and-media/cmb/171108-flexible-working.pdf

43   Working Families (2018) *Flexible working and performance* [online]. London: Working Families. [Viewed 9 October 2019]. Available from: https://www.workingfamilies. org.uk/wp-content/uploads/2014/09/Flexible-Working-Performance-2008.pdf

44   White, M., Hill, S., McGovern, P. G. and Mills, C. (2003). 'High-performance' management practices, working hours and work-life balance. *British Journal of Industrial Relations*, 41(2), 175–195. [Viewed 9 October 2019]. Available from: https://www. researchgate.net/publication/4737001_'High-performance'_Management_ Practices_Working_Hours_and_Work-Life_Balance

45   Chung, H. (2017). *Work autonomy, flexibility and work-life balance* [online]. Kent: University of Kent. [Viewed 9 October 2019]. Available from: http://wafproject. org/wordpress/wp-content/uploads/BT_1224371_WAF_report_Final.pdf

46   Grant Thornton (2015) *Women in business: The value of diversity* [online]. Grant Thornton. [Viewed 9 October 2019]. Available from: https://www. grantthornton.global/globalassets/wib_value_of_diversity.pdf

47   Credit Suisse and McKinsey, cited in CMI (2017). *Leadership for change* [online]. London: CMI. [Viewed 9 October 2019]. Available from: https://www. managers.org.uk/~/media/Files/PDF/CMI-Management-Manifesto.pdf

48   ONS (2006) *Labour market projections 2006–2020* [online]. London: ONS. [Viewed 9 October 2019]. Available from: http://stopstanstedexpansion.com/ documents/SSE10_Appendix_14.pdf

49   CBI/Pertemps (2017). *Employment trends survey* [online]. London: Pertemps. [Viewed 9 October 2019]. Available from: https://www.pertemps.co.uk/ about-us/latest-news/company-news/cbi-employment-trends-survey

50   Agile Future Forum (2013). *Understanding the economic benefits of workforce agility* [online]. Agile Future Forum. [Viewed 9 October 2019]. Available from: https://www.agilefutureforum.co.uk/wp-content/uploads/2014/11/Agile-Future-Forum-brochure.pdf

Part II

The impact of flexible working on health and productivity

3 Employees' psychological health and the impact of flexible working arrangements

Carolyn Timms, Paula Brough and Xi Wen (Carys) Chan

Introduction

In this chapter we discuss the construct of psychological health and its relationship with enhanced organisational productivity. Unlike previous generations where workforces were primarily male and work locations were fixed, modern workplaces are characterised by a greater diversity in personnel and locale. Many organisations have adopted flexible work arrangements (FWAs) which assist employees to balance their competing responsibilities. Commitments to work can be constrained by other compelling commitments in people's lives, commonly including demands arising from family responsibilities, sports activities, study, community work, and such like. However, in spite of the need, the take-up of FWAs can be varied. Many workers find alternative, but less satisfactory, ways of addressing the competing demands in their lives. In many cases, the reason for poor take-up is influenced by organisational cultures that covertly discourage employees from utilising FWAs (see, Cech and Blair-Loy, 2014; Fuller and Hirsh, 2018). Consequently, employees with few alternatives may experience a stigma when accessing FWAs, which can adversely affect their wellbeing and their career advancement. We begin this chapter by defining what we mean by psychological health and we discuss why organisations should be interested in their employees' levels of psychological health. We discuss the commonly available FWAs and their demonstrated impacts for levels of employee engagement and productivity. Finally, we review the common gender and generational differences which impact FWA offerings, and we suggest key issues for the consideration of future researchers in this field.

Psychological health

The term *psychological health* describes optimum human functioning and experience. Well recognised signs of optimum functioning include self-motivation, curiosity and active involvement in the social environment (Ryan and Deci, 2000), positive affect (Diener and Seligman, 2004), happiness (Ryan and Deci, 2001), flourishing/thriving (Fredrickson, 2001; May et al., 2004), ingenuity (Kim and Mauborgne, 2015), and resilience (Fredrickson et al., 2003). From an employer's perspective, these are all desirable attributes because workers with these qualities are creative, voluntarily share their ideas, and are productive, thereby enhancing organisational gains (Kim and Mauborgne, 1998, 2015).

According to Ryan and Deci's (2000) self-determination theory (SDT), desirable personal resources are not developed in isolation, but within structurally supportive social contexts (e.g., family and work). At the centre of SDT, competence, autonomy and relatedness are acknowledged as basic psychological needs, which when satisfied, enable people to succeed, thrive and contribute their best thinking and efforts to their organisations. Therefore, the effective managements of supportive workplaces recognise that workers' psychological health is essential to organisational prosperity (Dikkers et al., 2004). It is only when people are enabled to function at an optimum level, that they are actively engaged, doing their best work, eagerly advancing organisational goals, and thereby enabling strategic organisational advantage over commercial competitors (Kim and Mauborgne, 1998, 2015).

Why should organisations be interested in workers' psychological health?

The short answer as to why organisations should be interested in their workers' psychological health is an economic one. The costs of a chronically mentally unwell workforce are considerable, and unfortunately, are steadily increasing. Occupational stress (workplace mental ill health) claims by employees, organisational mental health insurance premiums, and other indirect costs attributable to occupational stress alone, cost industrialised countries billions each year. Recent estimates, for example, suggest occupational stress costs the Australian economy approximately AU$15 billion per annum (Safe Work Australia, 2013). International estimates are comparable to these Australian figures, demonstrating that occupational stress remains a global predicament: Canadian work stress annual costs equate to AU$11 billion, Netherlands AU$23 billion, and UK AU$46 billion (EU, 2014). In a recent review, Hassard et al. (2018, p. 1) described occupational stress as (still) being a "sizeable financial burden on society". Lost productivity specifically attributable to *employee absenteeism*, caused by the physical and mental health impacts of occupational stress, costs Australian organisations approximately AU$5 billion per annum (PricewaterhouseCoopers, 2014). Recent calculations also indicate that approximately 6% (AU$890 million) of the annual costs of depression experienced by employed Australians, is specifically attributable to occupational stress (Cocker et al., 2017).

We acknowledge that these economic costs of psychological health are influenced by national legislation, which defines an employer's legal responsibilities for their workers' mental health. Where such legal responsibilities are breached, workplace mental ill-health claims by employees seeking financial compensation may be submitted. For countries without this national legislation, economic costs are estimated primarily by employee work withdrawals (examples include low productivity, absenteeism, presenteeism, sick leave, turnover), and the costs of staff replacements, including employee recruitment and training costs. The costs to an organisation for *not* being suitably interested in their employee's good psychological health are therefore, considerable, regardless of the national legislative context.

For organisational scholars, the measurement of work engagement provides an efficacious snapshot of employees' psychological health and wellbeing within the social context of work (Bakker and Schaufeli, 2008; Downey et al., 2015; Timms et al., 2015b). The construct captures a sense of positivity that is characteristic of thriving workplaces (Salanova and Schaufeli, 2008; Schaufeli and Bakker, 2003) as well as people (May et al., 2004). It also contributes to the collective phenomenon of morale (Hart et al., 2000), and a demonstrable impression of cohesiveness, cooperation, vibrancy and enthusiasm that is immediately obvious to any visitors to the worksite (Dinham et al., 1995). Employees who are engaged in their work find it energising, challenging in a satisfying way, are proud of the work they do, and report that their work time passes quickly (Schaufeli and Salanova, 2014).

There is, therefore, a strong business case for organisations to pay attention to employee wellbeing. Harter et al.'s (2013) meta-analysis established substantial relationships between workers' engagement and performance. Harter et al. (2013) found positive relationships between work engagement and customer loyalty, productivity and profitability. They also reported negative relationships between work engagement and negative workplace events such as employee turnover rates, accidents, absenteeism, theft, mortality and product defects. This suggests that strategic planning for productivity gains must necessarily consider the psychological health of workers. Traditional paradigms (which assume that the two driving forces within organisations are economic concerns and self-interest (Kim and Mauborgne, 1998, 2015)) are misleading and essentially destructive in terms of organisational prosperity (see also, Harter et al., 2002). Unfortunately according to Schein (1996), a lack of alignment between different work levels (e.g., management, middle management and workers) can lead to internal differences in organisational culture, thereby subverting innovation and hindering the potential for growth (see, for example, Biggs et al., 2014). It seems that the misalignment described by Schein (1996), has led to frustratingly flat-footed responses by organisations to strategies designed to accommodate the needs of the modern workforce.

Flexible working arrangements

Flexible working arrangements (FWAs) are organisational strategies devised to assist workers in managing their disparate responsibilities. FWAs often appear prominently in company policies where their inclusion signals to prospective employees that the interwoven nature of the domains of their lives are respected, valued and accounted for (Brough et al., 2005; Timms et al., 2015a). In addition, as workforces have increasingly diversified, governments have recognised the need for FWAs to enable successful synchronisation between work and non-work responsibilities. Hegewisch and Gornick (2008) reported that 17 Western countries have granted workers the statutory right to request FWAs. Indeed, under the conditions of the *Fair Work Act* (Australian Government, 2009), workers in Australia can request FWAs on the basis of parenthood, caring responsibilities, disability, domestic violence or age.

Flexible work arrangements typically encompass: flexitime (i.e., work hours determined by employees), flexiwork (i.e., location or tasks of work determined by employees), job-sharing (i.e., tasks of one job are covered by two or more employees), compressed work week (i.e., a standard number of hours is compressed into a reduced number of days per week), tele-working (i.e., employees work away from their workplace for some or all of the work week, while being electronically linked), direct provision of care-giving and health benefits, and monetary and informational support for non-work roles (e.g., vouchers and referrals (McCarthy et al., 2010)). FWAs can also be categorised according to whether they are longer term, formalised arrangements or short-term/ad-hoc informal arrangements (Townsend et al., 2017). FWAs are now widely implemented across all types of organisations including governmental, private, not-for-profit, large corporations, and small-and-medium businesses in most industrialised countries, and are mostly used by working parents in these organisations (Joyce et al., 2010).

However, there is a troubled history concerning the implementation of FWAs and their expected benefits for employee wellbeing (Blair-Loy and Wharton, 2004; Cech and Blair-Loy, 2014). Research has demonstrated that actual use of FWAs may communicate a negative narrative (e.g., Brough, O'Driscoll and Biggs, 2009; Pocock, 2016). Thus (consistent with Schien's 1996 prediction), the *on-paper* existence of FWAs belies *the reality* of levels of organisational cultures tacitly discouraging their use (see also, Timms et al., 2015a). While Schien (1996) was clearly discussing organisational policies more broadly than FWAs, he did note that tacit assumptions about "how the world is and ought to be" influenced perceptions, thinking and behaviour within organisations, and could well sabotage an organisation's formal policies. For example, Cech and Blair-Loy (2014) observed that while organisations may attempt to facilitate workers' needs by providing FWAs, co-workers and supervisors may well regard the *need* for flexibility as a sign of reduced commitment to the organisation. Cech and Blair-Loy (2014) called this "*flexibility stigma*". Such an atmosphere at work inevitably has ripple effects affecting employee wellbeing. Timms et al. (2015a), for example, found a negative relationship they termed a *backlash* between FWA use and employee engagement over a period of 12 months. Field and Chan (2018), whose participants were all using FWAs (a few worked entirely from home), also found that some knowledge workers made themselves constantly available even after work hours. This was because they felt that virtual displays of employee engagement had become a proxy for organisational commitment. It is, therefore, observed that hindering cultures (Dikkers et al., 2004) or sub-cultures (Schein, 1996) within organisations can in reality be dysfunctional and destructive in their attitudes towards FWA utilisation.

Kim and Mauborgne (1998, 2015) also warned that workers who do not experience a sense of inclusion at work will hoard ideas and withdraw co-operation. The logical (and circular) consequence of such worker behaviour being the imposition of punitive measures to ensure compliance with company guidelines and expectations. As the management model involving coercive strategies for enforcing employee compliance is a common one (Albrecht, 2002), it remains difficult to convince organisational managements of benefits gained by enhancing employee wellbeing. However, Fink (2003) observed that a top-down mentality such as this inevitably leads to people working-to-rule, thus effectively withdrawing their voluntary cooperation (see also Kim and Mauborgne, 1998).

FWAs and their effects on workers' health and wellbeing

Although FWAs are now common in industrialised economies, a thorough understanding of their impacts on employee health and wellbeing is still lacking. Joyce et al. (2010) conducted a systematic review on the effects of FWAs. They found FWAs that increased workers' control and choice (e.g., flexible scheduling or early/partial/gradual retirement) were shown to have significant positive effects on workers' physical, mental and general health (e.g., systolic blood pressure, heart rate, tiredness, mental health, sleep duration, sleep quality, alertness and self-rated health status). Moen et al. (2011) also found that a results only work environment (ROWE) that does not restrict workers to where and when they work (i.e., organisation-wide flexible working) enhanced workers' health-related behaviours (e.g., getting enough sleep, exercising more, going to the doctor when sick, not going to the workplace when ill) through increasing workers' schedule control and decreasing negative work-to-home spillover.

By contrast, FWAs that were determined by organisational interests (specifically, involuntary part-time employment, contractual flexibility and fixed-term contract) either had no significant effects or negative effects on workers' physical and mental health (Joyce et al., 2010). In many cases, the nature of the relationship between FWAs and health and wellbeing is also not self-evident. For example, Moen et al. (2011) found that if FWAs were offered to help individual workers on a selective basis, there were no significant effects between these FWAs (i.e., ROWE) and workers' health and wellbeing outcomes. Further, Rudolph and Baltes (2017) found that access to and use of FWAs were contingent upon workers' age and health, and they jointly influenced one another, which subsequently had implications for work outcomes. Putting gender into context, Chung and Van der Lippe (2018) consistently found that women were expected to carry out more domestic responsibilities whilst using FWAs, while men were expected to prioritise and expand their work spheres. Consequently, women were more likely to fear and face negative career consequences due to their use of FWAs, consistent with Timms et al.'s (2015a) *backlash* effect. Therefore, future studies examining the influence of FWAs on workers' health and wellbeing need to be contextualised at both the macro and micro levels.

Employee engagement, productivity and flexible work arrangements

Sonnentag et al. (2008) observed that being able to "switch off" during non-work time was a key factor in producing high levels of employee engagement. They noted that employees who were unable to achieve psychological detachment experienced a reduction of their work engagement. This concurs with associations observed between long-hours work cultures and employee psychological ill health (Brough et al., 2005; McDonald et al., 2007; Peetz and Allan, 2005) and echoes warnings about the 24/7 connectivity with employees available to organisations through modern technology (Leiter et al., 2014; O'Driscoll et al., 2010). While the need for tractability in regard to working arrangements coincides with social and political drivers seeking workplace flexibility, it can meet with passive resistance on the part of supervisory staff (Cooper and Baird, 2015; Schein, 1996; Timms et al., 2015a). According to Cech and Blair-Loy (2014), for example, staff members who are visible for long hours in workplaces are still generally regarded as being more committed and, therefore, are more likely to achieve promotion. Other researchers (e.g., Donnelly et al., 2012; Fuller and Hirsh, 2018) have also associated this sort of supervisory judgement with a burden of shame and stigma endured by employees who use FWAs. Consistent with Schein's (1996) observation of misalignment, Dikkers et al. (2004) referred to this sort of work culture as *hindering* because its characteristic feature is mutual suspicion. According to Dikkers et al. (2004), workers dominated by a hindering work culture are compelled by expectations that they will submit to long hours at work and (by means of modern technology) be available around the clock (see also Bessa and Tomlinson, 2017; Fenner and Renn, 2010; Leiter et al., 2014).

According to Pocock (2016), about one third of workers (both women and men) report that they do require some flexibility in order to achieve a better fit between their work and non-work lives, but they do not ask for it. In smaller workplaces this could be because highly skilled workers are legally required to be on site at all times (as can be the case in the nursing profession, see Weale et al., 2017), and any absence from only a small mass of skilled employees can be incompatible with organisational flexibility. These restraints would usually be apparent to employees, would contribute to their expectations, and would generally be accepted. However, the bulk of existing research has found other explanations for workers' reluctance to avail themselves of their legal right to request FWAs.

Gender/generational differences and their FWA needs

Canibano (2019) investigated the experiences of workers in a large global international consulting firm. Within this setting, FWAs afforded benefits both to individuals, and to the company. Canibano noted that female employees with family responsibilities were able to use a combination of telecommuting and flexible hours, and could also be available to communicate with company personnel in different time zones. According to Canibano (2019), this also provides an example of evolving combinations of individual and organisational FWAs, which successfully negotiate the individual needs of the worker and those of the company.

Other research demonstrates indirect benefits to organisations that encourage FWA use. Castillo et al. (2012), for example, observed that FWA provision in organisations enabled non-custodial fathers to have higher levels of involvement with their children, thereby contributing to the psychological health of both employees and their families. Morelock et al. (2017) found that FWA provision enabled workability in older adults who have important organisational contributions to make but no longer wish to be in the full-time workforce. In both these cases, the provision of FWAs and encouragement of their use convey a message to workers that their needs are prioritised, demonstrates respect and contributes to organisational trust, thereby enabling an organisational culture of voluntary cooperation (Kim and Mauborgne, 1998).

Future Research in FWAs

The ability for some workers to conduct their work from their local café, home or shopping mall was unimaginable less than one generation ago. Similarly, the ease with which we now conduct work with colleagues in different parts of the country, or indeed internationally, and in different time zones, was also unimaginable. We are the last generation who were dependent on submitting our work in hard copy via the postal services, an act which now seems quite archaic. Technology has thus generated huge changes in the methods of our work. As discussed above, technology has been significant in providing flexibility to both our work locations and work hours, producing both positive and negative outcomes for employees (see also Brough and O'Driscoll, 2015). Future technological developments will also likely produce a change in our work methods, which we cannot readily conceive of today. These changes and the appropriate management of their impacts are clearly a point of interest for future FWA research.

It has been suggested that each generation of workers has an increased interest in improving the balance of their work and non-work responsibilities – primarily by their increased use of FWAs. A generational change of individual career attitudes and goals has also been observed, albeit with some mixed findings. It has been observed, for example, how securing a job with suitable FWAs to support family commitments, sporting, study and/or travel pursuits is increasingly a "standard" requirement for young employees entering the workforce (Brough et al., 2014). Organisations in information technology (IT), marketing and social media who seek to primarily employ young workers, are flaunting their creative FWAs options. This is a marked change when considering, for example, that it is only recently that employees in some countries (e.g., Australian and New Zealand) received statutory paid parental leave (Brough et al., 2009). Whilst US employees, of course, are still without this national provision. A pertinent consideration for future researchers, then, will be to assess the impact of FWAs as these young workers age and potentially their FWA preferences (and those of their employers) change (Khallash and Kruse, 2012). What will be the preference for the even younger generations entering the workforce in 10–15 years? Will FWAs in new organisations be markedly different? Perhaps, for example, the increasingly ageing population and/or the declining birth rates will encourage the use of different and/or more generous leave and FWAs? Also, while it is simple for a technology firm to offer FWAs to their employees since the nature of IT work is portable, how would organisations in customer-facing service industries such as retail, manufacturing and healthcare cope if their employees demanded more FWAs?

A final issue to consider for the future is if the impact of ecological/climate change will influence FWAs offerings and employee preferences. There is not, to date, any specific published research on this issue. However, the impact of how green spaces (both inside and outside workplaces) positively impact workers' wellbeing has gained considerable momentum in recent years (Buckley et al., 2018; Gilchrist et al., 2015). The inclusion of ecological activities within FWAs could be justified, for example, for locations where the impact of a changing ecological climate is severe; for locations experiencing regular flooding, fires, etc. The benefits to organisations for their employees to work on community tasks, whilst experiencing a suitable mental recovery from their work demands, could perhaps be substantial. We therefore anticipate that ecological/climate change may have an impact of future offerings of FWAs, in order to promote employee psychological health.

Conclusions

In this chapter, we have reviewed some of the key positive and negative impacts of FWAs for employee psychological health. We discussed both the monetary and psychological impacts for why organisations should be considerate of employee mental health. We indicated how the inclusion of formal FWA polices, and clear support for their use, are associated with positive benefits for both employees, their families and their organisations. These benefits primarily consist of increased motivation, engagement, creativity, and service by employees, resulting in enhanced productivity. FWAs also assist organisations to recruit and retain employees, especially younger and older workers and employees with significant non-work responsibilities. Finally, we identified three key issues for future researchers to consider: technological changes that will further impact where and how we conduct our work; changes in FWA offerings shaped by the new emerging generations of workers; and how ecological/climate change may directly impact both FWAs and employee wellbeing.

Recommendations

The extant organisational culture is an important consideration for managements in developing appropriate responses to employees' legitimate take-up of FWAs. Therefore organisation-wide training is indicated. While provision for FWAs is legislated by governments and articulated in company documents, many organisational cultures tacitly discourage their use (Brough and O'Driscoll, 2010). The unsatisfactory presence of any experienced *flexibility stigma* (Cech and Blair-Loy, 2014) or *backlash* (Timms et al., 2015a) signals a need for an increase in organisation-wide education charting the benefits to both the organisation and to employees of policies that consider the non-work responsibilities of staff members. This falls in the realm of communication and training. It is therefore recommended that companies address the need for education within their organisation and clearly communicate to all levels that the benefits of FWAs go far beyond personal advantage.

It is also recommended that training provisions to *direct supervisors/managers* be increased. The primary hurdle faced by employees seeking FWA access is a lack of supervisor approval of this access (Thompson, Brough & Schmidt, 2006). In many cases, supervisors react to the most apparent problem of physically absent employees, without due consideration of the range of human resource options available to support employees, or of the benefits arising from employees successfully accessing FWAs. When supervisors/managers are better educated about these benefits, then approval for FWA access can increase, producing flow-on benefits for both employees and their organisations.

Finally, an assessment of the specific FWAs desired by employees is also strongly recommended. Blanket provisions of common FWAs, such as flexi-time, tele-working and compressed weeks may not necessarily be applicable to all organisations. For example, Field and Chan (2018) noted that tele-working appears to have fewer negative consequences compared to working reduced (e.g., part-time) hours, and suggested that future studies should look at the mechanisms that drive these varying outcomes across different cohorts and types of FWAs. Further, a discrepancy between offered and desired FWAs can exist (Brough et al., 2005). An effective organisation should aim to reduce this discrepancy and offer FWAs of most benefit to their employees.

References

Albrecht, S.L. 2002. Perceptions of integrity, competence and trust in senior management as determinants of cynicism towards change. *Public Administration and Management: An Interactive Journal*, 7, 320–343.

Australian Government. 2009. *The Fair Work Act, 2009.* Canberra, Australia: Australian Government.

Bakker, A.B. & Schaufeli, W.B. 2008. Positive organizational behavior: Engaged employees in flourishing organizations. *Journal of Organizational Behavior, 29,* 147–154.

Bessa, I. & Tomlinson, J. 2017. Established, accelerated and emergent themes in flexible work research. *Journal of Industrial Relations, 59,* 153–169.

Biggs, A., Brough, P. & Barbour, J. 2014. Relationships of individual and organizational support with engagement: Examining various types of causality in a three-wave study. *Work & Stress, 28,* 236–254.

Blair-Loy, M. & Wharton, A.S. 2004. Organizational commitment and constraints on work-family policy use: Corporate flexibility policies in a global firm. *Sociological Perspectives, 47,* 243–267.

Brough, P. & O'Driscoll, M. 2010. Organisational interventions for balancing work and home demands: An overview. *Work & Stress, 24,* 280–297.

Brough, P. & O'Driscoll, M.P. 2015. Integrating work and personal life. In R.J. Burke, K.M. Page & C.L. Cooper (eds), *Flourishing in Life, Work, and Careers: Individual Wellbeing and Career Experiences.* Cheltenham, UK: Edward Elgar.

Brough, P., O'Driscoll, M. & Biggs, A. 2009. Parental leave and work-family balance among employed parents following childbirth: An exploratory investigation in Australia and New Zealand. *Kotuitui: New Zealand Journal of Social Sciences Online, 4,* 71–87.

Brough, P., O'Driscoll, M. & Kalliath, T. 2005. The ability of "family friendly" organisational resources to predict work-family conflict and job and family satisfaction. *Stress and Health, 21,* 223–234.

Brough, P., Timms, C., O'Driscoll, M., Kalliath, T., Siu, O.L., Sit, C. & Lo, D. 2014. Work-life balance: A longitudinal evaluation of a new measure across Australia and New Zealand Workers. *International Journal of Human Resource Management, 25,* 2724–2744.

Buckley, R.C., Brough, P. & Westaway, D. 2018. Bringing outdoor therapies into mainstream mental health. *Frontiers in Public Health,* May, 1–4.

Canibano, A. 2019. Workplace flexibility as a paradoxical phenomenon: Exploring employee experiences. *Human Relations, 72,* 1–27.

Castillo, J., Welch, G. & Sarver, C. 2012. Walking a high beam: The balance between employment stability, workplace flexibility and nonresident father involvement. *American Journal of Men's Health, 6,* 120–131.

Cech, E. & Blair-Loy, M. 2014. Consequences of flexibility stigma among academic scientists and engineers. *Work and Occupations, 41,* 86–110.

Chung, H. & Van Der Lippe, T. 2018. Flexible working, work-life balance, and gender equality. *Social Indicators Research,* Special, 1–17.

Cocker, F., Sanderson, K. & Lamontagne, A.D. 2017. Estimating the economic benefits of eliminating job strain as a risk factor for depression. *Journal of Occupational and Environmental Medicine, 59,* 12–17.

Cooper, R. & Baird, M. 2015. Bringing the "right to request" flexible working arrangements to life: From policies to practices. *Employee Relations, 37,* 568–581.

Diener, E. & Seligman, M.E.P. 2004. Beyond money. Towards an economy of well-being. *Psychological Science in the Public Interest, 5,* 1–31.

Dikkers, J., Geurts, S., Den Dulk, L., Peper, B. & Kompier, M. 2004. Relations among work-home culture, the utilization of work-home arrangements, and work-home interference. *International Journal of Stress Management, 11,* 323–345.

Dinham, S., Cairney, T., Craigie, D. & Wilson, S. 1995. School climate and leadership: Research into three secondary schools. *Journal of Educational Administration*, *33*, 36–58.

Donnelly, N., Proctor-Thomson, S. & Plimmer, G. 2012. The Role of 'Voice' in Matters of 'Choice': Flexible Work Outcomes for Women in the New Zealand Public Services. *Journal of Industrial Relations*, *54*, 182–203.

Downey, S., Van Der Werff, L., Thomas, K. & Plaut, V. 2015. The role of diversity practices and inclusion in promoting trust and employee engagement. *Journal of Applied Social Psychology*, *45*, 35–44.

European Union (EU). 2014. *Calculating the Cost of Work-Related Stress*. European Agency for Safety & Health at Work. Report.

Fenner, G. & Renn, R. 2010. Technology-assisted supplemental work and work-to-family conflict: The role of instrumentality beliefs, organizational expectations and time management. *Human Relations*, *63*, 63–82.

Field, J.C. & Chan, X.W. 2018. Contemporary knowledge workers and the boundaryless work–life interface: Implications for the human resource management of the knowledge workforce. *Frontiers in Psychology*, *9*, 2414.

Fink, D. 2003. The law of unintended consequences: The "real" cost of top-down reform. *Journal of Educational Change*, *4*, 105–128.

Fredrickson, B.L. 2001. The role of positive emotions in positive psychology: The broaden-and-build theory of positive emotions. *American Psychologist*, *56*, 218–226.

Fredrickson, B.L., Tugade, M.M., Waugh, C.E. & Larkin, G.R. 2003. What good are positive emotions in crises? A prospective study of resilience and emotions following the terrorist attacks on the United States on September 11th, 2001. *Journal of Personality and Social Psychology*, *84*, 365–376.

Fuller, S. & Hirsh, C.E. 2018. "Family-friendly" jobs and motherhood pay penalties: The impact of flexible work arrangements. *Work and Occupations*, *46*, 1–42.

Gilchrist, K., Brown, C. & Montarzino, A. 2015. Workplace settings and wellbeing: Greenspace use and views contribute to employee wellbeing at peri-urban business sites. *Landscape and Urban Planning*, *138*, 32–40.

Hart, P., Wearing, A.J., Conn, M., Carter, N. & Dingle, R. 2000. Development of the school organisational health questionnaire: A measure for assessing teacher morale and school organisational climate. *British Journal of Educational Psychology*, *8*, 211–228.

Harter, J., Schmidt, F., Agrawal, S. & Plowman, S. 2013. *The Relationship Between Engagement at Work and Organizational Outcomes: 2012 Q12 Meta-Analysis*. Washington, DC: Gallup.

Harter, J., Schmidt, F. & Hayes, T. 2002. Business-unit-level relationship between employee satisfaction, employee engagement and business outcomes: A meta-analysis. *Journal of Applied Psychology*, *87*, 268–279.

Hassard, J., Teoh, K., Visockaite, G., Dewe, P. & Cox, T. 2018. The cost of work-related stress to society: A systematic review. *Journal of Occupational Health Psychology*, *23*, 1–17.

Hegewisch, A. & Gornick, J. 2008. *Statutory Routes to Workplace Flexibility in Cross-National Perspective*. Washington, DC: Institute for Women's Policy Research & Center for Workplace Law.

Joyce, K., Pabayo, R., Critchley, J. & Bambra, C. 2010. Flexible working conditions and their effects on employee health and wellbeing. Cochrane Reviews. Available at: https://www.cochrane.org/CD008009/PUBHLTH_flexible-working-conditions-and-their-effects-on-employee-health-and-wellbeing

Khallash, S. & Kruse, M. 2012. The future of work and work-life balance 2025. *Futures, 44*, 678–686.

Kim, W.C. & Mauborgne, R. 1998. Procedural justice, strategic decision making, and the knowledge economy. *Strategic Management Journal, 19*, 323–338.

Kim, W.C. & Mauborgne, R. 2015. *Blue Ocean Strategy, Expanded Edition: How to Create Uncontested Market Space and Make the Competition Irrelevant*. Boston, MA: Harvard Business School Publishing.

Leiter, M., Bakker, A. & Maslach, C. 2014. The contemporary context of job burnout. In M. Leiter, A. Bakker & C. Maslach (eds), *Burnout at Work: A Psychological Perspective*. London: Psychology Press.

McCarthy, A., Darcy, C. & Grady, G. 2010. Work-life balance policy and practice: Understanding line manager attitudes and behaviors. *Human Resource Management Review, 20*, 158–167.

McDonald, P., Pini, B. & Bradley, L. 2007. Freedom or fallout in local government? How work-life culture impacts employees using flexible work practices. *International Journal of Human Resource Management, 18*, 602–622.

May, D.R., Gilson, R.L. & Harter, L.M. 2004. The psychological conditions of meaningfulness, safety and availability and the engagement of the human spirit at work. *Journal of Occupational and Organizational Psychology, 77*, 11–37.

Moen, P., Kelly, E., Tranby, E. & Huang, Q. 2011. Changing work, changing health: Can real work-time flexibility promote health behaviors and well-being? *Journal of Health and Social Behavior, 52*, 404–429.

Morelock, J., Mcnamara, T. & James, J. 2017. Workability and requests for flexible work arrangements among older adults: The role of a time and place management intervention. *Journal of Applied Gerontology, 36*, 1370–1392.

O'Driscoll, M., Brough, P., Timms, C. & Sawang, S. 2010. Engagement with information and communication technology and psychological well-being. In P.L. Perrewé & D.C. Ganster (eds), *New Developments in Theoretical and Conceptual Approaches to Job Stress, Research in Occupational Stress and Well Being*. Bingley, UK: Emerald Group.

Peetz, D. & Allan, C. 2005. Flexitime and the long-hours culture in the public sector: Causes and effects. *The Economic and Labour Relations Review, 15*, 159–180.

Pocock, B. 2016. Holding up half the sky? Women at work in the 21st century. *The Economic and Labour Relations Review, 27*, 147–163.

PricewaterhouseCoopers. 2014. Creating a mentally healthy workplace: Return on investment analysis. Beyond Blue. Report. Available at: http://www.headsup.org.au

Rudolph, C. & Baltes, B. 2017. Age and health jointly moderate the influence of flexible work arrangements on work engagement: Evidence from two empirical studies. *Journal of Occupational Health Psychology, 22*, 40–58.

Ryan, R.M. & Deci, E.L. 2000. Self-determination theory and the facilitation of intrinsic motivation, social development and well-being. *American Psychologist, 55*, 68–78.

Ryan, R.M. & Deci, E.L. 2001. On happiness and human potentials: A review of research on hedonic and eudaimonic well-being. *Annual Review of Psychology, 52*, 139–170.

Safe Work Australia. 2013. The incidence of accepted workers compensation claims for mental stress in Australia. Safe Work Australia.

Salanova, M. & Schaufeli, W. 2008. A cross-national study of work engagement as a mediator between job resources and proactive behaviour. *The International Journal of Human Resource Management, 19*, 116–131.

Schaufeli, W. & Bakker, A. 2003. *Utrecht Work Engagement Scale: Preliminary Manual.* Utrecht, The Netherlands: Occupational Health Psychology Unit, Utrecht University.

Schaufeli, W.B. & Salanova, M. 2014. Burnout, boredom and engagement at the workplace. In M.C. Peeters, J. de Jonge & T. Taris (eds), *People at Work: An Introduction to Contemporary Work Psychology.* Chichester, UK: Wiley-Blackwell.

Schein, E. 1996. Three cultures of management: The key to organizational learning. *Sloan Management Review, 38,* 9–20.

Sonnentag, S., Mojza, E.J., Binnewies, C. & Scholl, A. 2008. Being engaged at work and detached at home. A week-level study on work engagement, psychological detachment and affect. *Work and Stress, 22,* 257–276.

Thompson, B.M., Brough, P. & Schmidt, H. 2006. Supervisor and subordinate work-family values: Does similarity make a difference? *International Journal of Stress Management, 13,* 45–63.

Timms, C., Brough, P., O'Driscoll, M., Kalliath, T., Siu, O., Sit, C. & Lo, D. 2015a. Flexible work arrangements, work engagement, turnover intentions and psychological health. *Asia Pacific Journal of Human Resources, 53,* 83–103.

Timms, C., Brough, P., O'Driscoll, M., Kalliath, T., Siu, O., Sit, C. & Lo, D. 2015b. Positive pathways to engaging workers: work-family enrichment as a predictor of work engagement. *Asia Pacific Journal of Human Resources, 53,* 490–510.

Townsend, K., McDonald, P. & Cathcart, A. 2017. Managing flexible work arrangements in small not-for-profit firms: The influence of organisational size, financial constraints and workforce characteristics. *The International Journal of Human Resource Management, 28,* 2085–2107.

Weale, V., Wells, Y. & Oakman, J. 2017. Flexible working arrangements in residential aged care: Applying a person-environment fit model. *Asia Pacific Journal of Human Resources, 55,* 356–374.

4 Workplace flexibility increases productivity throughout presenteeism[1]

A conceptual framework

Sara L. Lopes and Aristides I. Ferreira

Introduction

In the last few decades of research, the concept of presenteeism or attendance at work while sick has mainly been conceptualized as a variable with negative implications (e.g., productivity losses) (Aronsson & Gustafsson, 2005). Despite the advances in recent years, the presenteeism literature is still not conceptually grounded in a strong theory (Lohaus & Habermann, 2019). For example, some literature suggests that there is a lack of conceptual clarity around the topic of presenteeism in the current policy debate about workplace flexibility and productivity (Irvine, 2011). The relationship between workplace flexibility and presenteeism seems to be under studied. Therefore, this chapter draws upon the conceptual framework of positive presenteeism (Karanika-Murray & Biron, 2019; Karanika-Murray & Cooper, 2018), with the emphasis on those schools of thought on presenteeism that are more interested in studying reduced productivity losses associated with sickness presence (Turpin et al., 2004) and the consequences of these behaviours (Gosselin, Lemyre & Corneil, 2013; Lopes et al., 2018). These theoretical contributions have tried to conceptualize presenteeism as an adaptive behaviour (Karanika-Murray & Biron, 2019; Karanika-Murray & Cooper, 2018). Karanika-Murray and Biron developed a model where presenteeism is represented as a dynamic, balanced process of adaptation between health constraints and performance demands, depending on the availability of internal capacities and flexible work resources (Karanika-Murray & Biron, 2019). And, focusing on the positive side of presenteeism, these authors proposed a 2{x}2 presenteeism framework, built upon the axes of health and performance. For example, an optimal adjustment to health constraints and performance demands is related with functional presenteeism (e.g., being highly engaged with work to forget psychological and/or physical problems), and in contrast, poor health and poor performance are associated with dysfunctional presenteeism (Karanika-Murray & Biron, 2019).

Previous studies define organizational flexibility as the organizational capacity to adapt the internal structure of the company to the external environment (Broekaert, Andries & Debackere, 2016). Within the big umbrella of organizational flexibility, we will adopt the concept of workplace flexibility where flexible work arrangements are important measures to promote the employees' capacity to deal with their health problems, increased job demands and possible work-family conflicts (Butler et al., 2009). Examples of job arrangements include job crafting, flexible task management, schedule flexibility (e.g., flexitime) and location flexibility (e.g., the employee can choose the best physical location to work, such as telework or remote work through Internet).

The fast growth of the gig economy raises questions about the quality of jobs that are currently being created. Gig economy is generally characterized by temporary positions and short-term engagements among employers, workers and customers (Kalleberg & Dunn, 2016). However, gig economy is also seen as promoting jobs that offer considerable levels of flexibility, autonomy and work-life balance (Kalleberg & Dunn, 2016).With this in mind, we proposed an explanatory model that may provide guidance for managers and academicians and considers the role of individual productivity despite presenteeism and the contextual factors of flexibility. These factors, when embedded in strong climates of presenteeism (i.e., pressures to go to work while ill) may lead to different employee profiles and varying levels of productivity conditioned by environments with asymmetrical patterns of flexibility and presenteeism climates.

Based on these assumptions, we aim: i) to provide a clear picture of the constructs and to increase the debate around the topics of flexibility on presenteeism; ii) to develop individualized and contextualized profiles where presenteeism can be adaptive and functional (Karanika-Murray & Biron, 2019); and iii) to explain potential antecedents (e.g., presenteeism climate, bureaucracy) that may lead to each of the studied profiles.

Presenteeism and productivity

In the presenteeism literature, the construct can be operationalized solely as an attendance behaviour (e.g., Aronsson, Gustafsson & Dallner, 2000; McGregor, 2017), or as behaviour and consequent outcome (Ferreira et al., 2019; Hemp, 2004). In the latter approach, productivity loss is the consequence of sickness presence at work (Turpin et al., 2004). It is important to note that productivity will be considered only at an individual level, referring to the employee efficiency in the performance of tasks and functions at work (Gosselin et al., 2013). Since productivity loss due to absenteeism can be more easily calculated than productivity loss due to presenteeism (Hemp, 2004), researchers are striving to understand productivity losses attributed to presenteeism, and to develop better instruments to measure this. Moreover, there is a need for improved and, therefore, better models to evaluate the true impact of health on productivity costs. For example, what are the dynamics of individual sickness on team performance (McGregor, 2017)? Previous measures have only focused on the productivity outcomes of specific health conditions, such as chronic diseases (e.g., Stanford Presenteeism Scale [SPS-6] developed by Koopman et al., 2002), or confuse psychological and physical health problems (e.g., World Health Organization Health and Work Performance Questionnaire [HPQ] developed by Kessler et al., 2003).

Several studies provide evidences of weak psychometric properties (Ospina et al., 2015), suggesting that measures are merely evaluating financial metrics (Schultz, Chen & Edington, 2009), or were not specifically designed to measure productivity loss attributable to physical or psychological problems (Grawitch et al., 2017).

Our proposed presenteeism model describes the dynamic nature of presenteeism and focuses on how the dynamic process between productivity and flexibility can delineate different types of presenteeism behaviours. These presenteeism behaviours can be influenced by structural and contextual aspects of the organizations (their presenteeism climate) and individuals' own health status. To illustrate, the dynamic nature of presenteeism can depend if the sickness conditions employees are dealing with are temporary and 'unpredictable' conditions (e.g. epilepsy, vertigo attacks) and/or chronic (e.g., types of cancer, allergies) and also from the availability of organizational resources to protect workers' health and performance (e.g., high vs. low support from supervisors and peers).

Presenteeism behaviours can occur due to numerous reasons. For example, they can occur in employees who feel job insecurity, pressure by their peers or fear of being judged or criticized by their team/colleagues (Johns, 2011). Notwithstanding, increased workloads may also cause presenteeism, leading individuals to feel that they cannot afford to take sick leave regardless of their health status. Herewith, non-flexible work arrangements can lead to barriers in how workers manage their own health (Roelen & Groothoff, 2010).

With this in mind and following recommendations from Karanika-Murray and Biron (2019), our conceptual model can bring theoretical clarity to bear on the dynamic nature of presenteeism behaviour, with specific focus on the different levels of productivity losses a worker can present when they decide to go to work sick.

Presenteeism climate

Presenteeism climate, as linked to the individual practice of presenteeism, has been a rising research topic in the literature (Ferreira et al., 2015; Ferreira et al., 2017; Gosselin et al., 2013). Presenteeism is more usual in organizations that promote or have features such as co-worker competitiveness, difficulty of replacement and extra-time valuation (Ferreira et al., 2017). With all these features contributing to a presenteeism climate in the workplace, it follows that it is the result of the beliefs and values regarding certain features of the organization, and also of society pressuring employees to attend work despite suffering from health problems (Ferreira et al., 2017). Thus, a presenteeism climate is a multidimensional construct, and the pressure to be present at work can increase the levels of job-related stress, which can result in productivity losses (Johns, 2010; Koopman et al., 2002). Despite these evidences, the influence of a climate of presenteeism on employee behaviour remains to be explained, especially regarding its impact on leaders and co-workers.

Presenteeism climate is directly influenced by an organization's environment, in so far as it is the responsibility of companies to make explicit which health conditions are acceptable for employees to be present or absent from work (Ferreira et al., 2015). Studies indicate that employees may feel pressured to engage in presenteeism behaviours in situations where they think their colleagues would be affected if they call in sick (Nielsen & Daniels, 2016). There are a lot of factors that contribute to workers being present despite adverse health conditions: competitiveness within the organization, major responsibilities at work; preoccupations with career and performance; and lack of support from leaders (Ferreira et al., 2015; Koopman et al., 2002). Therefore, presenteeism is more common in organizations where employees and leaders feel there is pressure to go to work while ill, contributing to a presenteeism climate (Ferreira et al., 2017). The reciprocal influence between supervisors and employees, and between employees and co-workers can have a determinant role in shaping employee behaviours and productivity (Aronsson & Gustafsson, 2005; Hunter, Ansari & Jayasingam, 2013; Luksyte, Avery & Yeo, 2015).

When an employee is suffering from a health problem, s/he often has to decide to stay away from work, engaging in a sickness absence behaviour, or to continue to attend work, engaging in a sickness presence behaviour (MacGregor & Cunningham, 2018). Since organizations can encourage the existence of some conditions that promote a presenteeism climate within them, encouraging flexible work environments could be a way for managers and human resources (HR) departments to reduce the negative consequences of a presenteeism climate in the workplace. Giving the reciprocal influence between managers and employees, encouraging managers to work flexibly themselves can be a starting point, since they can act as role models (Clarke & Holdsworth, 2017).

Moreover, social support from supervisors and co-workers can result in flexible arrangements that can help to reduce the pressure on employees to go to work while sick (Gosselin et al., 2013; MacGregor & Cunningham, 2018). For example, a growing number of organizations are providing tools to allow employees to work from home, which often makes workers feel more productive and creates a more positive attitude towards work, promoting a better work-life balance (Clarke & Holdsworth, 2017).

Presenteeism and flexibility

In the current gig economy, technologies provide employees with full control over their own work and schedule. Examples of gig employees in the workforce could include freelancers, independent contractors, project-based workers and temporary or part-time hires. The literature distinguishes between worker-controlled flexible scheduling and manager-controlled flexible scheduling (Henly, Shaefer & Waxman, 2006). Most of the advantages of flexible scheduling, such as lower work-family conflict (Shockley & Allen, 2007), are more associated with worker-controlled flexibility. With manager-controlled flexibility, however, there is increased uncertainty and employees may feel inhibited with regard to planning their own daily schedules (Lehdonvirta, 2018). Structural pressures on the quantity of working time (e.g., due to unexpected workloads) influences the way working schedules are designed and may introduce a false sense of flexibility. In fact, employees with little bargaining power, and an incapacity to say no or to negotiate task demands, may turn what is known as worker-controlled flexibility into manager-controlled flexibility (Lehdonvirta, 2018), and consequently lead to the benefits associated with work flexibility being lost.

In the current chapter, we will highlight the dark side of flexibility and suggest it could lead to employees hiding illness which may, in turn, affect their productivity and increase burnout, and also affect their work-life balance (Blair-Loy, 2009). Should managers encourage their employees to work when they are ill? What can employers do to reduce the costs of presenteeism? According to Robertson (2011), the answer to these two questions is that the solution to enable both employers and employees to reduce the detrimental impact of both sickness absence and sickness presence is flexibility. In other words, managers should support their employees' return to work while ill in a phased way. Therefore, managers should incorporate a culture of common sense and flexibility where each health condition (either a chronic condition such as diabetes or a seasonal condition such as influenza) will be fairly assessed in order to ensure only legitimate sickness absence is authorized. Flexible HR policies would enable employees who took time off due to illness to return to work and make up for the time lost. This would send a message of fairness that everyone is allowed to recover properly when they are sick. Moreover, in contexts of chronic diseases and permanent sickness presence (for example, the case of different types of cancer or allergies), Oakman, Kinsman and Briggs (2017) identified six strategies to enable productivity despite presenteeism, namely: i) support from a supervisor; ii) job design; iii) physical environment changes; iv) medication/therapies; v) access to resources; and vi) personal characteristics. All these enabling aspects have one thing in common: flexibility. For example, supervisors should provide flexibility in the schedules and workloads, make it possible to adjust the number of hours and take regular breaks, and facilitate working from home. Also, employees while ill should have the opportunity to negotiate job design/ task characteristics in terms of variety, flexibility, autonomy, identity and feedback. Another important practice that would help towards increasing the productivity of employees who work while ill would be to take steps to modify the work environment, to include better access to the workplace, and to ensure more assistance from colleagues and provide appropriate equipment (i.e., ergonomic working tools). Companies should also promote non-threatening environments where professionals have the flexibility to discuss their health problems, and have access to important resources (e.g., medication and health professionals).

Johns (2010) identified adjustment latitude as the opportunities available to employees to change their work procedures to reduce their work outputs and thus reduce their productivity levels while ill. Accordingly, employers who allow adjustment latitude are somewhat promoting opportunities to take away and to reduce presenteeism. Another measure of flexibility highly associated with presenteeism is the ease of replacement, which means that the work not done due to absenteeism has to be done upon return to the company. The literature shows that lack of backup with regard to this, and the fear of heavier workloads, time pressure and absence of support from colleagues and supervisors are among the most common reasons for presenteeism (Caverley, Cunningham & MacGregor, 2007). Moreover, when working in high-dependent team cultures, employees may feel pressure from their peers for reliable and on-time attendance (Johns, 2010). The sense of urgency and mutual dependence in certain teams (e.g., surgery teams) stimulate a compulsion for presenteeism, which in turn may lead to long-term sickness absence.

A new presenteeism framework

Employees' thoughts and decisions around whether to go to work or to stay at home while ill may be influenced by structural and contextual aspects of their job status and task demands, as well as self-evaluation of their health condition (Irvine, 2011). Therefore, as we will explain in more detail below, we propose a conceptual approach (Figure 4.1) where the axes of productivity and flexibility suggest the existence of four different typologies of employee environments. Employees in environments with high flexibility may have reduced productivity (HiFlexRedPro) or have a different attitude with lower levels of productivity loss due to presenteeism (HiFlexHiPro). Contexts of low flexibility may lead to profiles where employees go to work, but due to an absence of flexibility and poor working conditions reveal low production (LoFlexRedPro). Alternatively, employees may be pressured by supervisors and peers to increase their productivity despite the absence of a flexible work setting (LoFlexHiPro).

HiFlexHiPro

HiFlexHiPro is a label attributed to those employees who, despite going to work while ill, know how to benefit from the positive strengths of flexible work settings. Hence, we may ask whether all employees should go to work despite being ill. Concerning this question, there is no magic formula, since several factors such as illness severity, labour legislation, pressure from peers and supervisors, and self-motivation may contribute to the decision whether to stay at home or to go to work while ill. The literature shows that going to

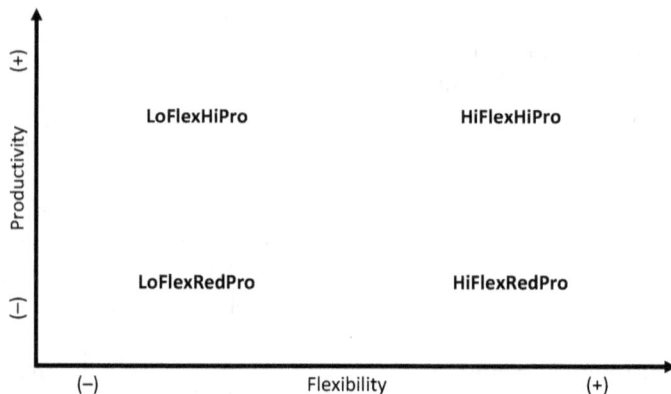

Figure 4.1 A conceptual model of presenteeism showing the impact of the dimensions of productivity and flexibility

work despite being ill can be an interesting strategy to recover from the health problem or possibly, even, to maintain wellbeing and good mental health (Sanderson & Cocker, 2013). In fact, a relevant faction of the presenteeism literature aims to provide suggestions to help managers and employees increase (or maintain) productivity despite illness. We know from the literature that employees with high job engagement (Ferreira et al., 2019), supervisor support, reduced task ambiguity (Zhou et al., 2016), low neuroticism, high conscientiousness, job security and low work-family conflict (Johns, 2011) reported fewer productivity losses despite going to work while ill. These findings emphasize that individual and contextual variables contribute towards reducing the negative impact of presenteeism at work. Therefore, in this chapter, we conceptualize that flexible work settings may provide good conditions for functional presenteeism (Karanika-Murray & Biron, 2019). Going to work may be seen as sustainable behaviour that allows employees to maintain their levels of productivity and, at the same time, recover from their health problems (Urtasun & Nuñez, 2018). Employees who find flexible and positive working conditions may be more likely to fall into the HiFlexHiPro category in that they have good employee experiences (Whysall, Bowden & Hewitt, 2018) because flexibility allows them to deal with their illness problems and thus maintain high levels of productivity. This can be particularly relevant for workers dealing with chronic health conditions such as diabetes, arthritis or depression, as they are likely to have more time to be distracted from the health condition while at work socializing with colleagues, customers and supervisors (McGregor et al., 2017).

HiFlexRedPro

Some companies, such as Google, have developed a fun park where employees can have moments of amusement and have the flexibility to choose from several activities, such as playing video games, bowling, basketball or running slides at the expense of short-term productivity, with apparent therapeutic gains (Fortune, 2017). In real work settings that have similar features to those of the fun park, we can easily find employees who have the flexibility to execute several tasks, manage their daily schedule and still prefer to go to work and rest or simply procrastinate even while ill. The literature suggests the concept of therapeutic presenteeism to describe those workers who go to work to recover from health problems and see their job therapeutically (Karanika-Murray & Biron, 2019). These employees may find that the contexts of good camaraderie, a strong commitment to team work and organizational climates characterized by flexibility and positive organizational climate help mitigate or even hide the negative effects of their health problem (Knani, Biron & Fournier, 2018).

Employees with this profile tend to find that a supportive work environment where low productivity and less desirable workplace behaviours, such as procrastination, are well accepted for the sake of a common good that is the healthy recovery of a colleague. In the long term, however, this therapeutically driven presenteeism may change to dysfunctional presenteeism (Karanika-Murray & Biron, 2019) where long-term sickness presence may become detrimental to health and performance (Taloyan et al., 2012). In the long term, HiFlexRedPro profiles may experience a downward spiral of reduced performance and subsequent increased vulnerability associated with the incapacity to recover their resources despite the flexibility found in their work setting (Hobfoll, 1989). The perception of continuous reduced productivity may lead to perceptions of injustice from colleagues and supervisors which, in turn, may lead to reduced social support and decreased emotional support (Demerouti, Mostert & Bakker, 2010). Therefore, although HiFlexRedPro profiles in contexts of high flexibility and a positive organizational climate may initially find a sanctuary for their health recovery at the expenses of the company, the same sources of support may disappear if, in the long term, employees do not change their attitude and take advantage of the good environmental conditions provided by a flexible work setting to start increasing productivity.

LoFlexRedPro

Low flexibility work contexts may trigger the appearance of employee profiles where, although they have made an effort to work while sick, there is low productivity because of the characteristics of the work environment. Some organizational policies, such as payment for sick leave, attendance control and downsizing have been associated with enhanced presenteeism (Johns, 2010).

Although presenteeism is seen as a behavioural response to perceived sickness, the extent to which it affects individuals' productivity may be related to the perception of their work environment characteristics (Jensen, Andersen & Holten, 2017). Therefore, workers who perceive their work environment as negative may make an effort to go to work while sick, although they are incapable of being productive since they feel confined. An employee feels that their work environment is negative when the physical and psychological working conditions are inadequate (Ali, Ali & Adan, 2013). Increased workloads, stressful work environments, poor relationships with colleagues and lack of support from supervisors are features of a negative work environment that have been linked to lower levels of productivity (Johns, 2010; Ma et al., 2018; Musich et al., 2006).

In low-flexibility work environments, higher bureaucracy, structural limitations and lack of resources are features that can lead workers to feel frustrated about their jobs, which can negatively affect their productivity levels (Jensen et al., 2017). One example can be found in public service jobs where there can be an increase in the occurrence of presenteeism behaviours because the act of absenteeism directly affects the cost and the quality of public service provision (Jensen et al., 2017). Likewise, employees with this presenteeism profile can have a tendency to be unsatisfied within their jobs, which can lead to a higher tendency for employee turnover (Ali et al., 2013; Sanderson & Cocker, 2013).

Thus, in work contexts with lower flexibility, presenteeism behaviours may arise as a coping behaviour to deal with the negative features of the work environment (Musich et al., 2006), although with negative consequences for employee productivity levels.

LoFlexHiPro

LoFlexHiPro is a label attributed to those work environments where there is no flexibility and which require that employees go to work while sick and still maintain high levels of productivity, despite the possible negative health consequences.

The reasons that lead employees to go to work even when experiencing moderate levels of physical and psychological discomfort, to the detriment of their own health, may be motivated by a stringent work environment that encourages a presenteeism climate. In such circumstances, the lack of social support from peers and supervisors can make employees feel they are 'slaves' to their own work environment and under pressure to not take sick leave or the appropriate time to recover (MacGregor & Cunningham, 2018). In work environments with low flexibility, individuals' motivations for presenteeism are related to a desire to avoid punishment from others (Ma et al., 2018), or team responsibilities (Bierla, Huver & Richard, 2013). Workplace settings where workers' own productivity determines team performance and goals can push individuals to maintain higher levels of productivity despite health problems, inducing workers to behave in ways contrary to their own will. Supervisors can also play a determinant role: if a supervisor is present at work despite their own health condition, their behaviour sets a standard for the team to meet, so employees will be constrained to act similarly (Bierla et al., 2013).

There are also organizational-related factors, such as organizational policies, job insecurity and time pressure (Johns, 2010) that can drive employees
to be forced to increase their productivity despite the absence of a flexible
work setting. For example, companies may have restricted policies regarding
sick leave, such as an attendance bonus or punishment for certain amounts of
sick leave (Ma et al., 2018).

However, this kind of extreme commitment regardless of an individual's
health problems may have strong implications for the person and also for their
colleagues and employers. Working when sick is a consequence of a more
immediate health problem (for instance, migraines or allergies) but can in
itself be a forthcoming risk for future adverse health problems (Sanderson &
Cocker, 2013). Individuals who feel obligated to go to work while sick can be
at increased risk of accidents or mistakes due to fatigue or difficulty in concentrating, not meeting deadlines and not being able to think clearly (Sanderson & Cocker, 2013). In the case of contagious diseases such as influenza,
they could possibly infect their colleagues, resulting in further absences in
the team (Bierla et al., 2013). Moreover, working while sick can develop the
risk of a poor quality of life (Lopes et al., 2018), and thus increase the risk of
future absence for ill health. Taking into account the dynamic nature of this
model, individuals who work in contexts that promote these types of presenteeism behaviours may also be more likely to develop higher levels of burnout
and work-related stress (Jensen et al., 2017). This could lead to the transition
from levels of higher productivity to levels of low productivity, which could
result in greater risk for the emergence of *LoFlexHiPro* presenteeism profiles.

Recommendations

In this chapter, we dedicated our attention to clarifying the topic of presenteeism in a new, under studied line of research that links organizational
flexibility and productivity. Based on previous research, we established a
presenteeism climate as a multidimensional construct directly influenced
by the organization environment, and one in which the existence of certain conditions can promote sickness presence behaviours (Ferreira et al.,
2015; Gosselin et al., 2013). In light of these evidences, encouraging flexible
work environments can be a way to reduce the negative consequences of a
presenteeism climate in the workplace. We reviewed several organizational
features that could explain the link between presenteeism and flexibility.
More importantly, we extended our understanding of presenteeism in an
integrated model where the intersection of different levels of productivity
and flexibility suggest the existence of four different typologies of employees
in the workplace.

HighFlexHiPro is a label attributed to those employees who, despite going
to work while ill, have lower levels of productivity losses because their flexible work setting allows them to benefit from the positive strengths associated
with those work environments.

HighFlexRedPro is a label characterized by work contexts with high flexibility and a positive organizational climate, which helps individuals to hide the negative effects of their health problem, which in turn can cause reduced productivity in employees who decide to go to work ill. Along the opposite axis of flexibility, *LoFlexRedPro* is associated with the appearance of employee profiles that, despite making an effort to work while sick, reveal lower levels of productivity due to an absence of flexibility and poor working conditions. Finally, the *LoFlexHiPro* is a label related to work environments with no flexibility, where the pressures from supervisors and peers require that employees go to work while sick and maintain higher levels of productivity.

In general, in this chapter, we highlight the importance of creating flexible organizational climates that can help to manage employees' health in the workplace in an appropriate manner. By developing more flexible arrangements, workers may deal with the negative effects of presenteeism in a more powerful way, which can help to prevent stress, burnout and long-term sickness absence (Jensen et al., 2017; MacGregor & Cunningham, 2018). Moreover, we believe that our productivity-flexibility framework of presenteeism adds to the literature by providing a more comprehensive understanding of the dynamics underlying the process of deciding to go to work while sick, as well as the trajectories between the different types of presenteeism behaviour.

We recommend organizations to foster a culture that supports individuals' wellbeing, allowing them to take time off from work when needed. Implementing these policies will help to manage presenteeism in organizations, increase productivity and contribute to a healthier life. For our final recommendation, companies can implement wellness programmes that can help workers to focus on their health, such as nutrition and exercise programmes, health assessments or free flu vaccinations. Healthier employees not only lead to lower rates of sick leave but also to a more engaged workforce. We believe that flexible work contexts can have a positive effect on health outcomes (Clarke & Holdsworth, 2017), contributing to healthier employees and greater work-life balance.

Note

1 Funding: This work was supported by Fundação para a Ciência e a Tecnologia, grant SFRH/BD/134420/2017.

References

Ali, A. Y., Ali, A. A., & Adan, A. A. (2013). Working conditions and employees' productivity in manufacturing companies in Sub-Saharan African context: case of Somalia. *Educational Research International, 2* (2).

Aronsson, G. & Gustafsson, K. (2005). Sickness presenteeism: prevalence, attendance-pressure factors, and an outline of a model for research. *Journal of Occupational and Environmental Medicine, 47*, 958–966.

Aronsson, G., Gustafsson, K., & Dallner, M. (2000). Sick but yet at work. An empirical study of sickness presenteeism. *Journal of Epidemiology & Community Health*, *54* (7), 502–509.

Bierla, I., Huver, B., & Richard, S. (2013). New evidence on absenteeism and presenteeism. *International Journal of Human Resource Management*, *24* (7), 1536–1550.

Blair-Loy, M. (2009). Work without end? Scheduling flexibility and work-to-family conflict among stockbrokers. *Work and Occupations*, *36* (4), 279–317.

Broekaert, W., Andries, P., & Debackere, K. (2016). 'Innovation processes in family firms: the relevance of organizational flexibility', *Small Business Economics*, *47* (3), 771–785.

Butler, A., Grzywacz, J., Ettner, S., & Liu, B. (2009). 'Workplace flexibility, self-reported health, and health care utilization', *Work & Stress*, *23* (1), 45–59.

Caverley, N., Cunningham, J. B., & MacGregor, J. N. (2007). Sickness presenteeism, sickness absenteeism, and health following restructuring in a public service organization. *Journal of Management Studies*, *44*, 304–319.

Clarke, S. & Holdsworth, L. (2017). Flexibility in the workplace: implications of flexible work arrangements for individuals, teams and organizations. Report. Alliance Manchester Business School, University of Manchester, UK.

Demerouti, E., Mostert, K., & Bakker, A. B. (2010). Burnout and work engagement: a thorough investigation of the independency of both constructs. *Journal of Occupational and Health Psychology*, *15*, 209–222.

Ferreira, A. I., da Costa Ferreira, P., Cooper, C. L., & Oliveira, D. (2019). How daily negative affect and emotional exhaustion correlates with work engagement and presenteeism-constrained productivity. *International Journal of Stress Management*, *26* (3), 261–271.

Ferreira, A. I., Mach, M., Martinez, L. F., Brewster, C., Dagher, C. Perez-Nebra, A., & Lisovskaya, A. (2017). Working sick and out of sorts: a cross-cultural approach on presenteeism climate, organizational justice and work–family conflict. *The International Journal of Human Resource Management*, *30* (19), 2754–2776.

Ferreira, A. I., Martinez, L. F., Cooper, G. L., & Gui, D. M. (2015). LMX as a negative predictor of presenteeism climate: a cross-cultural study in the financial and health sectors. *Journal of Organizational Effectiveness*, *3*, 282–302.

Fortune (2017). *100 Best companies to work*. Retrieved from https://fortune.com/best-companies/2017/google

Gosselin, E., Lemyre, L., & Corneil, W. (2013). Presenteeism and absenteeism: differentiated understanding of related phenomena. *Journal of Occupational Health Psychology*, *18*, 75–86.

Grawitch, M. J., Waldrop, J. S., Erb, K. R., Werth, P. M., & Guarino, S. N. (2017). Productivity loss due to mental- and physical-health decrements: distinctions in research and practice. *Consulting Psychology Journal: Practice and Research*, *69* (2), 112–129.

Hemp, P. (2004). Presenteeism: at work – but out of it. *Harvard Business Review*, *82* (10), 49–58.

Henly, J. R., Shaefer, H. L., & Waxman, R. E. (2006). Non-standard work schedules: employer- and employee-driven flexibility in retail jobs. *Social Service Review*, *80* (4), 609–634.

Hobfoll, S. E. (1989). Conservation of resources: a new attempt at conceptualizing stress. *American Psychologist*, *44*, 513–524.

Hunter, K., Ansari, M. A., & Jayasingam, S. (2013). Social influence tactics and influence outcomes: the role of leader-member exchange and culture. Conference Paper: Society for Industrial & Organizational Psychology, Houston, Texas.

Irvine, A. (2011). Fit for work? The influence of sick pay and job flexibility on sickness absence and implications for presenteeism. *Social Policy & Administration*, *45* (7), 752–769.

Jensen, U. T., Andersen, L. B., & Holten, A. L. (2017). Explaining a dark side: public service motivation, presenteeism, and absenteeism. *Review of Public Personnel Administration*, *39* (4), 1–24.

Johns, G. (2010). Presenteeism in the workplace: a review and research agenda. *Journal of Organizational Behavior*, *31* (4), 519–542. Retrieved from http://search.ebscohost.com/login.aspx?direct=true&db=bth&AN=48836930&site=ehost-live&scope=site

Johns, G. (2011). Attendance dynamics at work: the antecedents and correlates of presenteeism, absenteeism, and productivity loss. *Journal of Occupational Health Psychology*, *16* (4), 483–500.

Kalleberg, A. L. & Dunn, M. (2016). Good jobs, bad jobs in the gig economy. *Perspectives on Work*, *20*, 10–14.

Karanika-Murray, M. & Biron, C. (2019). The health-performance framework of presenteeism: towards understanding an adaptive behavior. *Human Relations*, 1–20.

Karanika-Murray, M. & Cooper, C. (2018). Presenteeism: an introduction to a prevailing global phenomenon. In L. Lu & C. Cooper (eds), *Presenteeism at Work*. Cambridge: Cambridge University Press.

Kessler, R. C., Barber, C., Beck, A., Berglund, P., Cleary, P. D., McKenas, D., & Wang, P. (2003). The World Health Organization health and work performance questionnaire (HPQ). *Journal of Occupational and Environmental Medicine*, *45* (2), 156–174.

Knani M., Biron, C., & Fournier, P. R. (2018). Presenteeism: a critical review of the literature. In L. Lu & C. Cooper (eds), *Presenteeism at Work*. Cambridge: Cambridge University Press.

Koopman, C., Pelletier, K. R., Murray, J. F., Sharda, C. E., Berger, M. L., Turpin, R. S., et al. (2002). Stanford presenteeism scale: health status and employee productivity. *Journal of Occupational and Environmental Medicine*, *44*, 14–20.

Lehdonvirta, V. (2018). Flexibility in the gig economy: managing time on three online piecework platforms. *New Technology, Work & Employment*, *33* (1), 13–29.

Lohaus, D. & Habermann, W. (2019). Presenteeism: a review and research directions. *Human Resource Management Review*, *29* (1), 43–58.

Lopes, S. L., Ferreira, A. I., Passos, A. M., Neves, M., Sousa, C., & Sá, M. J. (2018). Depressive symptomatology, presenteeism productivity and quality of life: a moderated mediation model. *Journal of Occupational and Environmental Medicine*, *60* (4), 301–308.

Luksyte, A., Avery, D. R., & Yeo, G. (2015). It is worse when you do it: examining the interactive effects of coworker presenteeism and demographic similarity. *Journal of Applied Psychology*, *100* (4), 1107–1123.

Ma, J., Meltzer, D., Yang, L.-Q., & Liu, C. (2018). Motivation and presenteeism: the whys and whats. In L. Lu & C. Cooper (eds), *Presenteeism at Work*. Cambridge: Cambridge University Press.

McGregor, A. (2017). An investigation into the phenomenon of presenteeism: examining antecedents and the operationalisation of presenteeism. PhD thesis, School of Psychology, University of Wollongong, Australia. https://ro.uow.edu.au/theses1/178

McGregor, A., Sharma, R., Magee, C., Caputi, P., & Iverson, D. (2017). Explaining variations in the findings of presenteeism research: a meta-analytic investigation into the moderating effects of construct operationalizations and chronic health. *Journal of Occupational Health Psychology*, *23* (4), 1–17.

MacGregor, J. & Cunningham, B. (2018) To be or not to be … at work while ill: a choice between sickness presenteeism and sickness absenteeism in the workplace. *Journal of Organizational Effectiveness: People and Performance, 5* (4), 314–327.

Musich S., Hook, D., Banner, S., Spooner, M., & Edington, D. W. (2006). The association of corporate work environment factors, health risks, and medical conditions with presenteeism among Australian employees. *American Journal of Health Promotion, 21* (2), 127–136.

Nielsen, K. & Daniels, K. (2016). The relationship between transformational leadership and follower sickness absence: the role of presenteeism. *Work & Stress, 30* (2), 93–208.

Oakman, J., Kinsman, N., & Briggs, A. M. (2017). Working with persistent pain: an exploration of strategies utilised to stay productive at work. *Journal of Occupational Rehabilitation, 27* (1), 4–14.

Ospina, M. B., Dennett, L., Waye, A., Jacobs, P., & Thompson, A. H. (2015). A systematic review of measurement properties of instruments assessing presenteeism. *The American Journal of Managed Care, 21,* 171–e185.

Robertson, I. (2011). Flexibility is the key to reducing absence. *Employee Benefits,* 15. Retrieved from http://search.ebscohost.com/login.aspx?direct=true&db=bth&AN=60388403&site=ehost-live&scope=site

Roelen, C. A. M. & Groothoff, J. W. (2010). Rigorous management of sickness absence provokes sickness presenteeism. *Occupational Medicine, 60* (4), 244–246.

Sanderson, K. & Cocker, F. (2013). Presenteeism: implications and health risks. *Australian Family Physician, 42,* 172.

Schultz, A. B., Chen, C. Y., & Edington, D. W. (2009). The cost and impact of health conditions on presenteeism to employers: a review of the literature. *PharmacoEconomics, 27,* 365–378.

Shockley, K. M. & Allen, T. D. (2007). When flexibility helps: another look at the availability of flexible work arrangements and work-family conflict. *Journal of Vocational Behavior, 71* (3), 479–493.

Taloyan, M., Aronsson, G., Leineweber, C., Magnusson, H. L., Alexanderson, K., & Westerlund, H. (2012). Sickness presenteeism predicts suboptimal self-rated health and sickness absence: a nationally representative study of the Swedish working population. *PLoS ONE, 7* (9), e44721.

Turpin, R. S., Ozminkowski, R. J., Sharda, C. E., Collins, J. J., Berger, M. L., Billotti, G. M., et al. (2004). Reliability and validity of the Stanford Presenteeism Scale. *Journal of Occupational and Environmental Medicine, 46,* 1123–1133.

Urtasun, A. & Nuñez, I. (2018). Healthy working days: the (positive) effect of work effort on occupational health from a human capital approach. *Social Science & Medicine, 202,* 79–88.

Whysall, Z., Bowden, J., & Hewitt, M. (2018). Sickness presenteeism: measurement and management challenges. *Ergonomics, 61* (3), 341–354.

Zhou, Q., Martinez, L. F., Ferreira, A. I., & Rodrigues, P. (2016). Supervisor support, role ambiguity and productivity associated with presenteeism: a longitudinal study. *Journal of Business Research, 69* (9), 3380–3387.

5 Flexible working and quality of life

Compatible?

Sarah Jackson and Jonathan Swan

In this chapter we explore flexible working and its relationship to work. Looking back over the preceding three decades we will examine how flexibility has changed both in its conception and utilisation, and how expectations of what flexible working can and should deliver have correspondingly altered. We will look at both the employee and employer perspective, and the surrounding policy and legislative developments that have shaped the way that flexibility has played out in the UK. Drawing on this we will examine whether the ability to access flexibility is equitably distributed, and how flexibility is differently conceived and utilised, and the attendant variation in the benefits it confers. We anticipate some international readers will recognise a similar trajectory in their own employment landscape, but will also see that development in any country is so shaped by "local" factors (such as childcare provisions, legislation, state support for non-workers, presence of collective bargaining, etc.) that it is difficult to draw a general picture.

In our conclusion we will set out a number of recommendations for the future development of flexibility from an organisational and policy perspective to make it more compatible with quality of life, drawing on current trends in organisational practice and the policy and legislative agenda.

Introduction

From its early days,[1] flexible working practices were developed to support two linked ideas: that they could help people (primarily mothers of young children) into employment; and that they could help workers achieve a better quality of life through improved work life balance.[2,3] Quality of life in this context is defined as the ameliorating of family and work conflict by the use of working practices that facilitate balance between home and work.[4] Flexible working practices were seen to be a way of opening up employment opportunity by breaking the link with "traditional" full-time work, allowing people (mothers) to combine non-typical working hours (such as reduced hours or flexi time) with their caring responsibilities.[5,6] This would also allow an enhanced quality of life, permitting a satisfying balance between paid work and family life. Other benefits were envisaged that included a new balance within couple households where fathers might increasingly share childcare responsibilities; and an erosion within the workplace of traditional working patterns, replaced by more flexible alternatives.[7]

However, as flexibility and flexible working have developed and become mainstream concepts and human resources (HR) practice, some of the expected benefits of flexible working have not materialised. These include greater equality between mothers and fathers in caring for children; a reduction in working time; and more autonomy over working time and working place for workers. In some cases they are absent,[8] in others they are changed and some are only still now in their infancy. For example, the use of technology has given workers the ability to flex their working place by being able to work remotely and from home. But the positive effects of this have been undermined by a detrimental blurring of the boundaries between work and home,[9] and an increase in overall working time as technology allows workers to be "always on".[10] This is a result of flexible working practices "running up against" a workplace and working structure that has in many instances been resistant to change, and in other places has evolved and been appropriated by other agendas that have co-opted flexibility and repurposed it, for example by emphasising organisational flexibility above individual.[11] In addition, the limited scope of flexible working, focusing primarily on mothers of young children, has limited the impact that could potentially be larger and more fundamental.

This understandable narrowness, concentrating largely on certain types of employee for whom there was an economic and business case, meant that policy and practice development within organisations was shaped and communicated towards their needs. As a result flexible working indeed became associated with mothers of young children, as something primarily designed for and used by them. Popular methods of flexible working, such as part-time work, job share and, to a lesser extent, term-time working that were (and, as we shall show, still are) commonly utilised by this group were perceived as "female" ways of working and, whilst not off limits to other types of worker, were less popular with them. Flexibility therefore became quite compartmentalised from the outset: primarily aimed at women with dependent children who needed to work less than full time.

Over time, family campaigners in the UK worked alongside early-adopter employers to broaden the categories of worker who might benefit from flexibility. Others with caring responsibilities (fathers, carers of other adults, grandparents) were identified as being potential beneficiaries.[12] This can be seen in the rise of "Family Friendly Working", as employers rebranded their communications whilst simultaneously developing new policies aimed at the new types of employees.[13] Employees with no caring responsibilities remained less visible in terms of policy provision, even though employers drew the boundaries around family ever more loosely. The belief and perception that flexibility was essentially a women's (mothers') issue was reinforced by the gap in policy provision within organisations, where work life and flexible working policies for mothers outstripped provisions for other types of carers.[14]

In the UK, legislation reinforced this gendered perception, the Right to Request Flexible Working initially (in 2003) being available to parents of young children only. Relatively toothless redress for employees treated unfairly meant effectively that it was easier (and remains so, despite the subsequent extension of the legislation – via carers, and then parents of older children – to all employees in 2014) for employers to reject requests from fathers, for example, than mothers[15] who are able to find better protection by recourse to indirect sex discrimination law in disputes.

Nevertheless, the development of the legislation, and of employer practice which followed (and in many cases anticipated) a similar path, shows a wider understanding that flexibility should be about more than childcare and can deliver wider opportunities to all.

However, access to flexibility remains piecemeal for many workers[16] with evidence that its formal reach has not expanded for almost two decades.[17] Less easily tracked – but likely to be increasing – is informal, non-contractual flexibility. Both approaches appear to offer some quality of life benefits to the individual.

Formal flexibility establishes an agreed pattern (what, when, where) via formal changes to the employment contract, particularly around the number of hours worked. This may also deliver control to the worker via both the initial renegotiation of their role with their manager, and via the protection and security, which should come with certainty about the agreed arrangement. Informal flexibility takes place within an unchanged work structure and culture, but it enables the worker to control when and where the work is delivered on an ad hoc basis, which may enable a better fit with life outside work.

Working Families and Cranfield[18] revealed that many employees work flexibly but without using formal policy procedures to do so. This was particularly a pattern favoured by men and was seen as being "below the radar" and thus more likely to be achievable than via a formal request. It was also perceived as being less likely to cause the kind of career damage which we shall show is so evident for women working part time. The researchers concluded that "the numbers of people working in this way suggests that for many it is a more practical solution than a formalised arrangement".

Whether flexible working arrangements are formal or informal, the benefit to the individual appears to derive from the degree of control and autonomy which they have over their working patterns and work-life fit. In this, there appear to be strong parallels with what many studies have identified as being necessary for a culture of wellbeing at work.[19] Control, in the context of flexible working and quality of life, may not rest upon the ability to flex at will. This kind of work "fluidity" as the basis of work-life satisfaction is predicated on assumptions about certain work cultures which are not representative of the workforce as a whole, but are common in, for example, Millennial start-ups, professional services and other knowledge industries. Similar fluidity, but without the personal control and autonomy, presents as zero-hours or gig economy employment. The Trades Union Congress (TUC) estimates that there are three million people in the UK's "precariat" (people whose income and employment is insecure) (*Living on the Edge*, 2016).[20] But even for those in contractual employment, control may not be accessible. The *British Social Attitudes* survey (2016)[21] shows that, while levels of perceived autonomy at work have risen over the last decade for those in managerial jobs, those in semi-routine and routine occupations have experienced an increase in employer control.

The links between flexibility, control, and autonomy are likely also to relate to workload. Where workload is too great, Health and Safety Executive (HSE) evidence is strong that stress-related ill health results (*Work-Related Stress, Anxiety or Depression Statistics in Great Britain 2019*, 2019).[22] The annual *Modern Families Index* published by Working Families consistently confirms that – in the face of work overload – flexible working does not help and may in fact make things worse, because of the mismatch between the individual's expectation about what flexibility should deliver in terms of quality of life, and the reality (*Modern Families Index 2013–19*). This suggests that predictable yet inflexible work may be better for quality of life than flexible work, which effectively offers only the flexibility to manage too much. It also highlights that even the commonly found definitions of flexible working (for example, that used by the Chartered Institute of Personnel and Development (CIPD): "'Flexible working' describes a type of working arrangement which gives a degree of flexibility on how long, where, when and at what times employees work.") miss out, crucially, *how much* work is to be done (*Flexible Working Practices*, 2019).[23]

This mixed picture surrounding flexibility demonstrates that it remains under-exploited as a potentially transformative new way of working.

Benefits and issues for individuals

The original expectation that flexible working would deliver improved quality of life to the individual was reflected in the concept of work life balance, which has become widely used as an indicator of a "good" employer.[24] And indeed we see today that flexible working is used to permit time not simply for parenting or caring, but also to enable individuals to undertake wider training or further education, to develop new businesses or side hustles while retaining the security of their existing employment, or to participate in sport or community volunteering. In this respect, it can be argued that flexible working is delivering as promised.

If it were as straightforward as suggested by the UK government's simple definition of flexible working[25] (*Flexible Working*, 2019) – "flexible working is a way of working that suits an employee's needs" – we should expect to see widespread patterns of work which demonstrably enhance individual quality of life across age ranges and social class. The difficulty is encapsulated by the contradiction inherent in the idea of balance, as a zero–sum trade-off between time and money, twin currencies which are necessary both for families to thrive and for effective teams and performance at work. Evidence is extensive[26] of the damage caused by financial poverty to health, life chances, and relationships. Where time is in short supply, family relationships and parental mental and physical wellbeing also suffer.[27,28] In particular, one third of parents who do work flexibly, nevertheless report no improvement in their work–life balance.[29] This suggests that flexibility in and of itself does not always deliver the desired outcome.

Where the individual's approach to the trade-off is to sacrifice money for increased time, via reduced-hours or part-time working, negative consequences may result. The majority of reduced-hours flexible working (with the proviso that many such arrangements may not in fact be flexible at all) is carried out by women with dependent children. The number of people working part time has remained steady since the late 1990s at around one quarter of the workforce, although over that period there has been a gradual reduction in the percentage who are women, and by 2016 nearly one quarter of part-time workers were men, although those working part time and on low wages would prefer to be in better-earning full-time work.[30] Part-time jobs and zero-hours contracts are also especially common among those just starting out in employment (aged 16–19), and the over 65s towards the end of their working lives.[31]

Part-time work, in the sense of hours set by the employer, may not offer the kind of fluidity which has come to be identified with flexible working. This does not mean that such work arrangements do not support improved balance and quality of life. They may well do so, because they can provide the dual income required for family life, time and money, as well as the control which comes from having predictable working hours.

Part-time work continues to be less common in more highly paid or managerial roles (it is estimated that only 11.1% of part-time roles which are advertised are "quality" jobs, commanding a minimum of £20,000 per annum for the full-time equivalent role[32,*]), and, despite legislation which has outlawed discrimination against part-time employees since 2000, the part-time "pay penalty" is still very real in the UK when part-time earnings are compared to full-time.[33]

For women in particular, part-time work can bring long-term negative impacts on lifetime earnings, on pensions, and on poverty in old age. Over half of part-time workers earn less than £10,000 per annum, and 81% of part-time workers are women.[34] The Resolution Foundation has shown that 48% of mothers on low to middle incomes, and 42% of mothers educated to degree level, take a lower-skilled part-time job on their return to work after having children.[35] (*The Price of Motherhood*, 2012). Mayhew[36] (*The Dependency Trap*, 2018) points out that "Gender variations in total life-time earnings remain substantial, with men earning – on average – 80% more than women.

This reflects the impact of career breaks, part-time jobs and lower-paid work on the average total earned by women". As a result, the average pension pot of a 65-year-old woman in the UK is £35,800, one fifth of that of a 65-year-old man.[37]

Women with dependent children are most likely to use *all* of the forms of flexible working covered in the CIPD's first *UK Working Lives* survey 2018.[38] Analysis by Scotcen for Family Friendly Working Scotland of the Growing Up in Scotland dataset shows that low paid fathers and mothers are equally likely to have access to forms of flexible working, but that mothers are more likely to use them.[39] Focus group work for the same study showed that fathers were reluctant to ask for flexible working because it was not the norm in their workplace, although some wished they could do so – and some mothers wished that they could work longer hours rather than being the one in the couple to reduce or even give up paid work. Lower paid workers in the focus groups tended to be uncertain about what flexible arrangements might be available to them and viewed arrangements such as job sharing as more for managerial staff than for people like themselves.

Managers and people who are in higher paid roles are less likely to work part time, but are more likely to use all other kinds of flexible working.[40] Access to such flexibility is highly dependent on already being employed: but the availability of advertised flexible roles decreases as salary increases, from around one in five for roles paying under the full-time equivalent of £20,000 per annum to fewer than one in ten for roles paying at least £75,000 per annum full-time equivalent.[41] For the spread of flexible working, it is important that more managers work flexibly. Of those surveyed, 82% believe that flexible working benefits their organisation, but 27% of those without personal experience of flexible working believe it has no benefit at all.[42]

There is evidence of increasing interest in flexible working from younger fathers with young children. Fathers surveyed in the *Modern Families Index 2017–19* expressed their wish to play a more active role at home and their frustration that work is not flexible enough. A minority have taken action, reducing their working hours or moving to a new employer; a larger number intend to take action within two years to find a better balance between work and home.

Where and in what sector people work contributes to whether they have access to flexibility. Part-time work is more available in smaller workplaces; other forms of flexible working are slightly more common in larger workplaces, suggesting that availability may be dependent on engagement by organisational leadership or at least senior HR with strategic responsibility for people development and its impact on business outcomes.[43] Workers in the public sector are twice as likely to have a flexible working arrangement as those in the private sector, although a study comparing the experience of fathers and flexibility in two large organisations, one public sector and one private sector, identified that the public sector workers were more likely to perceive their flexible working as "part of the furniture" than as a benefit, reporting that it had little impact on their resilience in the face of organisational change and turbulence.[44]

People who are self-employed appear to benefit from the control that flexible working can offer, and CIPD suggests that this is the main reason people become self-employed[45] (*Megatrends*, 2019). However, around a third of self-employed people today, 1.7 million out of 5 million, are better described as the "precariat", who have little control over when and how much they work. A study of working patterns, earnings, and work-life balance in the performing arts shows the difficulty of combining self-employment with caring, with high numbers of freelancers having to turn down paid work because of care responsibilities. Median annual earnings of self-employed parents and carers in this industry are significantly less on average (£15,000) than for those who are employed (£35,000 full time, £18,500 part time).[46]

In general it can be said that low-value workers have neither the money nor the time they need for quality of life, and they also lack the protections that come from employment, whether or not it is flexible. For these workers in particular, the legal Right to Request Flexible Working has little value when there is an imbalance in power and risk between employer and employee. Evidence of the opportunities in unionised workplaces for strengthening the Right can be seen in the 2019 agreement[47] between the Society of London Theatres and Equity, which enshrines in West End theatre contracts the day-one right of the worker to ask, and an obligation on the employer to consider the request seriously. (Legislation requires an employee to have been employed for at least 26 weeks before having this right.) It will be interesting to track the impact of this strengthened right in practice.

For high value workers – professionals, but also high-skilled craftspeople and knowledge workers – there has been a sea-change in the availability of flexible working, underpinned by developments in the technology that enable remote working, and driven by increased understanding of the business benefit of giving the individual greater control and autonomy, whether for reasons of wellbeing, of engagement, or of performance. Also important has been the increased understanding of the business necessity of diversity, widely and compellingly evidenced by McKinsey & Co.[48] (*Women in the Workplace*, 2018) among others, which requires the career progression of women in particular to be better supported. Flexible working can be seen to play a central part in gender equality and wider wellbeing strategies.[49]

How are organisations using flexibility?

The way that employers have used flexibility has changed over time. Partly this has been driven by the changes discussed earlier, as attitudes changed about who could and should benefit from flexible working practices. Other developments, such as the rapid expansion of the role of technology, have opened up new ways of working such as remote and home working. It is important to recognise that the business case for flexibility has evolved over time too, shifting the way that organisations seek advantage from utilising flexible working practices.

The business case has been important in encouraging organisations to adopt flexible working practices, emphasising from the early days the advantages it would bring.[50] It has formed a central part of UK government efforts to encourage the use of flexible working practices,[51] promoting business benefits supplemented by only light touch regulation.[52] Over time it has adapted to tackle a number of employment issues, recommending adopting flexible working practices to benefit organisations in areas such as recruitment, retention, wellbeing and health, organisational agility, carbon footprint, diversity, and, most recently, gender equality.

Flexible working practices have long been associated with improved retention and recruitment.[53] Offering flexibility makes employers a more attractive destination as an employer of choice, and more recent developments have seen flexibility in where work is done extend to recruitment, with initiatives such as the Scottish Government's "location neutral" policy.[54] Simply put, people no longer have to be geographically near a workplace to be able to do the job. Flexibility is further extending into recruitment through the adoption of schemes such as Happy to Talk Flexible Working,[55] where employing organisations specifically offer the possibility of flexibility during the recruitment process and in so doing extend the pool of potential recruits who might otherwise rule themselves out of applying for full-time or fixed-location work. The widening of the potential recruitment pool has always been implicit for organisations who offer flexible working. The drive is to make this more explicit, and in 2018 the UK government convened a Flexible Working Taskforce[56] to increase the uptake of flexible working and explore making it mandatory for employers to advertise jobs as being able to be done on a flexible basis. Flexible working is also seen as a retention tool, allowing the reconciliation of life and work over the life course without employees having to leave employment in order to fulfil their outside responsibilities. It also acts a retention tool through a wellbeing lens, with flexibility viewed as a way to positively manage issues of work volume and intensity, as well as facilitating issues such as phased return to work after long sickness absence.

That the business case has periodically refocused is both a strength and a limitation. Many organisations are able to find beneficial uses that are relevant to their own operational situation; but there is no one-size-fits-all business case, which for some organisations can be problematic. This is particularly the case for those moving beyond basic legislative compliance and introducing policies and practices for the first time, who find themselves unable to discover a business case that will unequivocally tell them that introducing flexible working will quantifiably enhance the financial bottom line. A business case for specific activities like recruitment and retention is easier to demonstrate, while wider organisation-wide benefits are harder to show, particularly in areas such as productivity and financial performance.[57] Many organisations with decades of experience still find it difficult to locate whole organisation benefits, as they are unable to disentangle the effects of flexible working practices from other activities.[58] There is a tension between these claims for improved effectiveness and organisational support for expanding flexible working programmes suggesting that "belief" in flexible working practices is not universal within organisations and amongst senior decision makers. This may be a result of the relative lack of HR metrics around flexibility, leaving its advocates relying on qualitative rather than quantitative data when trying to make the argument to senior leaders.

Whilst many organisations have developed flexible working polices, take up in practice has not reached the levels that might be expected. In terms of formal flexible working requests men are underrepresented, for example.[59] This is a result of the workplace culture issue discussed previously, where flexible working is perceived by employees to be an unrealistic option despite organisational policies existing.[60] Employee surveys[61] show that these beliefs often originate from the way that line managers support flexible working and employees' own observations of what the culture of the organisation is around working time and career progression. For example, using flexible working arrangements, especially reduced hours, is negatively perceived for men who feel that they will be identified as less committed to work if they do not adhere to traditional gendered norms of full-time breadwinner, with attendant career penalties.[62]

However, not all informal flexible working is a response to the difficulty of moving flexible working policy into practice. Organisations in the vanguard increasingly talk about "embedded" flexibility, where flexible working is the norm and employees do not need to seek permission, nor make contractual changes to use it. Organisations variously claim that "flexibility is in our DNA" and "our culture is a flexible one" and other similar statements. The intention is to demonstrate that flexibility is part of the culture, with deeply understood values shared by the workforce and management around the positive benefits of flexible working. Such values may encompass: the ability to work flexibly is open to all employees; permission to work flexibly is assumed; workers have autonomy around working time and place; performance is evaluated on the basis of outputs. Such informal flexibility is the preferred "default" mechanism, although it may remain vulnerable to individual managers who do not share the organisational view and manage their teams in ways that discourage flexible working. The aspiration towards embedded flexibility has largely come as result of what may be called the policy/practice gap: in response both to growing employee demands for flexible working and maintaining a position as an employer of choice, organisations developed comprehensive policy offerings. However, policy utilisation did and does not take place at the levels expected. Practice falls short of policy. The process of embedding flexibility can therefore be viewed as a cultural change activity, where organisations endeavour to weave flexible working into the everyday way in which the organisation as a whole works, through the use of the policies provided, as well as other informal mechanisms. Embedded flexibility might be viewed as the "gold standard", allowing all workers to use flexibility in any way they want to achieve the work-life balance they desire, ultimately delivering a better quality of life. However, achieving embedded flexibility is difficult: significant barriers need to be overcome, in particular around line manager capability, workload, and job design, where practical actions and investment are required to underpin culture change.

Conclusion

At least some flexible working practices are available in most organisations today[63] and they continue to be adopted and adapted as a way of improving organisational effectiveness and individual wellbeing.

The business-focused utilitarian drivers within most organisations do not mean flexible working cannot deliver genuine improvements to quality of life. Encouragingly we see that this is not restricted solely to high-value workers, with good practice in the employment of semi-routine workers being developed by employers such as Enterprise Rent-A-Car, Arnold Clark motor retailer, and Timpson shoe repair shops.[64,65,66]

Some organisations are beginning to think beyond flexibility into workload and the twin currencies of time and money. Those trying out the four-day week[67] are the most obvious; while the Agile Future Forum[68] approach identifies the "sweet spot", which enables an organisation to align the needs of its workforce with customer demand. It is a version of the familiar "win-win" but one that is based on a deconstruction and then rebuilding of the organisation's processes and work structures.

Evidence of different uses can easily be found, and the "best practice" approach is a well-established one.[69] It is important to recognise in any discussion of the benefits of flexible working practices, and the way that they are used, that benefits can accrue for the employer or for the employee. Ideally they will benefit both (the dual agenda[70]) but it may be that the benefits of flexibility for employers constrain choice and opportunity for individuals.[71]

Flexible organisations do not therefore necessarily mean flexible working is available to all employees to use as they choose, and so quality-of-life gains continue to be unrealised. Ability to access flexible working is not equitably distributed: lower paid workers are less likely to do so, other than by taking on part-time roles (which may not in themselves be flexible), while for women in general a career penalty is associated with flexible working. Although there has been an increase in men working part time, and there is evidence of a desire on the part of younger fathers to be able to play a more active part in family life, traditional expectations and assumptions around gendered caring roles remain.

For professional workers, digital technologies have enabled a decoupling of work from location and from employer-defined working times, but often at the cost of work overspill into life "outside work". Many who work flexibly report no improvement in their quality of life.

There are some organisations who are beginning to think differently about work, but the majority (including, we would suggest, even those who talk about embedded flexible working) have done little to challenge traditional thinking about how work is structured, designed, and delivered. In almost all organisations, flexibility remains an individual accommodation or variation from the norm. Employees may have some control and choice around where and when they work, but how much remains a challenge; as does the dominant location-based and manager-controlled culture.

Over the past 30 years, the flexible working revolution has not in fact delivered significant quality of life gains for workers. Where flexible working has succeeded, has been in supporting more women into paid employment. But the promised changes around enabling men and women to share care more equally, and of greater leisure or non-work time for all, have not come about.

Recommendations

1. Public policy should be developed to actively support the equalisation of caring, based on at least 12 weeks of properly paid, independent leave for fathers and second carers, as a day-one employment right. Requiring employers to publish details about the parental leave and pay they offer (as proposed by Jo Swinson MP) is a sensible and practical way to build on the recruit and retain aspects of the business case. Employers such as Diageo, Aviva, and The Telegraph Group are beginning to establish a norm for men and women of 26 weeks fully paid leave; it will be hard for many smaller or public sector organisations to follow suit, unless and until government establishes its societal value, as with the Right to Request Flexible Working.

2. The critical next step for employers who wish to create a truly flexible culture will be to address work design, and in particular workload, because of its impact on wellbeing and performance. In fact, this need not be directly related to flexible working. Even within a traditional Monday–Friday, 9–5 culture, work overload is damaging. Tackling overload – and flexibility – via work design requires increased support and training for managers to strengthen their ability to be clear about role purpose and outputs.

3. Employers should consider whether a job can be done flexibly and make that clear when advertising; and jobs should be recruited flexibly by default – with the starting point being consideration of why a job *cannot* be done flexibly. This would kickstart a fundamental flexible working shift with an ensuing workplace culture change. Some individual employers are already taking this approach.

Taken together, action under these headings should take us back to the original conception, where flexible working was to result in increased quality of life for everyone, without the negative, gendered disbenefits from which it currently suffers.

Note

* Regular research on the Minimum Income Standard (MIS) produces budgets for different household types, based on what members of the public think is needed for a minimum acceptable standard of living in the UK. For a two-parent household with two dependent children, each parent needs to earn £20,600 to meet the Standard.

References

1. Working Families, 2019. *Celebrating 30 years* [online]. Available at: https://www.workingfamilies.org.uk/wp-content/uploads/2017/12/WF-35thAnniversary_6ppA5-FINALforweb.pdf [Accessed 13 September 2019].
2. New Ways to Work, 1981. *Job sharing: a guide for employers*. Sheffield, UK: New Ways to Work.
3. Clutterbuck, D (ed.), 1985. *New patterns of work*. Aldershot, UK: Gower Publishing.
4. Kossek, EE, Hammer, LB, Kelly, EL, & Moen, P, 2014. Designing work, family & health organizational change initiatives, *Organizational Dynamics*, *43*, 53–63.
5. New Ways to Work, 1981. *Job sharing: a guide for employees*. Sheffield, UK: New Ways to Work.
6. New Ways to Work, 1981. *Job sharing: a guide for employers*. Sheffield, UK: New Ways to Work.
7. New Ways to Work, 1988. *Men: choosing flexible work patterns*. London: New Ways to Work.
8. Chung, H, 2017. *Work autonomy, flexibility and work life balance*. Canterbury, UK: University of Kent.
9. Working Families, 2019. *Modern families index*. London: Working Families.
10. Chung, H, 2017. *Work autonomy, flexibility and work life balance*. Canterbury, UK: University of Kent.
11. Lyonette, C, Anderson, D, Lewis, S, Payne, N, & Wood, S, 2017. Work life balance and austerity: implications of new ways of working in British public sector organisations. In *Work life balance in times of austerity and beyond*. New York: Routledge.
12. New Ways to Work, 1995. *Balanced lives: changing working patterns for men*. London: New Ways to Work.
13. Web.archive.org, 2019. *Wayback machine* [online]. Available at: https://web.archive.org/web/20030130221726/http://www.parentsatwork.org.uk [Accessed 13 September 2019].
14. Working Families, 2015. *Top employers for working families benchmark report*. London: Working Families.
15. Trades Union Congress (TUC), 2005. *Flexible working report*. London: TUC.
16. Working Families, 2019. *Modern families index*. London: Working Families.
17. Chartered Institute of Personnel and Development (CIPD), 2019. *Megatrends flexible working*. London: CIPD.
18. Kelliher, C, Anderson, D, & Swan, J, 2008. *Flexible working and performance*. London: Working Families.

19. Kossek, EE, Valcour, M, & Lirio, P, 2014. The sustainable workforce. In CL Cooper (ed.), *Wellbeing*. doi:10.1002/9781118539415.wbwell030
20. Trades Union Congress (TUC), 2016. *Living on the edge: the rise of job insecurity in modern Britain*. London: TUC.
21. Curtice, J, Phillips, M, & Clery, E, 2015. *British social attitudes: the 33rd report*. London: NatCen Social Research.
22. Health and Safety Executive (HSE), 2019. *Work-related stress, anxiety or depression statistics in Great Britain, 2019*. London: HSE. Available at: https://www.hse.gov.uk/statistics/causdis/stress.pdf
23. Chartered Institute of Personnel and Development (CIPD), 2019. *Flexible working practices*. London: CIPD.
24. Great Place to Work, 2019. *What is a great workplace?* [online] Available at: https://www.greatplacetowork.co.uk/about/what-is-a-great-workplace/ [Accessed 13 September 2019].
25. GOV.UK, 2019. *Flexible working* [online]. Available at: https://www.gov.uk/flexible-working [Accessed 6 September 2019].
26. Joseph Rowntree Foundation, 2018. *UK Poverty 2018*. York, UK: JRF.
27. Working Families, 2019. *Modern families index*, p. 16. London: Working Families.
28. Cooper, C & Swan, J, 2005. *Time, health and the family*. London: Working Families.
29. Working Families, 2019. *Modern families index*. London: Working Families.
30. Resolution Foundation, 2018. *Counting the hours* [online]. Available at: https://www.resolutionfoundation.org/app/uploads/2018/01/Counting-the-hours.pdf [Accessed 6 August 2019].
31. Chartered Institute of Personnel and Development (CIPD), 2019. *Megatrends flexible working*. London: CIPD.
32. Timewise, 2018. *Flexible jobs index 2018*. London: Timewise.
33. Chartered Institute of Personnel and Development (CIPD), 2019. *Megatrends flexible working*. London: CIPD.
34. Chartered Insurance Institute and Insuring Women's Futures, 2018. *Solving women's pension deficit to improve retirement outcomes for all*. London: Chartered Insurance Institute.
35. Resolution Foundation, 2012. *The price of motherhood: women and part time work*. London: Resolution Foundation.
36. Mayhew, L, 2018. *The dependency trap – are we fit enough to face the future?* London: Centre for the Study of Financial Innovation (CSFI).
37. Chartered Insurance Institute and Insuring Women's Futures, 2018. *Solving women's pension deficit to improve retirement outcomes for all*. London: Chartered Insurance Institute.
38. Chartered Institute of Personnel and Development (CIPD), 2018. *UK working lives 2018*. London: CIPD.
39. Family Friendly Working Scotland, 2017. *Family friendly working and low income families*. Glasgow, Scotland: Family Friendly Working Scotland.
40. Chartered Institute of Personnel and Development (CIPD), 2019. *Megatrends flexible working*. London: CIPD.
41. Timewise, 2018. *Flexible jobs index 2018*. London: Timewise.
42. Institute of Leadership and Management, 2016. *Flexible working: goodbye nine to five*. Tamworth, UK: Institute of Leadership and Management.
43. Chartered Institute of Personnel and Development (CIPD), 2019. *Megatrends flexible working*. London: CIPD.
44. Lancaster University Management School and Working Families, 2011. *Working and fathers. Combining family life and work*. London: Lancaster University Management School and Working Families.

45. Chartered Institute of Personnel and Development (CIPD), 2019. *Megatrends flexible working.* London: CIPD.
46. McDowall, A, Gamblin, D, & Teoh, K, 2019. *Balancing act.* London: Parents in the Performing Arts.
47. Hemley, M, 2019. West End deal secures 9% pay rise and paves the way for flexible working [online]. *The Stage,* 11 June. Available at: https://www.thestage.co.uk/news/2019/west-end-deal-secures-9-pay-rise-and-paves-the-way-for-flexible-working [Accessed 5 August 2019].
48. McKinsey & Co., 2018. *Women in the workplace in 2018.* Available at: https://www.mckinsey.com/featured-insights/gender-equality/women-in-the-workplace-2018 [Accessed 20 June 2019].
49. Barclays Bank PLC, 2018. *Dynamic working. How do you work your life?* London: Barclays Bank PLC.
50. New Ways to Work, 1993. *Changing times: a guide to flexible work patterns for human resource managers.* London: New Ways to Work.
51. Department of Trade and Industry, 2004. The evaluation of the work life balance challenge fund. *Employment Relations Research* series, No. 32. London: The Tavistock Institute.
52. Higginbottom, K, 2001. Members and aims of working parents taskforce announced [online]. *Personnel Today,* 28 June. Available at: https://www.personneltoday.com/hr/members-and-aims-of-working-parents-taskforce-announced [Accessed 27 June 2019].
53. New Ways to Work, 1993. *Changing times: a guide to flexible work patterns for human resource managers.* London: New Ways to Work.
54. Working Families, 2019. *Working Families|Scottish Government, Winner 2014, The DTCC Best for Innovation Award – Working Families* [online]. Working Families. Available at: https://www.workingfamilies.org.uk/employers/case-studies/case-studies-flexible-working/scottish-government-winner-2014-the-dtcc-best-for-innovation-award [Accessed 13 September 2019].
55. Working Families 2019. Working Families|West Dunbartonshire Council, Winner 2017, Best Public Sector Employer - Working Families [online]. Working Families. Available at https://workingfamilies.org.uk/employers/case-studies/best-public-sector-employers/west-dunbartonshire-council-winner-2017-best-public-sector-employer [Accessed 13 September 2019].
56. Chartered Institute of Personnel and Development (CIPD), 2019. *Flexible working task force* [online]. Available at: https://www.cipd.co.uk/news-views/policy-engagement/flexible-working [Accessed 13 September 2019].
57. de Menezes, LM & Kelliher, C, 2019. *Flexible working in organisations: a research overview.* Abingdon and New York: Routledge Focus.
58. Working Families, 2018. *Top employers for working families benchmark report.* London: Working Families.
59. UK Parliament, 2018. *The Right to Request Flexible Working,* para 91. Report from Women and Equalities Committee 2018. London: UK Parliament.
60. Kelliher, C, Anderson, D, & Swan, J, 2008. *Flexible working and performance.* London: Working Families.
61. Working Families, 2019. *The modern families index.* London: Working Families.
62. Kelland, J, 2016. "Fatherhood forfeits" and "motherhood penalties": an exploration of UK management selection decision-making on parent applicant. Conference paper number: CIPD/ARC/2016/2. London: CIPD.
63. Department for Business, Innovation and Skills, 2014. *The fourth work-life balance employer survey.* London: Department for Business, Innovation and Skills.
64. Smail, J, 2019. *Enterprise Rent-A-Car announces new benefits for working parents* [online]. Employee Benefits. Available at: https://www.employeebenefits.co.uk/enterprise-benefits-working-parents [Accessed 13 September 2019].

65. Working Families, 2019. *Arnold Clark Finalist 2019, Best Innovation* [online]. Available at: https://www.workingfamilies.org.uk/employers/case-studies/arnold-clark-finalist-2019-best-innovation [Accessed 13 September 2019].
66. Department for Culture Media and Sport, 2019. *My role on the Women's Business Council – DCMS blog* [online]. Available at: https://dcmsblog.uk/2014/02/my-role-on-the-womens-business-council [Accessed 13 September 2019].
67. Booth, R, 2019. *UK call centre to trial four-day week for hundreds of staff* [online]. *The Guardian*. Available at: https://www.theguardian.com/money/2019/may/03/uk-call-centre-to-trial-four-day-week-for-hundreds-of-staff [Accessed 13 September 2019].
68. The Agile Future Forum, 2019. *Agile Future Forum supporting UK business growth* [online]. Available at: https://www.agilefutureforum.co.uk [Accessed 13 September 2019].
69. Working Families, 2019. *Winners of 2019 Best Practice Awards* [online]. Available at: https://www.workingfamilies.org.uk/news/working-families-best-practice-awards-2019 [Accessed 13 September 2019].
70. Rapoport, R, Bailyn, L, Fletcher, JK, & Pruitt, BH, 2002. *Beyond work-family balance: advancing gender equity and workplace performance.* San Francisco, CA: Jossey-Bass.
71. Lewis, S, Anderson, D, Lyonette, C, Payne, N, & Wood, S (eds), 2017. *Work-life balance in times of recession, austerity and beyond.* New York: Routledge, https://doi.org/10.4324/9781315683263

Part III

What makes flexible working work?

6 Leadership in flexible work systems

Anika Cloutier and Julian Barling

On June 30th, 2017, Madalyn Parker (@madalynrose) tweeted a screenshot of an email exchange between her and her boss, Ben Congleton, CEO. This screenshot contained an initial email from Madalyn detailing her desire to take the next two days off, to focus on her mental health as a means of refreshing herself to come back to work at 100%. Contained in this tweet was her boss's response to her request. Ben both thanked Madalyn for her email, specifying the importance of using sick days for mental health and questioning why this is not a more standard practice across organizations. Notably, Ben praised Madalyn for being an example to all team members, and that emails such as hers help cut through the stigma of mental illness to ensure that employees can bring their whole selves to work.

This tweet went viral, being shared over 15,000 times, receiving more than 44,000 likes, and catching the attention of several traditional media outlets. The general sentiment was an overwhelmingly positive endorsement of the CEO's response. Sheryl Sandberg, COO of Facebook, praised Ben saying "… Ben showed such compassion and is a great example of why we need more leaders who encourage employees to bring their whole selves to work."

(cited in McGregor, 2017)

Although the story of CEO Ben Congleton is, of course, not explicitly about flexible work schedules, the lesson we can draw from it is just how critical leaders at all levels of the organization are in implementing and supporting broad alternate work arrangements. The purpose of this chapter is to discuss the role of organizational leaders in flexible work systems more specifically.[1] Flexible work is now widely recognized as not only a workplace benefit, but an expectation, and in response many organizations are developing policies and opportunities for workers to vary the hours they choose to work during the day. For example, recent surveys suggest that 50–90% of organizations across Europe (Organisation for Economic Co-operation and Development (OECD), 2016) and North America (MacLean, 2018) now offer at least one type of flexible work option. However, as we will illustrate, the existence of such policies is only half of the battle. After they have been formally instituted, organizational leaders will serve as gatekeepers, allowing employees who access them to feel psychologically safe, with no implicit threats to their reputations and jobs. In all of this, leaders' own personal attitudes and behaviors will be critical and will determine whether they support or sabotage the successful implementation of a flexible workplace policy.

Consider the opening story about Madalyn and Ben. Although this story is about using sick days for mental health, it illustrates how comfortable Madalyn was not only to use sick days to fit her personal needs, but also to share why she needed to do so with her boss and colleagues. In response, her CEO not only accepted her reasoning, but praised Madalyn for her candor, suggesting that Madalyn should serve as a role model for other employees in the organization.

What if Ben had been less supportive? Would the existence of such policies still be used if a leader sent a different signal? Alternatively, what if it was Ben who had sent out an email similar to that of Madalyn? Might leaders benefit from flexible work policies in the same way as employees? And what signal would that send to others?

In this chapter, we respond to such questions, and consider the role leaders play within a flexible work system. We believe that flexible work structures for individuals at all levels of the organization can benefit from such programs, enabling their ability to live healthier work, personal, and family lives. We have divided our chapter to enhance our understanding of two topics: (1) how leaders can facilitate flexible work systems for others; and (2) how leaders can take advantage of flexible work systems for themselves. We first discuss why leaders serve a pivotal role in flexible work systems including the benefits for enabling such systems, and the challenges they face in doing so. We then shift focus and consider how individuals in leadership roles themselves may take advantage of flexible work, including the unique benefits to leaders, and the challenges they may face as well. Finally, given its prominence in research attention (Barling, 2014), and the direct benefits to well-being (e.g., Arnold, Turner, Barling, Kelloway, & McKee, 2007), we conclude by suggesting four transformational leadership behaviors leaders can enact to facilitate the successful implementation and use of a flexible work system within their organization.

Leaders facilitating flexible work systems for followers

Leaders at all levels of the organization fulfil a critical role in facilitating access to flexible work systems for others. In the presence of formal flexible work policies, leaders act as gatekeepers. Although policies may exist that allow workers to start or end work at different times during the day, whether employees take advantage of this flexibility is largely determined by their leaders' implicit or explicit permission to do so. Employees need to believe that accessing flexible schedules will not result in adverse effects on their current experiences and future opportunities at work. Leaders' support for employees accessing flexible work opportunities cannot necessarily be taken for granted: In a recent global survey of over 31,000 employees across 22 developed and developing countries (Willis Towers Watson, 2017), less than half of employees (44%) believed that senior leadership at their organization sincerely endorsed policies that benefit their well-being. If employees sense this ambiguity or lack of concern, they are less likely to approach their leaders with issues regarding their well-being, and less likely to take steps to change the situation, which could include choosing not to access flexible work arrangements. Indeed, research shows that despite their desire to do so, employees will not take advantage of breastfeeding (Weber et al., 2011), personal day (Eaton, 2003), and family-friendly (Wang & Walumbwa, 2007) policies, unless their leaders explicitly encourage their use.

In order for employees to gain real benefit from flexible work policies and programs, leaders need to show active support – in short, they need to display leadership on this issue, the type of leadership that will create a sense of psychological safety among employees (Nembhard & Edmondson, 2006) when considering whether to access flexible work opportunities. We now discuss the benefits of leaders encouraging flexible work systems, and the challenges they may face in doing so.

The benefits

There is no reason for us to provide a comprehensive review of the many benefits associated with flexible work systems; that case is made in a number of chapters in this book. What we do, however, is review the benefits that followers experience when leaders specifically enable and endorse flexible work systems, including the improvements to employees' mental health, workplace attitudes, and performance.

Employee mental health

Perhaps the most well-documented benefit of flexible work systems for employees is to their mental health, specifically in improving psychological well-being. Across the board, supervisor endorsement of flexible work enhances the benefits these policies generate. For example, research reliably demonstrates that work-family conflict is reduced in the presence of flexible work policies, with these effects strengthened by managerial support (Julien, Somerville, & Culp, 2011; Mesmer-Magnus & Viswesvaran, 2006). In a meta-analysis combining 85 studies and comprising 72,507 employees, Kossek, Pichler, Bodner, and Hammer (2011) found that not all supervisor support generates equal reductions to work-family conflict; instead, supervisor support needs to specifically target work-family concerns. In other words, leaders need to articulate their specific support for work-family balance and the use of flexible hours. Breaugh and Frye (2008) focused on four alternative work policies, namely telecommuting, ability to take work home, flexible work hours, and family leave. Their findings showed that whether or not a supervisor supported these specific alternative work arrangements predicted whether employees would use them.

Breaugh and Frye (2008) went even further, concluding that "the informal actions taken by a supervisor to accommodate family responsibilities may have greater influence on work–family conflict than the use of formal practice" (p. 352). Their statement is important, as it speaks to the indirect or symbolic benefits that accrue when leaders support flexible work.

Supervisor endorsement of flexible work systems also improves other dimensions of health. In one study of 1,200 parents in the US, employees with greater access to work-schedule flexibility that was explicitly supported by their supervisor reported greater work-life balance and, in turn, experienced lower levels of stress, minor physical illnesses, and sleep disorders (Jang, 2009). Additional benefits include reductions in depression, somatic complaints, and blood cholesterol for women (Thomas & Ganster, 1995). Again, all of the beneficial outcomes to mental and physical health are enhanced when the leader encourages the use of such policies.

Employee's individual workplace attitudes

Research has consistently shown over decades that greater flexibility in work scheduling is associated with positive individually held workplace attitudes. Leader support, again, enhances such benefits. Indeed, when supervisors endorse flexible work schedules, individuals enjoy even greater job satisfaction (Thomas & Ganster, 1995), work engagement (Swanberg, McKechnie, Ojha, & James, 2011), affective commitment and decreased work withdrawal (Wang & Walumbwa, 2007), and turnover intentions (Choi, 2018).

Organizational and employee performance

The literature on flexible work systems and work performance benefits is more mixed, with few studies investigating the collective benefits of flexible work arrangements and supervisor support on objective measures of work performance. However, in one large survey of 92,000 US employees, the effects of family-friendly work policies on organizational performance was moderated by support from top management endorsement and direct supervisor support (Ko, Hur, & Smith-Walter, 2013). Intriguingly, top management support for family-friendly work policies was a better moderator of employee satisfaction, whereas direct supervisor support was stronger in moderating the relationship between family-friendly work policies and organizational performance. Regardless, these findings again point to the importance of leaders at all levels of the organization endorsing flexible work policies if employees are to benefit to the maximum extent possible from their use. That is, although potentially distant in the organizational hierarchy from followers, it is likely that top-level leaders' attitudes trickle down and affect all other employee attitudes and behaviors regarding flexible work (Schaubroeck et al., 2012).

The challenges

Although the documented benefits of flexible work policies are encouraging, leaders could face several challenges when trying to implement them. These include endorsing and actively encouraging the use of such policies, creating fair and equitable access across employees, trusting employees and relinquishing control, and maintaining effective communication.

Active encouragement

An immediate and in some cases unexpected challenge leaders will face when flexible work schedules are introduced is endorsing their use. Indeed, a survey on flexible work arrangements conducted by the Conference Board of Canada identified managerial resistance as a primary obstacle in their implementation, with 64% of respondents indicating this as a primary issue (MacLean, 2018). In order for leaders to endorse flexible work systems, an important cognitive shift in how work is understood and evaluated needs to occur. No longer can units of time (i.e., number of hours worked) form a significant part of evaluating performance. Old assumptions, whether implicit or explicit, that equated arriving before or staying later than others with attitudes (e.g., loyalty, job satisfaction), work effort, or the quality of work performance are no longer viable. Within the context of a system that allows for flexible work scheduling, such assumptions would be both unfair and inaccurate. Leaders would now have to let go of the notion that performance monitoring necessitates shared face-time.

Supporting this, several studies have shown that the relationship between hours worked and production or output is non-linear (e.g., Pencavel, 2014). Specifically, below a certain threshold, hours worked are linearly associated with output; in contrast, output decreases once the threshold of hours (~6 hours) is crossed. In addition, evidence is mixed as to whether observing others' task performance affects the quality of their performance (for simple tasks, observation improves performance while for complex tasks, observation harms performance; Markus, 1978); there would appear to be no evidence to suggest that the more hours a leader observes followers' work performance, the better that performance. Shifting such beliefs can be challenging given cognitive biases such as the confirmation bias (the tendency to only pay attention to information that confirms originally held beliefs) and conservatism bias (the tendency to overvalue traditional information above novel evidence). Still, such changes would be necessary if leaders are to successfully support employees accessing flexible work opportunities.

Leaders resistant to the idea of flexible work may need to ask themselves why they are resistant. Are their attitudes based on negative anecdotes or difficult personal experiences? Might the leader fear their role will decrease in significance, or that employees will take advantage of them? One possibility is that providing leaders with disconfirming evidence will change such beliefs in some cases. Regardless, the larger lesson is that leaders themselves need to be supported in any transition by their organization when implementing flexible work systems.

The most effective leaders will ensure that accessing flexible work opportunities becomes the norm for their employees. Leaders do so by actively communicating and clearly outlining the flexible options available. They articulate the boundaries of such policies to reduce any ambiguity associated with their use; reward and recognize individuals who use such policies and discourage others from criticizing those who do so; and ensure performance expectations are not greater for those who choose to work flexible hours. In addition, they ensure equal or equivalent access to flexible work opportunities to all employees in the work group. Most importantly, they ensure that they themselves serve as models in the use of flexible systems – a topic to which we will return to later.

The importance of these leadership behaviors (e.g., feedback, reward, and recognition) should not be discounted. Across several studies, research shows that there is a persistent gap between what leaders think they have expressed to employees in terms of family-friendly work policies, and what programs and opportunities employees think they can actually access (Budd & Mumford, 2006; Sánchez-Vidal, Cegarra-Leiva, & Cegarra-Navarro, 2012). Leaders need to be careful to avoid any suggestion that accessing flexible work opportunities could harm employees' careers in any way (e.g., work evaluation, promotional possibilities). Negative feedback, in whatever form it occurs, is invariably perceived more strongly than positive (Baumeister et al., 2001) and as such, leaders need to carefully consider how policy information is communicated and reinforced through their behaviors.

Fairness

Another challenge that leaders could well face when administering flexible work structures is that of ensuring that all employees are treated fairly. Leaders may realistically fear that the application of flexible work systems could cause difficulties with ensuring equity. These issues should not be taken lightly. Achieving fairness in the workplace is indeed a complicated challenge (Brockner, 2006) and the consequences of perceiving unfairness among employees can have very significant effects for employees and their organizations (e.g., Colquitt, 2001). For flexible work systems to achieve their intended benefits, all workers need to feel they enjoy equal access to the policies, with the acknowledgment that the most successful implementations will individualize access for different employees with different needs rather than impose a single rigid template. Indeed, fairness does not mean treating everyone the same.

Acknowledging that leaders are unlikely to control the general policy, individual discussions with each of their employees on how they can access and use the flexible work benefits that exist, and actively encourage them to do so, should be considered. It is critical to assure team members that the system is meant to suit their needs, rather than their individual needs bending to the flexible work policy. After all, this is the basic purpose of flexible work programs – to ensure that working hours can be customized to individuals' unique needs. In doing so, the reasons why employees are seeking flexibility should be much less important than how that flexibility can be provided. Making individuals defend their motivation for seeking flexible hours will only discourage employees from initiating the discussion in the first instance.

One way to enhance the likelihood that leader behaviors will be perceived as being fair is to explicitly consider each of the four elements of organizational fairness (or justice) (Colquitt, 2001).

1. Distributive justice: perceptions that the distributions of tangible (e.g., pay) or intangible (e.g., working hours) resources are fair.
2. Procedural justice: perceptions that the decisions and processes that lead to outcomes of distribution are fair.
3. Interpersonal (interactional) justice: perceptions that one is treated with respect and propriety regarding distributive decisions.
4. Informational (interactional) justice: perceptions that one is receiving adequate, timely, and accurate information regarding distributive decisions.

Applying these principles to flexible work systems – leaders should ensure policies are fairly applied across all employees; that the ways in which unique schedules are set are agreed upon with each individual worker; that each employee's unique needs are considered with sensitivity and respect; and that information regarding decision-making is clearly communicated in a timely fashion.

Relinquishing control and trusting employees

Surely, one of the biggest personal challenges any leader will face in applying flexible work systems is relinquishing managerial control and trusting that employees will not abuse these systems. Greater organizational control is an inherent part of the leadership role – the authority and power to make decisions for others, and to direct others (Christie & Barling, 2009). For some leaders, relinquishing the responsibility in determining when employees work will be experienced as a status loss. Because people seek to gain power and status (Magee & Galinksy, 2008), and feel badly when they are accorded lower status (Hoption, Christie, & Barling, 2015), relinquishing such control may be uncomfortable and unpleasant for leaders, resulting in negative psychological (Pettit, Yong, & Spataro, 2010) and physiological responses (Scheepers, Ellemers, & Sintemaartensdijk, 2009). Moreover, those in higher status positions suffer the consequences of status loss more than those in lower status positions (Marr & Thau, 2014). Despite all this, it is questionable whether leaders can successfully encourage and facilitate their employees' access to flexible work policies unless they manage to relinquish control.

One prerequisite if leaders are to relinquish control is that they trust their employees. Although there are several definitions of trust, we adopt Mayer, Davis, and Schoorman's (1995) definition as

> the willingness of a party to be vulnerable to the actions of another party based on the expectation that the other will perform a particular action important to the trustor, irrespective of the ability to monitor or control that other part.
>
> (p. 712)

Trusting others can be very difficult. It requires the trustor to want to trust the trustee, and that the trustee has the perceived ability, benevolence, and integrity to reduce the risk associated with trusting. In the context of leaders facilitating the implementation of flexible work systems, leaders have to be willing to trust initially. In most situations, leaders will have an established relationship with followers that will likely leave them having different levels of trust in different employees, making some leaders more risk averse in the adoption of flexible work schedules. Setting clear guidelines about what they expect from followers in accessing flexible work policies could enhance the likelihood that trust occurs and is maintained. Leaders may be helped by remembering (a) that followers are initially required to trust in their leaders' decision making, and (b) that the development of trust naturally occurs over time, and in this instance by granting employees the opportunity to prove that they deserve to be trusted. Ultimately, the more trusted an employee feels by their leader, the more empowered they will feel over their work (Gomez & Rosen, 2001).

Communication and feedback

One additional challenge that leaders may experience when implementing and administering flexible work systems is maintaining effective communication, feedback, and performance evaluations in a context in which shared face time decreases. This is a legitimate concern for a couple of reasons. First, leaders may have less direct, face-to-face opportunity to communicate regular feedback with employees with somewhat differing work hours. The responsibility to ensure high quality communication with their followers is now more complicated when active performance monitoring is not always possible. Sara Sutton Fell, founder and CEO of FlexJobs suggests that "proactive communication, time management, and creating a clear understanding of goals and milestones are all 'best practice' management skills that become more important when managing flexible workers" (National Federation of Independent Business (NFIB), 2018).

Second, regular communication and opportunities to socialize with peers within work groups is an important social practice that is central to the fundamental need to belong (Baumeister & Leary, 1995). A potentially unavoidable consequence of varying schedules within a work group will be reduced opportunities for such social interactions, not only with one's leader, but amongst team members as well. Organizational belongingness is critical to psychological well-being (Harris & Cameron, 2005), can mitigate the negative effects of work stressors (Armstrong, Shakespeare-Finch, & Shochet, 2016), and are significant predictors of physical health and wellness (Steffens et al., 2017). As such, leaders must ensure that they create regular opportunities to facilitate social interactions amongst peers to maintain the social benefits of work and maintain an organizational climate.

We recommend that leaders take an experimental approach to testing flexible work schedules in their organizations. This would involve surveying team members to identify their flexible work needs; pre-testing attitudes, well-being, and performance. Thereafter, flexible work schedules could be implemented for a period of time, after which surveys could be re-administered to assess whether employees' attitudes, well-being, and performance have changed in the desired direction. Findings from studies over several decades suggest that the likelihood is that this will help leaders appreciate the positive effects of their actions, and help them maintain their support for flexible work policies as they move forward.

Leaders experiencing flexible work systems for themselves

When thinking about the role of leaders in flexible work systems, researchers, policy makers, and the general public are more likely to focus on the role leaders play in facilitating others' access to such systems – as we have done so far in this chapter. But doing so exclusively ignores the fact that leaders themselves can also benefit from flexible work. One reason that leaders may be overlooked in this regard is that leadership roles are already invested with greater decision latitude (Christie & Barling, 2009) and the ability to schedule their own work hours, especially as they ascend the organizational hierarchy (Yukl, 2012). However, autonomy and flexible work systems are not synonymous, making it equally important to focus on leaders' use of flexible work systems. Although research on this topic is limited, there are some studies demonstrating the benefits and challenges leaders may face when taking advantage of flexible work for themselves.

Benefits

Perhaps unsurprisingly, the mental health, work-family balance, attitudinal, and performance benefits of flexible work that exist for followers also exist for leaders. Although these benefits should be sufficient to suggest that leaders, just like others holding other work roles, deserve equal access to flexible work, there are additional reasons why flexible work schedules may be uniquely beneficial for leaders, including improvements in the quality of their leadership behaviors, greater diversity in leadership roles, and organizational benefits of role modeling.

Leadership behaviors

One benefit of allowing leaders access to flexible work schedules may be to the quality of leadership behaviors. Leadership behaviors can take several positive and negative forms. The most widely studied theory of positive leadership is transformational leadership (Barling, 2014), which involves four behaviors, namely idealized influence (behaving ethically), inspirational motivation (being charismatic and inspiring), individualized consideration (being concerned with the individual needs of followers), and intellectual stimulation (developing followers to think critically for themselves). Such leadership behaviors are ideal in a workplace as they improve employee attitudes (Dumdum, Lowe, & Avolio, 2013), and performance outcomes (Wang, Oh, Courtright, & Colbert, 2011). But leadership behaviors can also take negative form. That is, leaders can engage in abusive supervision which involves "the sustained display of hostile verbal and nonverbal behaviors" (Tepper, 2000, p. 178), or passive leadership behaviors, which involves inactive or nonresponsive leadership behaviors that deny followers the recognition they deserve for good performance (reward omission) and the punishment they warrant for poor performance (punishment omission) (Hinkin & Schriesheim, 2008). Such negative leadership behaviors have negative consequences for employee attitudes (Mackey, Frieder, Brees, & Martinko, 2017) and organizational outcomes (e.g., workplace injuries, Kelloway, Mullen, & Francis, 2006). As such, researchers have recently concentrated efforts into understanding what factors may predict positive – and prevent negative – leadership behaviors (Barling, 2014).

Although at this time there is no known research directly testing whether leaders' adoption of flexible work arrangements cause changes to their leadership behaviors, some research suggests when leaders strike a better work-life balance – a primary benefit of flexible work systems – they do engage in more positive and fewer negative leadership behaviors. For example, a recent study by Dionisi and Barling (2019) using leader and follower dyads showed that when leaders experienced greater family-work conflict, they were more likely to experience depressive symptoms, which in turn predicted abusive supervision, as well as increased cognitive distraction at work, which resulted in passive leadership behaviors.

A different study testing leader and follower dyads (ten Brummelhuis, Haar, & Roche, 2014) investigated the effects of leaders' family-work conflict and family-work enrichment on their experience of burnout, work engagement, and supportive leadership behaviors. Ten Brummelhuis et al. found that leaders with greater family-work enrichment come to work more engaged, enthusiastic, vigorous, and dedicated to their work. In turn, this results in more energy invested in supporting followers. Importantly, these authors also found that leaders who experienced higher levels of family-work conflict also reported feeling more burnt out at work, resulting in less supportive leadership behaviors.

The effects of burnout and depletion are not limited to reductions in supportive leadership behaviors. Across one longitudinal and one daily diary study, Courtright et al. (2015) showed that greater family-to-work conflict was indirectly associated with abusive supervision, with this effect being as mediated by daily ego depletion.

Although the causal effects of a flexible work system on leadership behaviors remains to be directly tested, we suggest that some of the lessons drawn from the above studies predict a similar pattern of findings. Drawing on principles from the conservation of resources theory (Hobfoll, 2002), we believe that when leaders enjoy greater flexibility in setting their work schedules, the increase in family time would serve to regenerate psychological resources and energy (ten Brummelhuis et al., 2014). In turn, these extra psychological resources could help leaders refrain from enacting bad leadership behaviors, and provide the necessary energy to engage in good leadership behaviors (Lin, Scott, & Matta, 2019).

Leader diversity

Perhaps one of the most socially important benefits of leaders' using flexible work schedule themselves would be the increased likelihood of diversifying the potential pool of organizational leaders. Specifically, female leaders, who still shoulder more home responsibilities than their male counterparts, may benefit especially from flexible work hours, enabling them to ascend the organizational hierarchy and break the glass ceiling more easily.

There is strong evidence indicating that flexible work hours help females as they move up the organizational and leadership hierarchy. Compared to males, females place greater value on flexible working hours to meet the needs of their demanding schedules beyond work (e.g., Lombard, 2001). Females whose organization offers greater flexible work hours report higher organizational commitment and job satisfaction than females who have less access to such flexibility (Scandura & Lankau, 1997), as a result of which females may stay longer in organizations that provide flexibility. In addition, the availability of flexible work policies also affects females' leadership aspirations more greatly than it does for males (Fritz & van Knippenberg, 2017), such that females feel more motivated to seek leadership roles in their organization if flexible work schedules are available. Importantly, the development of more work-life policies over time has been associated with the rise of females holding lower-level and senior-level managerial roles (Dreher, 2003), but the benefits to female leadership emergence can take several years to appear (Kalysh, Kulik, & Perera, 2016).

The existence of flexible work schedules and policies may also support female leaders ascending into higher executive leadership roles. In a cross-national examination of 9,627 managers in 33 countries, Lyness and Judiesch (2008) showed that managers who can establish a work-life balance are ultimately rated as higher in career-advancement potential. This was specifically the case for females in egalitarian cultures. Although some research contradicts these findings (e.g., females who take advantage of flexible work schedules are perceived as less motivated towards career advancement; Rogier & Padgett, 2004), Lyness and Judiesch's (2008) findings suggest that females who can achieve a work-life balance send signals to others that they are capable of handling greater leadership responsibilities. By implementing strategic workplace flexibility policies, organizations can retain talented females, and increase their likelihood of advancing into leadership positions over time.

Flexible work schedules may also promote religious diversity in organizations. Many employees have religious beliefs and obligations that require regular and frequent prayer during working hours. This is a significant issue, as research has documented that prayer practices at work can result in discriminatory behaviors by others (Ghumman, Ryan, Barclay, & Markel, 2013). Although speculative, we suggest that meeting religious obligations at work may indirectly reduce the likelihood of being selected for leadership roles if short-term absence from one's work tasks or station are perceived as a lack of commitment, or a dual commitment that places work secondary. However, flexible work schedules would seamlessly integrate religious obligations with work, such that employees meeting those obligations would be at no disadvantage in ascending the organizational hierarchy.

Role modeling

Another meaningful benefit of leaders using flexible work schedules for themselves is the role modeling effect it will inspire. Individuals romanticize the role of leaders in organizations (Meindl, Ehrlich, & Dukerich, 1985), and look to their behaviors as indicators of what is considered acceptable, normative, and encouraged, especially with regards to ethical behavior (Treviño & Brown, 2005). If leaders themselves take the opportunity to work flexible hours, and these same policies are available to followers, the leaders' behaviors will legitimize and reinforce their use for others because of the important role leaders' values and behaviors fulfil in setting and maintaining company culture (Schein, 1992), especially when these values and behaviors are rewarded and/or punished. Thus, when leaders take the opportunity to use flexible working hours, they normalize the use of such policies (Allen, 2001).

The challenges

Finally, there are some challenges unique to leaders when taking advantage of flexible work systems, including managing boundaries between work and non-work, understanding the advantages afforded to one's self in a leadership role, and re-conceptualizing one's role as a leader.

Managing boundaries

Perhaps counterintuitively, managing the boundaries between work hours and personal hours can be more challenging within flexible work systems (Desrochers, Hilton, & Larwood, 2005). This is because greater flexibility can engender greater role ambiguity. Although leaders are more likely to use flexible work policies than non-leaders (Lambert, Marler, & Gueutal, 2008), the benefits of these policies for leaders themselves has been mixed. For example, in a qualitative study conducted on Australian managers, increased flexibility resulted in the perception that managers have less control over time demands, and the feeling that they could not as easily access flexible work hours as compared to other work roles (e.g., subordinates) in their organization (Parris, Vickers, & Wilkes, 2008). Similarly, the availability of flexible work hours increased managers' feelings of anxiety and external pressures (Ford & Collinson, 2011), as such policies (a) threatened their self-perceived organizational status, and (b) left leaders feeling as though they had higher expectations of achieving a perfect work-family balance by both employees and their family members alike. Thus, organizational leaders need to pay special attention when creating boundaries between work and personal/family time.

Understanding role differences

There are two important challenges leaders may face as a function of their work role. First, the opportunities available to them may not extend to the employees they supervise. This might immediately raise concerns around perceived fairness in the workplace for their subordinates. Second, the flexible work hours worked by a leader may encourage followers to work similar hours, which may not be ideal. For example, if a leader chooses to work late at night, followers may implicitly get the impression that this is expected from them. Being unable to participate, or having unreasonable expectations, can ultimately jeopardize any benefits that might accrue from the leader serving as an ethical role model, once again emphasizing the importance of customizing flexible work for each employee.

Changing how leaders think about their role

At one level, leaders need to reconceptualize how their own work is evaluated in order to successfully implement and maintain flexible work systems and policies – from hours present on the job to the actual productive output of workers. At a more personal level, this means that leaders need to change how they go about fulfilling their leadership role on a day-to-day basis – the same reconceptualization of self-evaluation needs to occur. Specifically, their role might be less about continual performance monitoring, and more about creating and fostering those work conditions that bring out the best in their followers, and that help new leaders develop. This initially involves the difficult personal challenge of relinquishing control and replacing it with trust in and opportunities for autonomy for team members.

Conclusion

Traditionally, a chapter like ours would emphasize just how much leaders could do to facilitate benefits for others through using flexible work opportunities, and the first part of our discussion does just that. However, consistent with the notion that leaders matter just as much as anyone else in organizations, we also considered what all this would mean for leaders themselves in their leadership roles and in their personal lives. As such, we argue that the use of flexible work structures is of significant importance to individuals at all levels of the organization, contributing to their ability to live healthier work, personal, and family lives. Expanding our focus in this way is critical: as stated by Ben Congleton at the opening of this chapter, we should all be able to bring our whole selves to work – whatever time that may be.

Recommendations

Throughout this chapter we have offered several suggestions as to how leaders might successfully implement and maintain flexible work systems and policies. We suggest that with its focus on four different leadership behaviors, transformational leadership (Bass & Riggio, 2006) may be an ideal framework on which to summarize our recommendations. Accordingly, we close off this chapter by outlining how these behaviors are relevant in the context of leaders implementing and supporting flexible work systems for their team members. These recommendations may be particularly relevant to human resource professionals as well, who play a significant role in ensuring leaders are trained to apply the leadership behaviors discussed below.

(1) Idealized influence includes behaving ethically and practicing what one preaches. As noted throughout the chapter, one critical initial step in promoting flexible work is by doing the right thing, as a result of which the leader would serve as a role model for followers' behaviors. By personally making use of flexible work opportunities, leaders legitimize the same choice for their followers.
(2) Inspirational motivation involves inspiring and motivating others to achieve certain goals. If leaders wish to facilitate flexible work structures,

they must actively encourage team members to work flexibly. Going beyond this, leaders could praise those who take advantage of such policies, and discuss the benefits of such policies with team members. Together, this will work towards creating a culture of flexible work, and eliminate any fears associated with using these policies.

(3) Intellectual stimulation reflects the most developmental dimension of transformational leadership (Barling, 2014), and refers to leaders helping employees think about their work in new ways, and encouraging and facilitating active involvement by followers in decision making. Within the context of flexible work systems, leaders can interact individually and collectively with followers, and explicitly engage in discussions on the benefits of accessing flexible work opportunities, and how this is consistent with a new way of thinking about work that goes beyond a traditional "unit of time" based approach. Leaders can then discuss with their employees how to actively craft an individualized flexible work schedule. By involving followers in all of these decisions, followers may be more likely to adhere to a schedule, which in turn will engender leaders' trust in them as they struggle to relinquish control.

(4) Individualized consideration is ideally suited to the challenge of supporting employees as they engage with flexible work opportunities as it involves supporting and developing employees' personal and work-related needs. Within the context of flexible work systems, leaders would appreciate that implementing a new system would involve change for many employees, and actively support them as they choose to engage in a different work system. Leaders could also ensure that even when team members start and end work at different times of the day, opportunities for work-related and social interactions among team members, and with themselves, are maintained, if not enhanced.

Note

1 Note – the examples of flexible work systems discussed in this chapter primarily consider time, however, we acknowledge that flexible work systems can involve geographical (e.g., location of work) flexibility as well.

References

Allen, T. D. (2001). Family-supportive work environments: The role of organizational perceptions. *Journal of Vocational Behavior, 58*, 414–435.

Armstrong, D., Shakespeare-Finch, J., & Shochet, I. (2016). Organizational belongingness mediates the relationship between sources of stress and posttrauma outcomes in firefighters. *Psychological Trauma: Theory, Research, Practice, and Policy, 8*, 343–347.

Arnold, K. A., Turner, N., Barling, J., Kelloway, E. K., & McKee, M. C. (2007). Transformational leadership and psychological well-being: The mediating role of meaningful work. *Journal of Occupational Health Psychology, 12*, 193–203.

Barling, J. (2014). *The science of leadership: Lessons from research for organizational leaders.* New York: Oxford University Press.

Bass, B. & Riggio, R. E. (2006). *Transformational leadership* (2nd ed.). New York: Taylor & Francis.

Baumeister, R. F., Bratslavsky, E., Finkenauer, C., & Vohs, K. D. (2001). Bad is stronger than good. *Review of General Psychology, 5*, 323–370.

Baumeister, R. F. & Leary, M. R. (1995). The need to belong: Desire for interpersonal attachments as a fundamental human motivation. *Psychological Bulletin, 117*, 497–529.

Breaugh, J. A. & Frye, N. K. (2008). Work–family conflict: The importance of family-friendly employment practices and family-supportive supervisors. *Journal of Business and Psychology, 22*, 345–353.

Brockner, J. (2006). Why it's so hard to be fair. *Harvard Business Review, 84*, 122–129.

ten Brummelhuis, L. L., Haar, J. M., & Roche, M. (2014). Does family life help to be a better leader? A closer look at crossover processes from leaders to followers. *Personnel Psychology, 67*, 917–949.

Budd, J. W. & Mumford, K. (2006). Family–friendly work practices in Britain: Availability and perceived accessibility. *Human Resource Management, 45*, 23–42.

Choi, S. (2018). Managing flexible work arrangements in government: Testing the effects of institutional and managerial support. *Public Personnel Management, 47*, 26–50.

Christie, A. M. & Barling, J. (2009). Disentangling the indirect links between socioeconomic status and health: The dynamic roles of work stressors and personal control. *Journal of Applied Psychology, 94*, 1466–1478.

Colquitt, J. A. (2001). On the dimensionality of organizational justice: A construct validation of a measure. *Journal of Applied Psychology, 86*, 386–400.

Courtwright, S. H., Gardner, R. G., Smith, T. A., McCormick, B. W., & Colbert, A. E. (2015). My family made me do it: A cross-domain, self-regulatory perspective on antecedents to abusive supervision. *Academy of Management Journal, 59*, 1630–1652.

Desrochers, S., Hilton, J., & Larwood, L. (2005). Preliminary validation of the work–family integration-blurring scale. *Journal of Family Issues, 26*, 442–466.

Dionisi, A. M. & Barling, J. (2019). What happens at home doesn't stay at home: The role of family and romantic partner conflict in destructive leadership. *Stress and Health, 35*, 304–317.

Dreher, G. F. (2003). Breaking the glass ceiling: The effects of sex ratios and work-life programs on female leadership at the top. *Human Relations, 56*, 541–562.

Dumdum, U. R., Lowe, K. B., & Avolio, B. J. (2013). A meta-analysis of transformational and transactional leadership correlates of effectiveness and satisfaction: An update and extension. In *Transformational and Charismatic Leadership: The Road Ahead 10th Anniversary Edition* (pp. 39–70). Amsterdam: JAI Press.

Eaton, S. C. (2003). If you can use them: Flexibility policies, organizational commitment, and perceived performance. *Industrial Relations: A Journal of Economy and Society, 42*, 145–167.

Ford, J. & Collinson, D. (2011). In search of the perfect manager? Work-life balance and managerial work. *Work, Employment and Society, 25*, 257–273.

Fritz, C. & van Knippenberg, D. (2017). Gender and leadership aspiration: The impact of work–life initiatives. *Human Resource Management, 57*, 855–868.

Ghumman, S., Ryan, A. M., Barclay, L. A., & Markel, K. S. (2013). Religious discrimination in the workplace: A review and examination of current and future trends. *Journal of Business and Psychology, 28*, 439–454.

Gomez, C. & Rosen, B. (2001). The leader-member exchange as a link between managerial trust and employee empowerment. *Group & Organization Management, 26*, 53–69.

Harris, G. E. & Cameron, J. E. (2005). Multiple dimensions of organizational identification and commitment as predictors of turnover intentions and psychological well-being. *Canadian Journal of Behavioural Science, 37*, 159.

Hinkin, T. R. & Schriesheim, C. A. (2008). An examination of "non-leadership": From laissez-faire leadership to leader reward omission and punishment omission. *Journal of Applied Psychology, 93*, 1234–1248.

Hobfoll, S. E. (2002). Social and psychological resources and adaptation. *Review of General Psychology, 6*, 307–324.

Hoption, C., Christie, A., & Barling, J. (2015). Submitting to the follower label. *Zeitschrift für Psychologie, 220*, 221–230.

Jang, S. J. (2009). The relationships of flexible work schedules, workplace support, supervisory support, work-life balance, and the well-being of working parents. *Journal of Social Service Research, 35*, 93–104.

Julien, M., Somerville, K., & Culp, N. (2011). Going beyond the work arrangement: The crucial role of supervisor support. *Public Administration Quarterly, 35*, 167–204.

Kalysh, K., Kulik, C. T., & Perera, S. (2016). Help or hindrance? Work–life practices and women in management. *The Leadership Quarterly, 27*, 504–518.

Kelloway, E. K., Mullen, J., & Francis, L. (2006). Divergent effects of transformational and passive leadership on employee safety. *Journal of Occupational Health Psychology, 11*, 76–86.

Ko, J., Hur, S., & Smith-Walter, A. (2013). Family-friendly work practices and job satisfaction and organizational performance: Moderating effects of managerial support and performance-oriented management. *Public Personnel Management, 42*, 545–565.

Kossek, E. E., Pichler, S., Bodner, T., & Hammer, L. B. (2011). Workplace social support and work–family conflict: A meta-analysis clarifying the influence of general and work–family-specific supervisor and organizational support. *Personnel psychology, 64*, 289–313.

Lambert, A. D., Marler, J. H., & Gueutal, H. G. (2008). Individual differences: Factors affecting employee utilization of flexible work arrangements. *Journal of Vocational Behavior, 73*, 107–117.

Lin, S. H., Scott, B. A., & Matta, F. K. (2019). The dark side of transformational leader behaviors for leaders themselves: A conservation of resources perspective. *Academy of Management Journal, 62*, 1556–1582.

Lombard, K. V. (2001). Female self-employment and demand for flexible, nonstandard work schedules. *Economic Inquiry, 39*, 214–237.

Lyness, K. S. & Judiesch, M. K. (2008). Can a manager have a life and a career? International and multisource perspectives on work-life balance and career advancement potential. *Journal of Applied Psychology, 93*, 789–805.

McGregor, J. (2017). The mental health email shared 'round the world. *The Washington Post* (July 4). Retrieved from: https://www.washingtonpost.com/news/on-leadership/wp/2017/07/14/the-mental-health-email-shared-round-the-world

Mackey, J. D., Frieder, R. E., Brees, J. R., & Martinko, M. J. (2017). Abusive supervision: A meta-analysis and empirical review. *Journal of Management, 43*, 1940–1965.

MacLean, K. (2018). Flexible work arrangements: Transforming the way Canadians work. *The Conference Board of Canada* (May 30). Retrieved from: https://www.conferenceboard.ca/e-Library/abstract.aspx?did=9614

madalynrose (2017, June 30) When the CEO responds to your out of the office email about taking sick leave for mental health and reaffirms your decision [Twitter Post]. Retrieved from: https://twitter.com/madalynrose/status/880886024725024769?lang=en

Magee, J. C. & Galinsky, A. D. (2008). 8 social hierarchy: The self-reinforcing nature of power and status. *Academy of Management Annals, 2,* 351–398.

Markus, H. (1978). The effect of mere presence on social facilitation: An unobtrusive test. *Journal of Experimental Social Psychology, 14,* 389–397.

Marr, J. C. & Thau, S. (2014). Falling from great (and not-so-great) heights: How initial status position influences performance after status loss. *Academy of Management Journal, 57,* 223–248.

Mayer, R. C., Davis, J. H., & Schoorman, F. D. (1995). An integrative model of organizational trust. *Academy of Management Review, 20,* 709–734.

Meindl, J. R., Ehrlich, S. B., & Dukerich, J. M. (1985). The romance of leadership. *Administrative Science Quarterly, 30,* 78–102.

Mesmer-Magnus, J. R. & Viswesvaran, C. (2006). How family-friendly work environments affect work/family conflict: A meta-analytic examination. *Journal of Labor Research, 27,* 555–574.

National Federation of Independent Business (NFIB) (2018). Three ways business leaders are ensuring flexible work programs are successful. Retrieved from: https://www.nfib.com/content/benefits/technology/3-ways-business-leaders-are-ensuring-flexible-work-programs-are-successful/

Nembhard, I. M. & Edmondson, A. C. (2006). Making it safe: The effects of leader inclusiveness and professional status on psychological safety and improvement efforts in health care teams. *Journal of Organizational Behavior, 27,* 941–966.

Organisation for Economic Co-operation and Development (OECD) (2016). Be Flexible! Background brief on how workplace flexibility can help European employees to balance work and family. Retrieved from: https://www.oecd.org/els/family/Be-Flexible-Backgrounder-Workplace-Flexibility.pdf

Parris, M. A., Vickers, M. H., & Wilkes, L. (2008). Caught in the middle: Organizational impediments to middle managers' work-life balance. *Employee Responsibilities and Rights Journal, 20,* 101–117.

Pencavel, J. (2014). The productivity of working hours. *The Economic Journal, 125,* 2052–2076.

Pettit, N. C., Yong, K., & Spataro, S. E. (2010). Holding your place: Reactions to the prospect of status gains and losses. *Journal of Experimental Social Psychology, 46,* 396–401.

Rogier, S. A. & Padgett, M. Y. (2004). The impact of utilizing a flexible work schedule on the perceived career advancement potential of women. *Human Resource Development Quarterly, 15,* 89–106.

Sánchez-Vidal, M. E., Cegarra-Leiva, D., & Cegarra-Navarro, J. G. (2012). Gaps between managers' and employees' perceptions of work–life balance. *The International Journal of Human Resource Management, 23,* 645–661.

Scandura, T. A. & Lankau, M. J. (1997). Relationships of gender, family responsibility and flexible work hours to organizational commitment and job satisfaction. *Journal of Organizational Behavior, 18,* 377–391.

Schaubroeck, J. M., Hannah, S. T., Avolio, B. J., Kozlowski, S. W., Lord, R. G., Treviño, L. K., et al. (2012). Embedding ethical leadership within and across organization levels. *Academy of Management Journal, 55,* 1053–1078.

Scheepers, D., Ellemers, N., & Sintemaartensdijk, N. (2009). Suffering from the possibility of status loss: Physiological responses to social identity threat in high status groups. *European Journal of Social Psychology, 39*, 1075–1092.

Schein, E. H. (1992). How leaders create organizational cultures (ch. 11); How founders and leaders embed and transmit culture (ch. 12). *Organizational culture and leadership* (2nd ed.). San Francisco, CA: Jossey-Bass.

Steffens, N. K., Haslam, S. A., Schuh, S. C., Jetten, J., & van Dick, R. (2017). A meta-analytic review of social identification and health in organizational contexts. *Personality and Social Psychology Review, 21*, 303–335.

Swanberg, J. E., McKechnie, S. P., Ojha, M. U., & James, J. B. (2011). Schedule control, supervisor support and work engagement: A winning combination for workers in hourly jobs? *Journal of Vocational Behavior, 79*, 613–624.

Tepper, B. J. (2000). Consequences of abusive supervision. *Academy of Management Journal, 43*, 178–190.

Thomas, L. T. & Ganster, D. C. (1995). Impact of family-supportive work variables on work-family conflict and strain: A control perspective. *Journal of Applied Psychology, 80*, 6–15.

Treviño, L. K. & Brown, M. E. (2005). The role of leaders in influencing unethical behavior in the workplace. In R. E. Kidwell & C. L. Martin (eds), *Managing organizational deviance* (pp. 69–87). Thousand Oaks, CA: Sage.

Wang, G., Oh, I. S., Courtright, S. H., & Colbert, A. E. (2011). Transformational leadership and performance across criteria and levels: A meta-analytic review of 25 years of research. *Group & Organization Management, 36*, 223–270.

Wang, P. & Walumbwa, F. O. (2007). Family-friendly programs, organizational commitment, and work withdrawal: The moderating role of transformational leadership. *Personnel Psychology, 60*, 397–427.

Weber, D., Janson, A., Nolan, M., Wen, L. M., & Rissel, C. (2011). Female employees' perceptions of organisational support for breastfeeding at work: Findings from an Australian health service workplace. *International Breastfeeding Journal, 6*, 1–7.

Willis Towers Watson (2017). Global benefits attitudes survey. Retrieved from https://www.willistowerswatson.com/en/insights/2017/11/2017-global-benefits-attitudes-survey

Yukl, G. (2012). Effective leadership behavior: What we know and what questions need more attention. *Academy of Management Perspectives, 26*, 66–85.

7 Line managers and flexible working

Sharon Clarke

With the introduction of new legislation (for example, the US Telework Enhancement Act, 2010; the UK Flexible Working Regulations, 2014; and the Flexible Working Act, 2016, in the Netherlands), the opportunity to work flexibly has increased for many employees. In Europe, for example, 65% of employees report having access to flexible work, with 42% making use of flexible work arrangements (European Commission, 2018). Flexible working has been defined as "the opportunity of workers to make choices influencing when, where, and for how long they engage in work-related tasks" (Bal & de Lange, 2015, p. 127). Flexible working can take a number of different forms, including flexibility in when work is done (e.g., flexibility in start and finish times; compressed hours), where it is done (e.g., working from home; remote working), and for how long (e.g., part-time work; reduced load work). These arrangements may be formally reflected in employees' contracts or arranged informally at their line manager's discretion. In this chapter, we focus on the role of line managers in making flexible working "work". "Line managers" refers to those with direct managerial responsibility for other employee(s); the number of personnel within organizations who have line management responsibilities will vary depending on the size and structure of the organization (and in the smallest organizations this may be the owner-manager of the business). We draw on literature from a number of related contexts to evaluate the role of line managers, including research on specific forms of flexible working (e.g., part-time work; remote working/telecommuting; working from home; reduced-load work); research on work-family balance and flexible working, such as family-supportive supervision; and, research on idiosyncratic deals (or *i-deals*, defined as "voluntary, personalized agreements of a nonstandard nature negotiated between individual employees and their employers regarding terms that benefit each party" (Rousseau et al., 2006, p. 978)). We highlight ways in which the line manager plays a significant role in flexible working, from the influence on who takes up opportunities for flexible working and the form that flexible working takes through personal negotiations, to the ongoing support of flexible working within organizations. The pervasive influence of line managers in the success of flexible working policies provides a significant opportunity not only to improve productivity, but also to promote gender equality and mental well-being in organizations.

Much of the theorizing around line managers' roles in flexible working is based on a social exchange perspective (Blau, 1964/1986). Although flexible working policies are formulated at the organizational level, they are often implemented at a local level, where agreements must be reached between the line manager and the employee on an individual basis (i.e., an idiosyncratic deal, or i-deal; Rousseau et al., 2006). The quality of the relationship (as reflected in leader-member exchange) has been found to have a significant influence on the successful negotiation of i-deals, including those related to time and location flexibility (Hornung et al., 2014; Rosen et al., 2013). Based on social exchange theory, there is evidence to suggest that allowing employees to work flexibly creates perceived obligations, which leads to employees responding with increased work effort (Kelliher & Anderson, 2010), and more organizational citizenship, that is extra-role behaviours such as helping co-workers (Rousseau et al., 2006). Line managers use the negotiation of i-deals with specific individuals as a way of motivating them. Particularly when i-deals are more of a rarity, the employee will feel more highly valued in comparison to their co-workers, leading to increased motivation, and subsequently enhanced employee performance and engagement in organizational citizenship behaviours. Employees also report enhanced work-related attitudes, including job satisfaction (Singh & Vidyarthi, 2018), and affective commitment (Anand et al., 2010). Empirical work has supported the role of social exchange processes which mediate the effects of i-deals on employee performance and organizational citizenship behaviours (Singh & Vidyarthi, 2018). Gajendran et al. (2015) investigated the effects of remote working on individual effectiveness: they found positive effects on both task and contextual performance, but this was dependent on the relationship with the line manager. Individuals with a good supervisor relationship achieved higher levels of task and contextual performance regardless of the extent to which they worked remotely.

In the following sections we consider the role of line managers across all stages of exploration, negotiation, implementation, and maintenance of flexible working in organizations. Line managers often play a significant role in determining who is permitted to take up flexible working arrangements and in what format, given that many flexible working arrangements are negotiated on an individual basis. Granting the option to work flexibly has implications for managing staff effectively, as employees gain additional control over their work schedules and/or working hours, as well as the potential to decide where to work. Thus, the line manager must consider the effects on their own work, and also on the work of their team. Flexible working has positive benefits for the organization (e.g., attracting and retaining talented staff, more motivated and committed employees), and the employee (e.g., increased autonomy, improved work-life balance), but recent studies have also highlighted the "dark side" of flexible working. It creates management challenges for the line manager (e.g., difficulties with communication and coordination), and can be divisive in a team context, by creating perceptions of unfairness, competitive climate, and stigma. Research has also suggested that flexible working may not provide expected benefits for employees, as it can lead to work intensification and career "penalties". Over time, flexible workers may become marginalized by perceptions of reduced contribution from both colleagues and managers. These are all challenges for the line manager in terms of successfully managing teams of employees who work flexibly, not only in the early stages of implementing flexible working, but also over time as flexible working is integrated into daily operations.

Line managers influence who takes up flexible working

If an employee's line manager is perceived to hold negative attitudes towards flexible working, this can make them reluctant to take up the opportunity to work flexibly. In a study looking at reduced load work, Gascoigne and Kelliher (2018) found that manager views had a significant influence on employees' decisions about whether to ask for flexible working (or whether to consider alternative options, such as leaving the organization, remaining full-time, or delaying going part time). Kossek et al. (2016) interviewed line managers about their perceptions of using reduced load work; they found that managers were more likely to be supportive of this alternative work pattern if they perceived employees to be high performers, flexible in their use of reduced load work, and employed in suitable jobs. Less supportive managers expressed concerns that commitment to the organization and productivity would be adversely affected by reduced load work. They felt that a request for reduced load work acted as a warning of employees who were not coping with demands of the full-time job.

Earlier research suggested that managers' knowledge of flexible working practices was often variable, which could affect their ability to offer flexible working to their employees (Casper et al., 2004). Managers may be unsure how to put organizational flexible work policies into practice and believe that they will have difficulties supervising flexible workers and managing their performance (Van Dyne et al., 2007). Indeed, managers often hold negative views about flexible working due to the tension between granting autonomy and maintaining control as a manager (Peters et al., 2010). Negative views are also associated with line managers who believe that flexible working is being used out of self-interest rather than to increase productivity (Leslie et al., 2012). In making decisions about requests to work flexibly, Klein et al. (2000) found that managers were more likely to approve requests to work part time for employees whose performance was considered good, would be likely to leave if their request was denied, and would be difficult to replace.

There may be a trickle-down effect from the attitudes and actions of senior management to those managers who are tasked with implementing flexible work policies. Williams et al. (2017) found that even though senior executives recognized the strategic benefits of having flexible work policies, they still reported concern about the impact of flexible working on productivity.

This was reflected in differing practices across organizational divisions, indicating that implementation depended on the extent to which senior managers signalled support through open communication and encouragement of flexible working practices. The study concluded that senior management attitudes resulted in a tendency for inconsistent practice across the organization and for leaving decisions to local discretion. In addition, when executives did not work flexibly themselves, this tended to reinforce the message that flexible working is career limiting. However, when line managers themselves have caring responsibilities, they tend to be more amenable to flexible working (such as schedule i-deals), leading to greater satisfaction with work-family balance for employees (Las Heras et al., 2017). The development of an organizational culture that supports flexible working and encourages better work-life balance can help to mitigate negative managerial attitudes. For example, Bourdeau et al. (2019) found that line managers held differing attitudes to work-life balance policies depending on whether they were perceived as *enabling* policies (i.e., which allowed latitude in when, where, and how long employees work), and those which operated in an *enclosing* way (i.e., which promoted work intensification). They found that line managers tended to view the latter as a signal of work devotion, rather than the former, but that the subsequent impact on employees' career development was mitigated by organizational norms (for family supportiveness).

In contrast to quite a negative picture in terms of managerial attitudes towards flexible working, there is some evidence that increasing experience of managing flexible work and the increased incidence of flexible working practices being embedded in organizations, may lead to more positive attitudes. For example, Gascoigne and Kelliher (2018) found that their interviewees spoke of trying to identify managers who might be more amenable to flexible working due to cultural differences; one interviewee notes that a Swedish line manager was more receptive to the idea of flexible working compared to a UK manager within the same international company. Thus, we might expect that negative managerial attitudes may cease to act as a barrier to employees taking up flexible working opportunities over time, as line managers grow in confidence with further experience of flexible working in future.

Line managers influence flexible working through the negotiation of i-deals

Putnam et al. (2014) argue that organizations need to move away from defining flexible working as a special privilege, and enshrine it as an employee right. However, this is not currently the case in many organizations where flexible working is not written into organizational policies as an employee right, but is a special privilege which must be requested and negotiated on an individual basis. Such nonstandard arrangements are becoming increasingly frequent, with the reduction in collective bargaining to establish common working conditions, including Europe and the USA (Organisation for Economic Co-operation and Development (OECD), 2019; US Bureau of Labor Statistics, 2018). The positive effects of i-deals on work-related outcomes, such as job satisfaction and affective commitment, have been reported across both Western and Eastern cultures (Liao et al., 2016). These individual negotiations place line managers at the centre of decisions not only to approve flexible working, but also to define the content and boundaries of any flexible working arrangement. A substantial body of literature has developed around this topic of idiosyncratic deals (or i-deals). I-deals within the context of flexible working include: schedule and location flexibility, as well as reduced load arrangements (Hornung et al., 2010; Rosen et al., 2013). Taking a social exchange perspective emphasizes the importance of the relationship between the line manager and the employee, but it has been argued that social exchange mechanisms are not sufficient to explain i-deals; these need additional theoretical perspectives, such as employees pursuing their own personal goals, especially for flexibility or reduced workload contracts, or that the benefits derive from changes in job characteristics, such as autonomy (Liao et al., 2016).

Thus the negotiation of i-deals depends not only on social exchange mechanisms, but might be extended by using a Conservation of Resources framework (Hobfoll, 1989). Based on Conservation of Resources theory, the possibility to work flexibly entails valued resources (e.g., autonomy, flexibility, work-family balance, etc.), which flexible workers are motivated to defend from loss (Halbesleben et al., 2014). Therefore flexible workers take action to signal that their efficiency and productivity is not adversely affected (e.g., maintain visibility and presence, work to become more proficient and adaptable, show willingness to be flexible). The role of line managers in facilitating valued resources, such as autonomy, has been subject of limited research. However, a study conducted by Aryee et al. (2013) demonstrated that line managers' support for control over work time increased flexible workers' engagement in contextual work performance. In a further theoretical extension, Liu et al. (2013) considered both social exchange and self-enhancement as mediating mechanisms linking i-deals to employee work outcomes. They argued that because employees personally invest in their work, the negotiation of i-deals may lead to increased perceptions of self-worth, and high self-esteem. Their study supported these arguments such that organizational self-esteem mediated the effects of flexibility i-deals on employees' proactive behaviours over and above social exchange. Thus, flexible working affects employee behaviours not only through social exchange but also through perceptions of self-enhancement. Rofcanin et al. (2017a) argue that managers play a critical role not only in the negotiation, but also the successful implementation of i-deals. While most research focuses on the impact of i-deals on employees' attitudes and behaviours, Rofcanin et al. (2017a) focused on managers' emotions. The study found that managers' positive emotions were associated with employees' socially connecting behaviours (i.e., the extent to which employees engage with co-workers and improve team efficiency), while managers' negative emotions were associated with employees' socially disconnecting behaviours. Negotiated i-deals were more likely to be successfully executed where managers experienced positive rather than negative emotions.

Furthermore, most research has considered the effects of i-deals on individual employee performance, rather than team performance. Taking a social comparison perspective, Vidyarthi et al. (2016) suggested that having negotiated a successful i-deal raises the individual employee's standing relative to others within the team, but that little research has been done that has considered the consequences of such an effect within the team context. In their study, the authors focused on leader-member exchange social comparison (LMXSC) variable, which reflects team members' subjective assessment of their own LMX (leader-member exchange) compared to the LMX of their co-workers (Vidyarthi et al., 2010). They found that LMXSC only affected employee behaviour in groups characterized by low team orientation; in contrast, for closely connected and tight-knit groups, LMXSC had no effect on employee behaviour. Further work has also emphasized the influence of co-workers' i-deals. For example, Kong et al. (2018) found that for an individual employee, others' i-deals can have a negative influence by increasing their emotional exhaustion and deviant behaviours. Perceptions of co-workers' i-deals can also impact on employees' concerns regarding distributive justice and equity within teams, affecting their tendency to speak up about perceived unfairness (Marescaux et al., 2019). Thus, i-deals can have positive effects on individual employee performance, especially when they are loosely connected to their co-workers, but can have unintended consequences within closely interconnected teams, such as perceived inequity. This research aligns with findings from our own work (Clarke & Holdsworth, 2017) in which a key issue to emerge for managers of flexible work teams was that managers expect flexible workers to be "flexible with flexibility" in order to avoid a negative impact on team morale. The extent to which team effectiveness was perceived to be affected by flexible working depended on managers ensuring fairness and consistency in the implementation of flexible work, and avoiding ad hoc arrangements, to protect their team from negative consequences. They spoke about the importance of building trust and confidence not only for individuals, but also at a team level.

Line managers influence the ongoing effectiveness of flexible working

Flexible working is often used by employees to help them achieve a satisfactory balance between the work and non-work aspects of their lives. In this context, the extent of family-specific support from line managers is an important element of the organization's ongoing support for flexible working. Family-supportive supervisor behaviours (FSSBs) are those actions by line managers that are perceived to provide support for those working flexibly, including instrumental support, and proactive management of work-family arrangements (Hammer et al., 2009). FSSBs have been linked to the success of flexible working, especially time flexibility, such as reduced work hours (Allen, 2001; Breaugh & Frye, 2008). In a meta-analysis, general organizational and supervisory support was found to be important for reducing work-family conflict, but most important was family-specific support (Kossek et al, 2011). There is evidence that family-supportive supervisors enable employees to better balance work and family through the reduction of work-family interference (Greenhaus et al., 2012). Family-supportive supervisors are perceived as empathetic, and also actively help employees to manage their work and non-work time. For example, line managers might take action to ensure that flexible workers maintain control over their work time, which helps to increase employees' contextual work performance (Aryee et al., 2013). The positive effects of family-supportive supervision depends on the quality of the relationship with the line manager; for example, based on social exchange theory, Bagger and Li (2014) found that the influence of family-supportive supervision on employee work outcomes was mediated by leader-member exchange. While the literature has tended to focus on supporting families, the provision of supervisory support extends to employees who negotiate flexibility i-deals seeking work-life balance more generally (Crain & Stevens, 2018), such as working towards retirement. Indeed, research has demonstrated that flexibility i-deals can motivate employees to continue working beyond retirement (Bal et al., 2012).

While i-deals are specifically requested and negotiated with the line manager by the employee, and granted based on the employee's perceived value, FSSBs are initiated by the employee's line manager (Crain & Stevens, 2018). Limited research has focused on identifying the antecedents of FSSBs, but a theoretical model developed by Straub (2012) suggested that the quality of the relationship with the employee together with their felt responsibility would act as key mechanisms encouraging FSSBs. Felt responsibility would be increased when line managers developed a social bond based on perceptions of common experience and an understanding of the benefits of work-family enrichment; contextual factors, such as supportive senior managers and family-supportive organizational culture, would also encourage FSSBs. Line managers may be constrained by their ability to engage in role modelling if they lack dependant care responsibilities, face difficulties with managing flexible work teams, or experience increased workload and burnout themselves (Crain & Stevens, 2018). The value of demonstrating FSSBs is reflected in research conducted by Walsh et al. (2019), which provides evidence of a potential employee backlash when supervisors fail to engage in FSSBs; the study found that this can lead to workplace ostracism against supervisors with impacts on their well-being. This would suggest the possibility of a vicious cycle where line managers are too drained to engage in FSSBs, but this leads to negative employee reactions, which further drains the line managers' personal resources.

In managing flexible work over time, line managers face the reality of management challenges, including difficulty in managing an employee's work activities and preventing unproductive developments (Hertel et al., 2005). For example, Richardson (2010) found that managing employees who work remotely requires line managers to enhance communications, balance autonomy with micromanaging, and increase trust. Thus, it is important for flexible workers to agree with their line managers from the outset how they will work with their colleagues and their manager to maintain work productivity (Kossek & Thompson, 2016), such as when handing over incomplete work and information for others to deal with in order to hit deadlines. Rousseau et al. (2016) argue that the nature of the manager-employee relationship may change over time, given that those who work reduced hours or work remotely may feel less connected to their line manager and the organization, and so feel less committed, leading to the relationship becoming more transactional over time. This shifting in the quality of the manager-employee relationship may subsequently affect the line manager's ongoing provision of support, leading to potential marginalization of flexible workers. In addition to the relationship with the manager, flexible working may also affect relationships with co-workers, particularly where the implementation of i-deals leads to increased peer dissatisfaction, perceptions of inequity, and resentment from colleagues. Line managers who have good relationships with their team may be able to mitigate these effects as the i-deals of others may be more accepted as colleagues trust the manager. Thus, colleagues are less likely to perceive i-deals as favouritism, and may see their line manager as open to flexibility (and so amenable to negotiating an i-deal for others in the future). Line managers might also be well-placed to mitigate the "dark side" of flexible working, which has been identified as operating through three primary mechanisms (at a micro-level): inequity mechanism, a stigma mechanism, and a spillover mechanism (Perrigino et al., 2018). It is important for line managers to manage the team as a whole, and not just flexible working employees, to ensure that flexible working "works" for the team as well as the individual.

Kossek and Ollier-Malaterre (2019) studied line managers' work redesign tactics, which are manager-initiated activities aimed at ensuring that workload is decreased in line with reductions in work hours and pay for those with reduced-load work arrangements. This is important for flexible workers as the failure to manage workloads can lead to frustration and overwork for employees, as well as impacting on career progression and opportunities for networking (Gascoigne & Kelliher, 2018). Line managers discussed how they would proactively reorganize work such that reduced-load work still maintained an appropriate level of challenge without leading to work intensification, such as identifying tasks that could be removed from the scope of the job. These ongoing activities formed a stage of sustainable career embedding, which involved communication to resolve issues and cultural readjustment to ensure that flexible working did not become stigmatized over time. In addition, both line managers and employees would engage in collaborate job crafting to co-create sustainable careers (Kossek & Ollier-Malaterre, 2019), which takes place informally from implementation and through ongoing collaborative activities. The extent to which these collaborative activities are successful in building a sustainable and rewarding job depends on the quality of the manager-employee relationship.

The use of informal job crafting by employees is discussed by Gascoigne and Kelliher (2018); they highlight that some job crafting needs to be done by the employee on a day-to-day basis in order to "fine-tune" the arrangement (e.g., so that they are not seen to be doing less than colleagues). They emphasize how few flexibly working employees in their study were able to negotiate a workable i-deal, and that informal reworking of the "deal" would continue over time, which would involve both individual and collaborative job crafting by the employee. Flexible workers will continue to craft their jobs on a daily basis to optimize the fit between their own requirements and job characteristics (Wessels et al., 2019). This continues on a micro-level after the negotiation of an i-deal and allows employees to decide where and when to work on a daily basis. Wessels et al. define time-spatial job crafting as:

> [a] context-specific type of job crafting in which employees (a) reflect on specific work tasks and private demands; (b) select workplaces, work locations, and working hours that fit those tasks and private demands; and (c) possibly adapt either their place/location of work and working hours or tasks and private demands to ensure that these still fit to each other thereby optimizing time/spatial-demands fit.
>
> (p. 505)

They propose this as a specific type of person-environment fit (PE fit) that employees manage using job crafting to actively adapt their work environment to align with their personal work demands. As this job crafting is personalized and occurs on a daily basis, whilst optimizing fit for the individual, it may still create significant challenges for line managers in terms of coordination, and may exacerbate marginalization of employees from their colleagues. Gascoigne and Kelliher (2018) found that those employees who relied only on individual job crafting tended to focus on reducing demands (which had disadvantages, such as the potential for marginalization and/or work intensification). However, engaging in collaborative crafting with colleagues was a more successful tactic, such that their co-workers would be able to provide cover for the employee's absence within the team by substituting for them. Such tactics would depend on maintaining good relationships not only with the line manager, but also with co-workers.

We have focused on the role of line managers, highlighting their importance not only in managing special arrangements for flexible workers, but also in managing the broader needs of the team. Many aspects of the success of flexible working rely not only on the efforts of line managers, but also on the effects of collaborative job crafting with colleagues, which depend on building positive relationships within teams, and avoiding the development of resentment from colleagues. Although they have received less research attention, it is also important to note that line managers' efforts are much assisted by a positive team climate and a supportive organizational culture (Bal et al., 2012; Bourdeau et al., 2019; Rofcanin et al., 2017b). For example, Rofcanin et al. (2017b) examined the moderating effects of a family-supportive organizational culture, such that FSSBs had a stronger relationship with employee work engagement within a positive organizational culture. Thus, this research illustrates the additive effects of positive support from line managers together with a supportive organizational culture.

Recommendations

Organizations should consider the following recommendations when implementing flexible working, in order to maximize the positive influence of line managers in the negotiation and implementation of flexible working practices, and minimize potential "dark side" effects, such as: management challenges (e.g., difficulties with communication and coordination); perceptions of unfairness, competitive climate, and stigma; and, work intensification, career "penalties", and marginalization for employees. Our review suggests that there are positive benefits associated with flexible working for team effectiveness and organizational productivity, as well as benefits for individual employees in terms of job satisfaction and work-life balance, when flexible working is carefully managed.

- As part of negotiations with employees, ensure there are clear communications, including setting boundaries and managing expectations;
- Make formalized arrangements, but ensure that both parties maintain a willingness to be "flexible with flexibility";
- Implement consistent practices across teams to ensure perceived fairness, but remain open to ongoing "crafting" of jobs to ensure that practices may be adapted over time;
- Consider requests for flexible working on an individual basis, such that managers are open to requests for flexible working, and consider each request on its merits, using consistent principles;
- Encourage managers to work flexibly themselves, so they act as role models, and develop an understanding of the issues associated with flexible working;
- Develop a positive and supportive organizational culture, which will help to mitigate problems associated with flexible working.

References

Allen, T.D. (2001). Family-supportive work environments: The role of organizational perceptions. *Journal of Vocational Behavior, 58*(3), 414–435. DOI:10.1006/jvbe.2000.1774

Anand, S., Vidyarthi, P.R., Liden, R.C., & Rousseau, D.M. (2010). Good citizens in poor-quality relationships: Idiosyncratic deals as a substitute for relationship quality. *Academy of Management Journal, 53*(5), 970–988. DOI:10.5465/AMJ.2010.54533176

Aryee, S., Chu, C.W.L., Kim, T.-Y., & Ryu, S. (2013). Family-supportive work environment and employee work behaviors: An investigation of mediating mechanisms. *Journal of Management, 39*(3), 792–813. DOI:10.1177/0149206311435103

Bagger, J. & Li, A. (2014). How does supervisory family support influence employees' attitudes and behaviors? A social exchange perspective. *Journal of Management, 40*(4), 1123–1150. DOI:10.1177/0149206311413922

Bal, P.M., De Jong, S.B., Jansen, P.G.W., & Bakker, A.B. (2012). Motivating employees to work beyond retirement: A multi-level study of the role of i-deals and unit climate. *Journal of Management Studies, 49*(2), 306–331. DOI:10.1111/j.1467–6486.2011.01026.x

Bal, P.M. & de Lange, A.H. (2015). From flexibility human resource management to employee engagement and perceived job performance across the lifespan: A multi-sample study. *Journal of Occupational and Organizational Psychology, 88*(1), 126–154. DOI:10.1111/joop.12082

Blau, P. (1964/1986). *Exchange and Power in Social Life.* New York: Wiley.

Bourdeau, S., Ollier-Malaterre, A., & Houlfort, N. (2019). Not all work-life policies are created equal: Career consequences of using enabling versus enclosing work-life policies. *Academy of Management Review, 44*(1), 172–193. DOI:10.5465/amr.2016.0429

Breaugh, J.A. & Frye, N.K. (2008). Work-family conflict: The importance of family-friendly employment practices and family-supportive supervisors. *Journal of Business and Psychology, 22*(4), 345–353. DOI:10.1007/s1086900890811

Casper, W.J., Fox, K.E., Sitzmann, T.M., & Landy, A.L. (2004). Supervisor referrals to work-family programs. *Journal of Occupational Health Psychology, 9*(2), 136–151. DOI:10.1037/1076–8998.9.2.136

Clarke, S. & Holdsworth, L. (2017). Flexibility in work teams: Review and case studies of the effects of flexible working on team performance and organizational effectiveness. Report (ref: 3/17) published by ACAS. Full report available for download at: http://www.acas.org.uk/index.aspx?articleid=2056

Crain, T.L. & Stevens, S.C. (2018). Family-supportive supervisor behaviors: A review and recommendations for research and practice. *Journal of Organizational Behavior, 39*(7), 869–888. DOI:10.1002/job.2320

European Commission (2018). Eurobarometer report on work-life balance [online]. Retrieved from: https://www.eesc.europa.eu/en/news-media/news/release-eurobarometer-report-work-life-balance-european-commission

Flexible Working Act (Netherlands) (2016). Retrieved from: http://wetten.overheid.nl/BWBR0011173/2016-01-01

Flexible Working Regulations (UK) (2014). Retrieved from: http://www.legislation.gov.uk/uksi/2014/1398/pdfs/uksi_20141398_en.pdf

Gajendran, R.S., Harrison, D.A., & Delaney-Klinger, K. (2015). Are telecommuters remotely good citizens? Unpacking telecommuting's effects on performance via i-deals and job resources. *Personnel Psychology, 68*(2), 353–393. DOI:10.1111/peps.12082

Gascoigne, C. & Kelliher, C. (2018). The transition to part-time: How professionals negotiate "reduced time and workload" i-deals and craft their jobs. *Human Relations, 71*(1), 103–125. DOI:10.1177/0018726717722394

Greenhaus, J.H., Ziegert, J.C., & Allen, T.D. (2012). When family-supportive supervision matters: Relations between multiple sources of support and work–family balance. *Journal of Vocational Behavior, 80*(2), 266–275. DOI:10.1016/j.jvb.2011.10.008

Halbesleben, J.R.B., Neveu, J.-P., Paustian-Underdahl, S.C., & Westman, M. (2014). Getting to the "COR": Understanding the role of resources in Conservation of Resources theory. *Journal of Management*, *40*(5), 1334–1364. DOI:10.1177/0149206314527130

Hammer, L.B., Kossek, E.E., Yragui, N.L., Bodner, T.E., & Hanson, G.C. (2009). Development and validation of a multidimensional measure of Family Supportive Supervisor Behaviors (FSSB). *Journal of Management*, *35*(4), 837–856. DOI:10.1177/0149206308328510

Hertel, G.T., Geister, S., & Konradt, U. (2005). Managing virtual teams: A review of current empirical research. *Human Resource Management Review*, *15*(15), 69–95. DOI:10.1016/j.hrmr.2005.01.002

Hobfoll, S.E. (1989). Conservation of resources: A new attempt at conceptualizing stress. *American Psychologist*, *44*(3), 513–524. DOI:10.1037/0003–066X.44.3.513

Hornung, S., Rousseau, D.M., Glaser, J., Angerer, P., & Weigl, M. (2010). Beyond top-down and bottom-up work redesign: Customizing job content through idiosyncratic deals. *Journal of Organizational Behavior*, *31*(2–3), 187–215. DOI:10.1002/job.625

Hornung, S., Rousseau, D.M., Weigl, M., Müller, A., & Glaser, J. (2014). Redesigning work through idiosyncratic deals. *European Journal of Work and Organizational Psychology*, *23*(4), 608–626. DOI:10.1080/1359432X.2012.740171

Kelliher, C. & Anderson, D. (2010). Doing more with less? Flexible working practices and the intensification of work. *Human Relations*, *63*(1), 83–106. DOI:10.1177/0018726709349199

Klein, K.J., Berman, L.M., & Dickson, M.W. (2000). May I work part-time? An exploration of predicted employer responses to employee request for part time work. *Journal of Vocational Behavior*, *57*(1), 85–101. DOI:10.1006/jvbe.1999.1729

Kong, D.T., Ho, V.T., & Garg, S. (2018). Employee and coworker idiosyncratic deals: Implications for emotional exhaustion and deviant behaviors. *Journal of Business Ethics*, 1–17. DOI:10.1007/s10551-018-4033–9

Kossek, E.E. & Ollier-Malaterre, A. (2019). Desperately seeking sustainable careers: Redesigning professional jobs for the collaborative crafting of reduced-load work. *Journal of Vocational Behavior*. DOI:10.1016/j.jvb.2019.06.003

Kossek, E.E., Ollier-Malaterre, A., Lee, M.D., Pichler, S., & Hall, D.T. (2016). Line managers' rationales for professionals' reduced-load work in embracing and ambivalent organizations. *Human Resource Management*, *55*(1), 143–171. DOI:10.1002/hrm.21722

Kossek, E.E., Pichler, S., Bodner, T., & Hammer, L. (2011). Workplace social support and work-family conflict: A meta-analysis clarifying the influence of general and work-family-specific supervisor and organizational support. *Personnel Psychology*, *64*(2), 289–313. DOI:10.1111/j.1744–6570.2011.01211.x

Kossek, E.E. & Thompson, R.J. (2016). Workplace flexibility: Integrating employer and employee perspectives to close the research–practice implementation gap. In T.D. Allen & L.T. Eby (eds), *The Oxford Handbook of Work and Family*. New York: Oxford University Press.

Las Heras, M., Van der Heijden, B.I.J.M., De Jong, J., & Rofcanin, Y. (2017). "Handle with care": The mediating role of schedule i-deals in the relationship between supervisors' own caregiving responsibilities and employee outcomes. *Human Resource Management Journal*, *27*(3), 335–349. DOI:10.1111/1748–8583.12160

Leslie, L.M., Manchester, C.F., Park, T.Y., & Mehng, S.A. (2012). Flexible work practices: A source of career premiums or penalties? *Academy of Management Journal*, *55*(6), 1407–1428. DOI:10.5465/amj.2010.0651

Liao, C., Wayne, S.J., & Rousseau, D.M. (2016). Idiosyncratic deals in contemporary organizations: A qualitative and meta-analytical review. *Journal of Organizational Behavior, 37*(1), 9–29. DOI:10.1002/job.1959

Liu, J., Lee, C., Hui, C., Kwan, H.K., & Wu, L.-Z. (2013). Idiosyncratic deals and employee outcomes: The mediating roles of social exchange and self-enhancement and the moderating role of individualism. *Journal of Applied Psychology, 98*(5), 832–840. DOI:10.1037/a0032571

Marescaux, E., De Winne, S., & Sels, L. (2019). Idiosyncratic deals from a distributive justice perspective: Examining co-workers' voice behaviour. *Journal of Business Ethics, 154*(1), 263. DOI:10.1007/s10551-016-3400-7

Organisation for Economic Co-operation and Development (OECD) (2019). Collective bargaining coverage. Retrieved from: www.stats.oecd.org

Perrigino, M.B., Dunford, B.B., & Wilson, K.S. (2018). Work–Family Backlash: The "Dark Side" of Work–Life Balance (WLB) Policies. *Academy of Management Annals, 12*(2), 600–630. DOI:10.5465/annals.2016.0077

Peters, P., den Dulk, L., & Ruijter, J.D. (2010). May I work from home? Views of the employment relationship reflected in line managers' telework attitudes in six financial-sector organizations. *Equality, Diversity and Inclusion, 29*(5), 517–531. DOI:10.1108/02610151011052799

Putnam, L.L., Myers, K.K., & Gailliard, B.M. (2014). Examining the tensions in workplace flexibility and exploring options for new directions. *Human Relations, 67*(4), 413–440. DOI:10.1177/0018726713495704

Richardson, J. (2010). Managing flexworkers: Holding on and letting go. *Journal of Management Development, 29*(2), 137–147. DOI:10.1108/02621711011019279

Rofcanin, Y., Kiefer, T., & Strauss, K. (2017a). What seals the i-deal? Exploring the role of employees' behaviours and managers' emotions. *Journal of Occupational & Organizational Psychology, 90*(2), 203–224. DOI:10.1111/joop.12168

Rofcanin, Y., Las Heras, M., & Bakker, A.B. (2017b). Family supportive supervisor behaviors and organizational culture: Effects on work engagement and performance. *Journal of Occupational Health Psychology, 22*(2), 207–217. DOI:10.1037/ocp0000036

Rosen, C.C., Slater, D.J., Chang, C., & Johnson, R.E. (2013). Let's make a deal: Development and validation of the ex post i-deals scale. *Journal of Management, 39*(3), 709–742. DOI:10.1177/0149206310394865

Rousseau, D.M., Ho, V.T., & Greenberg, J. (2006). I-deals: Idiosyncratic terms in employment relationships. *Academy of Management Review, 31*(4), 977–994. DOI:10.5465/AMR.2006.22527470

Rousseau, D.M., Tomprou, M., & Simosi, M. (2016). Negotiating flexible and fair idiosyncratic deals (i-deals). *Organizational Dynamics, 45*(3), 185–196. DOI:10.1016/j.orgdyn.2016.07.004

Singh, S. & Vidyarthi, P.R. (2018). Idiosyncratic deals to employee outcomes: Mediating role of social exchange relationships. *Journal of Leadership & Organizational Studies, 25*(4), 443–455. DOI:10.1177/1548051818762338

Straub, C. (2012). Antecedents and organizational consequences of family supportive supervisor behavior: A multilevel conceptual framework for research. *Human Resource Management Review, 22*(1), 15–26. DOI:10.1016/j.hrmr.2011.08.001

US Bureau of Labor Statistics (2018). Union membership rate. Retrieved from: www.bls.gov

US Office of Personnel Management (2010). Telework Enhancement Act 2010. Retrieved from: https://www.telework.gov/guidance-legislation/telework-legislation/telework-enhancement-act

Van Dyne, L., Kossek, E., & Lobel, S. (2007). Less need to be there: Cross-level effects of work practices that support work-life flexibility and enhance group processes and group-level OCB. *Human Relations*, *60*(8), 1123–1154. DOI:10.1177/0018726707081657

Vidyarthi, P. R., Liden, R. C., Anand, S., Erdogan, B., & Ghosh, S. (2010). Where do I stand? Examining the effects of leader–member exchange social comparison on employee work behaviors. *Journal of Applied Psychology*, *95*(5), 849–861. DOI:10.1037/a0020033

Vidyarthi, P.R., Singh, S., Erdogan, B., Chaudhry, A., Posthuma, R., & Anand, S. (2016). Individual deals within teams: Investigating the role of relative i-deals for employee performance. *Journal of Applied Psychology*, *101*(11), 1536–1552. DOI:10.1037/apl0000145

Walsh, B.M., Matthews, R.A., Toumbeva, T.H., Kabat-Farr, D., Philbrick, J., & Pavisic, I. (2019). Failing to be family-supportive: Implications for supervisors. *Journal of Management*, *45*(7), 2952–2977. DOI:10.1177/0149206318774621

Wessels, C., Schippers, M.C., Stegmann, S., Bakker, A.B., van Baalen, P.J., & Proper, K.I. (2019). Fostering flexibility in the new world of work: A model of time-spatial job crafting. *Frontiers in Psychology*, *10*, 505. DOI:10.3389/fpsyg.2019.00505

Williams, P., McDonald, P., & Cathcart, A. (2017). Executive-level support for flexible work arrangements in a large insurance organization. *Asia Pacific Journal of Human Resources*, *55*(3), 337–355. DOI:10.1111/1744–7941.12125

8 The balanced communications diet for business

Principles for working smarter, not harder in a connected world

Nicola J. Millard

The problem of *workus interruptus*

Did you know that during an average working day we are allegedly interrupted once every three minutes (Mark et al., 2008) ... oh, hang on my phone just beeped ... now, where was I?

With agile and flexible working we may not be tethered to our offices or desks anymore, but the devices we have on us constantly have blurred the boundaries between our work life and the rest of our life. We have the pressure of responding to a multitude of beeps and buzzes whether we are in the boardroom, on the beach or in the bathroom. Communication is essential for healthy life and good business decisions, but being overwhelmed by communication is not. Just like food is essential for survival, too much of it can be bad for us.

Don't get me wrong, these technologies have made our working lives better in many ways. For a start, they put us in control of where, when and how we work. They are the foundation for flexible, agile and home working. They have changed the ways that we communicate and collaborate forever. The challenge isn't connection anymore; it is disconnection.

It may be easier to abstain from technology use outside the workplace but, when we often carry our offices around with us in our back pockets, disconnection can be challenging. It is more difficult than ever to define when we are working, and when we are not. This "always on" way of life can cause "techno-stress" – i.e. "stress caused by an inability to cope with the demands of organisational technology usage" (Tarafdar et al., 2010). To help combat this, we developed a set of simple principles – a "balanced communications diet for business" – to help us to become healthier and more productive in work.

When are we most productive?

"Productivity" is often defined in manufacturing terms as "the ratio of what is produced to what is required to produce it" (Hill, 1993). This is a simple concept when applied to a factory production line but, particularly when applied to knowledge work, it becomes more problematic. The only tangible input is the number of hours worked. Output is less easy to define. If people equate a clear email inbox, or constant availability on instant messenger, with productivity then that is probably what employees do all day. Is this really "productive work"?

In an attempt to understand productivity, BT and Cambridge University conducted a set of employee interviews (Mieczakowski et al., 2011). There were a wide variety of answers to the question *"Where, when and why are you most productive at work?"*

- *"I find I get a full day of work done between 6:00 and 9:30 in the morning. For my sanity as well, knowing I can get at least two productive hours of work in before breakfast, makes a huge difference to my day."*
- *"In the evening, hands down. Less interruptions and my natural time clock is at its peak then."*
- *"For ideas – it's before 9.30 am. For acting on those ideas, 10 am to 3 pm."*
- *"I need peace and quiet – interruptions just jumble my brain up and I get nothing done."*
- *"On a plane – it's the only safe haven now from calls and emails. Sadly, even that's changing now!"*
- *"I do all my thinking in the car – I have an hour's commute – once I get to the office it's all go, go, go! Do I want to work from home? No, I'd lose all that thinking time!"*
- *"I can tell you where I'm NOT productive – being tugged in all different places sitting in a 'team' set-up office with no privacy or physical barriers between myself and others."*

The general theme that emerges from these answers – aside from *"everyone is different"* – is that people regard themselves as most productive when they are free of interruption. This is often outside the office and the traditional 9-to-5 day. The problem is frequently that we can't get through the work for talking about the work. However, if you rephrase this question and ask people what motivates them about work over and above the money that they earn, they say that they *"like the people that they work with"*. These people, one assumes, are also generally the source of many of these interruptions!

A significant amount of research supports the idea that having time to think and reflect each day does a great deal for well-being, and constant interruptions can counter this (Mieczakowski et al., 2011; Tams et al., 2018; Galluch et al., 2015). This is the time that we seem to value, if the answers to these questions are to be believed. People who are always "plugged-in" often don't get this vital mental downtime. We all seem to recognise that we need peace and quiet sometimes to just think. But finding the time to do this can be easier said than done. We always seem to put a higher value on action rather than inaction. The value of reflection is underrated because business is so concerned with action and activity – things that are easy to measure – rather than thinking about action, which looks too much like staring into space.

This "cult of busyness" also means that we tend to get tugged in all directions during our working day. We can feel out of control. People are most likely to become enthusiastic about what they are doing when they are free to make decisions about the way that they do it. Classic psychology (Karasek & Theorell, 1990) tells us that high levels of demand and low levels of perceived control results in stress, burnout and emotional exhaustion.

Control is easier on some communication devices than others. It's easy to find the off switch on a laptop; but less so on a smart phone. Because we often can't be seen at our desks, or in the office anymore, there can be a pressure to be always on. Control can take other forms, though. Minimising distractions and interruptions could be one way of both taking control and becoming more productive.

Brain juggling

There is one thing that acts strongly against us simply choosing to switch off. Technology plays to the natural distractibility of human nature and our compulsion to embrace uncertainty and novelty (Fitz et al., 2019). Every time the new mail notification flashes up on screen, the red dot appears against an app, or our phone vibrates, we feel the need to take a look, regardless of what else we are doing. The vast majority of these alerts lead us to irrelevant, routine or junk stuff. However, there is the occasional "reward" – an important document or good news – that motivates us to keep checking for incoming messages even when we should really be paying attention to other things (like walking in a straight line or being at a meeting). In addition, the accomplishment we feel when we reach the end of our email inbox or send that witty tweet tends to be easier to achieve than doing all those other, more complex tasks on our "to do" list.

One problem with this is that the frequency of distraction is inversely correlated with productivity (Duke and Monta, 2017; Fitz et al., 2019). As we compulsively check incoming messages, the less productive we become. A number of studies have also cited a close relationship between stress and the amount of times we check our devices (e.g. Lee et al., 2014; Brod, 1984; Thomee et al., 2011). Turning alerts off is an obvious solution, but there is evidence that this can make people more anxious, as FOMO (Fear Of Missing Out) kicks in (Fitz et al., 2019). The most stressed individuals can even imagine "phantom" alerts and compulsively check their devices even when there is nothing coming in (Kruger & Djerf, 2017).

One of the big reasons that technology is more distracting now than it used to be is that the alerts from devices are increasingly social in nature. Devices alert us to messages, voicemails and even the locations of our friends and colleagues, whereas previously they might only send out alerts when they were out of batteries. These social alerts are hard to tune out. You can ignore the ping of a washing machine when it has finished a spin cycle, but you can't ignore your boss. This tends to result in us attempting to multitask.

Multitasking (attempting to perform two or more tasks simultaneously), or task switching (when you are interrupted mid-task) are effectively the mental equivalent of juggling. If you have ever closed your laptop down at the end of the day and found a multitude of half-finished email replies, chat sessions and half-completed documents, you have probably been doing one or the other. Academics have long known that task-switching has a detrimental effect on productivity, even for simple tasks (e.g. Rogers & Monsell, 1995). The results are even worse for complex tasks (e.g. Rubinstein et al., 2001). Although switch costs may be small, sometimes just a few tenths of a second per switch, they can add up to large amounts of time wasted when people switch repeatedly back and forth between tasks. Task switching can also impede memory and knowledge retention, particularly for interruptions mid-task. Interruptions reduce our ability to pay attention (Ophir et al., 2009), complete tasks, reduce task accuracy (Montag & Walla, 2016), and increases the time we take to complete tasks (Cellier & Eyrolle, 1992).

This means that multitasking may look productive, but it may actually take more time and involve more errors. Research from Stanford University (Ophir et al., 2009) has shown that people who regard themselves as good at multitasking are generally worse at judging the quality of information that they are reading and worse at recalling what they have done. This means that they are often less productive than people who are single taskers.

Multitasking can also be exhausting (Mark et al., 2008; Monicque et al., 2009). Paying attention to one thing whilst doing another means that we need to do more work to maintain any level of attention on either task. Sitting in a meeting doing email on your phone generally means either the meeting or the email gets short shrift. The lesson here? The average person is generally unaware of the cognitive effect that technology is having on their life.

Ultimately, much of this boils down to stress because of the sheer number of things that are simultaneously competing for our attention – "information overload" (Tarafdar et al., 2010). Being able to prioritise in overload situations is extremely difficult and can result in us going up a number of productivity cul-de-sacs. Having the self-control to close everything down and concentrate on a single task until it is finished is probably the biggest challenge but the key to better productivity.

How do we prefer to communicate at work?

Ultimately, old fashioned face-to-face communication still emerges as essential for building trust, and delivering important or emotionally sensitive messages (Pentland, 2015). But getting people in the same room together can be almost impossible, especially in highly virtualised and globalised businesses. Inevitably, much of business today is conducted over digital communication channels.

Text-based communications – especially chat – tends to be a favourite for pure information exchange (Hickman & Davies, 2018). It is an easy way to get messages to a lot of people with minimal effort. But it's difficult to convey much in terms of nuance and emotion in text, unless you pepper it with emoticons.

Text-based communications can also create excessive demands on the receivers of them. This is sometimes called "techno-overload" (Tarafdar et al., 2010). As technology makes us more productive and more efficient, things that used to take days now take minutes. This can create a sudden influx of demand on us, can lead managers to communicate more than is necessary (Davis, 2002) and get more information than they can process and use effectively (Fisher & Wesolkowski, 1999). We also tend to become increasingly unable to identify information that is actually useful, rather than spam.

This often results in us getting both tired and stressed, as well as working longer hours. The productivity benefits of agile and flexible working can potentially be displaced by the resulting pressure to keep on top of things. This "techno-invasion" (Tarafdar et al., 2010) can result in people feeling as if they are tethered permanently to work. They may leave the office, but they can't leave the office behind.

Being "always on" can significantly impinge on family time. The "speed trap" of quick reflex responses has brought pressure to respond immediately. This belief tends to create a false sense of urgency, puts pressure on us to respond fast (with no time to think carefully about our responses) and means that we can spend more time reading and responding to it than actually getting any other work done.

This sense of urgency can have a negative impact on the quality of decision-making (Perlow et al., 2002). Speed and quality are two key variables when people make important decisions, and they often come into conflict. Fast decisions are not always ideal, but more decisions are, of necessity, being made quickly. Faster communication provides more information for decision-makers to use, but their decisions might lack detail or adequate consideration. Combine that with the inevitable shortening of attention spans and we get a shallow, 180-character elevator pitch style of communication. Worse still, key people may not respond in time and decisions are then made without their potentially critical input.

The cost to users is also a factor which needs to be considered. In order to communicate with others in the past there was a cost incurred by both the sender and receiver of information. This was in terms of effort and often financially as well. Today, people can send huge amounts of material to others quickly and with almost zero additional cost. It is easier than ever before to burden other people with a deluge of information that might be important but that they never see because of inbox overload.

The great thing – and the problem – with email is that it covers a kind of middle ground between other more instant forms of communication (chat, social media, telephone, meetings) and more traditional written communications like post (Newport, 2019). For one thing, you can communicate with a lot of people at a single click of the "send" key without the need for them to be there, or the niceties and small talk that frequently occur with more synchronous forms of communication, like the phone. The fact that it leaves an audit trail is also flagged as an advantage (Mieczakowski et al., 2011).

The demise of email has been long forecast, but old channels often stick around. It is gradually being eclipsed by chat, though. Chat is very much where it's at in the consumer space – with the proliferation of messaging apps such as WhatsApp, WeChat and Facebook Messenger. Inevitably, many of these tools are being brought into the workplace (Hickman & Davies, 2018). Chat can have some advantages. It is short, easy and quick but, as a tool of mass distraction, it still has many of the same disadvantages as email.

Social media has also been mooted as the ultimate collaboration tool within enterprises. Its significant strength is that you don't actually have to know who to contact in order to message them and it can cross organisational silos (and defy spam filters). Finding the right person to talk to without cc'ing the whole company is sometimes very difficult in the email universe.

However, social media also has similar weaknesses in terms of information overload and as a task interrupter, with some people reporting "stream stress" as they attempt to keep up on Twitter, Facebook, Yammer, LinkedIn, Instagram and the multitude of other social tools. The danger is that we may just end up with a raft of emails being replaced with a stream of messages from multiple different sources.

Introducing the balanced communications diet for business

The way that we work has been changed fundamentally by the technologies that we use. Ways of communication with others have changed. Knowledge access has increased, but being awash with too much data has threatened our ability both to process everything and also to acquire new knowledge. There are clear positives and negatives here.

This is where well-being at work comes in. Well-being is defined by the Cambridge Dictionary as "the state of feeling healthy and happy". It is more than just personal happiness and takes into account factors such as sense of purpose and direction. Those who report "techno-stress" at work frequently feel overwhelmed or constantly distracted by communications technology and are more likely to report lower perceptions of well-being (Tarafdar et al., 2010).

Throwing away technology is neither desirable, nor practical, but changing our use of it could result in better productivity and more time to ourselves. To improve well-being, we need to look at how we are using technology and whether or not we can improve our perception of control over its use.

The main problem highlighted by the BT/Cambridge research was that ubiquitous connectivity made it easy to check on things at work at any time of the day (Mieczakowski et al., 2011). Moreover, a "quick phone check" could easily turn into several hours of use.

What can we do to achieve a better communications diet for business? There are five things to consider:

- Location
- Rules
- Awareness
- Education
- Balance.

Location

Location is becoming a very key aspect to ensuring that business communication is effective. Just because we *can* work anywhere doesn't mean we *should*.

Work can literally be defined by space. With the rise of flexible working, that space may not be within the four walls of an office anymore. If you live and work in the same place, establishing boundaries between the "office" and the "home" can be important. Some flexible workers can go to extreme strategies to separate the two. Anecdotally, I know people who have established their office in a shed in their back garden, dress in a suit during working hours, or work from co-working spaces or coffee shops. Closing the office door at the end of the day and leaving the phone and laptop behind is a powerful way of exerting control. The same rule applies when you are on holiday.

Location can also be determined by the device. Doing a considered reply to a complex topic is probably better done on a better and bigger screen than on a smartphone – so may not be appropriate whilst you are on the move. It is often easier to send a one-sentence message on a smart phone because you are attempting to type using a tiny keypad whilst squinting at a small screen. Many of these curt replies can cause significant misunderstandings and result in yet more messages to distract you.

Another way of exerting a degree of control over location is to move from a default of always on, to choosing when you are on. Turn your phone off when in meetings so that there is no temptation to be distracted by your device silently flashing at you at inappropriate moments. Turn alerts off rather than having them continuously beckoning you to look at them. That way you have to consciously log on to access it rather than simply flick from one app to another. Disconnect when you are doing tasks that require concentration so that you are forced to concentrate on a single task rather than succumb to the temptation to surf.

Research from the universities of Würzburg, Germany, and Nottingham Trent, UK, has gone so far as to suggest that removing the smartphone from the room you are in entirely could significantly improve productivity (Carolus et al., 2018).

Rules

Establish rules for yourself. Set times when you are "on" and when you are "off". Some people are choosing to go back to an old-fashioned feature phone with no internet connectivity, so that they can't access online content. Others have taken to carrying two devices around; one for work and one for personal activities. Aside from the inconvenience of an extra slab of technology to lug about, this can strictly partition the working day from family time.

Ironically one thing that is coming along to help us manage our technology is more technology. Having a virtual desktop in the cloud for work can ensure that you are logged in to that space by choice rather than by default. There are also intelligent personal assistants which can automatically tag and prioritise incoming messages as urgent, non-urgent, spam, or personal.

Using presence information to define times when you are available for interruption can provide people with a guide as to when and how is the best time to contact you. Appearing offline on instant messenger is not a crime and "busy" really does mean that you don't want to be interrupted. Similarly, setting time limits for doing email can also prove beneficial. Some people schedule email free days once a week.

Some corporates and countries have gone one step further and imposed rules to help employees to turn off. European countries such as France have established a "right to turn off" policy as part of their flexible working initiatives. Some companies will only allow employees access to their email accounts half an hour before and half an hour after a shift. Others automatically delete email when people are on leave. These top-down strategies may not work for all organisations, however, particularly those who operate flexible working hours, or work across global boundaries and time zones.

Awareness

Understand how you are using technology when you are working. Awareness of use is the key to achieving balance and well-being when using communications technology, largely because most people appear to be unaware just how much they use it and how habitual their use is. Try recording the ways in which you are using technology at work for a few days. Some apps will automatically record screen time for you to save you having to think about it. You can then try to aim for a more ideal level, whatever you define that level to be.

Education

This is really around establishing guidelines and cultural norms around acceptable use of communication channels. Establishing conventions such as "no email after 5.30 pm", asking "is this the right channel for this message" and allowing individuals to broadcast their communication preferences are all part of the process of educating the workforce.

Many organisations are establishing organisational communication etiquette and even providing training courses on the appropriate use of communication and clear language within their business. Even simple things like establishing rules on when, or when not, to use "reply to all" in email messages or how to construct meaningful subject lines can make a huge difference. Behaviours often come from the top, so it is critical for leaders to display appropriate communication behaviours themselves (Schwartz & Porath, 2014). They shouldn't bombard their people with email at all times of the day and night, micro-manage their employees on instant messenger, or schedule meetings at anti-social hours (particularly challenging when global virtual teams are involved as it's always five o'clock somewhere).

Balance

As with everything else, moderation is key. Moderation of communications technology, whether it is by location, rules or something else, is ultimately a way to achieve a certain sense of balance. Self-control plays a critical part in this. If we want to become more productive and lessen the potential negative impact of technology, we need to make a conscious effort to control how we use it. The larger problem is that we really are not aware of when we are in control of technology and when technology is in control of us.

There is no perfect way to exert self-control. We are better at controlling ourselves in certain situations than others. People who are more easily distracted by technology must, first, become aware of it before they can start to control their behaviour.

However, behavioural economists will tell you that self-control may be less straightforward than we may think (Ariely & Wertenbroch, 2002). What looks like exquisite self-control can actually just be an instance of rule-following. For example, if someone is told that they must check their email only twice a day and then does so, they are not exhibiting traditional self-control, but are simply following a rule. Self-control has to do with being aware of the potential long-term consequences of an action and acting accordingly, even when the short-term consequences would be pleasurable. Rule-following only requires us to do what we are told. While self-control will likely play a big role in how much modern technology affects any one individual, it is important to keep in mind how self-control is characterised and how it differs between individuals.

Many of the concerns about what communications technology is doing to us are about the degree to which it stops us talking to each other in a traditional way. Emailing or messaging the person sitting opposite us makes no sense and yet we often do exactly that. This could be due to lack of privacy in the office space we are in (Bernstein & Turban, 2018), or simply that we can establish an audit trail of the conversation.

Establishing a balance around communications use at work is vital. Anyone who has sat through a conference doing their emails only to suddenly realise they have no concept of what has actually happened in the real world needs to ask themselves why they were at that event. This is sometimes called "continuous partial attention" (Hemp, 2009). Establishing boundaries for acceptable use of communications technologies is important. In meetings, both face-to-face and virtual, switching everything off should be acceptable behaviour.

However, the point that balance is achieved is probably unique to each and every one of us. Some people feel lost without their smartphones, while others relish time out. Regardless of your preference, there is evidence that having at least some technology down time is beneficial to well-being (Tarafdar et al., 2010; Thomée et al., 2011; Fitz et al., 2019). Taking a tech break can also reduce feelings of dependence on technology (Carolus et al., 2018).

Recommendations

As employees further blur the lines between work and play by working flexible hours, home working, or bringing their own devices, apps and tools to work, there is a risk that switching off from the digital business world entirely will become more and more difficult. The productivity penalties of being "always on" are still being uncovered. Indeed, one recommendation for future research is to reinvent and redefine productivity in the context of the digital workplace. Measuring the number of hours worked, or sick days logged is easy to do, but not necessarily relevant for a rigorous investigation of productivity in an era where people work more flexibly and virtually. Establishing measures, or proxies, for productivity and connecting them to areas such as well-being are vital, but extremely difficult (especially for knowledge workers).

The impact of multitasking is another area of concern which deserves more research attention since it can be a significant time devourer in an increasingly distracting world. Mistaking activity for productivity – whatever that means in a digital world – may mean that we have little time to "unplug" and unwind.

Leadership inevitably plays a huge part in this. Leaders need to role model a balanced workstyle in order for their employees to do the same.

All of this becomes more important as we consider the future world of work. Artificial Intelligence (AI) may help us become more productive but it may also cause more intensification of our work (Waytz, 2019). It is likely to leave human workers with an increasingly messy, complex, emotive and even less quantifiable workload. This means that there is likely to be more focus in the future on employee well-being, burn out prevention and the importance of down time.

Ultimately, it is up to us to establish a balance that suits us as individuals. This means that consideration of principles such as the "balanced communications diet" – i.e. location, rules, awareness, education and balance – will become increasingly important to help individuals to work smarter, not harder.

Acknowledgements

The author would like to thank Mary Lumkin, Jeff Patmore, Anna Mieczakowski, Tanya Goldhaber and John Clarkson for their work on the original "Balanced Communications Diet" research, which inspired "The Balanced Communications Diet for Business" paper.

References

Ariely, D. & Wertenbroch, K. (2002), Procrastination, deadlines and performance: Self-control by precommitment, psychological science, *American Psychological Society*, *13*(3), May, 219–244.

Bernstein, E.S. & Turban, S. (2018), The impact of the "open" workspace on human collaboration, *Philosophical Transactions of the Royal Society B Biological Sciences*, *373*, http://doi.org/10.1098/rstb.2017.0239

Brod, C. (1984), *Technostress: The human cost of the computer revolution*, Reading, MA: Addison-Wesley.

Carolus, A., Binder, J.F., Muench, R., Schmidt, C., Schneider, F. & Buglass, S. (2018), Smartphones as digital companions: Characterizing the relationship between users and their phones, *New Media and Society*, *21*(4), 914–938.

Cellier, J. & Eyrolle, H. (1992), Interference between switched tasks. *Ergonomics*, *35*(1), 25–36.

Davis, G. (2002), Anytime/anyplace computing and the future of knowledge work, *Communications of the ACM*, *45*(2), 67–73.

Duke, É. & Monta, C. (2017), Smartphone addiction, daily interruptions and self-reported productivity, *Addictive Behaviours Reports*, *6*(December), 90–95.

Fisher, W. & Wesolkowski, S. (1999), Tempering technostress, *IEEE Technology and Society Magazine*, *18*(1), 28–33.

Fitz, N., Kushlev, K., Jagannathan, R., Lewis, T., Paliwal, D. & Ariely, D. (2019), Batching smartphone notifications can improve well-being, *Computers in Human Behaviour*, *101*(December), 84–94.

Galluch, P.S., Grover, V. & Thatcher, J.B. (2015), Interrupting the workplace: Examining stressors in an information technology context, *Journal of the Association for Information Systems*, *16*(1), 1–47.

Hemp, P. (2009), Death by information overload, *Harvard Business Review*, *87*(September), 49–53.

Hickman, M. & Davies, J. (2018), *People, productivity and the digital workplace: How mobile and collaboration services can boost productivity*, Digital Employee Research 2018, BT White Paper, https://www.globalservices.bt.com/en/insights/whitepapers/people-productivity-in-digital-workplace

Hill, T. (1993), *Manufacturing Strategy: The Strategic Management of the Manufacturing Function* (2nd ed.), London: Open University/Macmillan.

Karasek, R.A. & Theorell, T.G. (1990), *Healthy Work: Stress, Productivity and the Reconstruction of Working Life*, New York: Basic Books.

Kruger, J.M. & Djerf, J.M. (2017), Bad vibrations? Cell phone dependency predicts phantom communication experiences, *Computers in Human Behaviour*, *70*(May), 360–364.

Lee, Y., Chang, C., Lin, Y. & Cheng, Z. (2014), The dark side of smartphone usage: Psychological traits, compulsive behaviors and techno-stress, *Computers in Human Behaviour*, *31*(February), 373–383.

Mark, G., Gudith, D. & Klocke, U. (2008), The cost of interrupted work: More speed and stress, *Proceedings of CHI 08, Proceedings of the SIGCHI Conference on Human Factors in Computing Systems*, New York: ACM, pp. 107–110.

Mieczakowski, A., Goldhaber, T. & Clarkson, J. (2011), *Culture, Communication and Change: Report on an Investigation of the Use and Impact of Modern Media and Technology in Our Lives*, Cambridge, UK: Engineering Design Centre, University of Cambridge/BT, https://www-edc.eng.cam.ac.uk/downloads/culturebook.pdf

Monicque, M., Lorista, B., Bezdana, E., ten Caat, M., Spana, M.M., Roerdink, J.B.T.M. & Maurits, N.M. (2009), The influence of mental fatigue and motivation on neural network dynamics; an EEG coherence study, *Brain Research*, *1270*(May), 95–106.

Montag, C. & Walla, P. (2016), Carpe diem instead of losing your social mind: Beyond digital addiction and why we all suffer from digital overuse, *Cogent Psychology*, *3*(1).

Newport, C. (2019), Was e-mail a mistake? The mathematics of distributed systems suggests that meetings might be better, *The New Yorker*, August 6.

Ophir, E., Nass, C. & Wagner, A.D. (2009), Cognitive control in media multitaskers, *PNAS*, *106*(37), 15 September, 15583–15587, www.pnas.org_cgi_doi_10.1073_pnas.0903620106

Pentland, A. (2015), *Social Physics: How Social Networks Can Make Us Smarter*, New York: Penguin Random House.

Perlow, L., Okhuyson, G. & Repenning, N. (2002), The speed trap: Exploring the relationship between decision making and the temporal context, *Academy of Management Journal*, *45*(5), October, 931–955.

Rogers, R.D. & Monsell, S. (1995), Costs of a predictable switch between simple cognitive tasks, *Journal of Experimental Psychology*, *124*(2), 207.

Rubinstein, J., Evans, J. & Meyer, D. (2001), Executive control of cognitive processes in task switching, *Journal of Experimental Psychology Human Perception & Performance*, *27*(4), September, 763–797.

Schwartz, T. & Porath, C. (2014), Your boss's work-life balance matters as much as your own, *Harvard Business Review*, July 10.

Tams, S., Grover, V. & Thatcher, J.B. (2018), Concentration, competence, confidence, and capture: An experimental study of age, interruption-based technostress, and task performance, *Journal of the Association for Information Systems*, *19*(9), 857–890.

Tarafdar, M., Tu, Q. & Ragu-Nathan, T.S. (2010), Impact of technostress on end-user satisfaction and performance, *Journal of Management Information Systems*, *27*(3), Winter, 303–334.

Thomée, S., Härenstam, A. & Hagberg, M. (2011), Mobile phone use and stress, sleep disturbances, and symptoms of depression among young adults – a prospective cohort study, *BMC Public Health*, *11*, article 66, https://bmcpublichealth.biomedcentral.com/articles/10.1186/1471-2458-11-66

Waytz, A. (2019), Leisure is our killer app, *MIT Sloan Management Review*, Summer, https://sloanreview.mit.edu/article/leisure-is-our-killer-app

9   The impact of the commute on our mental health and physical health within the context of flexible and non-flexible working

Anna Mary Cooper-Ryan, Charlotte Stonier and Abolanle Gbadamosi

Introduction

With continuing advancements in technology, the workplace is evolving, with many employers and employees looking at how they can work smarter and more flexibly. In conjunction with this, we are seeing changes occurring in workplaces that include: changes in office space usage (for example, hot-desking and break-out rooms); and a move away from large head office buildings, often with expensive running costs due to their size and location, and a move towards incorporating elements of more remote working (where practical) (Citrix Systems, 2009). Many of these changes have been influenced by the rise in technologies that enable people to work remotely (e.g. high speed internet, online platforms for meetings and collaborations) (The Work Foundation, 2016), and can increase our ability to have global employee communications without the physical relocation of offices (examples of this type of working can be found in the report "Working beyond walls: The government workplace as an agent of change", DEGW, 2008). But do these continuing changes in the workplace and technological advancements disrupt or assist our work-life balance, do they impact our commute in a positive way or negative way and, as a result, is there an impact on our health?

Building on this, this chapter will briefly consider how our commute impacts on our mental health and our physical health. We will consider this in relation to those who commute regularly and those who have more flexible working patterns where a commute is less regular. In this chapter, we take the premise that flexible working is a way for employees to have greater flexibility over where, when and how long they work and for employers to be more flexible about how they use office space and support the work-life balance of employees.

Looking at rates of flexible working in 2010 within the European Union, employees in Finland were most likely to have some flexibility in working time arrangements, with those from Hungary being the least likely to have flexibility (Chartered Institute of Personnel and Development (CIPD),

2019). In addition to leading the way with rates of flexible working, Finland is also providing examples of critical legislation such as the new Working Hours Act 2020 that is designed to improve the ability for employers and employees to work together to find a flexible working pattern, which suits both needs – notably, to enable working hours not to be tied to a specific place of work (and is expected to smooth the navigation of agreements around work done from home) (Ministry of Economic Affairs and Employment of Finland, 2019). A further European survey exploring those who take advantage of home or mobile teleworking in 2015 found that more employees in Denmark than anywhere else in Europe reported working this way (37% of employees) (employees from Denmark also reported in 2014 having the most satisfaction with work-life balance across Europe), with the lowest reported uptake being found in Italy (7%) (CIPD, 2019). Interestingly, a United Kingdom survey in 2016 around flexible working (which asked for the five biggest benefits of flexible working to the person), found the top three reasons to be reducing stress/pressure (29%), better work-life balance (54%), and an influencing factor for staying with employer (28%); with 23% of those who responded feeling that flexible working helped them reduce commuting time (CIPD, 2016).

Taking the reducing commuting reason from above, it could be said that flexible working and changes to how and where people work, by its very nature, will have an effect on the daily commute: this could be the mode of commute, whether there is a need for a commute, a change in commuting time or the number of days where a commute is needed, or the distance travelled during the commute. Considering changes to commute time as an example, current data show that there has been no significant change over the last decade within major UK cities in relation to commute time, with the average only differing by a few minutes between 2007 and 2016 (for example, Birmingham 27 vs. 29 minutes, Manchester 30 vs. 29 minutes, Edinburgh 27 vs. 31 minutes) (Office for National Statistics (ONS), 2018). In a similar vein, in the United States, average commute times have not changed significantly (25.2 minutes in 2007 to 26.6 minutes in 2016) (Florida Department of Transportation (FDOT), 2018). Changes in commuting time, mode and distance are likely to have a knock-on effect on both our mental health and levels of physical activity/sedentary behaviour; for example, although active commuting (defined as walking, cycling and the use of public transport, which almost invariably involves elements of walking and cycling (Flint et al., 2014)), has been found to increase physical activity and mental health. Research has shown that long-distance commutes negatively impacts our mental health and health-related outcomes. Longer commutes may be impractical for walking or cycling and therefore can increase time spent sedentary, which can lead to negative health consequences, and potential exposure to overcrowding on public transport that can also impact on mental health (Rafferty et al., 2016; King & Jacobson, 2017; Norgate et al., 2019).

Work in the context of commuting

In this section we will briefly consider the workplace, flexible working and how this can impact and change our commute. For instance, despite there being a growing awareness by key stakeholders and employees around flexible working, and the impact of commuting on our health and well-being at present, for many of us our day still contains an element of commuting (Eurostat, 2016), with this aspect of our day having a propensity to have a knock-on effect on other parts of the day (Guell et al., 2012). It is also predicted by Williams and Jach (2017) that for the next five years there will still be a reliance on commuting to a specific location for work (with the majority of workers travelling by car), but that in ten years we are likely to see changes around how we commute (mode shift in line with a growing desire to consider the environment and our health/well-being) and work (growing uptake of flexible working and changes in workplace real estate).

Currently there are a number of factors that interplay in relation to our commute and our work. The time of day people work is known to have an impact on the length and ease of commute (e.g. within or outside rush hour), with the period when we commute being impacted by our working model (i.e. nine to five, shift work, part time, flexible working etc.). However, control of our own working hours still sees an uneven distribution of flexible working across the employment landscape – between private and public sectors, large and small organisations, and men and women. For example, employees in smaller organisations are more likely to work part time; however, employees in large organisations are more likely to have a variety of flexible working contracts available (CIPD, 2019). A second factor that impacts our working patterns, and as such our commute, is gender, with women more likely to use flexible working arrangements (e.g. to balance work and childcare). For example Roberts and Taylor (2017) and Jacob et al. (2019) found that commute times in England and Wales were closely linked to local labour market conditions (e.g. local unemployment rates, "female friendliness" of local employment sector), and that the impact on the commute length is not gender neutral (with local unemployment rates having differing effects on men's and women's commutes, and the "female friendliness" only affecting women's commutes not men's). This study further reported that although there is a growing female workforce, on the whole, women commute less than men, both in relation to time and distance (Roberts & Taylor, 2017). A recent ONS analysis (2019) found that men, in return for higher pay, are more likely to tolerate longer commutes (over an hour), and women consider the commute more (e.g. length) when deciding about whether to leave a job and favour shorter (15 minutes or less) flexible commutes. The ONS found that the gender commute gap and the gender pay gap follow the same age-pattern, with a potential explanation being when people on average have children.

Despite variability in working hours by gender and country, additional time spent commuting can become burdensome and impact on the ability to undertake activities outside of work (e.g. socialising and physical activity). In conjunction with this, for some workers who use public transport, our commute has become a balancing act between work time (e.g. catching-up on emails) or undertaking personal activities (e.g. reading). Linked to this is the often unclear question around how commuting counts in a working day, and the hours of a standard working week (taken as 48 hours over 7 days in Europe); for example, Gripsrud and Hjorthol's (2012) time-use study in Norway in 2008 found that over a third of train users worked on board, with 25% of those commuting having their travel time approved as working hours. Inclusion or exclusion of the commute as working hours will often vary within different countries, different sectors and different companies, making calculating true working hours challenging for some. Within the European Union, in relation to the EU Working Time Directive (2003/88/EC), the Court of Justice of the European Union ruled that some forms of commuting time should be classed as working time (Eurofound, 2015); however, this legislation only applies to those without a fixed place to commute to each day.

In view of time as a factor, several studies exploring the implications of commuting suggest that employees are typically better able to meet the multiple demands of work and personal life when time constraints, commonly associated with "traditional" employment practices are alleviated (Halpern, 2005; Taylor et al., 2017). A study that examined "flexible" choices (such as part-time work or compressed hours) found that this usually translated to fewer commuting hours; however, the same study found that flexible working had no significant impact on commuting satisfaction (Russell et al., 2009). This could imply that whilst flexible working may limit commuting hours, the common negative perceptions associated with commuting experiences are perhaps not negated.

Interestingly, home-based employees have been found to be happier to experience slightly longer work commute times if they are able to have at least one day a week working from home (de Vos et al., 2018). Whilst the benefits of flexible working arrangements are observable, some employees can in fact experience greater work "intensity" and consequently more stress when employed on fewer hours (such as part-time hours) and can feel obliged to work harder because of less time commitment (Kelliher & Anderson, 2010). It has also been found that constraints to flexible working include communication problems, misinformation, lack of team coordination, and lack of social support from co-workers (Clarke & Holdsworth, 2017; The Work Foundation, 2016).

Our commute length is a direct result of where we live, and for many of us we often do not choose the location we want to live solely, or even at all, in relation to how it will impact our commute. Factors such as local social opportunities, schools, amenities, costs and the area can often be considerations (Roberts & Taylor, 2017). The Population Reference Bureau (2000) suggests that the commute and location can often be trade-offs that need to be made to achieve a required work-life balance. In line with this, Williams and Jach (2017) predict our commutes will move from passive to active modes due to pressures (e.g. overcrowding) and changes in transport systems. This need can be seen with UK rail journeys being the most time-consuming commuting method compared to driving, bus and cycling, reaching in excess of two hours for an average two-way journey in 2017 (Trades Union Congress (TUC), 2018). Lengthy travel times are not limited to the UK: it has been reported that public transport users in Melbourne, Australia, spend on average 80 minutes travelling to and from work and 28% of commuters travel for over 2 hours per day on a train, bus or tram (Moovit Insights, n.d.).

The impact of commuting on mental health

As previous research suggests, commuting can occupy a substantial amount of time in an employee's day and, for some, the journey to and from work is rarely straightforward; adverse conditions such as congested roads, over-crowded train carriages and/or busy foot traffic in and around public transport hubs are often antecedents of employee stress (Legrain et al., 2015; Novaco & Gonzalez, 2009), negative workplace behaviour (Hennessy, 2008), and occupational burn-out (Amponsah-Tawiah et al., 2016). Furthermore, research indicates that challenging travel conditions can also significantly impact the mental health and well-being of commuters (Chatterjee et al., 2019; Paton, 2017; Royal Society for Public Health (RSPH), 2016; Urhonen et al., 2016; Wang et al., 2019). Interestingly "years spent commuting" can also affect commuter health. Urhonen et al. (2016) found that whilst physical complaints increased with years spent commuting (10+ years), mental health complaints such as stress diminished as the years increased, potentially through travel adaptation and learning to use the time more efficiently (Sposato et al., 2012). As such, this section will consider the impact of the commute on our mental health and the impact of flexible vs. non-flexible working.

Within this section we take the definition that mental health relates to a person's "state of mind" and a level of psychological well-being that forms an essential part of an individual's overall health (World Health Organization (WHO), 2018). Stable emotional and psychological health is typically partnered with positive social functioning and the ability to appropriately operate in personal and professional circumstances; and usually in the absence of mental disorders, such as depression and anxiety (Barry, 2009; National Institute for Health and Care Excellence (NICE), 2019). Mental health disorders, which affect approximately 450 million people worldwide, can also have a significant impact on workplace performance, causing a decrease in job satisfaction and workplace productivity, and an increase in levels of absenteeism (Friman et al., 2017; Szeto & Dobson, 2010; Taylor et al., 2017; WHO, 2001; Wright & Cropanzano, 2000). In relation to flexible working, Milner et al. (2015), suggest that reduced working hours can help to support better employee mental health and also typically equates to decreased commuting time (Organisation for Economic Co-operation and Development (OECD), 2016).

Looking more closely at how flexible working may support mental health, Barck-Holst et al. (2017) propose that stress, negative emotions, exhaustion levels and memory difficulties are less prevalent when "time demands" of work are reduced. Additionally, research by Schiller et al. (2017) found that a 25% reduction to working time improves sleep quality and reduces the experience of stress. Flexible working options also provide employees with a greater degree of autonomy when selecting work patterns to suit their personal and family life (International Workplace Group (IWG), 2019; Feng & Boyle, 2014; Rüger et al., 2017; Stutzer & Frey, 2008).

Considering our working-day, long commutes by definition occupy long periods of time and, as a consequence, often lead to personal "time losses" (Besser et al., 2008; Cassidy, 1992). These can disrupt our work-life balance, commonly leading to family tensions and decreased levels of satisfaction with personal/family activities (Christian, 2012a; Jang & Zippay, 2011). This may also feel especially burdensome for commuters who do not perceive the commute as "quality" (e.g. due to mode choice and related issues) (Handy & Thigpen, 2019; Lorenz, 2018). In a study involving 5,216 survey participants from the 16 wave version (1991–2006) of the British Household Panel Survey (BHPS), researchers identified that journey times of over one hour were likely to cause commuter distress, in particular for women with children, who showed higher risk of poor mental health in all of the commuting times analysed (0–29 minutes, 30–59 minutes and 60+ minutes) compared to their peers with no children (Feng & Boyle, 2014). These findings suggest that women who have other time-pressured commitments (e.g. child care) may be more sensitive to adverse travel events (such as traffic congestion and travel unpredictability) during the commute (Evans et al., 2002). In addition to these findings it is important to recognise that gender disparity in employment is slowly declining, evidenced by a developing female workforce and shared work-life responsibilities between men and women, where men are also taking the lead at home with domestic duties (Lyness & Judiesch, 2014). Haar et al. (2014) further highlight that a positive "work-life balance" and job satisfaction is more likely for those in a high gender-egalitarian culture compared to areas with traditional gender "norms".

Whilst flexible working hours commonly reduce commuting time and therefore help both male and female employees to achieve a better work-life balance, this method of working is not without risk. Working patterns (such as compressed hours) are often presented as a compact working week, therefore requiring longer hourly attendance in a shorter space of time with the potential for more stress, exhaustion and psychological strain (Golden, 2012). Additionally, the decreased commuting hours commonly associated with flexible working may in fact deprive employees of certain travel benefits (i.e. opportunity to unwind, work day preparation or reading). Linked to this, Jachimowicz et al. (2018) claim that some commuters typically lack a clearly defined "role" when travelling between home and the workplace; during a commute, they are not an employee nor are they occupying personal roles (e.g. a parent). Jachimowicz et al. (2018) found that those who were able to focus on role-clarification prospection during the journey, were better able to prepare for, and potentially improve, their workplace experience. These viewpoints highlight that an overlap of roles may contribute to issues of work-life conflict, particularly if the "employee role" is functioning within a home environment (e.g. cannot switch off from work), therefore potentially affecting the stress levels and mental health of the commuter and family members. Similarly, these principles feature in the "inter-domain transfer effect" framework (Novaco et al., 1990), and more recently, the "work–family enrichment theory" (Greenhaus & Powell, 2006), where each model considers emotion and experience to be transferable between separate domains. A negative experience in the home domain (e.g. a personal dispute), can be transferred to the commute and/or work domain, thus making the journey and/or workplace seem negative. Conversely, a positive commute/work experience may encourage positivity and improved performance in subsequent domains.

It also remains relevant that, alongside flexible working patterns and "travel activity/behaviour", environmental and organisational conditions are also adapted to ease the burden of long commutes. Research suggests, that developments in transport infrastructure may help to alleviate some of the adverse conditions of lengthy commutes, whilst also implementing future sustainable commuting options (Rahman et al., 2015; Yigitcanlar & Kamruzzaman, 2018). For example, mayors and academics in Japan proposed a "Smart Wellness City" in 2009 to support the mental and physical health of residents (Koike et al., 2017). These changes include improved public transport access to avoid the stress and anxiety commonly associated with congestion through car dependency (Higgins et al., 2018), and the development of a more "walking friendly" environment (Hopkins & Mckay, 2019; Koike et al., 2017). The expansion of "smarter" cities and public mobility projects have also become more popular in Melbourne, Australia, where flexible working or "anywhere working" arrangements are intended to challenge the increasing issue of traffic congestion, including public transport (Hopkins & Mckay, 2019).

As evidenced above, stressors associated with commuting are not exclusive to a single modality or context. A 2006 study of rail commuters travelling into Manhattan, New York, found that passenger stress levels, as indicated by raised cortisol readings, were higher following a long commute (45 to 180 minutes) (Evans et al., 2006). Additionally, a decline in post-commute task outcomes (a proofreading task) and an increase in self-reported stress perception (irrespective of gender) further confirmed the negative impact of extended travel time on mental health and motivation. These findings are again indicative of commuting stressors, particularly in connection to long commutes, which are perhaps less emotionally tolerable (Norgate et al., 2019), and less physiologically tolerable due to the prolonged exposure to environmental contaminants, noise pollution, lack of facilities and/or overcrowding (Cantwell et al., 2009; Cox et al., 2006).

Despite numerous unfavourable outcomes associated with commuting, it is important to consider the benefits, many of which are linked to active commuting and can be enjoyed in both flexible and traditional working arrangements (which will be picked up in more detail in the next section) (Lancée et al., 2017; Martin et al., 2014; Olsson et al., 2013; Smith, 2017). Cycling and walking are considered common forms of active commuting that help to reduce cortisol levels (related to stress) and increase endorphins (related to mood). Active commuting also allows people to connect with natural spaces to help improve mental health (Triguero-Mas et al., 2015; Triguero-Mas et al., 2017), cognitive functioning (Zijlema et al., 2017), and reduce stress, particularly for those who cycle on a consistent basis (e.g. 4+ days per week) (Avila-Palencia et al., 2017). Cycling and walking to work may also provide the commuter with more privacy for self-reflection and relaxation, although in some cities, there can be a risk of exposure to pollution and large numbers of other commuters.

Section conclusion and practical initiatives

Despite the variety of adverse conditions associated with certain commuting conditions (i.e. extended time travel), researchers have attempted to establish several practical recommendations to help alleviate the concerns associated with work travel, particularly those that impact commuter mental health and well-being. One of the more significant findings to emerge is commuting duration, identified as a leading risk to commuter mental health; weighing particularly heavy on those with other time-sensitive commitments (Feng & Boyle, 2014). Research highlights that flexible working arrangements can perhaps mitigate these outcomes by reducing the frequency of commuting hours, thus making space for more leisure and family orientated activities (CIPD, 2016; Wielers & Raven, 2011). However, in the absence of flexible working options, long commutes can significantly impact commuter mental health, typically presenting as anxiety, stress and exhaustion (Gottholmseder et al., 2009; Hilbrecht et al., 2014; Nomoto et al., 2015).

One intervention, which may support commuters, is the use of cognitive and behavioural strategies, such as "mindfulness-based" therapy. Techniques used within mindfulness-based cognitive therapy can help a person to manage stress by encouraging positive physical and psychological behaviours when exposed to adverse experiences. In a commuting context, an example of this would be to identify, process and ultimately accept some of the common commuting stress triggers (i.e. inevitable time delays and/or an over stimulating/noisy environment) in order to discard negative stimuli and direct attention to more constructive "present moment" experiences of the journey (Boe & Hagen, 2015; Paredes et al., 2017; Sagui-Henson et al., 2018).

Evidence also suggests that people are psychologically influenced by their surroundings and/or perception of commute characteristics (Handy & Thigpen, 2019; Zijlema et al., 2018; Wei et al., 2019). Excessively polluted cities, for example, make active commuting options much less desirable. Furthermore, commuters who are bound by economic/personal circumstances (e.g. lower-income families) may have to walk or cycle through necessity rather than choice, thus restricting travel autonomy. There are, however, very clear physical benefits to active commuting, most of which also positively impact mental health, as mental and physical health are fundamentally linked.

The impact of commuting on physical health

Building on the previous section, this section will consider the impact of commuting on our physical health. This is because, for many of us, our commute provides an opportunity to combine travel to and from our workplace with physical activity either in part or as a whole. Active commuting has been recognised as a feasible way of incorporating greater levels of physical activity into daily life, thereby helping meet recommended levels (NICE, 2012; WHO Regional Office for Europe, 2017). Undertaking physical activity has been well evidenced to be associated with: a reduction in various health outcomes, including cardiovascular disease, diabetes, some cancers and reducing the risk of premature mortality (Warburton et al., 2006; WHO, 2010; Department of Health (DH), 2011; Garber et al., 2011; Lee et al., 2012); improved mental health (Anokye et al., 2012; Cooper & Barton, 2015); and a reduction in anxiety (Anderson & Shivakumar, 2013). Previous studies have shown that significant levels of physical activity can be accrued during commuting, for example, 5 out of 26 workers in a UK-based study achieved minimum recommended physical activity guidelines (30 minutes of moderate-to-vigorous physical activity (MVPA) per day) in their commute alone, with commuting; accounting for 68% of total time in MVPA (Rafferty et al., 2016). Another study reported that participants recorded 55 minutes of MVPA per day and 30% of the recommended level of MVPA was accrued in commute (Yang et al., 2012). Therefore, the amount of physical activity accumulated during commuting could help to improve the health of the population in terms of both physical and mental health.

Despite the benefits of active commuting, travel distance from home to work, ineffective public transportation system, and convenience can act as barriers to uptake. Lengthy commute journeys can result in commuters taking a non-active mode of transport (Rafferty et al., 2016; RSPH, 2016); for example, in the UK from 1998 to 2016, of those who always used only one commute mode, 69% commuted to work as car/van drivers (the largest percentage) compared to 6% who walked (lowest 0% taxi/minicab) (Department for Transport, 2019). A major disadvantage of "non-active" lengthy commute journeys is also the association with increased levels of stress and increased time spent being sedentary (Christian, 2012b; The Work Foundation, 2016).

To support physical activity, allowing employees the flexibility of structuring their day by avoiding a rush-hour commute may enable workers to undertake activities that support healthier lifestyles (e.g. going for a run/swim or going to the gym, attending to other personal commitments, attending medical appointments or making a healthy meal) (RSPH, 2016). Further flexible working has been recognised as a way of reducing time spent during commuting, with almost 60% of commuters reporting that working remotely or flexibly helps to increase productivity (The Work Foundation, 2016), improve job satisfaction, and reduce stress (CIPD, 2019; Kelliher & Anderson, 2010). Although it should be noted that while different flexible working arrangements have been found to be beneficial, this is not always the case with flexible work hours that involve night shifts, often resulting in excessive fatigue, sleep disturbance, and gastrointestinal disorders (Costa et al., 2001).

Looking more specifically at the physiological effects of active commuting, it has been associated with a reduction in body mass index (BMI) and body fat percentage (BFP) (Flint et al., 2014; Flint et al., 2016; Mytton et al., 2018), reduced levels of hypertension and diabetes (Honda et al., 2015; Laverty et al., 2013), reduced cardiovascular risk (Celis-Morales et al., 2017; Gordon-Larsen et al., 2009; Panter et al., 2018), and reduced risk of metabolic syndrome (Garcia-Hermoso et al., 2018; Sadarangani et al., 2018; Steell et al., 2017).

Taking body fat as an example, evidence to support the benefits of active commuting by mode is seen in a cross-sectional study in the UK, which reported that commuters who cycled had lower body fat than those using a car, while those who walked regularly had no reduction in body fat (Mytton et al., 2018). A study conducted in India found that commuting by walking, cycling and public transport was associated with a lower likelihood of being overweight or obese and the associations remained after adjustment for potential confounders, including age, sex, standard of living, occupation, leisure-time physical activity, diet, and alcohol intake (Millett et al., 2013). Similarly, Rissel et al. (2014) used data from the New South Wales Continuous Health Survey to examine trends of walking and cycling over time from 2005 to 2010, concluding that Australian male and female workers that walked to work had a significantly lower BMI; however, cycling to work was associated with lower BMI in men only compared to other modes of commuting. This gender split was also found in a nationally representative UK study, which reported that compared to using private transport, walking and cycling to work were associated with lower BMI in men only (Flint et al., 2014). In a similar vein, a prospective UK cohort study that followed participants between April 2007 and December 2010 found that commuting by cycling and walking was associated with a lower risk of cardiovascular diseases, cancer outcomes and all-cause mortality, independent of BMI (Celis-Morales et al., 2017). In line with this finding, a longitudinal study that stratified commuters into regular (at least three days a week) and non-regular commuters, depending on whether they reported exclusive car use for commuting, found that regular commuters with active patterns of commuting had a lower risk of cardiovascular disease, and non-regular commuters with active patterns were associated with a lower risk of all-cause mortality compared to exclusive car users (Panter et al., 2018). This observation suggests that the frequency of commuting – at least three times a week – may influence our health differently. Finally, for those commuters who do not have the option to actively commute, the adoption of flexible working may allow them the opportunity to engage in healthier activities during the day (Hilbrecht et al., 2014; RSPH, 2016).

Section conclusion and practical initiatives

From the evidence it can be seen that there are significant benefits of active commuting on physical health, which are impacted by commute mode. However, most studies have classified active commuting as walking or cycling, with only a few including public transport. This has resulted in not capturing mixed-mode journeys, which is a major limitation. While commuting can be beneficial in terms of increasing physical activity levels, long commute journeys can increase the use of more passive modes of transport. Flexible working can provide an opportunity to engage in healthier activities, such as preparing healthy meals and exercising during what would have been the commute time.

Going forward, a recommendation to increase active and mixed-mode commuting may help to address environmental sustainability and increase physical activity in the population (Woodcock et al., 2007). We do recognise there are always likely to be commutes where active transport is not suitable, but future public policy and infrastructure should explore ways to encourage the use and development of low-energy transportation systems. Further to this consideration is the need to look into how to achieve commute modal shift on a population level. An example of this can be seen in countries such as the Netherlands, Denmark and Germany, where there are established infrastructures for transport such as safe and designated cycle lanes and a culture socialised towards cycling, the environment lends itself to active commuting, which is also coupled with the government having deterrents for driving in cities (e.g. taxes, and restrictions on parking and car ownership) (Pucher & Buehler, 2008). Finally, flexible working arrangements and having effective transportation systems can help improve the health of the working population, reallocate some rush-hour commutes to off-peak times, help increase the uptake of public transport due to less congestion outside of the rush-hour, and allow time for more active modes of commute (Ben-Elia & Ettema, 2011).

Chapter conclusion

Until such time as there is more widespread legislation along the lines of the Finnish Flexible Working Hours Act 2020 (Ministry of Economic Affairs and Employment of Finland, 2019), which enables working hours not to be tied to a specific place of work (and is expected to smooth the navigation of agreements around work done from home), commuting is still likely to be a prominent feature of working life. Notably, the mode, distance and time of commutes is increasing in many places due to the number of people who are commuting and the pressures on travel modes. A person's commute can have a profound effect on their mental and physical health, both in terms of the short-term impact each day, which may change depending on the characteristics of a journey, to accumulative effects longer term. Although our desire for flexible working may be impacted by such factors as life priorities and age (CIPD, 2019), flexible working arrangements will be likely to mitigate aspects of commuting challenges by calling into question the need to commute (e.g. greater uptake of remote or virtual working) and reducing the frequency of commuting hours, thus making space for more leisure and family orientated activities (CIPD, 2016; Wielers & Raven, 2011). We also observed that if no commute takes place, flexible working provides opportunity for other personal activities to take the place of commutes, which can promote health and well-being.

Changing our options for flexible working and/or improving commutes will require multi-agency working, time and investment, but ultimately investing in understanding and improving workers' options is something that will benefit health, economies and productivity.

Recommendations

The recommendations below are designed to provide discussion points and suggestions for key stakeholders around future scenarios for flexible working and/or improving commutes in relation to mental health and physical health.
  Going forward companies could:

- Explore how the provision of flexible working could provide value to all stakeholders and reduce the need for commuting (e.g. more uptake of remote or virtual working, thus potentially reducing the strain on transport systems, and supporting improved mental and physical health of workers).
- Explore how to improve the uptake and management of flexible working to support employees and employers, or to explore where the time/mode of commutes can be varied to support employees.
- Explore how organisations could learn good practice from companies who already implement practices that limit staff being able to work outside their working hours (which may help encourage a better work-life balance and the use of a commute to help transition into personal roles).
  - For example, Daimler (German automotive company) have installed software to auto-reply to emails and then delete them while employees are away, and for some companies in France a deal has been made between employers' federation and unions to enforce a 35-hour week and no emails after 6 pm (except in exceptional working hours) (Gibson, 2014). Companies taking these stances are allowing commuters to

use this time as a transition period to allow a change in mindset, and ultimately support health and well-being.

- To further encourage active commuting, companies may want to consider exploring how to support this choice (e.g. through storage and shower facilities, and guides developed with local organisations around travel routes).

Key stakeholders can help improve the experience of commuting, reduce the impact and support its integration into flexible working patterns through:

- Considering how to challenge some of the environmental pressures, for example, those demonstrated in Australasia around "smart city" planning policies that integrate public transport.
  - Through this, there is the potential that infrastructural adjustments, such as natural/green spaces, walkways (positioned away from traffic) and additional cycle lanes will help to combat the burden of busy and often polluted urbanised commutes (particularly for the active traveller who is closely exposed to environmental contaminants).
- Local governments, transport sectors and employers coming together to explore how infrastructure and the built environment can be developed to support more active commuting, or to reduce known stressors during commuting (e.g. overcrowding and lateness of public transport services).
- Health and transport policies could benefit from being adapted to mitigate the impacts of commuting duration (e.g. for it to be considered within working hours or flexible working policies).

Finally, thinking about the individual:

- Where workers can take advantage of flexible working practices they should explore if there is a need to commute when remote and virtual working may be possible, or if changing their commute pattern (e.g. mode, time) would reduce the physical and mental impact of commuting.
- Interventions should help support commuters to develop tools to allow them to better transition through different roles on journeys to and from work.
- Commuters could consider their role during the commute and how they could use the commute to transition from home to work and vice versa to reduce the mental health impact of the commute (e.g. listening to an audiobook, carrying out mindfulness, reading a book/magazine).

Acknowledgement

The authors would like to acknowledge Dr Alex Clarke-Cornwell for her helpful comments and suggestions on this chapter.

References

Amponsah-Tawiah, K., Annor, F., & Arthur, B. (2016). Linking commuting stress to job satisfaction and turnover intention: The mediating role of burnout. *Journal of Workplace Behavioural Health*, *31*(2), 104–123.

Anderson, E.H. & Shivakumar, G. (2013). Effects of exercise and physical activity on anxiety. *Frontiers in Psychiatry*, *4*(27).

Anokye, N.K., Trueman, P., Green, C., Pavey, T.G., & Taylor, R.S. (2012). Physical activity and health related quality of life. *BMC Public Health*, *12*(1), 624.

Avila-Palencia, I., de Nazelle, A., Cole-Hunter, T., Donaire-Gonzalez, D., Jerrett, M., Rodriguez, D., & Nieuwenhuijsen, M. (2017). The relationship between bicycle commuting and perceived stress: A cross-sectional study. *BMJ Open*, *7*(6), E013542.

Barck-Holst, P., Nilsonne, Å., Åkerstedt, T., & Hellgren, C. (2017). Reduced working hours and stress in the Swedish social services: A longitudinal study. *International Social Work*, *60*(4), 897–913.

Barry, M.M. (2009). Addressing the determinants of positive mental health: Concepts, evidence and practice. *International Journal of Mental Health Promotion*, *11*(3), 4–17.

Ben-Elia, E. & Ettema, D. (2011). Rewarding rush-hour avoidance: A study of commuters' travel behavior. *Transportation Research Part A: Policy and Practice*, *45*(7), 567–582.

Besser, L.M., Marcus, M., & Frumkin, H. (2008). Commute time and social capital in the US. *American Journal of Preventive Medicine*, *34*(3), 207–211.

Boe, O. & Hagen, K. (2015). Using mindfulness to reduce the perception of stress during an acute stressful situation. *Procedia – Social and Behavioural Sciences*, *197*, 858–868.

Cantwell, M., Caulfield, B., & O'Mahony, M. (2009). Examining the factors that impact public transport commuting satisfaction. *Journal of Public Transportation*, *12*(2), 1.

Cassidy, T. (1992). Commuting-related stress: Consequences and implications. *Employee Counselling Today*, *4*(2), 15–21.

Celis-Morales, C., Lyall, D., Welsh, P., Anderson, J., Steell, L., Guo, Y. et al. (2017). Association between active commuting and incident cardiovascular disease, cancer, and mortality: Prospective cohort study. *British Medical Journal*, *357*, j1546.

Chartered Institute of Personnel and Development (CIPD) (2016). Employee outlook: Focus on commuting and flexible working – Survey report. Retrieved 21 August 2019 from: https://www.cipd.co.uk/Images/employee-outlook-focus-on-commuting-and-flexible-working_tcm18-10886.pdf

Chartered Institute of Personnel and Development (CIPD) (2019). Mega trends: Flexible working. Retrieved 21 August 2019 from: https://www.cipd.co.uk/Images/megatrends-report-flexible-working-1_tcm18-52769.pdf

Chatterjee, K., Chng, S., Clark, B., Davis, A., De Vos, J., Ettema, D. et al. (2019). Commuting and wellbeing: A critical overview of the literature with implications for policy and future research. *Transport Reviews*, *40*(1), 1–30.

Christian, T.J. (2012a). Automobile commuting duration and the quantity of time spent with spouse, children, and friends. *Preventive Medicine*, *55*(3), 215–218.

Christian, T.J. (2012b). Trade-offs between commuting time and health-related activities. *Journal of Urban Health*, *89*(5), 746–757.

Citrix Systems (2009). The office of the future: The critical factors behind our changing work environment. Retrieved 16 September 2019 from: http://www.axisfirst.co.uk/technology/pdfs/The_Office_of_the_Future_Whitepaper.pdf

Clarke, S. & Holdsworth, L. (2017). Flexibility in the workplace: Implications of flexible work arrangements for individuals, teams and organisations. Retrieved 21 August 2019 from: https://www.acas.org.uk/media/4901/Flexibility-in-the-Workplace-Implications-of-flexible-work-arrangements-for-individuals-teams-and-organisations/pdf/Flexibility-in-the-Workplace.pdf

Cooper, K. & Barton, G.C. (2015). An exploration of physical activity and wellbeing in university employees. *Perspectives in Public Health, 136*(3), 152–160.

Costa, G., Åkerstedt, T., Nachreiner, F., Baltieri, F., Folkard, S., Dresen, M.F. et al. (2001). Flexible work hours, health and well-being in the European Union: Preliminary data from a SALTSA project. *Journal of Human Ergology, 30*(1–2), 27–33.

Cox, T., Houdmont, J., & Griffiths, A. (2006). Rail passenger crowding, stress, health and safety in Britain. *Transportation Research Part A: Policy and Practice, 40*(3), 244–258.

DEGW (2008). Working beyond walls: The government workplaces as an agent of change. Retrieved 16 September 2019 from: https://assets.publishing.service.gov.uk/government/uploads/system/uploads/attachment_data/file/394153/Working-beyond-Walls.pdf

Department for Transport (2019). Analyses from the National Travel Survey. Retrieved 2 June 2019 from: https://assets.publishing.service.gov.uk/government/uploads/system/uploads/attachment_data/file/775032/2019-nts-commissioned-analyses.pdf

Department of Health (DH) (2011). UK physical activity guidelines. Retrieved 2 June 2019 from: https://assets.publishing.service.gov.uk/government/uploads/system/uploads/attachment_data/file/213740/dh_128145.pdf

Eurofound (2015). EU level: ECJ rules that travel time is treated as working time. Retrieved 2 June 2019 from: https://www.eurofound.europa.eu/it/publications/article/2015/eu-level-ecj-rules-that-travel-time-is-treated-as-working-time

Eurostat (2016). Statistics on commuting patterns at regional level. Retrieved 21 August 2019 from: https://ec.europa.eu/eurostat/statistics-explained/index.php/Statistics_on_commuting_patterns_at_regional_level#General_overview

Evans, G., Wener, R., & Kaplan, R. (2006). Rail commuting duration and passenger stress. *Health Psychology, 25*(3), 408–412.

Evans, G., Wener, R., & Phillips, D. (2002). The morning rush hour: Predictability and commuter stress. *Environment and Behaviour, 34*(4), 521–530.

Feng, Z. & Boyle, P. (2014). Do long journeys to work have adverse effects on mental health? *Environment and Behaviour, 46*(5), 609–625.

Flint, E., Cummins, S., & Sacker, A. (2014). Associations between active commuting, body fat, and body mass index: Population based, cross sectional study in the United Kingdom. *British Medical Journal, 349*, g4887. Article correction: https://www.bmj.com/content/bmj/350/bmj.h2056.full.pdf

Flint, E., Webb, E., & Cummins, S. (2016). Change in commute mode and body-mass index: Prospective, longitudinal evidence from UK Biobank. *The Lancet: Public Health, 1*(2), e46–e55.

Florida Department of Transportation (FDOT) (2018). Commuting trends in Florida. Retrieved 16 August 2019 from: https://fdotwww.blob.core.windows.net/sitefinity/docs/default-source/content/planning/trends/special/acs022818.pdf?sfvrsn=47db27fd_0

Friman, M., Gärling, T., Ettema, D., & Olsson, L.E. (2017). How does travel affect emotional well-being and life satisfaction? *Transportation Research Part A: Policy and Practice*, *106*, 170–180.

Garber, C.E., Blissmer, B., Deschenes, M.R., Franklin, B.A., Lamonte, M.J., Lee, I.-M. et al. (2011). Quantity and quality of exercise for developing and maintaining cardiorespiratory, musculoskeletal, and neuromotor fitness in apparently healthy adults: Guidance for prescribing exercise. *Medicine & Science in Sports & Exercise*, *43*(7), 1334–1359.

Garcia-Hermoso, A., Quintero, A.P., Hernandez, E., Enrique Correa-Bautista, J., Izquierdo, M., Tordecilla-Sanders, A. et al. (2018). Active commuting to and from university, obesity and metabolic syndrome among Colombian university students. *BMC Public Health*, *18*(1), 523.

Gibson, M. (2014). Here's a radical way to end vacation email overload. Retrieved 2 June 2019 from: https://time.com/3116424/daimler-vacation-email-out-of-office

Golden T.D. (2012). Altering the effects of work and family conflict on exhaustion: Telework during traditional and nontraditional work hours. *Journal of Business & Psychology*, *27*(3), 255–269.

Gordon-Larsen, P., Boone-Heinonen, J., Sidney, S., Sternfeld, B., Jacobs, D.R., & Lewis, C.E. (2009). Active commuting and cardiovascular disease risk: The CARDIA study. *Archives of Internal Medicine*, *169*(13), 1216–1223.

Gottholmseder, G., Nowotny, K., Pruckner, G.J., & Theurl, E. (2009). Stress perception and commuting. *Health Economics*, *18*(5), 559–576.

Greenhaus, J.H. & Powell, G.N. (2006). When work and family are allies: A theory of work–family enrichment. *The Academy of Management Review*, *31*(1), 72–92.

Gripsrud, M. & Hjorthol, R. (2012). Working on the train: From "dead time" to productive and vital time. *Transportation*, *39*(5), 941–956.

Guell, C., Panter, J., Jones, N.R., & Ogilvie, D. (2012). Towards a differentiated understanding of active travel behaviour: Using social theory to explore everyday commuting. *Social Science & Medicine*, *75*(1), 233–239.

Haar, J.M., Russo, M., Suñe, A., & Ollier-Malaterre, A. (2014). Outcomes of work–life balance on job satisfaction, life satisfaction and mental health: A study across seven cultures. *Journal of Vocational Behavior*, *85*(3), 361–373.

Halpern, D.F. (2005). How time-flexible work policies can reduce stress, improve health, and save money. *Stress and Health*, *21*(3), 157–168.

Handy, S. & Thigpen, C. (2019). Commute quality and its implications for commute satisfaction: Exploring the role of mode, location, and other factors. *Travel Behaviour and Society*, *16*, 241–248.

Hennessy, D.A. (2008). The impact of commuter stress on workplace aggression. *Journal of Applied Social Psychology*, *38*(9), 2315–2335.

Higgins, C., Sweet, D., & Kanaroglou, M. (2018). All minutes are not equal: Travel time and the effects of congestion on commute satisfaction in Canadian cities. *Transportation*, *45*(5), 1249–1268.

Hilbrecht, M., Smale, B., & Mock, S.E. (2014). Highway to health? Commute time and well-being among Canadian adults. *World Leisure Journal*, *56*(2), 151–163.

Honda, T., Kuwahara, K., Nakagawa, T., Yamamoto, S., Hayashi, T., & Mizoue, T. (2015). Leisure-time, occupational, and commuting physical activity and risk of type 2 diabetes in Japanese workers: A cohort study. *BMC Public Health*, *15*(1), 1004.

Hopkins, J. & Mckay, J. (2019). Investigating "anywhere working" as a mechanism for alleviating traffic congestion in smart cities. *Technological Forecasting & Social Change*, *142*, 258–272.

International Workplace Group (IWG) (2019). The IWG global workspace survey. Welcome to Generation Flex – The Employee Power Shift. Retrieved from: http://assets.regus.com/pdfs/iwg-workplace-survey/iwg-workplace-survey-2019.pdf

Jachimowicz, J., Lee, J.J., Staats, B.R., Menges, J., & Gino, F. (2018). Between home and work: Commuting as an opportunity for role transitions. *Harvard Business School NOM Unit Working Paper* (16-077), pp. 16–17.

Jacob, N., Munford, L., Rice, N., & Roberts, J. (2019). The disutility of commuting? The effect of gender and local labor markets. *Regional Science and Urban Economics*, 77, 264–275.

Jang, S. & Zippay, A. (2011). The juggling act: Managing work-life conflict and work-life balance. *Families in Society*, 92(1), 84–90.

Kelliher, C. & Anderson, D. (2010). Doing more with less? Flexible working practices and the intensification of work. *Human relations*, 63(1), 83–106.

King, D.M. & Jacobson, S.H. (2017). What is driving obesity? A review on the connections between obesity and motorized transportation. *Current obesity reports*, 6(1), 3–9.

Koike, H., Osada, T., & So, T. (2017). Smart wellness city – new healthy community movements in Japan (breakout presentation). *Journal of Transport & Health*, 7(SS), S66.

Lancée, S., Veenhoven, R., & Burger, M. (2017). Mood during commute in the Netherlands: What way of travel feels best for what kind of people? *Transportation Research Part A*, 104, 195–208.

Laverty, A.A., Mindell, J.S., Webb, E.A., & Millett, C. (2013). Active travel to work and cardiovascular risk factors in the United Kingdom. *American Journal of Preventive Medicine*, 45(3), 282–288.

Lee, I.M., Shiroma, E.J., Lobelo, F., Puska, P., Blair, S.N., Katzmarzyk, P.T., & Lancet Physical Activity Series Working Group (2012). Effect of physical inactivity on major non-communicable diseases worldwide: An analysis of burden of disease and life expectancy. *The Lancet*, 380(9838), 219–229.

Legrain, A., Eluru, N., & El-Geneidy, A.M. (2015). Am stressed, must travel: The relationship between mode choice and commuting stress. *Transportation Research Part F: Traffic Psychology and Behaviour*, 34, 141–151.

Lorenz, O. (2018). Does commuting matter to subjective well-being? *Journal of Transport Geography*, 66(C), 180–199.

Lyness, K.S. & Judiesch, M.K. (2014). Gender egalitarianism and work–life balance for managers: Multisource perspectives in 36 countries. *Applied Psychology*, 63(1), 96–129.

Martin, A., Goryakin, Y., & Suhrcke, M. (2014). Does active commuting improve psychological wellbeing? Longitudinal evidence from eighteen waves of the British Household Panel Survey. *Preventive Medicine*, 69, 296–303.

Millett, C., Agrawal, S., Sullivan, R., Vaz, M., Kurpad, A., Bharathi, A. et al. (2013). Associations between active travel to work and overweight, hypertension, and diabetes in India: A cross-sectional study. *PLoS medicine*, 10(6), e1001459.

Milner, A., Smith, P., & LaMontagne, A.D. (2015). Working hours and mental health in Australia: Evidence from an Australian population-based cohort, 2001–2012. *Occupational and Environmental Medicine*, 72(8), 573–579.

Ministry of Economic Affairs and Employment of Finland (2019). Working Hours Act to be updated. Retrieved 3 October 2019 from: https://valtioneuvosto.fi/en/article/-/asset_publisher/1410877/tyoaikalaki-uudistuu

Ministry of Economic Affairs and Employment of Finland (n.d.) Working hours are regulated by the Working Hours Act and collective agreements. Retrieved 28 January 2020 from: https://tem.fi/en/working-hours

Moovit Insights (n.d.). Facts and usage statistics about public transport in Melbourne, Australia. Retrieved 14 August 2019 from: https://moovitapp.com/insights/en-gb/Moovit_Insights_Public_Transport_Index-2803

Mytton, O.T., Ogilvie, D., Griffin, S., Brage, S., Wareham, N., & Panter, J. (2018). Associations of active commuting with body fat and visceral adipose tissue: A cross-sectional population based study in the UK. *Preventive Medicine, 106*, 86–93.

National Institute for Health and Care Excellence (NICE) (2012). Physical activity: Walking and cycling (PH41). Retrieved 14 August 2019 from: www.nice.org.uk/guidance/ph41

National Institute for Health and Care Excellence (NICE) (2019). NICEimpact. Mental health. Retrieved 2 June 2019 from: https://www.nice.org.uk/Media/Default/About/what-we-do/Into-practice/measuring-uptake/NICEimpact-mental-health.pdf

Nomoto, M., Hara, A., Kikuchi, K., & Ergol, J.H. (2015). Effects of long-time commuting and long-hour working on lifestyle and mental health among school teachers in Tokyo, Japan. *Journal of Human Ergology, 44*(1), 1–9.

Norgate, S.H, Cooper-Ryan, A.M., Lavin, S., Stonier, C., & Cooper, C.L. (2019). The impact of public transport on the health of work commuters: A systematic review. *Health Psychology Review, 12*, June, 1–20.

Novaco, R.W. & Gonzalez, O.I. (2009). Commuting and well-being. In Y. Amichai-Hamburger (ed.), *Technology and Psychological Well-being* (pp. 174–205). Cambridge: Cambridge University Press.

Novaco, R.W., Stokols, D., & Milanesi, L. (1990). Objective and subjective dimensions of travel impedance as determinants of commuting stress. *American Journal of Community Psychology, 18*(2), 231–257.

Office for National Statistics (ONS) (2018). Travel to work methods and the time it takes to commute from home to work, Labour Force Survey, 2007 to 2016. Retrieved 2 June 2019 from: https://www.ons.gov.uk/employmentandlabourmarket/peopleinwork/labourproductivity/adhocs/008005traveltoworkmethodsandthetimeittakestocommutefromhometoworklabourforcesurvey2007to2016

Office for National Statistics (ONS) (2019). The commuting gap: Women are more likely than men to leave their job over a long commute. Retrieved 2 June 2019 from: https://www.ons.gov.uk/employmentandlabourmarket/peopleinwork/earningsandworkinghours/articles/thecommutinggapwomenaremorelikelythanmentoleavetheirjoboveralongcommute/2019-09-04

Olsson, L.E., Gärling, T., Ettema, D., Friman, M., & Fujii, S. (2013). Happiness and satisfaction with work commute. *Social indicators research, 111*(1), 255–263.

Organisation for Economic Co-operation and Development (OECD) (2016). Be flexible! Background brief on how workplace flexibility can help European employees to balance work and family. Retrieved 2 June 2019 from: https://www.oecd.org/els/family/Be-Flexible-Backgrounder-Workplace-Flexibility.pdf

Panter, J., Mytton, O., Sharp, S., Brage, S., Cummins, S., Laverty, A.A. et al. (2018). Using alternatives to the car and risk of all-cause, cardiovascular and cancer mortality. *Heart, 104*(21), 1749–1755.

Paredes, P.E., Hamdan, N.A.H., Clark, D., Cai, C., Ju, W., & Landay, J.A. (2017). Evaluating in-car movements in the design of mindful commute interventions: Exploratory study. *Journal of Medical Internet research, 19*(12), e372.

Paton, N. (2017). Long commutes to work take toll on employee health. *Occupational Health & Wellbeing, 69*(7), 4. Retrieved 16 September 2019 from: https://search.proquest.com/docview/1923938544?accountid=8058

Population Reference Bureau (2000, December). The future of commuting. Retrieved 2 June 2019 from: https://www.prb.org/thefutureofcommuting

Pucher, J. & Buehler, R. (2008). Making cycling irresistible: Lessons from the Netherlands, Denmark and Germany. *Transport Reviews*, *28*(4), 495–528.

Rafferty, D., Dolan, C., & Granat, M. (2016). Attending a workplace: Its contribution to volume and intensity of physical activity. *Physiological Measurement*, *37*(12), 2144–2153.

Rahman, A.N.N.A., Yusoff, Z.M., & Omar, D. (2015). Smart commuting for urban working family to workplace. *Procedia – Social and Behavioral Sciences*, *184*(C), 252–258.

Rissel, C., Greenaway, M., Bauman, A., & Wen, L.M. (2014). Active travel to work in New South Wales 2005–2010, individual characteristics and association with body mass index. *Australian and New Zealand Journal of Public Health*, *38*(1), 25–29.

Roberts, J. & Taylor, K. (2017). Intra-household commuting choices and local labour markets. *Oxford Economic Papers*, *69*(3), 734–757.

Royal Society for Public Health (RSPH) (2016). The impact of rush hour commuting on health and wellbeing. Retrieved 2 June 2019 from: https://www.rsph.org.uk/uploads/assets/uploaded/b1320af3-7ba3-4b4e-a14351e7d8cfb24b.pdf

Rüger, H., Pfaff, S., Weishaar, H., & Wiernik, B. (2017). Does perceived stress mediate the relationship between commuting and health-related quality of life? *Transportation Research Part F: Psychology and Behaviour*, *50*, 100–108.

Russell, H., O'Connell, P., & McGinnity, F. (2009). The impact of flexible working arrangements on work–life conflict and work pressure in Ireland. *Gender, Work & Organization*, *16*(1), 73–97.

Sadarangani, K.P., Von Oetinger, A., Cristi-Montero, C., Cortinez-O'Ryan, A., Aguilar-Farias, N., & Martinez-Gomez, D. (2018). Beneficial association between active travel and metabolic syndrome in Latin-America: A cross-sectional analysis from the Chilean National Health Survey 2009–2010. *Preventive Medicine*, *107*, 8–13.

Sagui-Henson, S., Levens, S., & Blevins, C. (2018). Examining the psychological and emotional mechanisms of mindfulness that reduce stress to enhance healthy behaviours. *Stress and Health*, *34*(3), 379–390.

Schiller, H., Lekander, M., Rajaleid, K., Hellgren, C., Åkerstedt, T., Barck-Holst, P., & Kecklund, G. (2017). The impact of reduced worktime on sleep and perceived stress – a group randomized intervention study using diary data. *Scandinavian Journal of Work, Environment & Health*, *43*(2), 109–116.

Smith, O. (2017). Commute well-being differences by mode: Evidence from Portland, Oregon, USA. *Journal of Transport & Health*, *4*, 246–254.

Sposato, R.G., Röderer, K., & Cervinka, R. (2012). The influence of control and related variables on commuting stress. *Transportation Research Part F: Traffic Psychology and Behaviour*, *15*(5), 581–587.

Steell, L., Garrido-Méndez, A., Petermann, F., Díaz-Martínez, X., Martínez, M.A., Leiva, A.M. et al. (2017). Active commuting is associated with a lower risk of obesity, diabetes and metabolic syndrome in Chilean adults. *Journal of Public Health*, *40*(3), 508–516.

Stutzer, A. & Frey, B.S. (2008). Stress that doesn't pay: The commuting paradox. *Scandinavian Journal of Economics*, *110*(2), 339–366.

Szeto, A.C. & Dobson, K.S. (2010). Reducing the stigma of mental disorders at work: A review of current workplace anti-stigma intervention programs. *Applied and Preventive Psychology*, *14*(1–4), 41–56.

Taylor, E., Mulvihill, C., Baillie, N., & Irwin, H. (2017). NICE public health guidance: Healthy workplaces. *Journal of Public Health, 39*(1), 215–216.

Trades Union Congress (TUC) (2018, November 13). Annual commuting time is up 18 hours compared to a decade ago, finds TUC. Retrieved 2 June 2019 from: https://www.tuc.org.uk/news/annual-commuting-time-18-hours-compared-decade-ago-finds-tuc

Triguero-Mas, M., Dadvand, P., Cirach, M., Martínez, D., Medina, A., Mompart, A. et al. (2015). Natural outdoor environments and mental and physical health: Relationships and mechanisms. *Environment International, 77*, 35–41.

Triguero-Mas, M., Donaire-Gonzalez, D., Seto, E., Valentín, A., Martínez, D., Smith, G. et al. (2017). Natural outdoor environments and mental health: Stress as a possible mechanism. *Environmental Research, 159*, 629–638.

Urhonen, T., Lie, A., & Aamodt, G. (2016). Associations between long commutes and subjective health complaints among railway workers in Norway. *Preventive Medicine Reports, 4*, 490–495.

de Vos, D., Meijers, E., & van Ham, M. (2018). Working from home and the willingness to accept a longer commute. *The Annals of Regional Science, 61*(2), 375–398.

Wang, X., Rodríguez, D.A., Sarmiento, O.L., & Guaje, O. (2019). Commute patterns and depression: Evidence from eleven Latin American cities. *Journal of Transport & Health, 14*, 1–19.

Warburton, D.E.R., Nicol, C.W., & Bredin, S.S.D. (2006). Health benefits of physical activity: The evidence. *Canadian Medical Association Journal, 174*(6), 801.

Wei, D., Cao, X., & Wang, M. (2019). What determines the psychological well-being during commute in Xi'an: The role of built environment, travel attitude, and travel characteristics. *Sustainability, 11*(5), 1328.

Wielers, R. & Raven, D. (2011). Part-time work and work norms in the Netherlands. *European Sociological Review, 29*(1), 105–113.

Williams, J. & Jach, J. (2017, March). How will we commute to the workplace in the future? *Work Design Magazine: Expert Insights.* Retrieved 2 June 2019 from: https://workdesign.com/2017/03/will-commute-workplace-future

Woodcock, J., Banister, D., Edwards, P., Prentice, A.M., & Roberts, I. (2007). Energy and transport. *The Lancet, 370*(9592), 1078–1088.

The Work Foundation (2016). Working anywhere: A winning formula for good work? Retrieved 2 June 2019 from: http://www.theworkfoundation.com/wp-content/uploads/2016/02/398_Working-Anywhere.pdf

World Health Organization (WHO) (2001). The World Health Report 2001: Mental health: New understanding, new hope. Retrieved 2 June 2019 from: https://www.who.int/whr/2001/en/whr01_en.pdf?ua=1

World Health Organization (WHO) (2010). Global recommendations on physical activity for health. Retrieved 2 June 2019 from: http://apps.who.int/iris/bitstream/handle/10665/44399/9789241599979_eng.pdf;jsessionid=B1034C3A5029E99349E179567934AF35?sequence=1

World Health Organization (WHO) Regional Office for Europe (2017). Towards more physical activity in cities. Retrieved 2 June 2019 from: http://www.euro.who.int/__data/assets/pdf_file/0018/353043/2017_WHO_Report_FINAL_WEB.pdf?ua=1

World Health Organization (WHO) (2018). Mental health: Strengthening our response. Retrieved 2 June 2019 from: https://www.who.int/news-room/fact-sheets/detail/mental-health-strengthening-our-response

Wright, T.A. & Cropanzano, R. (2000). Psychological well-being and job satisfaction as predictors of job performance. *Journal of Occupational Health Psychology, 5*(1), 84–94.

Yang, L., Panter, J., Griffin, S.J., & Ogilvie, D. (2012). Associations between active commuting and physical activity in working adults: Cross-sectional results from the Commuting and Health in Cambridge study. *Preventive Medicine, 55*(5), 453–457.

Yigitcanlar, T. & Kamruzzaman, M. (2018). Smart cities and mobility: Does the smartness of Australian cities lead to sustainable commuting patterns? *Journal of Urban Technology, 26*(2), 21–46.

Zijlema, W.L., Avila-Palencia, I., Triguero-Mas, M., Gidlow, C., Maas, J., Kruize, H. et al. (2018). Active commuting through natural environments is associated with better mental health: Results from the PHENOTYPE project. *Environment International, 121*(Part 1), 721–727.

Zijlema, W.L., Triguero-Mas, M., Smith, G., Cirach, M., Martinez, D., Dadvand, P. et al. (2017). The relationship between natural outdoor environments and cognitive functioning and its mediators. *Environmental Research, 155*, 268–275.

10 Flexible working and skill-biased inequality

Causes and consequences

Egidio Riva and Marcello Russo

Introduction

Research, across a wide range of disciplines, has examined flexible working, here defined as the level of control that employees have over the timing, location and amount of their work (Allen et al., 2013; Hill et al., 2008). Overall, while findings are mixed and the size of the effects in relation to outcomes for employers is somewhat disputed (Bloom & Van Reenan, 2006; de Menezes & Kelliher, 2011), there is some evidence that providing employees with greater discretion over when, where, how much and for how long they work according to personal needs or preferences may be conducive to the attainment of individual and organizational goals. Despite these potential mutual gains for both employers and employees related to the adoption of flexible working arrangements, current literature signals that there is both a poorly met and a weak demand for more flexible working across the workforce (Kossek & Lautsch, 2018; Sweet et al., 2014; Eurofound, 2017). On one hand, there is a large and documented flexibility gap, i.e., a gap between the demand and supply of flexible working arrangements. Indeed, many employers do not introduce flexible working arrangements at all and/or deliver them to some but not all employees (Eurofound, 2015). On the other hand, a weak demand results when employees perceive flexible working as inaccessible (Budd & Mumford, 2006). In this regard, prior research has widely demonstrated that, even when entitled to flexible working options, employees may be reluctant to use them. A widespread concern is that taking advantage of flexible working arrangements may expose them to the risk of being negatively stereotyped and penalized (Blau & Kahn, 2013), with possible repercussions on career prospects. Hence, the literature reports large variations across different groups of employees in terms of access to flexible work options. Moreover, employees are also becoming more divided concerning the degree of uptake. In both cases, in addition to key demographics such as gender and age, skills are a crucial factor explaining such divides (Chung, 2019; Golden, 2008; Swanberg et al., 2005).

According to diverse schools of thoughts, skills can be broadly defined as human capital endowments, and specifically the qualities (i.e., cognitive, interactive, and physical abilities) employees possess that make them productive

at work (Green, 2013). All these qualities, which are typically operationalized by educational attainment (i.e., level of qualification held or duration of
education) or requirements needed to carry out job tasks, situate employees
in the labour market along different positions or occupations, ranked by income, social status, and power. Within the traditional human capital framework, the main assumption is that the higher employees' skills are, the better
will be their expected returns in both monetary and non-monetary terms.
In fact, if employers are demanding more or better knowledge and attitudes
to improve the economic performance of the organization, they then have
an incentive to invest in skill acquisition and development and provide better
working and employment conditions, including flexible working arrangements, to those employees who can best deploy the knowledge and attitudes
that are productive of value. Thus, flexible working can possibly reinforce the
patterns of inequality that characterize the occupational structure.

Against this background, this chapter addresses the issue of skill-biased
inequality in entitlement to and usage of flexible working, and examines,
within a multilevel and multifaceted framework comprising structural and
cultural or interactional elements (Bourdeau et al., 2019), its main causes and
(unintended) consequences. In the skill debate, a considerable amount of the
literature does not provide fine-grained accounts of the entire hierarchical
structure resulting from the uneven distribution of skills; rather, it usually
offers, with a few notable exceptions (e.g., Kossek & Lautsch, 2018), a less
nuanced picture built around the dichotomy of "high-skilled" versus "low-
skilled" jobs, employees, and/or occupations. Such a simplified framework
will be adopted in this chapter for the sake of brevity. However, it may ne-
glect the complexity, variety, and changing nature of skills (Payne, 2017).
Moreover, it may also obfuscate the fact that virtually no job or employee
should be classified as low-skilled or unskilled (Green, 2013: 25), considering that any personal quality may produce value (depending on the specific
requirements of the organization in which it is exercised) and can potentially
be improved over time. Accordingly, in the final section of this chapter, we
will broaden our narrative and offer some implications for policy and practice that could help organizations ensure a higher, more equal, and effective
use of flexible working for the best possible interests of both employees and
employers.

The flexibility gap: the employer perspective

There is a certain degree of variation in the extent to which flexible working
can accommodate the interests of both employers and employees, which may
explain why, as previously mentioned, not all employers tend to offer flexible
working arrangements, and not all employees, even in the same organization,
gain access to these flexible working arrangements. From an employer perspective, relative to the magnitude of the demand for a work schedule that
could better align with personal needs and aspirations, the supply of flexible

working is limited by structural or external constraints (Hill et al., 2008). These constraints are linked to the nature of jobs and to business-related variables (such as industry, types of market, and types of production), which may hamper the ability of workplaces to implement flexible working, restrict the range of flexible options available or limit the number of employees eligible for flexible working (Chung et al., 2007). For instance, in the case of occupations whose operational nature requires that most job-related tasks are performed at the employer's premises, employees cannot be given much choice over when and where they work. Flexibility in relation to the timing and/or location of work may simply not be introduced for most employees in certain sectors (e.g., education, social care, and health) given that customers/students/patients need support during specific/regular work hours and/or in person. Employees involved in teamwork or with low levels of autonomy generally need to maintain regular interaction and to receive systematic supervision and monitoring, which may require predictability in work schedules and make remote working problematic. Consequently, employers usually choose whether to allow flexible working and what different types of flexible work arrangements may be feasible, in addition to deciding which employees are the most suitable for flexible working.

Swanberg and colleagues (2005) suggest that, within an organizational justice framework, three principles may motivate decisions about whether, how, and to whom to distribute flexible work options: equality, need, and equity. Employers may decide to respond to the preferences and demands of all their employees and make flexible working accessible to everyone (principle of equality). Alternatively, they may agree that flexible work arrangements should be primarily offered to those who need them the most (principle of need). However, a large body of research has found that the equity principle prevails, meaning that the provision of flexible working is generally contingent on the potential contribution of the employee to the organization (Kossek & Lautsch, 2018). When meeting employee demands produces concurrent benefits to the employer, there may be, in fact, a business case for introducing flexible working (Kossek & Friede, 2006). Hence, core employees (i.e., those who are most valuable to the organization) are most likely to be entitled to flexible working. In particular, after controlling for a wide range of individual and organizational factors, high-skilled employees seem privileged, as they have comparatively greater access to flexible working (Chung, 2019; Golden, 2008). Indeed, an increasing number of employers use flexible working, as part of high-performance work systems, as a valued tool to attract, engage, reward, and retain better educated and qualified employees (Sweet et al., 2014). Moreover, in tight labour markets, high-skilled employees, based on the demand for human capital as a leverage for workplace competitiveness, usually have relative bargaining power to push for their interests. Therefore, they are usually able to win better and more flexible working schedules compared to low-skilled employees (Budd & Mumford, 2006).

The different meanings of flexible working and the employee experience

Less traditional ways of working may result in increased efforts to coordinate employees' flexible schedules with those of their co-workers and supervisors, as well as in growing human resource management problems, such as those deriving from the need to hire additional staff or to redistribute tasks and responsibilities. Accordingly, once again building on the logic of the business case, the expected costs and benefits may allow employers (and employees) to take, or prevent them from taking, full advantage of flexible working. Nonetheless, numerous studies indicate that, above and beyond economic factors and rationales, the inconsistent provision of flexible working is related to organizational culture factors, which contribute to shaping and influencing how flexible working is enacted and responded to in the workplace (Williams et al., 2013).

Undoubtedly, flexible working questions the conventional model of working and the ideal worker culture (Blair-Loy, 2003). As such, there is considerable divergence concerning employers' views about it. As anticipated, some employers consider flexible working as an integral component of their business strategy, motivated by the belief that redesigning work may be conducive to better performance by means of a more engaged, committed, and diverse workforce (de Menezes & Kelliher, 2019). On the other hand, many employers perceive flexible working as irrelevant or even counterproductive for meeting business needs. The underlying assumption in this perception is that alternative work schedules distract employees from dedicating time and energy to their work (Bourdeau et al., 2019). Within this framework, flexible working may be socially constructed, in the organizational context, either as the norm, to be provided on a regular basis and in a formalized way as part of some strategic human resource management approach, or as the exception, to be permitted on a contingent, casual, or ad hoc basis (Kossek & Friede, 2006).

From an employee perspective, organizational culture provides both opportunities and constraints for individual agency. In particular, different conceptualizations of flexible working translate into different attributions – by employers, managers, and co-workers – about the reasons why employees make use of or request flexible working. These attributions differ depending on the differential nature of flexible working options. In this regard, enclosing (i.e., promoting greater availability for work) versus enabling (i.e., giving employees more chances to spend time and energy outside work) (Bourdeau et al., 2019) or work-facilitating versus work-reducing (Chung, 2019) policies are associated with varied experiences of flexible working in the workplace, which are coherent with the organizational culture. For instance, despite the presence of a strong interest, employees may reveal a weak demand for flexible working, as they may not consider flexible working to be viable due to shared assumptions, beliefs, and values in the workplace regarding individual preferences and behaviours for managing work and non-work roles (Bourdeau et al., 2019;

Williams et al., 2013). This holds true for high-skilled employees. When requesting and/or having flexibility and control over one's schedule and work environment may conflict with the "work devotion schema" (Blair-Loy, 2003), employees in more demanding and rewarding jobs may not fully benefit from the wide range of flexible arrangements available or may even end up working harder or longer rather than modelling working patterns that suit them best. This brings us to the issue of the so-called implementation gap as well as to the paradoxes and other unintended negative consequences with which flexible working is associated when it is implemented ineffectively.

The implementation gap

The implementation gap is generally defined as a discrepancy between the availability and actual use of flexible work arrangements (Allen et al., 2013). The distinction between availability and use is important for at least two reasons. First, despite the fact that the presence of flexible working is associated with more positive attitudes at work (Grover & Crooker, 1995), it is the actual use of these policies that can help employees to manage their work and personal life goals successfully (Allen et al., 2013). Second, the theoretical reasons explaining the positive outcomes associated with flexible working availability and use are different (Allen & Shockley, 2009). The presence of positive effects of flexible working on individual outcomes – which also depend upon the form of flexibility chosen (if to satisfy organizational needs vs. personal needs) (Bourdeau et al., 2019) – are mostly explained by the norms of reciprocation and social exchange mechanisms (Cropanzano & Mitchell, 2005). That is, employees appreciate the availability of flexible working and, in return, tend to reciprocate the presence of such arrangements with more positive attitudes and behaviours at work. In contrast, the benefits associated with the use of flexible working can be explained by control theory (Carver & Scheier, 1982) and conservation of resource theory (Hobfoll, 1989). Using the flexible working policies available at work can provide employees with more resources and control over their work and family demands, which can facilitate the management of their work and non-work roles according to their preferences and needs.

The implementation gap is common in several organizations, wherein those employees who have access to flexible work options (typically those with higher level skills and qualifications) are also those who use these policies less often due to the presence of a stigma associated with such arrangements. Williams et al. (2016) argue that one of the reasons for this stigma is the persistence of a traditional corporate culture built on the "work devotion" (Blair-Loy, 2003) or "ideal worker" schema (Dumas & Sanchez-Burks, 2015). This schema is based on the idea that the ideal worker is a man (or, in rare cases, a single work-centric woman) who is available to work 24/7, who has a stay-at-home partner, and who is ready to sacrifice the family when needed. As a consequence, any behaviour that deviates from this image, like the decision to make use of flexible working arrangements (when not driven by organizational motives), is perceived to signal a low commitment to the job.

Role congruity theory elucidates the reason for this negative association (Eagly & Karau, 2002). This theory suggests that employees can be considered less suitable for high responsibility positions when they display behaviours and/or attitudes that are incongruent with general expectations about the behaviours that a manager should have. Using flexible working to accommodate personal needs and aspirations (especially enabling policies that give employees more personal discretion over when and where to work) can convey the sense that a person has more communal (i.e., caring, compassionate, sensitive) rather than agentic (i.e., assertive, competitive, determined, and aggressive) traits (Hideg et al., 2018). Since the predominant stereotypes about managers describe them as agentic and not communal, it is possible that flexible employees may be regarded as less appropriate for managerial roles (Rudman & Mescher, 2013). That is a possibility that employees in promising jobs usually consider, given that those who use flexible working have been shown to suffer wage penalties (Leslie et al., 2012), experience lower performance evaluations (Wharton et al., 2008), and receive fewer promotions (Lyness & Judiesch, 2008).

Work intensification

Kossek and Thompson (2016) maintain that the implementation gap also exists when there is a contradiction between the goals and outcomes that organizations hope to achieve in theory with the adoption of flexible work and the benefits actually experienced by employees. In this respect, it is not rare to observe that, although flexible working can increase individuals' performance responsiveness to work (Turel et al., 2011), it does not necessarily result in better work-life balance (Kossek & Lautsch, 2018). An explanation for this paradox concerns the negative effects of flexible working on work intensification.

Work intensification refers to the effort that employees put into their jobs during the time they are working (Burchell, 2002). In a recent report on European countries, Chung (2019) has shown that, on average, there is a significant increase in working hours for employees using flexible work. In particular, longitudinal data collected in Germany (2003–2011) revealed that employees with flexible schedules worked longer hours in comparison with those having a fixed schedule. Such increased work hours are not without consequences for employees' health, as demonstrated by prior research (e.g., Kattenbach et al., 2010) highlighting that flexibility can be associated with greater exhaustion and stress.

There is much debate about the causes of increasing work intensification for flexible employees (Kelliher & Anderson, 2010). Flexible working is likely to blur the boundary between work and home life (Fonner & Stache, 2012), making it difficult for teleworkers to navigate the micro transitions between work and family roles and potentially creating more challenges rather than reducing them. Another reason for the greater work intensification associated with flexible work relates to the "autonomy paradox" experienced by flexible employees (Mazmanian et al., 2013). On the one hand, flexibility gives employees greater discretion over when to work and how to organize the working day, as well as more control in the simultaneous management of both work and family activities. On the other hand, working remotely can lead employees to work longer hours due to the use of information and communication technologies that make people constantly connected to their work (Morandin et al., 2018), the removal of workplace distractions (i.e., social interactions), and the saving of commuting time that results in more hours to devote to work. In addition to depending upon the availability of enabling technologies that allow flexible employees to work anywhere and at any time, work intensification can also derive from the need for flexible employees to convey a more positive image and disprove some negative stereotypes associated with flexibility. For example, telecommuters might work longer hours and be more responsive to any work-related messages than traditional employees, so as to prove to their supervisor they are working even more and harder than usual. Finally, flexible employees tend to be driven to work harder and with more intensity due to a sense of moral obligation to reciprocate the favourable working conditions provided by the employer (Kelliher & Anderson, 2010).

An example of higher work intensification associated with flexible working is the case of the recently introduced "discretionary time off" policy, aimed at giving employees greater discretion over their vacation time. This policy – adopted by several corporations, including Virgin, General Electric, LinkedIn, and Netflix – provides employees with the freedom to choose how many days off to take without being required to justify their decision (upon the timely delivery of their expected results). While this policy can generate significant benefits for employees and employers, it is also susceptible to abuse; as a result, some companies, like the Chicago Tribune, have decided to discontinue it. Interestingly, and in support of our claim, this abuse came not in the form of employees taking too many days off; rather, many so-called "happy workaholic" employees (Friedman & Lobel, 2003) were taking fewer days off than required, resulting in a significant increase in work intensification and fatigue.

Perceptions of organizational unfairness

Organizational justice reflects employees' perceptions of fairness in three important aspects of the employment relationship: how resources are distributed at work (distributive justice), how decisions about the distribution of those resources are made (procedural justice), and how employees are treated overall in this process (interpersonal justice) (Greenberg & Colquitt, 2005). The current way flexible working policies are designed, and very often implemented, may be at odds with these three important principles, leading to an overall perception of unfairness of the company.

To illustrate, consider the famous *Harvard Business Review* case, Mommy Track Backlash (Hayashi, 2001), frequently used in business school to discuss the breadth and fairness of flexible work options. The case begins with the following quote:

> *Everybody at ClarityBase seemed to understand when one account manager – a working mother – got a special deal: Fridays off, limited travel, easy clients. But when other employees – namely, nonparents – started asking for similar treatment, the company found itself on the brink of an organizational firestorm.*

While it does not directly focus on high- vs. low-skilled employees, this case illustrates the disparity that often exists in the workplace regarding those who are entitled to flexible programmes because of their family situations. Indeed, there is wide consensus among researchers that, in many organizations, flexible working arrangements continue to be designed for employees with family caregiving responsibilities (Blair-Loy & Wharton, 2002) without taking into account the real needs and preferences of employees.

Moreover, since low-skilled employees often occupy temporary positions and work "bad" jobs, they often have very limited access to these policies (Muse & Pichler, 2011). Even when not explicitly excluded, low-skilled employees have *de facto* no entitlement to these programmes. For example, Muse and Pichler (2011) argued that the US Family Medical Leave Act (FMLA), which gives employees up to 12 weeks of unpaid time off for medical conditions (including the birth of a new child), is almost impossible for low-skilled employees to obtain. On the one hand, this act has restrictive eligibility criteria that significantly reduce these employees' potential access to this benefit. On the other hand, taking an unpaid leave of 12 weeks creates significant and often insurmountable financial constraints for low-skilled employees. Therefore, low-skilled employees receive less formal workplace support to meet their work and non-work responsibilities (Griggs et al., 2013).

The perception of unfairness concerns not only employees that have limited access to flexible programmes but also, in some cases, those who actually use them. While in the first case the perception of low fairness concerns the entitlement to flexible working options (i.e., distributive justice) and the procedures followed to grant access to some people and not others (i.e., procedural justice), in the second case the perception of injustice refers to the relations occurring between flexible employees and those with fixed schedules (i.e., interpersonal justice). For instance, prior research (i.e., Golden et al., 2008) has shown that telecommuters tend to experience lower workplace inclusion due to the lack of frequent physical interaction and the jealously of non-teleworking counterparts (Gajendran & Harrison, 2007).

Recommendations

In sum, the effectiveness of flexible working, measured in terms of the potential gains for both employers and employees, is impaired by the unequal access and ability of usage across employees of different skill levels. Before addressing what employers and managers could do to put flexible working in place in the most effective way possible, it is worthwhile to briefly discuss the importance of the external environment of the organizations.

Flexible working, like any other human resource management practice, is implemented and functions within organizational structures and cultures, which are embedded in specific national contexts, encompassing economic, cultural, and institutional factors. These factors shape the way in which flexible working is conceived and implemented across organizations and, therefore, create more or less favourable conditions for workplace intervention (den Dulk et al., 2013). For instance, welfare regimes have been found to influence the level of provision and the range of flexible working arrangements available in the workplace as well as the proportion and profile of the workforce to which flexible working is offered (Abendroth & den Dulk, 2011; Chung, 2019). In addition, industrial relations arrangements (such as the levels and styles of collective bargaining and the power relations between union and employer organizations) and labour laws (e.g., those regulating leave schemes and part-time employment) may alter, in favour of employees, the relative bargaining power over the work schedule (Berg et al., 2014; Budd & Mumford, 2006) and also contribute to tackling unequal access to flexible working across employees of different skill levels (Riva et al., 2018). Labour laws or the agreements produced through collective bargaining have binding effects on employers and guarantee consistent implementation of flexible working. Furthermore, they set standard rights and working conditions, thus ensuring that all employees, irrespective of their skills, have equitable access to more discretion and control over their work schedule.

Having said this, in an attempt to overcome the implementation gap and make flexible working equally usable and used across the workforce, we conclude by presenting some recommendations for successful design and successful workplace implementation.

First, there is reason to believe that it is not sufficient to widen the typology, the scope, and the range of employees benefiting from flexible working arrangements. To really make a change in the effectiveness of flexible working and reduce the implementation gap, it is also necessary to promote a cultural change in organizations (Russo & Morandin, 2019; Williams et al., 2016) to ensure that, after the use of these arrangements, employees do not incur negative evaluations and are not stigmatized because of their choice. A necessary step in this direction consists of discrediting the false assumptions that presentism is associated with better performance and that flexible working is linked to low work commitment (Hideg et al., 2018). Only when employees perceive psychological safety in the use of flexible working arrangements will it be possible to reduce the implementation gap.

Second, although there can be many reasons for enhanced work intensification resulting from the use of flexible working options, technology plays a major role in this process (Morandin et al., 2018). A possible remedy to this situation requires the strong commitment of flexible workers to develop greater awareness of their own connectivity behaviours and to identify specific strategies that can help them reduce the work intensification. For example, Russo, Ollier-Malaterre, and Morandin (2019) found that, on the basis of personal motivation (i.e., improving role performance, enhancing the quality of family relationships, etc.), both the strategies enacted to reduce the dependency on technological devices (e.g., smartphones) and the effectiveness of such strategies can vary. It is thus necessary that flexible workers learn how to better manage expectations of being connected with the stakeholders on the job to prevent their personal lives becoming totally dominated by work. In so doing, they can prevent the autonomy paradox, wherein employees who theoretically have more autonomy due to flexible job configurations end up being even more tied to their work and less able to maintain a healthy work-life balance (Mazmanian et al., 2013).

Finally, we recommend that employers should unlink the provision of flexible working from employees' skill level, as a variety of emotional, manual, cognitive, and creative skills is necessary for organizations to excel. In a rapidly changing environment, emphasis needs to be placed on ensuring that employees of any skill level could be equally eligible to benefit from flexible working options. Since increasing numbers of employees are interested in flexible working regardless of their family or work configuration, a new approach should be used in the design and implementation of flexible working policies in order to make them fairer and more effective. For instance, several scholars suggest that a promising approach could consist of developing idiosyncratic deals, or so-called *ideals* (Rousseau et al., 2006). Ideals, in this context, refer to customized, flexible agreements negotiated by employees and employers on several aspects of the employment relationship, including the work location and schedule as well as the workload, which could be lighter in some stages of the employee's career and life (e.g., after the birth of a child). More specifically, ideals can enable companies to promote flexible solutions that allow them not only to attain organizational goals but also, at the same time, to respond to the employee's mix of personal needs and preferences, thus making it possible to reduce the gap between the intended scope of flexible working and the real outcomes experienced by employees (Kossek & Thompson, 2016). Although high-skilled employees generally have a much better capacity to engage in a fruitful negotiation with employers, it is necessary to extend the range of application of these agreements to all workers, given that the impact of ideals on the improvement of work and family outcomes is strong and important (Las Heras et al., 2017). This could help organizations to create a more inclusive work environment and reduce the perception of organizational unfairness, enabling all employees – especially some engaged in lower-level jobs – to feel valued and cared for by their employer. This is especially important in order to foster greater gender equality in the workplace, as several organizations are now finding that ensuring greater access to flexible work to fathers (who, as mentioned previously, are not the primary target of these interventions) can help to reduce turnover among working mothers and caregivers (Stych, 2019). This could contribute to making the achievement of the desired level of work-life balance a concrete possibility for all rather than a privilege reserved for only a few.

References

Abendroth, A.K. & den Dulk, L. (2011) "Support for the work-life balance in Europe: The impact of state, workplace and family support on work-life balance satisfaction", *Work, Employment & Society*, 25(2), 234–256.

Allen, T.D. & Shockley, K. (2009) "Flexible work arrangements: Help or hype?". In R. Crane & J. Hill (eds), *Handbook of Families and Work: Interdisciplinary Perspectives* (pp. 265–284). Lanham, MD: University Press of America.

Allen, T.D., Johnson, R.C., Kiburz, K.M., & Shockley, K.M. (2013) "Work-family conflict and flexible work arrangements: Deconstructing flexibility", *Personnel Psychology*, 66(2), 345–376.

Berg, P., Bosch, G., & Charest, J. (2014) "Working time configurations: A framework for analyzing diversity across countries", *Industrial & Labour Relations Review*, 67(3), 805–837.

Blair-Loy, M. (2003) *Competing Devotions*. Cambridge, MA: Harvard University Press.

Blair-Loy, M. & Wharton, A.S. (2002) "Employees' use of work- family policies and the workplace social context", *Social Forces*, 80(3), 813–845.

Blau, F.D. & Kahn, L.M. (2013) "Female labor supply: Why is the United States falling behind?", *The American Economic Review*, 103(3), 251–256.

Bloom, N. & Van Reenan, J. (2006) "Management practices, work-life balance, and productivity: A review of some recent evidence", *Oxford Review of Economic Policy*, 22(4), 457–482.

Bourdeau, S., Ollier-Malaterre, A., & Houlfort, N. (2019) "Not all work-life policies are created equal: Career consequences of using enabling versus enclosing work-life policies", *Academy of Management Review*, 44(1), 172–193.

Budd, J.W. & Mumford, K. (2006) "Family-friendly work practices in Britain: Availability and perceived accessibility", *Human Resource Management*, 45(1), 23–42.

Burchell, B. (2002) "The prevalence and redistribution of job insecurity and work intensification". In B. Burchell, D. Ladipo, & F. Wilkinson (eds), *The Prevalence and Redistribution of Job Insecurity and Work Intensification: Job Insecurity and Work Intensification* (pp. 61–76). London: Routledge.

Carver, C.S. & Scheier, M.F. (1982) "Control theory: A useful conceptual framework for personality-social, clinical, and health psychology", *Psychological Bulletin*, 92(1), 111–135.

Chung, H. (2019) "National-level family policies and workers' access to schedule control in a European comparative perspective: Crowding out or in, and for whom?", *Journal of Comparative Policy Analysis: Research and Practice*, 21(1), 25–46.

Chung, H., Kerkhofs, M., & Ester P. (2007) *Working Time Flexibility in European Companies*. Luxembourg: Office for Official Publications of the European Communities.

Cropanzano, R. & Mitchell, M.S. (2005) "Social exchange theory: An interdisciplinary review", *Journal of Management*, *31*(6), 874–900.

den Dulk, L., Groeneveld, S., Ollier-Malaterre A., & Valcour, M. (2013) "National context in work-life research: A multi-level cross-national analysis of the adoption of workplace work-life arrangements in Europe", *European Management Journal*, *31*(5), 478–494.

Dumas, T.L. & Sanchez-Burks, J. (2015) "The professional, the personal, and the ideal worker: Pressures and objectives shaping the boundary between life domains", *The Academy of Management Annals*, *9*(1), 803–843.

Eagly, A.H. & Karau, S.J. (2002) "Role congruity theory of prejudice toward female leaders", *Psychological Review*, *109*(3), 573–598.

Eurofound (2015) *Third European Company Survey. Overview Report: Workplace practices – Patterns, Performance and Well-being*. Luxembourg: Publications Office of the European Union.

Eurofound (2017) *Sixth European Working Conditions Survey. Overview Report (2017 Update)*. Luxembourg: Publications Office of the European Union.

Fonner, K.L. & Stache, L.C. (2012) "All in a day's work, at home: Teleworkers' management of micro role transitions and the work-home boundary", *New Technology, Work and Employment*, *27*(3), 242–257.

Friedman, S.D. & Lobel, S. (2003) "The happy workaholic: A role model for employees", *Academy of Management Executive*, *17*(3), 87–98.

Gajendran, R.S. & Harrison, D.A. (2007) "The good, the bad, and the unknown about telecommuting: Meta-analysis of psychological mediators and individual consequences", *Journal of Applied Psychology*, *92*(6), 1524–1541.

Golden, L. (2008) "Limited access: Disparities in flexible work schedules and work-at-home", *Journal of Family and Economic Issues*, *29*(1), 86–109.

Golden, T.D., Veiga, J.F., & Dino, R.N. (2008) "The impact of professional isolation on teleworker job performance and turnover intentions: Does time spent teleworking, interacting face-to-face, or having access to communication-enhancing technology matter?", *Journal of Applied Psychology*, *93*(6), 1412–1421.

Green, F. (2013) *Skills and Skilled Work: An Economic and Social Analysis*. Oxford: Oxford University Press.

Greenberg, J. & Colquitt, J.A. (2005) *Handbook of Organizational Justice*. Mahwah, NJ: Lawrence Erlbaum Associates.

Griggs, T.L., Casper, W.J., & Eby, L.T. (2013) "Work, family and community support as predictors of work–family conflict: A study of low-income workers", *Journal of Vocational Behavior*, *82*(1), 59–68.

Grover, S.L. & Crooker, K.J. (1995) "Who appreciates family-responsive human resource policies: The impact of family-friendly policies on the organizational attachment of parents and non-parents", *Personnel Psychology*, *48*(2), 271–288.

Hayashi, A.M. (2001) "Mommy-track backlash", *Harvard Business Review*, *79*(3), March, 33–42.

Hideg, I., Kristic, A., Trau, R., & Zarina, T. (2018) "The unintended consequences of maternity leaves: How agency interventions mitigate the negative effects of longer legislated maternity leaves", *Journal of Applied Psychology*, *103*(10), 1155–1164.

Hill, E.J., Grzywacz, J.G., Allen, S., Blanchard, V.L., Matz-Costa, C., Shulkin, S., & Pitt-Catsouphes, M. (2008) "Defining and conceptualizing workplace flexibility", *Community, Work & Family*, *11*(2), 149–163.

Hobfoll, S.E. (1989) "Conservation of resources. A new attempt at conceptualizing stress", *The American Psychologist*, *44*(3), 513–524.

Kattenbach, R., Demerouti, E., & Nachreiner, F. (2010) "Flexible working times: Effects on employees' exhaustion, work-nonwork conflict and job performance", *Career Development International*, *15*(3), 279–295.

Kelliher, C. & Anderson, D. (2010) "Doing more with less? Flexible working practices and the intensification of work", *Human Relations*, *63*(1), 83–106.

Kossek, E.E. & Friede A. (2006) "The business case: Managerial perspectives on work and the family". In M. Pitt-Catsouphes, E.E. Kossek, & S. Sweet (eds), *The Work and Family Handbook* (pp. 611–626). Mahwah, NJ: Lawrence Erlbaum Associates.

Kossek, E.E. & Lautsch, B.A. (2018) "Work-life flexibility for whom? Occupational status and work-life inequality in upper, middle, and lower level jobs", *Academy of Management Annals*, *12*(1), 5–36.

Kossek, E.E. & Thompson, R.J. (2016) "Workplace flexibility: Integrating employer and employee perspectives to close research-practice implementation gap". In T. Allen & L.T. Eby (eds), *The Oxford Handbook of Work and Family* (pp. 255–270). Oxford: Oxford University Press.

Las Heras, M., Rofcanin, Y., Matthijs Bal, P., & Stollberger, J. (2017) "How do flexibility i-deals relate to work performance? Exploring the roles of family performance and organizational context", *Journal of Organizational Behavior*, *38*(8), 1280–1294.

Leslie, L.M., Manchester, C.F., Park, T., & Mehng, S.A. (2012) "Flexible work practices: A source of career premiums or penalties?", *Academy of Management Journal*, *55*(6), 1407–1428.

Lyness, K.S. & Judiesch, M.K. (2008) "Can a manager have a life and a career? International and multisource perspectives on work-life balance and career advancement potential", *The Journal of Applied Psychology*, *93*(4), 789–805.

Mazmanian, M., Orlikowski, W.J., & Yates, J. (2013) "The autonomy paradox: The implications of mobile email devices for knowledge professionals", *Organization Science*, *24*(5), 1337–1357.

de Menezes, L.M. & Kelliher, C. (2011) "Flexible working and performance: A systematic review of the evidence for a business case", *International Journal of Management Reviews*, *13*(4), 452–474.

de Menezes, L.M. & Kelliher, C. (2019) *Flexible Working in Organisations: A Research Overview*. London: Routledge.

Morandin, G., Russo, M., & Ollier-Malaterre, A. (2018) "Put down that phone! Smart use of smartphones for work and beyond", *Journal of Management Inquiry*, *27*(3), 352–356.

Muse, L.A. & Pichler, S. (2011) "A comparison of types of support for lower-skill workers: Evidence for the importance of family supportive supervisors", *Journal of Vocational Behavior*, *79*(3), 653–666.

Payne, J. (2017) "The changing meaning of skill: Still contested, still important". In C. Warhurst, K. Mayhew, D. Finegold, & J. Buchanan (eds), *The Oxford Handbook of Skills and Training* (pp. 54–71). Oxford: Oxford University Press.

Riva, E., Lucchini, M., den Dulk, L., & Ollier-Malaterre, A. (2018) "The skill profile of the employees and the provision of flexible working hours in the workplace: A multilevel analysis across European countries", *Industrial Relations Journal*, *49*(2), 128–152.

Rousseau, D.M., Ho, V.T., & Greenberg, J. (2006), "I-deals: Idiosyncratic terms in employment relationships", *Academy of Management Review*, *31*(4), 977–994.

Rudman, L.A. & Mescher, K. (2013) "Penalizing men who request a family leave: Is flexibility stigma a femininity stigma?", *Journal of Social Issues*, *69*(2), 322–340.

Russo, M. & Morandin, G. (2019) "Better work-life balance starts with manager", *Harvard Business Review*, https://hbr.org/2019/08/better-work-life-balance-starts-with-managers

Russo, M., Ollier-Malaterre, A., & Morandin, G. (2019) "If you want to use your phone less, first figure out why", *Harvard Business Review*, https://hbr.org/2019/06/if-you-want-to-use-your-phone-less-first-figure-out-why?ab=hero-subleft-2

Stych, A. (2019) "More leave for dads means ow turnover for moms", *The Biz Journals*, https://www.bizjournals.com/bizwomen/news/latest-news/2019/06/more-leave-for-dads-means-lowturnover-for-moms.html?page=all

Swanberg, J.E., Pitt-Catsouphes, M., & Drescher-Burke, K. (2005) "A question of justice: Disparities in employees' access to flexible schedule arrangements", *Journal of Family Issues*, *26*(6), 866–895.

Sweet, S., Pitt-Catsouphes, M., Besen, E., & Golden, L. (2014) "Explaining organizational variation in flexible work arrangements: Why the pattern and scale of availability matter", *Community, Work & Family*, *17*(2), 115–141.

Turel, O., Serenko, A., & Bontis, N. (2011) "Family and work-related consequences of addiction to organizational pervasive technologies", *Information & Management*, *48*(2–3), 88–95.

Wharton, A.S., Chivers, S., & Blair-Loy, M. (2008) "Use of formal and informal work-family policies on the digital assembly line", *Work and Occupations*, *35*(3), 327–350.

Williams, J.C., Berdahl, J.L., & Vandello, J.A. (2016) "Beyond work-life 'integration'", *Annual Review of Psychology*, *67*(1), 515–539.

Williams, J.C., Blair-Loy, M., & Berdahl, J.L. (2013) "Cultural schemas, social class, and the flexibility stigma", *Journal of Social Issues*, *69*(2), 209–234.

11 Control over working time – a twenty-first-century issue

Kate Bell

The history of workers' struggles over working time

"Eight hours' work, eight hours' rest, eight hours for what we will." The rallying call of the trade union movement in the late nineteenth-century for an eight-hour day put the issue of working time at the centre of working people's concerns.

When the Trades Union Congress (TUC) was founded in 1868, working hours averaged 62 hours a week. It is therefore unsurprising that campaigns on the length of the working day, crystallised in the eight-hour movement, were one of the trade union movement's early goals.

In 1890, the international trade union movement called for an international demonstration to demand an eight-hour day. But it was not until 1919, and the founding of the International Labour Organisation (ILO), that this was recognised. The first convention of the new tri-partite organisation was on working time ensuring that (with certain exceptions), "the working hours of persons employed in any public or private industrial undertaking or in any branch thereof ... shall not exceed eight in the day and forty-eight in the week" (ILO, 2019).

Improvements in workers' ability to control their working time advanced throughout the century – with new ILO conventions on "weekly rest" (in 1921 and 1957), holidays with pay (1970), night work (1990) and part time work (1994) (ILO, 2019a). Legislation in the UK in 2002 gave workers the right to request more flexible working patterns (Employment Act, 2002). By 2018, almost one in four of the UK workforce was engaged in some form of flexible working arrangement (Low Pay Commission, 2018) and the average working week had almost halved to 32 hours (TUC, 2018).

Contemporary issues in working time

While progress has been made, the battles over working time are far from won. And while the first industrial revolution gave birth to the trade union movement, the fourth industrial revolution, and advances in new technology including the rise of big data, robotics and artificial intelligence are reshaping the terrain on which these battles are fought.

One current issue is the encroachment of work into non-working time. This can lead to additional stress and often leaves workers conducting unpaid labour. The rise of communications technology that enables you to access emails or other work when not in the office means that the end of the working day can be an elastic concept. Research by the Chartered Institute of Personnel and Development (CIPD) in 2017 found that almost a third of workers believed that having remote access to the workplace means they cannot switch off in their personal time. This "always on" culture may also be contributing to the rise in work intensity identified by the Skills and Employment Survey in 2017, which found that "the proportion of workers in jobs where it was required to work at 'very high speed' for most or all of the time rose by 4 percentage points to 31 percent in 2017" (Green et al., 2018). The TUC's own research found that workers in the UK worked two billion hours unpaid in 2018 (Sellers, 2019).

A related issue is the unpredictability of working hours, also enabled by new technological innovations, in particular scheduling systems and platforms that enable faster interactions between an employer and large groups of people. These technologies help to enable extreme forms of labour flexibility, with the primary aim of reducing employer costs. There are now 974,000 people on zero-hours contracts in the UK (Office for National Statistics (ONS), 2020), which provide no guaranteed hours of work each week. This has pushed the risk of managing inconsistent demand within a company from the employer to the worker, who is offered work only within the hours where it is profitable for the employer. Over half of these workers have had a shift cancelled at less than 24 hours' notice, and 75 per cent have been offered work within the same time period, making it hard to plan either working or non-working time (Collinson, 2019).

The rise of platform-based working seeks to follow the same strategy. Work is parcelled into ever smaller tasks, with workers only paid while it can be demonstrated that they are delivering profit for the company. This is not innovation – the dock workers schemes of the nineteenth century saw dockers queuing for work, and only paid once hired. Companies have sought to claim that people working in these forms of work are "independent contractors" and therefore not eligible for the minimum wage and holiday pay – key legal protections that ensure working time is paid. Unions across Europe have been demonstrating in the courts that these claims are bogus. In the UK, a case against Uber found that its drivers should be classified as workers – meaning they are entitled to core protections – rather than as self-employed (though Uber are currently appealing this judgement at the Supreme Court) (British Broadcasting Corporation (BBC), 2018). In the Netherlands, the union Federatie Nederlandse Vakbeweging (FNV) has won a similar case against Deliveroo (Fair Transport Europe, 2019). But as these cases apply to individual workers only, many workers are still missing out on key protections.

Conclusion: a workers' agenda for working time

The early wins for the trade union movement in reducing the working day were won through a combination of collective bargaining at workplace level and campaigning for legal change. Similar strategies will be needed to ensure that today's workers enjoy predictable, paid, shorter working time.

We have already seen some notable union victories. Unions in France were instrumental in winning a "right to switch off" – meaning that employers must negotiate agreements on the use of technology outside working hours with workers (Eurofound, 2014). And union organising has been critical in establishing good practice in many German companies, including in Volkswagen, where the email server is switched off half an hour after the end of the working day (avoiding late night emailing), and Daimler, where any emails received while a staff member is on holiday are responded to with an automatic message telling the sender the email will be deleted (Froger-Michon & Jordan, 2018).

But there is clearly a need for further workplace and legislative change. The ILO's 2019 report on the future of work called for a move towards "expanding time sovereignty," stating that:

> Workers need greater autonomy over their working time, while meeting enterprise needs. Harnessing technology to expand choice and achieve a balance between work and personal life can help them realize this goal and address the pressures that come with the blurring of boundaries between working time and private time. It will take continued efforts to implement maximum limits on working time alongside measures to improve productivity, as well as minimum hour guarantees to create real choices for flexibility and control over work schedules.
>
> (ILO, 2019b, p. 12)

These ambitions could take the form of bans on work practices like zero-hours contracts that do not guarantee workers a minimum number of hours a week. We also need better enforcement of existing working time provisions, including the European working time directive, alongside stronger rights to ensure that working time can be organised in a way that suits the needs of workers. At present in the UK workers have a right to request flexible working after six months in the job. But this request can be turned down if the employer states that it does not fit with the needs of the business, and at present very few jobs at decent rates of pay are advertised as flexible (Timewise, 2016). Stronger rights are needed.

Technology should not only be seen as threatening to roll back hard-won victories in the fight for control over working time. Instead, new innovations and production techniques should give rise to greater productivity at work – just like in the first industrial revolution – and this should enable trade unions to pursue a more ambitious agenda in shortening the working week.

The UK government has estimated that robotics and autonomous systems could deliver a 15 per cent boost in output (gross value added (GVA)) by 2025 (Johnson, 2016) and the consultancy firm PricewaterhouseCoopers (PwC) has estimated that UK gross domestic product (GDP) will be £200 billion higher by 2030 as a result of artificial intelligence (PwC, 2017). One way to share this wealth with the workers who help generate it would be to enable us to work shorter hours for the same pay. The TUC's 150th Congress called for trade unions to set a twenty-first-century ambition for a four-day week. It's an ambition that our history suggests we can achieve.

Recommendations

- Strengthen collective bargaining within firms and across sectors as the most effective way to deliver reductions in working time where desired by workers.
- Ban zero-hours contracts to give workers more control over when they work.
- Set an ambition to deliver shorter working weeks as a key means of sharing the wealth generated by technological innovation.

References

British Broadcasting Corporation (BBC) (19 December 2018) "Uber loses latest legal bid over driver rights" [online]. Available at: https://www.bbc.co.uk/news/business-46617584 [last accessed 16 August 2019].

Chartered Institute of Personnel and Development (CIPD) (2017) "Logged on but can't turn off? A third of UK employees say remote access to work means they can't switch off" [online]. Available at: https://www.cipd.co.uk/about/media/press/270417-remote-work-issues [last accessed 4 July 2019].

Collinson, A. (2019) "Zero hours contracts: Time to stamp them out" [online]. Available at: https://www.tuc.org.uk/blogs/zero-hours-contracts-time-stamp-them-out [last accessed 16 August 2019].

Employment Act (UK) (2002) "c. 47" [online]. Available at: http://www.legislation.gov.uk/ukpga/2002/22/contents [last accessed 20 September 2019].

Eurofound (2014) "France: A legal right to switch off from work" [online]. Available at: https://www.eurofound.europa.eu/fr/publications/article/2014/france-a-legal-right-to-switch-off-from-work [last accessed 16 August 2019].

Fair Transport Europe (15 January 2019) "FNV wins two lawsuits against Deliveroo" [online]. Available at: https://www.fairtransporteurope.eu/fnv-wins-two-lawsuits-against-deliveroo [last accessed 16 August 2019].

Froger-Michon, C. & Jordan, C. (March 29 2018) "Switching on to switching off: Disconnecting employees in Europe?" [online]. Available at: https://www.lexology.com/library/detail.aspx?g=2f2f48c4-9e5b-4a1f-b166-a2b0fec80ce5 [last accessed 4 July 2019].

Green, F., Felstead, A., Gallie, D. & Henseke, G. (2018) *Work Intensity in Britain: First Findings from the Skills and Employment Survey 2017* [online]. Available at: https://www.cardiff.ac.uk/__data/assets/pdf_file/0009/1309455/4_Intensity_Minireport_Final.pdf [last accessed 4 July 2019].

International Labour Organisation (ILO) (1919) "001 – Hours of Work (Industry) Convention, 1919 (No. 1)" [online]. Available at: https://www.ilo.org/dyn/normlex/en/f?p=NORMLEXPUB:12100:0::NO::P12100_ILO_CODE:C001 [last accessed 4 July 2019].

International Labour Organisation (ILO) (2019a) "International labour standards on working time" [online]. Available at: https://www.ilo.org/global/standards/subjects-covered-by-international-labour-standards/working-time/lang--en/index.htm [last accessed 20 September 2019].

International Labour Organisation (ILO) (2019b) *Work for a brighter future – Global Commission on the Future of Work*, Geneva, Switzerland: International Labour Office, p. 12. Available at: https://www.ilo.org/wcmsp5/groups/public/---dgreports/---cabinet/documents/publication/wcms_662410.pdf [last accessed 4 July 2019].

Johnson, J. (2016) "Letter submitted by Jo Johnson MP, Minister of State for Universities Science, Research and Innovation (ROB0076)" [online], Science and Technology Select Committee. Available at: http://data.parliament.uk/writtenevidence/committeeevidence.svc/evidencedocument/scienceand-technology%20-committee/robotics-and-artificial-intelligence/written/37004.pdf [last accessed 4 July 2019].

Low Pay Commission (2018) "A Response to Government on 'One-sided Flexibility'", Table 1 [online]. Available at: https://assets.publishing.service.gov.uk/government/uploads/system/uploads/attachment_data/file/765193/LPC_Response_to_the_Government_on_one-sided_flexibility.pdf [last accessed 4 July 2019].

Office for National Statistics (ONS) (August 2020) "EMP17 People in employment on zero hours contracts" [online]. Available at: https://www.ons.gov.uk/employmentandlabourmarket/peopleinwork/employmentandemployeetypes/datasets/emp17peopleinemploymentonzerohourscontracts [last accessed 16 August 2019].

PricewaterhouseCoopers (PwC) (2017) "The economic impact of artificial intelligence on the UK economy" [online]. Available at: https://www.pwc.co.uk/economic-services/assets/ai-uk-report-v2.pdf [last accessed 4 July 2019].

Sellers, P. (2019) "Work your proper hours day – let's get tough on unpaid overtime" [online]. Available at: https://www.tuc.org.uk/blogs/work-your-proper-hours-day-%E2%80%93-let%E2%80%99s-get-tough-unpaid-overtime-1 [last accessed 4 July 2019].

Timewise (2016) "The Timewise flexible jobs index 2016" [online]. Available at: http://timewise.co.uk/wp-content/uploads/2016/05/Timewise_Flexible_Index_2016.pdf [last accessed 16 August 2019].

Trades Union Congress (TUC) (2018) "A future that works for working people" [online]. Available at: https://www.tuc.org.uk/research-analysis/reports/future-works-working-people [last accessed 4 July 2019].

Part IV

Flexible working for particular groups of workers

12 Supporting employees with invisible disabilities via flexible work

Alexandra Duval, Duygu Biricik Gulseren, and E. Kevin Kelloway

Introduction

Disability is broadly defined as impaired physical or psychological functioning (Bautista et al., 2019). Although traditionally people tend to associate the term 'disability' with visible disabilities such as amputation, or blindness, many disabilities have no visible characteristics. In the literature, the former is referred to as visible and the latter as invisible disability (Saal et al., 2014). Individuals with invisible disabilities face with unique challenges in the workplace. However, researchers as well as managers and policy makers have just recently started recognizing these challenges. Although there are some efforts to define invisible disabilities (Lingsom, 2008) and include them in workplace disability legislation (Catano et al., 2017; McDowell & Fossey, 2015), the needs of employees with invisible disabilities are not yet well understood.

One of the reasons behind the slow, and imperfect, progress addressing the needs of invisibly disabled workers is that the term invisible disabilities covers a diverse group of people with complex needs. From stage 4 cancer to mild depression, invisible disabilities can be in many forms, shapes, and levels (Santuzzi et al., 2014). Moreover, individuals experience each of these disabilities in an idiosyncratic way (i.e. two people with the "exact" same condition can have significantly different capacities (Goodman et al., 2015)). Therefore, finding a common solution to this problem may not be easy.

Efforts to find a common solution that will address the unique needs of all workers with different types of invisible disabilities contribute to the difficulty of finding such a solution. It is an unrealistic objective to expect managers and policy makers to come up with a one-size-fits-all solution when employees with invisible disabilities and their medical professionals struggle to find optimal solutions. Recognizing the diverse needs that can result from a single condition, let alone the many conditions covered under the umbrella term of invisible disabilities, we suggest workplaces provide flexibility (i.e. flexible work arrangements; Timms et al., 2015) to their employees and let them choose the best arrangement that works for them.

Throughout this chapter, we will briefly present the unique challenges associated with invisible disabilities at work. Then, we will provide an overview of different flexible work arrangement types. The third section will explore the barriers preventing individuals with invisible disabilities from accessing flexible work arrangements. The chapter will conclude with recommendations for future research and organizational practice.

Understanding the challenges for workers with invisible disabilities

Invisible disabilities are defined as "a wide range of physical and psychological conditions that often have no visible manifestation or have visible features that are not clearly connected to a disability" (Santuzzi et al., 2014, p. 204). Examples of some conditions which could qualify as an invisible disability include mental health disorders such as attention deficit disorder, or post-traumatic stress disorder, autoimmune diseases such as arthritis or AIDS, other chronic conditions such as cardiovascular disease, multiple chemical sensitivity, allergies, diabetes, or sleep disorders (Santuzzi et al., 2014). As one can see, invisible disabilities covers a wide range of conditions that may prevent people from fully engaging in their work.

The defining characteristics of invisible disabilities is that observers are unable to tell whether a person has a disability or not (Santuzzi et al., 2014). Although this may seem like an unimportant distinction, employees with invisible disabilities experience unique challenges at work. First, invisibly disabled employees can be, and typically are, perceived as healthy, abled individuals (Prince, 2017). Therefore, supervisors may not recognize fluctuations in performance as related to an invisible disability. When a disability is visible, the visual cues serve as a reminder and a form of proof that functional limitations exist and will impact how any employee is able to complete their work (e.g., using an elevator if they are unable to use the stairs). However, when the functional limitation is invisible, observers can easily forget about the disability. Even when workers decide to share their condition with their employers, because it is unseen, managers and colleagues may struggle to understand the difficulties experienced by employees with invisible disabilities (Lindsay et al., 2018). For example, in Biricik Gulseren and Kelloway's (2017) qualitative study on chronic pain sufferers, one participant reported that despite being open and candid about how light triggers her migraines, her colleagues needed to be reminded to leave the lights off every time she had a migraine.

Second, unlike visibly disabled employees, employees with invisible disabilities have the option to withhold their condition from their employer (Bonaccio et al., 2019). Although at first glance, the autonomy of deciding to disclose or not seems like an advantage for invisibly disabled employees, this is problematic from an identity as well as a legal protection perspective. From a legislative perspective, many developed countries such as Canada, the USA, and the UK require disclosure of the disability as the first step in asking for accommodation or adjustments in the workplace (Prince, 2017). Besides accommodation, the positive outcomes of disclosure include legal protection, greater freedom, increased comfort, and reduced stress due to concealment. Additionally, a greater understanding of employee capabilities will allow supervisors to provide the needed supports for performance enhancement and equitable career advancement (Prince, 2017).

Despite the advantages of disclosure, many workers still avoid sharing details of their condition with their employers (Lingsom, 2008). One of the most commonly cited reasons motivating concealment is the fear of stigmatization (Davis, 2005). Stigmatization refers to negative evaluations by others based on an individual's characteristics (Lingsom, 2008). For invisibly disabled employees, fear of stigmatization is common (Davis, 2008; Dimoff et al., 2016). Previous research has confirmed that the fear of stigmatization is grounded. For example, in Pescosolido et al.'s (2010) study, they found that between 47% and 74% of the general public were unwilling to work with a person who has a type of mental disability.

Choosing to conceal one's status as an individual with an invisible disability can result in mental health issues resulting from the gap between disabled identity and abled reputation. Workers with invisible disabilities are likely to incorporate this into their identity and live authentically (Prince, 2017). Additionally, concealing aspects of one's identity is an effortful experience that requires constant monitoring, and active concealment. Several studies show that invisibly disabled individuals suffer from feelings of isolation (Beatty & Kirby, 2006), psychological strain at work (Ragins et al., 2007), and cognitive exhaustion (Smart & Wegner, 2000) due to the mismatch between how they see themselves and how others see them. Some studies have demonstrated higher prevalence rates of mental health issues among invisibly disabled workers compared to those with a visible disability (e.g., Quinn & Ernshaw, 2011).

Invisible disabilities and legislation

In many industrialized countries, such as the United States, Canada, Australia, Europe, and the United Kingdom, employees with disabilities are protected by disability legislation. In general terms the aim of this type of legislation is to prevent discrimination against employees with disabilities. This protection requires employers to provide reasonable accommodation to their employees with disabilities so that they can still be in the workforce.

When one thinks about making the workplace more accessible to employees living with disabilities, the focus is typically on accommodations like elevators and ramps as many associate disabilities with physical limitations. This issue is highlighted in the way disability prevalence data is collected with many measures focusing on physical limitations (Santuzzi et al., 2014). However, legislation on disabilities like the Americans with Disabilities Act Amendments Act of 2008 (ADAAA, 2008) or the Equality Act (2010) have been expanding to include both physical and mental impairments. Under updated legislation, many conditions perhaps not typically associated with disability, which are invisible, are now covered.

The United States enacted the Americans with Disabilities Act of 1990 (ADA, 1990) with the intent of providing individuals with disabilities equal opportunities to work. However, following a series of Supreme Court decisions, the intent behind this act was significantly limited due to ever-narrowing interpretations of the Act. This led to the Americans with Disabilities Act Amendment Act (ADAAA, 2008). Changes in the 2008 Act broaden the scope to apply to individuals with physical or mental impairments that significantly impact major life activities and goes on to clarify that "major life activities include, but are not limited to, caring for oneself, performing manual tasks, seeing, hearing, eating, sleeping, walking, standing, lifting, bending, speaking, breathing, learning, reading, concentrating, thinking, communicating, and working" (ADAAA, 2008). The 2008 Amendment Act further clarifies that major life activities also include "the operation of a major bodily function, including but not limited to, functions of the immune system, normal cell growth, digestive, bowel, bladder, neurological, brain, respiratory, circulatory, endocrine, and reproductive functions" (ADAAA, 2008). In the ten years preceding this amendment, an average of 16,371 charges related to disabilities were brought to the US Equal Employment Opportunity Commission (EEOC), compared to 25,655 cases per year in the ten years since the enactment of the ADAAA (EEOC, 2019). Under this act employers must provide "reasonable accommodation" to employees with disabilities up to the point of "undue hardship" for known disabilities with specific mention that accommodation may include "job restructuring, part-time or modified work schedules" (ADAAA, 2008).

Similarly, the United Kingdom implemented the Disabled Persons Employment Act in 1944, which required all organizations with 20 or more employees to maintain a 3% quota of individuals registered as having a disability. This was replaced by the Disability Discrimination Act (DDA, 1995). An interesting feature of this legislation was the requirement under the Code of Practice that employers try to ascertain the existence of a disability if one was likely to exist (Woodhams & Corby, 2007). The DDA (1995) was most recently replaced by the Equality Act (2010). Though the Equality Act (2010) does not provide a list of examples similar to those found in the ADAAA (2008), it similarly applies to individuals with "physical or mental impairment which has a substantial and long-term adverse effect on his ability to carry out normal day-to-day activities" (Equality Act, 2010, p. 4). Another similarity is the responsibility of the employer to provide accommodation to the point of undue hardship, which is referred to as a duty to make adjustments. The Equality Act (2010) is enforced by Employment Tribunals.

Despite the increased legal protections afforded to individuals with invisible disabilities related to employment and the expansion of protections to include invisible disabilities; individuals living with disabilities continue to be disproportionately excluded from the workforce (Markel & Barclay,

2009). The dearth of research examining the impact of accommodations on the employment circumstances of individuals with invisible disabilities may in part explain the continued discrepancy in employment rates for individuals with and without disabilities. As of the most recent US census information (US Census Bureau, 2018), 81% of individuals without a disability were in the workforce compared to only 41.2% of individuals living with a disability. These statistics may imply that the current accommodation practices are insufficient in supporting workers with disabilities, particularly invisible disability, at work.

Current legislation may also be limited to a narrow focus on accommodation of individuals with disabilities. In a broader context, there is a movement to a more inclusive view (see, for example, the United Nations report, United Nations General Assembly (UNGA), 2018), which encourages the full participation of individuals with disabilities in the workplace. It is likely legislation will increasingly adopt this perspective.

Barriers to accommodation at work

Accommodations facilitate the full employment of individuals living with disabilities. However, access to accommodation has been identified as a key employment barrier (Garcia et al., 2005). The issue of access, however, is complex and represents many different barriers. These barriers are the manifestation of negative attitudes held by supervisors and coworkers (Colella, 2001). Barriers include scepticism, the repetitive need to disclose and request accommodation, attitudinal barriers, identity issues, and work motivation.

Supervisors and coworkers are more likely to be sceptical towards individuals with invisible disabilities, holding them responsible for their limitations (Colella & Stone, 2005). Negative perceptions are exacerbated by a predominance of individuals with invisible disabilities choosing not to disclose their condition unless it begins to affect their work (Beatty & Joffee, 2006). Colella (2001) noted that peers and coworkers are more likely to suspect an individual with an invisible disability of faking. Interestingly, this fallacy can be so strong that despite clear evidence of an invisible disability, an employee may still be perceived as a "liar" (Santuzzi et al., 2014). For example, in a study on accommodation fairness, researchers had to remove some participants from analysis because they simply did not believe that the individual receiving accommodation had an invisible disability, *despite having been told they did* (Paetzold et al., 2008). The issue is further highlighted in a qualitative analysis on invisible disabilities with participants saying that a significant barrier in accessing accommodations was policing by others (i.e. family, friends, and coworkers) regarding their actual need for such accommodations (Kattari et al., 2018). For example, some individuals with invisible disabilities did not feel they could use disability seating when commuting to work. Because their condition is invisible, they feared negative reactions from fellow commuters (Lacaille et al., 2007).

Furthermore, as Beatty and Kirby (2006) argue, disclosure is neither a binary concept nor a one-time event. As supervisors and coworkers change or as symptoms related to the invisible disability fluctuate, employees with invisible disabilities are repeatedly required to decide whether or not they will out themselves. If they choose to disclose, the next decision relates to whether or not they will seek an accommodation. Many invisible disabilities, such as chronic pain and anxiety disorder, often ebb and flow (Vajravelu et al., 2016); thus, the need for accommodations also fluctuate (Santuzzi et al., 2014). Need fluctuations may happen over longer periods of time or could vary weekly or even daily (Beatty & Joffe, 2006). The transience or fluctuation in support needs means that the employees must ask for accommodation every time there is a need. For example, an employee with migraines may need to leave work early and make up the missed work time later. If migraines occur regularly, three times a week for example, this employee will need to ask for an accommodation three times in the same week. That means she or he will have to disclose the condition to the employer three times a week, which is likely to force the employee to give unwanted details about their condition.

In addition to external barriers, individuals may internally struggle with the disability label (Kattari et al., 2018). During multiple focus groups, with individuals working with arthritis, an issue discussed was reluctance to use disability seating in public transportation. Though this was in part motivated, as discussed above, by fear of judgement from others it also represented an identity struggle. Despite the fact that prolonged standing increased their pain levels, they reported experiencing feelings of guilt and shame for using available disability seating. This internal clash is potentially motivated by a rejection of the disability label (Lacaille et al., 2007).

Much like the identity issues discussed above, the desire to be a good team member and employee can also generate internal struggle that manifests as an accommodation barrier. This is evident in the many team- and organizational-based factors that are considered when making an accommodation request. Employees have been found to consider both the cost to the organization and any inconvenience they perceive it may cause for supervisors, coworkers or clients (Baldridge & Veiga, 2006). Despite real accommodation needs even minor costs can result in employees choosing not to access accommodations. Additionally, belief that an accommodation, if granted, would have an impact on supervisors and coworkers also motivated withholding of accommodation requests (Baldridge & Veiga, 2006). In the next section we will propose flexible work arrangements as a potential solution to prevent the challenges outlined above. Flexible work arrangements are a promising way of accommodating employees with invisible disabilities.

Flexible work arrangements

The term "flexible work arrangements" refers to different systems put in place by employers to provide flexibility to their employees at work (Timms et al., 2015). In general, flexible work arrangements allow employees to set their own hours and work from a location that is convenient for them. The most commonly known flexible work arrangements include working from home (i.e. telework; Anderson et al., 2015), starting and finishing the work at non-standard hours (i.e. flextime; Spieler et al., 2017), or working long hours some days to take extended weekend breaks (i.e. compressed work weeks; Wadsworth & Facer, 2016). Flexible leave (e.g., short-term family responsibility leave, education leave, court leave) and flexible rest periods (e.g., division of vacation leave, postpone or interrupt vacation leave if eligible for another leave; Mihychuk, 2016) are also considered as flexible work arrangements. Flexible work arrangements can be part of an organization's official policies and procedures. It can also be organized between supervisors and employees informally (Weeden, 2005). Although some organizations may offer multiple types of flexible work arrangements (i.e. flextime and telecommute), others may only offer one (e.g., compressed work weeks).

An initiative at an American Fortune 500 company addresses this issue with a deliberate cultural overhaul. The company decided to shift the focus away from where and when people were getting their work done and instead focus on outcomes. This initiative aimed at creating a Results Only Work Environment (ROWE) where changes in work hours and location were the norm and did not need to be requested (Moen et al., 2013). This initiative resulted in many positive health outcomes for participants over time including smoking reduction/cessation, reduced alcohol consumption, reduced work-family conflict, increased exercise, increased perceptions of sufficient sleep, and time to cook healthy meals.

Flexible work arrangements serve as recruitment and retention tools for current and prospective employees (Thompson et al., 2015). Flexible work arrangements represent part of the organizational script whereby organizations communicate to their employees that they are valued and respected (Beatty & Joffee, 2006). The available evidence on the effectiveness of the flexible work arrangements is promising. For example, research conducted across multiple countries demonstrated that flexible work arrangements enabled employees to work the equivalent of up to two additional work days without experiencing work-life conflict (Hill et al., 2010). This research found that flexible work arrangements were maximized when employed synergistically (i.e. flexible location and flexible scheduling).

Several studies also reported positive outcomes of individual flexible work arrangement types. For example, Coenen and Kok (2014) observed that telework increased new product development performance through increased functional cooperation among team members, knowledge sharing, and inter-organizational involvement. Similarly, Bloom, Liang, Roberts, and Ying (2014) found that working from home increased the job performance of a sample of call centre employees in China. In another study, Gajendran, Harrison, and Delaney-Klinger (2015) showed that telework increased task and contextual job performance via increased autonomy perceptions. Besides enhanced performance, research shows that telework is also associated with other desired outcomes such as work-family effectiveness (Kossek et al., 2006), job satisfaction (Azar et al., 2018), organizational commitment (Harker Martin & MacDonnell, 2012), perceived autonomy (Gajendran & Harrison, 2007), and concentration (Biron & van Veldhoven, 2016). Reduced role stress (Gajendran & Harrison, 2007) and less need for recovery (Biron & van Veld-hoven, 2016) are also listed as favourable outcomes of telework.

Not only telework, but also other types of flexible work arrangements have encouraging results. For example, Casper and Harris (2008) demonstrated a positive relationship between flexible work schedules and affective organizational commitment (i.e. feeling emotionally attached to, and identifying with the goals of, the organization) (Allen & Meyer, 1990). Similarly, Halpern (2005) observed that flextime leads to reduced work stress, higher organizational commitment, and fewer days lost to absenteeism and tardiness. Similarly, the meta-analytic research on flextime has found that it can improve performance, job satisfaction, as well as decrease absenteeism (Baltes et al., 1999). Lastly, McNall, Nicklin, and Masuda (2010) demonstrated that even the existence of flexible work arrangements such as flextime and compressed work weeks was related to higher job satisfaction and reduced turnover.

Flexible work arrangements to support employees with invisible disabilities

Researchers have primarily focused on the potential for flexible work arrangements to diminish conflict between work and non-work life (Las Heras et al., 2017). Although a focus on reducing work/non-work conflict is laudable, it may miss the opportunity to understand and directly address the diverse needs of employees beyond familial or leisure activities. In particular, a focus on work-family issues may fail to recognize the spectrum of abilities employees have and the differing ways people can equally contribute. Workers with invisible disabilities are likely to benefit from flexible arrangements as control/flexibility are particularly important when managing invisible disabilities (Lacaille et al., 2007).

The availability of flexible work arrangements provides more autonomy to the employees over their work time and location and can benefit many different invisible disabilities (Timms et al., 2015). An example from clinical practice is a client living with Obsessive Compulsive Disorder (OCD) who, while driving, felt compelled to retrace her steps to ensure she had not hit anyone, which caused her to be late for work (Neal-Barnett & Mendelson, 2003). She could benefit from flexible scheduling that enabled her to travel to work outside of traffic windows (i.e. flextime) or, if possible, could benefit from working from home (i.e. flexplace or telework). Another example could be an individual living with arthritis who struggles in the morning when they are especially stiff, which makes getting ready and commuting to work very challenging and painful. For this individual, starting work later – through flexible scheduling – could contribute to improved quality of life and work outcomes (Lacaille et al., 2007).

The availability and use of flexible work arrangements can address many of the challenges of invisible work disabilities. First, employees with invisible disabilities may not feel compelled to disclose their conditions to their employer as long as the available options accommodate their needs. For example, flextime can empower employees to stop working and take care of themselves as needed. Similarly, telework allows them to create the optimal work atmosphere (e.g., reduced noise, lighting, scents). Diverse flexibility options enable employees with invisible disabilities to maintain their confidentiality if that is their desire.

Moreover, flexible work arrangements allow employees with invisible disabilities to manage their work performance. Instead of being forced to work by organizationally defined terms, employees can manage the demands of their condition and work more efficiently (Timms et al., 2015). Employees with visible conditions can also benefit, achieving higher work performance when they are given the opportunity to use their resources such as time, energy, and health autonomously.

Lastly, flexible work arrangements can take the pressure of finding reasonable accommodations off the shoulders of managers. Instead of trying to create resources that will address the unique needs of their employees with invisible disabilities, managers can let the employees find the arrangement that works best for them. For example, by allowing telework, an employee with back pain can create their optimal work setting (e.g., purchasing an ergonomic chair, working from bed, switching positions during the day). This way, the employer enjoys the benefits of increased productivity and decreased administrative burden.

Despite the many potential advantages, there is currently a substantial gap in research related to the impact that flexible work arrangements have on individuals with invisible disabilities. As discussed above, flexible work arrangements have the potential to provide much needed support to individuals living with invisible disabilities, which could enable them to join and remain in the workforce. Beatty and Joffe (2006) note that the lack of research on the impact of invisible disability on work outcomes may in part stem from a belief that people with invisible disabilities leave the workforce or are so few as to not substantially impact organizational outcomes. What little research does exist points to many potential benefits for individuals with invisible disabilities given the opportunity to use flexible work arrangements.

Conclusion

Invisible disabilities are unique in that they provide no external markers of limited functionality. Moreover, the functional limitation associated with a disability such as chronic pain may vary from day to day or with the nature of the task. As a result, it is difficult to craft an accommodation that suits a wide variety of disabilities, and individuals experiencing an invisible disability may be reluctant to self-identify as an individual requiring such accommodation. Widely available flexible work arrangements offer considerable potential for allowing individuals with invisible disabilities to craft an employment experience that maximizes their participation in the workforce without experiencing the potentially negative consequences of self-disclosure.

Recommendations

Research

Perhaps the most overriding need is the need for research to focus on and distinguish between visible and invisible disabilities. Such research may require specialized recruiting as those with invisible disabilities may be reluctant to self-identify. However, a specific focus on invisible disabilities is required in order to understand the different experiences and challenges posed by invisible disabilities. Moreover, more focused research would be useful in exploring the use, benefits, and outcomes associated with flexible work arrangements by individuals with invisible disabilities.

Practice

In practice, employees with invisible disabilities would benefit from having access to a range of flexible work arrangements so that they could craft their work experience to fit with their health status. Flexible work arrangements that are available to all employees would minimize the need for individuals to self-identify as having a disability. Moreover, the availability of flexible work arrangements for all employees would limit the need for individual employees to justify their use of an alternate schedule or work arrangement.

References

Allen, N.J. & Meyer, J.P. (1990). The measurement and antecedents of affective, continuance and normative commitment to the organization. *Journal of Occupational Psychology, 63*(1), 1–18.

Americans with Disabilities Act of 1990 (ADA) (1991). Pub. L. No. 101–336, §2, 104 Stat. 328.

Americans with Disabilities Act Amendments Act of 2008 (ADAAA) (2008). Pub. L. No. 110–325, 122 Stat. 3553.

Anderson, A.J., Kaplan, S.A., & Vega, R.P. (2015). The impact of telework on emotional experience: When, and for whom, does telework improve daily affective well-being? *European Journal of Work and Organizational Psychology, 24*(6), 882–897.

Azar, S., Khan, A., & van Eerde, W. (2018). Modelling linkages between flexible work arrangements' use and organizational outcomes. *Journal of Business Research, 91*, 134–143.

Baldridge, D. & Veiga, J. (2006). The impact of anticipated social consequences on recurring disability accommodation requests. *Journal of Management*, *32*(1), 158–179.

Baltes, B., Briggs, T., Huff, J., & Neuman, G. (1999). Flexible and compressed work-week schedules: A meta-analysis of their effects on work-related criteria. *Journal of Applied Psychology*, *84*(4), 496–513.

Bautista, A.F., Abd-Elsayed, A., & Chang Chien, G.C. (2019). Psychosocial factors as the main determinant of disability. In A. Abd-Elsayed (ed.), *Pain: A Review Guide* (pp. 1065–1067). Cham, Switzerland: Springer.

Beatty, J.E. & Joffe, R. (2006). An overlooked dimension of diversity: The career effects of chronic illness. *Organizational Dynamics*, *35*(2), 182–195.

Beatty, J.E. & Kirby, S.L. (2006). Beyond the legal environment: How stigma influences invisible identity groups in the workplace. *Employee Responsibilities and Rights Journal*, *18*(1), 29–44.

Biricik Gulseren, D. & Kelloway, E.K. (2017). Working through pain: The experience of chronic pain in the workplace. Poster presented at the Occupational Health Summer Institute, Halifax, Canada.

Biron, M. & van Veldhoven, M. (2016). When control becomes a liability rather than an asset: Comparing home and office days among part-time teleworkers. *Journal of Organizational Behavior*, *37*(8), 1317–1337.

Bloom, N., Liang, J., Roberts, J., & Ying, Z.J. (2014). Does working from home work? Evidence from a Chinese experiment. *The Quarterly Journal of Economics*, *130*(1), 165–218.

Bonaccio, S., Lapierre, L., & O'Reilly, J. (2019). Creating work climates that facilitate and maximize the benefits of disclosing mental health problems in the workplace. *Organizational Dynamics*, *48*(3), 113–122. https://doi.org/10.1016/j.orgdyn.2019.03.006

Casper, W.J. & Harris, C.M. (2008). Work-life benefits and organizational attachment: Self-interest utility and signaling theory models. *Journal of Vocational Behavior*, *72*(1), 95–109.

Catano, V., Kelloway, E.K., Biricik Gulseren, D., Day, A., Cameron, J., & Francis, L. (2017). The duty to accommodate psychological disorders and Canadian workplaces (unpublished).

Coenen, M. & Kok, R.A. (2014). Workplace flexibility and new product development performance: The role of telework and flexible work schedules. *European Management Journal*, *32*(4), 564–576.

Colella, A. (2001). Coworker distributive fairness judgments of the workplace accommodation of employees with disabilities. *The Academy of Management Review*, *26*(1), 100–116.

Colella, A. & Stone, D.L. (2005). Workplace discrimination toward persons with disabilities: A call for some new research directions. In R.L. Dipboye & A. Colella (eds), *Discrimination at Work: The Psychological and Organizational Bases* (pp. 227–253). Mahwah, NJ: Lawrence Erlbaum Associates.

Davis, N.A. (2005). Invisible disability. *Ethics*, *116*(1), 153–213.

Dimoff, J.K., Kelloway, E.K., & Burnstein, M.D. (2016). Mental health awareness training (MHAT): The development and evaluation of an intervention for workplace leaders. *International Journal of Stress Management*, *23*(2), 167–189.

Disability Discrimination Act 1995 (DDA) (1995). Retrieved from: http://www.legislation.gov.uk/ukpga/1995/50/pdfs/ukpga_19950050_en.pdf

Equality Act (2010). London: The Stationery Office Limited.

Gajendran, R.S. & Harrison, D.A. (2007). The good, the bad, and the unknown about telecommuting: Meta-analysis of psychological mediators and individual consequences. *Journal of Applied Psychology, 92*(6), 1524–1541.

Gajendran, R.S., Harrison, D.A., & Delaney-Klinger, K. (2015). Are telecommuters remotely good citizens? Unpacking telecommuting's effects on performance via i-deals and job resources. *Personnel Psychology, 68*(2), 353–393.

Garcia, M.F., Paetzold, R.L., & Colella, A. (2005). The relationship between personality and peers' judgments of the appropriateness of accommodations for individuals with disabilities. *Journal of Applied Social Psychology, 35*(7), 1418–1439.

Goodman, R.A., Posner, S.F., Huang, E.S., Parekh, A.K., & Koh, H.K. (2013). Defining and measuring chronic conditions: Imperatives for research, policy, program, and practice. *Preventing Chronic Disease, 10*, E66.

Halpern, D.F. (2005). Psychology at the intersection of work and family: Recommendations for employers, working families, and policymakers. *American Psychologist, 60*(5), 397–409.

Harker Martin, B. & MacDonnell, R. (2012). Is telework effective for organizations? A meta-analysis of empirical research on perceptions of telework and organizational outcomes. *Management Research Review, 35*(7), 602–616.

Hill, E., Erickson, J., Holmes, E., & Ferris, M. (2010). Workplace flexibility, work hours, and work-life conflict: Finding an extra day or two. *Journal of Family Psychology, 24*(3), 349–358.

Kattari, S., Olzman, M., & Hanna, M. (2018). "You Look Fine!": Ableist experiences by people with invisible disabilities. *Affilia, 33*(4), 477–492.

Kossek, E.E., Lautsch, B.A., & Eaton, S.C. (2006). Telecommuting, control, and boundary management: Correlates of policy use and practice, job control, and work–family effectiveness. *Journal of Vocational Behavior, 68*(2), 347–367.

Lacaille, D., White, M., Backman, C., & Gignac, M. (2007). Problems faced at work due to inflammatory arthritis: New insights gained from understanding patients' perspective. *Arthritis Care & Research, 57*(7), 1269–1279.

Las Heras, M., Rofcanin, Y., Matthijs Bal, P., & Stollberger, J. (2017). How do flexibility i-deals relate to work performance? Exploring the roles of family performance and organizational context. *Journal of Organizational Behavior, 38*(8), 1280–1294.

Lindsay, S., Cagliostro, E., & Carafa, G. (2018). A systematic review of workplace disclosure and accommodation requests among youth and young adults with disabilities. *Disability and Rehabilitation, 40*(25), 2971–2986.

Lingsom, S. (2008). Invisible impairments: Dilemmas of concealment and disclosure. *Scandinavian Journal of Disability Research, 10*(1), 2–16.

McDowell, C. & Fossey, E. (2015). Workplace accommodations for people with mental illness: A scoping review. *Journal of Occupational Rehabilitation, 25*(1), 197–206.

McNall, L.A., Nicklin, J.M., & Masuda, A.D. (2010). A meta-analytic review of the consequences associated with work–family enrichment. *Journal of Business and Psychology, 25*(3), 381–396.

Markel, K. & Barclay, S. (2009). Addressing the underemployment of persons with disabilities: Recommendations for expanding organizational social responsibility. *Employee Responsibilities and Rights Journal, 21*(4), 305–318.

Mihychuk, M. (2016). Flexible work arrangements: What was heard. Retrieved from: https://www.canada.ca/en/employment-social-development/services/consultations/what-was-heard.html#h2.0

Moen, P., Fan, W., & Kelly, E.L. (2013). Team-level flexibility, work–home spillover, and health behavior. *Social Science & Medicine, 84,* 69–79.

Neal-Barnett, A. & Mendelson, L. (2003). Obsessive compulsive disorder in the workplace. *Women & Therapy, 26*(1–2), 169–178.

Paetzold, R., Garcia, M., Colella, A., Ren, L., Triana, M., & Ziebro, M. (2008). Perceptions of people with disabilities: When is accommodation fair? *Basic and Applied Social Psychology, 30*(1), 27–35.

Pescosolido, B.A., Martin, J.K., Long, J.S., Medina, T.R., Phelan, J.C., & Link, B.G. (2010). "A disease like any other"? A decade of change in public reactions to schizophrenia, depression, and alcohol dependence. *American Journal of Psychiatry, 167*(11), 1321–1330.

Prince, M.J. (2017). Workplace accommodation of persons with invisible disabilities: A literature review. *Journal of Vocational Rehabilitation, 46*(1), 77–86.

Quinn, D.M. & Earnshaw, V.A. (2011). Understanding concealable stigmatized identities: The role of identity in psychological, physical, and behavioral outcomes. *Social Issues and Policy Review, 5*(1), 160–190.

Ragins, B.R., Singh, R., & Cornwell, J.M. (2007). Making the invisible visible: Fear and disclosure of sexual orientation at work. *Journal of Applied Psychology, 92*(4), 1103–1118.

Saal, K., Martinez, L.R., & Smith, N.A. (2014). Visible disabilities: Acknowledging the utility of acknowledgment. *Industrial and Organizational Psychology, 7*(2), 242–248.

Santuzzi, A., Waltz, P., Finkelstein, L., & Rupp, D. (2014). Invisible disabilities: Unique challenges for employees and organizations. *Industrial and Organizational Psychology, 7*(2), 204–219.

Smart, L. & Wegner, D.M. (2000). The hidden costs of hidden stigma. In T.F. Heatherton, R.E. Kleck, M.R. Hebl, & J.G. Hull (eds), *The Social Psychology of Stigma* (pp. 220–242). New York: Guilford Press.

Spieler, I., Scheibe, S., Stamov-Rossnagel, C., & Kappas, A. (2017). Help or hindrance? Day-level relationships between flextime use, work–nonwork boundaries, and affective well-being. *Journal of Applied Psychology, 102*(1), 67–87.

Thompson, R.J., Payne, S.C., & Taylor, A.B. (2015). Applicant attraction to flexible work arrangements: Separating the influence of flextime and flexplace. *Journal of Occupational and Organizational Psychology, 88*(4), 726–749.

Timms, C., Brough, P., O'Driscoll, M., Kalliath, T., Siu, O.L., Sit, C., & Lo, D. (2015). Flexible work arrangements, work engagement, turnover intentions and psychological health. *Asia Pacific Journal of Human Resources, 53*(1), 83–103.

United Nations General Assembly (UNGA) (2018). *United Nations 2018 flagship report on disability and development: Realization of the Sustainable Development Goals by, for and with persons with disabilities,* UN Doc. A/73/220.

US Census Bureau (2018). American Community Survey 1-Year Estimates. Retrieved from: https://www.census.gov/library/visualizations/2018/comm/disability.html

US Equal Employment Opportunity Commission (EEOC) (2019). Americans with Disabilities Act of 1990 (ADA) Charges (Charges filed with EEOC) (includes concurrent charges with Title VII, ADEA, EPA, and GINA) FY 1997–FY 2018. Retrieved from: https://www.eeoc.gov/eeoc/statistics/enforcement/ada-charges.cfm

Vajravelu, S., O'Brien, K., Moll, S., & Solomon, P. (2016). The impact of the episodic nature of chronic illness: A comparison of Fibromyalgia, Multiple Sclerosis and Human Immunodeficiency Virus (HIV). *Edorium Journal of Disability and Rehabilitation*, *2*, 53–65.

Wadsworth, L.L. & Facer, R.L. (2016). Work–family balance and alternative work schedules: Exploring the impact of 4-day workweeks on state employees. *Public Personnel Management*, *45*(4), 382–404.

Weeden, K. (2005). Is there a flexiglass ceiling? Flexible work arrangements and wages in the United States. *Social Science Research*, *34*(2), 454–482.

Woodhams, C. & Corby, S. (2007). Then and now: Disability legislation and employers' practices in the UK. *British Journal of Industrial Relations*, *45*(3), 556–580.

13 Workers with disabilities

The role of flexible employment schemes

Eleftherios Giovanis and Oznur Ozdamar

Introduction

The International Classification of Functioning, Disability and Health (ICF) defines disability as problems in human functioning that are categorised as impairments, activity limitations and participation restrictions. Participation restriction specifically includes problems with involvement in any area of life, such as facing discrimination in employment. According to the World Health Organization (WHO) in 2010, approximately 1 billion people, which consists of 15 percent of the global population, have some form of disability and employment rates for people with disabilities are below that of the overall population (WHO, 2011). The ratio of the employment rate of people with disabilities to the employment rate of people without disabilities ranges between 0.46 to 0.91 for the population aged 20–54 in European Countries (Scharle & Csillag, 2016).

One of the biggest challenges for labour market policies has always been the integration of disabled people. Disabled people facing barriers and possible discrimination in the labour market are likely to remain unemployed, especially in the long-term, which has adverse consequences for the individual, the society and the economic system. Therefore, some governments pay special attention to people with disabilities who need to be better integrated into the labour market. For instance, encouraging full participation of people with disabilities in the labour market is a key element of EU policies (Official Journal of EU, Art. 8, 2003).

Policies addressing disabled people are various in the form of *active labour market policies*, such as "supported employment", which supports the adaptation of the person in the workplace, "subsidised employment" that removes barriers during the recruitment processes, "vocational rehabilitation and training", which aims to improve the job skills of the people with disabilities, "quota schemes" that require employers to employ a certain minimum number of *workers* ensuring that a given proportion of *employees* consists of designated *persons* with *disabilities. Other policies* include "anti-discrimination schemes", which provide conditions for equal participation to work and "flexible employment schemes (flexible working conditions)", which refers to flexible working hours and working at home or other remote locations instead of the firm's premises.

Sheltered employment, incentives for job search assistance and counselling and for start-ups are also other examples of the active labour market policies (Thornton & Lunt, 1997; Greve, 2009; WHO, 2011). Moreover, there are *passive labour market policies* where disabled people rely on social benefits, such as unemployment, disability, sickness and injury allowances. The main criticism of social benefits is that they may prevent the unemployed from searching for jobs, therefore increasing unemployment duration and demotivating the unemployed from returning to work (Ljungqvist & Sargent, 2008). The evidence shows that the employment rates among disabled people were higher in countries in which spending on "active" labour policies was the highest, such as Sweden and Denmark compared with France, Greece, Italy and the UK (Eurostat, 2011).

The use of flexible employment schemes is one of the active labour market policies and this chapter discusses its role on the labour outcomes of disabled workers, such as job satisfaction, absenteeism, employee loyalty and performance at work. The evaluation of flexible employment schemes will be carried out based on earlier studies in the related literature and the empirical work done by Giovanis and Ozdamar (2019). A number of qualitative research studies based on interviews with disabled people show that more flexible working conditions would be extremely valuable due to various problems, such as accessibility, transportation, physical conditions of many working places, stigma and discriminatory practices, that exist in the workplace (Leicester, 1999; Marsay, 2014).

Positive inference from this chapter's evaluation about flexible employment schemes would provide some supportive evidence for their assumptive benefits and would be suggestive for starting to remove barriers to using them. The traditional work environment has barriers such as culture of presenteeism, a risk-averse culture, a lack of guidance at the level of individual employee and a lack of senior sponsorship at the highest level of a company to undertake flexible employment schemes (Future of Work Institute, 2012). Moreover, there are barriers for employees to request work flexibility in many countries in the world except for selected countries, such as New Zealand, Australia and the European Union member states, where all employees have the legal right to request a flexible work arrangement.[1] Thus, revealing the positive effect of flexible employment schemes on labour outcomes would confront and overcome those barriers.

The role of flexible employment in job satisfaction

Job satisfaction is an indicator that shows how an employee is content, satisfied and self-motivated with the job he/she does. There are factors (inputs and outputs) affecting job satisfaction and it changes based on the balance between *work-role inputs* (such as education, working time, effort) and *work-role outputs* (such as wages, work compensation, job security, promotion opportunities, job interest, independent work, feeling useful to society, good relationship with managers and colleagues – organisational socialisation). An increase in the *work-role outputs* increases job satisfaction level, while an increase in the *work-role inputs* decreases the level of satisfaction (Sousa-Poza & Sousa-Poza, 2000). Considering job satisfaction in the disability context, the *work-role inputs* category can include more factors for the people with disabilities unlike people without any physical or mental impairment. Physical and attitude obstacles, impairments and health problems that restrict daily activities and productivity, absence of proper accommodation and training in the workplace can be examples of factors that lower job satisfaction.

The findings of the empirical research in job satisfaction between disabled workers and their counterparts supports contradictory conclusions. The first conclusion of the related research is that workers with disabilities are more satisfied with their job. This is explained by the fact that people with disabilities have lower expectations due to their disadvantaged situation and position in the workplace and in society (Pagán & Malo, 2009). This is consistent with the theoretical perspective of the lower expectations, where members belonging to disadvantaged groups, such as disabled, low income and those with low educational attainment level, tend to be much happier to have a job at all, leading to higher levels of job satisfaction compared to those belonging to advantaged socio-economic groups (Giovanis & Ozdamar, 2019). Empirically this is supported in previous studies. Perry, Hendricks and Broadbent (2000) used a sample of college students who graduated from a large public midwestern university – without revealing which one – between 1951 and 1993. The authors found higher levels of job satisfaction in graduates with physical disabilities compared to their non-disabled peers when access discrimination was controlled for. Similarly, Pagán and Malo (2009), using data for Spain derived from the European Community Household Panel during the period of 1995–2001, found that disabled workers report high levels of job satisfaction when they control for productivity differences.

The second conclusion of the related research is that workers with disabilities are more satisfied with their job compared to the workers without disabilities. Due to *health restrictions, absence of assistive technology, wage inequality* and *difficulties in socialising in organisations*, workers with disabilities report lower levels of job satisfaction compared to their non-disabled counterparts (McAfee & McNaughton, 1997; Uppal, 2005). Considering the dissatisfaction effects of disability, it is important to explore the relationship between flexible employment schemes and job satisfaction for two main reasons. First, improvement in job satisfaction will help to reduce the dissatisfaction gap between disabled and non-disabled workers. Second, job satisfaction is a strong driver of employee loyalty and absenteeism and hence, of performance at work. More satisfied workers who perform better will also contribute positively to the firm performance.

Various studies emphasise the importance of working flexibility for the successful inclusion of people with disabilities (Wooten, 2008; Kulkarni & Lengnick-Hall, 2011). However, even though there is a growing interest in the implementation of flexible employment schemes, especially in the USA, there are few research studies exploring their relationship to job satisfaction of disabled workers around the globe. Therefore, based on three reasons (*health restrictions, absence of assistive technology* and *wage inequality*) that create job dissatisfaction for disabled workers, this section reveals how flexible employment schemes can be useful to solve dissatisfaction problems.

As the first reason of dissatisfaction, *health restrictions* reduce not only job satisfaction, but also the overall life satisfaction (Faragher, Cass & Cooper, 2005). If health restrictions are due to the physical conditions (e.g. mobility disability), flexible employment arrangements, such as teleworking, can be beneficial for both disabled workers and the for employer, increasing the job and life satisfaction of the worker.

Wage inequality between people with disabilities and non-disabilities is shown as the second reason for job dissatisfaction. McAfee and McNaughton (1997), using data on 236 individuals from 159 businesses in the US, revealed that disabled workers expressed strong dissatisfaction with pay and mild dissatisfaction with promotions. It is empirically documented that workers with disabilities earn lower salaries than non-disabled people (Hale, Hayghe & McNeil, 1998; Baldwin & Johnson, 2006). Regarding the pay and promotion dissatisfaction, flexible employment schemes might act again as one possible solution. If wages and promotions are determined based on the performance rather than the number of working hours, or presence in the employer's premises, disabled workers may exhibit higher levels of job satisfaction within the wage flexibility environment[2] (Ali, Schur & Blanck, 2011).

As the third reason for the dissatisfaction, Uppal (2005) found that *absence of assistive technology* in the workplace increased the dissatisfaction of disabled workers. Although, the role of flexible employment schemes on job satisfaction is not analysed, flexible employment arrangements can be a solution reducing the negative consequences of the absence of these technologies. This is especially the case where disabled workers have specific technological needs due to certain health limitations (Stone & Colella, 1996; Böhm et al., 2011; Baumgärtner, Böhm & Dwertmann, 2014), such as elevators or ramps and adjustable height desks. Their absence in the work environment can create job dissatisfaction and the solution can be suitable accommodations (e.g. home/ office endowed with these technologies) provided with flexible employment schemes (Wooten, 2008; Boehm et al., 2014). Assistive technologies are technical solutions and one of the main types of reasonable accommodation that can assist individuals with disabilities to succeed in their jobs. Under the EU's Employment Equality Directive (The Council of the European Union, 2000), employers have to provide reasonable accommodation to employees with disabilities. Reasonable accommodation is also an obligation under Article 5 of the United Nations Convention on the Rights of Persons with Disabilities (2007).[3] Besides technical solutions, working arrangements, such as flexible working hours are also one of the important types of the reasonable accommodation. Thus, absence of conditions, equipment and technical environments for disabled workers can be substituted with flexible working arrangements, such as teleworking, relocation to a new office or redeployment to a different job.

Difficulties in socialising in organisations is another reason for job dissatisfaction. Kulkarni and Lengnick-Hall (2011) discuss the role of flexible employment in the process of the organisational socialisation which is defined by Louis (1980) as "the process by which an individual comes to appreciate the values, abilities, expected behaviours, and social knowledge essential for assuming an organisational role and for participating as an organisational member". In particular, this process affects the disabled workers' adjustment and tasks in their job, which involves job satisfaction, performance and role innovation. Hence, the main conclusion and implication derived in the study by Kulkarni and Lengnick-Hall (2011) is that flexible employment should be the main central practice that will empower people with disabilities helping them to cope with their needs and to adjust in a successful manner in the organisational context and the tasks of the job. Difficulties in organisational socialisation can be caused by many factors and the behaviours and attributes of the employer or peers can affect the organisational socialisation of the disabled workers. Stone and Colella (1996) proposed a model that examines various factors about how they affect the reaction of employers and peers of disabled workers. Behaviours of the disabled worker and attributes of his/her employer or colleagues are counted in *personal characteristics* that affect the treatment of the disabled worker. Factors such as norms, values, policies in the workplace and reward systems are presented as the *organisational characteristics* and legislation/laws are taken into account as *environmental factors* that affect the way that disabled individuals are treated in organisational settings. Consequently, their model predicts that disabled individuals are often treated unfairly due to the biased perceptions of their employers and peers.

Organisations may use training programmes to change the stereotypic beliefs of employers and peers about disabled individuals, convincing them that disabled individuals have many job-related skills and competencies capable of adding value to organisations. Moreover, increasing organisational and job flexibility through flexible employment schemes can be useful to change their beliefs about workers with disabilities by assigning disabled workers to suitable jobs able to reveal their skills and competencies and contribute to the organisation. Schur et al. (2009) employed data from surveys on 30,000 employees in 14 companies in the USA over the period 2001–2006 and found that the differences in job satisfaction between disabled and non-disabled people are reduced when workplaces include corporate cultures that consider the employees' needs, such as those living with disabilities.

To sum up, due to their above-mentioned roles in solving job dissatisfaction reasons, flexible employment schemes can be a good solution to improve the job satisfaction of workers with disabilities who suffer from health restrictions, absence of assistive technology, lack of accommodations in the workplace, wage inequality and difficulties in socialising within organisations. According to Gewurtz and Kirsh (2009), a successful development in solutions for individual needs of workers with disabilities depends on the fact that flexibility exists in the workplace and work setting. In other words, the more flexible the organisation seems to be in the process of identifying, recognising, approving and applying custom-made, non-bureaucratic alternatives, the more successful the overall business will be. This flexibility can be accomplished by the working schedules we discuss in this chapter. Moreover, Giovanis and Ozdamar (2019), using data from the European Working Conditions Survey (EWCS) in 35 countries over the period of 2000–2015, empirically show the positive effects of flexible working schemes on the job satisfaction of workers with disabilities compared to their counterparts who are employed under fixed working schedules. Additionally, they found that the job satisfaction differences between disabled workers and workers without disabilities are reduced when the flexible employment schemes are in place.

The role of flexible employment in absenteeism, employee loyalty and performance at work

The second objective is to explore the impact of flexible employment on the absenteeism, employee loyalty and job performance of workers with disabilities, compared to the same group of workers and also non-disabled workers who are employed under traditional or fixed working schedules. Absenteeism in the work concept is defined "as the amount of time away from work; accidentally or intentionally" (Hernandez & Peele, 2009). Moreover, Martensen and Grønholdt (2006) define employee loyalty as "the identification with involvement in and commitment to the company and by being motivated to perform beyond expectations". Absenteeism, loyalty and performance are linked to each other, whereas absenteeism indirectly refers to lower levels of loyalty and low performance as well. Thus, reduction of absenteeism can be used also as a proxy for performance/productivity and loyalty to the organisation.

Earlier studies show that workers who experience work-life conflicts report lower levels of loyalty to the organisation, resulting in a reduction of performance and an increase in absenteeism (Beauregard & Henry, 2009). Research shows that flexible employment schemes may have positive impact on work-life balance and reduction of absenteeism (Lambert, 2000; Greenhaus & Powell, 2006; Kossek, Lautsch & Eaton, 2006). Lambert (2000) and Greenhaus and Powell (2006) argue that flexible employment schemes may improve workers' loyalty by having a positive effect on both job satisfaction and their personal lives. Similarly, Kossek, Lautsch and Eaton (2006) indicate that flexible arrangements at work give the ability to workers to cluster personal needs and appointments by gaining control over their time and place of work. Hence, disabled people employed in flexible working schedules will have more resources, in terms of time, place, comfort and more support, therefore they will be less likely to face work-life related conflicts.

Consequently, the assumptions lie in the fact that flexible employment arrangements can be used to reduce work-life conflict and enhance the work-life balance, such as devoting time that disabled people need, including home care, hospital and nursing services and reducing, if not eliminating, commuting time to work. Furthermore, special attention should be given to the fact that employees have different preferences in work-life practices and thus, employment schemes may not be efficient if they do not meet each worker's needs (Hill et al., 1998). Therefore, we assume that flexible employment arrangements can reduce the absence rates at work, since these meet specific needs of each worker and allow them to manage disability, chronic illnesses and long-term health conditions, limit their stress and anxiety and improve their mental health (Giardini & Kabst, 2008; Chartered Institute of Personnel and Development (CIPD),[4] 2018).

Employers' concerns are often expressed in relation to the employment performance of disabled workers; as they are assumed to be less productive than non-disabled staff (Stone & Colella, 1996; Lengnick-Hall, Gaunt & Kulkarni, 2008; Domzal, Houtenville & Sharma, 2008). Similarly, employers often associate other performance issues, such as work slowing down (Hernandez et al., 2008), higher absenteeism and lateness with disabled workers (Hernandez et al., 2008; Kaye, Jans & Jones, 2011; Gröschl, 2013) rather than non-disabled employees. In other words, disabled workers can occasionally be seen by managers as "problem" employees (Kaye, Jans & Jones, 2011).

However, earlier studies show that stereotypes and the beliefs of the employers are not valid regarding the loyalty or performance differences between disabled and non-disabled workers. The evidence shows that workers with disabilities do not present lower loyalty levels, higher staff turnover or higher levels of lateness compared to their non-disabled counterparts when flexible employment schemes are applied in the workplace (Kaletta, Binks & Robinson, 2012). In particular, the authors evaluated the productivity gaps between staff with and without disabilities in the Supply Chain and Logistics Division at Walgreens Co., which is a 10,000-employee unit of a national retail pharmacy chain. In the 31 sites of three distribution centres explored around the USA, there was not productivity distinction between employees with and without disabilities at 18 sites. When differences in productivity have occurred, disabled workers were more productive in ten places, while non-disabled employees were more productive only in three places. Hernandez and McDonald (2007) employed a focus group study based on 21 administrators from 16 companies in the USA. Employees with disabilities held various positions including service workers, administrative support workers, professionals, and officials and managers. The authors have found an even better record of attendance for disabled workers, except for those organisations where flexible employment applications were not reported. Thus, one of the main causes explaining these low levels of turnover intentions and absenteeism is the flexible accommodations provided by the firms and managers, such as the flexible employment schemes we discuss in this chapter.

Nevertheless, flexible employment schemes may not be always associated with better labour outcomes if some specific conditions are not satisfied. Giovanis (2018) explored the role of flexible employment schemes on firm performance using data from the Work Employment Relations Survey (WERS) in Great Britain in the years 2004 and 2011. In particular, the author examines the effect of teleworking and compressed hours, representing flexible working conditions on labour productivity and financial performance of the firms. In the case of teleworking, if the employees have very low influence in their job tasks, the effect of teleworking on labour productivity and firm performance becomes negative. Thus, this indicates that flexible employment schemes are not always enough to enhance performance, and managers should also consider other characteristics, such as influence, control, creativity and others. This is consistent with the theory by Stone and Colella (1996) that disabled workers are better off in firms that are perceived as responsive to all employees' needs and special requirements because accommodation in the workplace is less likely to be seen as unique care, while disabled people are probably worse off in unresponsive and more rigid organisations. Therefore, organisations interested both in the long-term integration and economic achievement of all employees must ensure that they understand and recognise whether and why different employee groups' job satisfaction may vary and identify the possible ways to enhance their employee satisfaction rates.

Furthermore, Giovanis and Ozdamar (2019) have explored the impact of three flexible employment schemes: working at home, teleworking and flexi-time on absenteeism using data from the European Working Conditions Survey over the period of 2000–2015 covering the 28 European Union member states and 7 associated countries. The results confirm the positive impact of those flexible employment schemes on absenteeism, improving the well-being of disabled employees and reducing the discrepancies between disabled and non-disabled workers. However, their findings also suggest that the success of the flexible employment implementation relies on the industry and the background of the employees. More specifically, the authors found that there are differences within the firms operating in the same industry, as more educated and high-skilled people are more likely to be employed under flexible working schedules, and especially in teleworking. Similarly, a strong heterogeneity is present between industries, as firms operating in the services sector are more likely to implement flexible employment schemes compared to firms in the mining, farming and manufacturing sectors.

Conclusions

Earlier findings suggest there is a positive impact from the flexible employment arrangements in the outcomes explored in this chapter. In particular, Giovanis and Ozdamar (2019) reveal a positive effect of flexible employment schemes on the job satisfaction and organisational loyalty of workers with disabilities compared to their counterparts who are employed under fixed working schedules. Furthermore, flexible employment schemes are useful to reduce job satisfaction differences between employees with and without disabilities.

There are two main types of policies for social support, also including people with disabilities. The first one is the *"active" policies* as described before and the second category includes the *"passive" policies*, where disabled people rely on social benefits, such as disability, sickness and injury allowances. A large proportion of the disabled people around the globe would be at risk of poverty in the absence of those benefits. However, our argument is that these social benefits cannot be effective and sustainable in the long term for two main reasons. First, the continuous reliance on government support increases the burden of the government budget, which could have been allocated to other more productive socio-economic activities, unless people are completely unable to work, which actually consists of a small proportion over the total population. Second and most important, people with disabilities will rely on social benefits, keeping them out of employment, losing their skills, prohibiting them from gaining valuable working experience, which will impact their socioeconomic well-being and psychological and mental health in the long-run period. In the case of flexible employment, which is an *active policy*, workers with disabilities will become less dependent on social benefits, improving their job satisfaction and thus, their organisation loyalty, performance and their overall well-being.

One of the factors related to job satisfaction is the degree to which employees perceive the job fits their needs, is inclusive and that they are treated fairly. Employees seek systems and policies that they perceive to be fair, which will likely increase their job satisfaction reducing the incidence of absenteeism (Bakker et al., 2003; VanWormer et al., 2011). Hence, "active" policies need to be prioritised, including training programmes, flexible employment schemes and proper accommodation at the workplace. It is apparent that the quota and the equality of opportunity approaches are not enough to address the special needs and demands of this group of workers. Therefore, both governments and firms should encourage policies designed to make workplaces more flexible and accommodating, combined with financial incentives that will allow workers with disabilities and their families to cope with the extra costs associated with disability.

There is a scepticism from both sides, employers and employees, about flexible employment. On the one hand, employees may feel they will be disadvantaged if utilising these types of schemes, such as job insecurity, wage inequality and the fear that their job could be at risk. However, we have shown that disabled workers may not differ from their counterparts in terms of productivity/performance and absenteeism when flexible working arrangements are applied. Flexible employment schemes can overcome the problems and concerns of job insecurity and wage levels. On the other hand, lack of flexible employment can exist due to unsupportive manager attitudes, as they are sceptical about the benefits of those schemes. Hence, employers and employees should engage in open discussions about the measurement of effectiveness and adaptation to the needs of both parties. Furthermore, the flexible arrangements should be designed, not only to fit with employees' needs, but also to enable them to be accountable for their performance and results, motivating them to improve their productivity and organisational loyalty.

Recommendations

We have shown how the flexible employment schemes have an impact on job satisfaction, employee loyalty, absenteeism and performance. Furthermore, this section provides several interesting directions for future studies and practical policy implications.

The first suggestion is to extend the investigation on the effect of flexible employment schemes on job satisfaction, employee loyalty, absenteeism and performance in developing countries, while the majority of the previous studies focussed on developed economies, including the USA, Europe and Australia.

The second suggestion is to consider examining whether workplaces offer flexible employment and what the main factors are that hinder their implementation. Some firms may not be aware of the potential benefits of flexible employment, or are very sceptical about their success or they may be unable to offer them, possibly due, for example, to the financial constraints that information and communication technology tools may require (these could include data storage or processing of large databases in some cases).

To overcome these obstacles, different policy implementations should be addressed and designed at government level. Governments should support firms in terms of financial and economic development incentives and subsidies if they face financial constraints. Furthermore, the related public institutions should provide guidance and information on firms about the possible benefits of flexible employment, especially to the managers and employers who are not aware of those schemes. One important benefit of flexible employment schemes that firms and managers should be aware of is their power to create diversity, which will increase job satisfaction, employee loyalty and productivity among all workers and particularly among those with disabilities. A more diverse and decentralised organisational setting is useful to all staff members and demonstrates that elevated centralisation is negatively linked to these outcomes.[5]

To convince managers who are sceptical about the success of flexible work arrangements, governmental research centres could conduct pilot studies by choosing randomly a sample group employed under flexible schemes and a control group employed under fixed schemes to analyse whether flexible work arrangements improve outcomes such as performance, loyalty, absenteeism and job satisfaction compared to the fixed arrangements.

In addition to policies at government level, firm-level policies are also necessary. Earlier studies have shown that not all flexible working schemes have the same impact on the outcomes of people with different disabilities. This may differ not only by the type of flexible employment scheme, but also by the type of disability, implying that systems and policies should be focussed and adjusted according to specific impairments. Thus, the policy implementation and management strategy at firm level should vary depending on the disability type, severity and the type of flexible employment arrangement. To implement customisable policies, firms must understand the diversity of their workforce and realise that different employees may desire different flexible arrangements for various reasons. One possible way to achieve this, in the case where flexible schemes are absent, is by conducting employee surveys. This will allow firms to identify the employees' demographics in order to implement customisable flexible arrangements that fit the specific needs of each worker.[6] While implementing the customisable flexible arrangements, the managers should also consider the professional sector and the education level of the workers. Some workers with disabilities, based on their specific needs, may demand flexible arrangements, including teleworking or home-office working, which mostly require knowledge in the use of information and communication technology (ICT). Workers who are not trained and capable of using ICT can be supported with additional policies, such as training programmes that aim to educate people in the use of ICT.

Furthermore, employers and employees should agree on the type of flexible employment by identifying the specific needs of the workers and ensuring their continuous support, but also to enable them to be accountable for their results and engage in actions that continuously improve their loyalty and performance. However, it is understandable that these types of flexible employment schemes cannot be implemented in all cases and their success, as our discussion indicates, strongly depends on the professional sector, education, industry, the product and service offered by the workplace. Moreover, not only the workers' experience, but also the infrastructure and the ability of the workplace to offer this type of employment, matter for the success of flexible employment implementation. Therefore, a policy recommendation that should be considered, by the state, industry and managers, is to provide training and education to firms to offer flexible employment arrangements, in case these are absent.

Notes

1 In the US, San Francisco, Vermont, New Hampshire and federal government, employees have the related right to request work flexibility, https://www.un. org/esa/socdev/enable/rights/ahc7bkgrndra.htm
2 Dutch sociologist Ton Wilthagen offered a matrix of four types of flexibility and four types of security, where wage flexibility is defined as performance-related pay.
3 Reasonable accommodation in the Convention refers to "necessary and appropriate modification and adjustments not imposing a disproportionate or undue burden, where needed in a particular case, to ensure to persons with disabilities the enjoyment or exercise on an equal basis with others of all human rights and fundamental freedoms".
4 The Chartered Institute of Personnel and Development (CIPD) is the professional body for the human resources sector in the UK.
5 Previous studies exploring the effect of diversity within organisations on productivity (Mor Barak, Cherin & Berkman, 1998; Boehm et al., 2014) show that the diversity environment is particularly useful to minority groups in terms of organisational characteristics (McKay et al., 2007).
6 Even though this chapter has focussed on workers with disabilities, we highlight that each disability type may require different needs and adjustments and this can be extended for the whole workforce, including healthy people with other needs, including caring for children and old people and to gain control over their work-life balance.

References

Ali, M., Schur, L. & Blanck, P. 2011. What types of jobs do people with disabilities want? *Journal of Occupational Rehabilitation*, 21(2), 199–210.
Bakker, A.B., Demerouti, E., de Boer, E. & Schaufeli, W.B. 2003. Job demands and job resources as predictors of absence duration and frequency. *Journal of Vocational Behavior*, 62(2), 341–356.
Baldwin, M.L. & Johnson, W. 2006. A critical review of studies of discrimination against workers with disabilities. In W.M. Rodgers III (ed.), *Handbook on the Economics of Discrimination* (pp. 119–160). Northampton, MA: Edgar Elgar Publishing.
Baumgärtner, M.K., Böhm, S.A. & Dwertmann, D.J.G. 2014. Job performance of employees with disabilities: Interpersonal and intrapersonal resources matter. *Equality, Diversity and Inclusion: An International Journal*, 33(4), 347–360.
Beauregard, T.A. & Henry, L.C. 2009. Making the link between work-life balance practices and organisational performance. *Human Resource Management Review*, 19(1), 9–22.
Boehm, S.A., Dwertmann, D.J.G., Kunze, F., Michaelis, B., Parks, K. & McDonald, D. 2014. Expanding insights on the diversity climate performance link: The role of workgroup discrimination and group size. *Human Resource Management*, 53(3), 379–402.
Böhm, S.A., Dwertmann, D.J.G. & Baumgärtner, M.K. 2011. How to deal with disability-related diversity: Opportunities and pitfalls. In T. Geisen & H.G. Harder (eds), *Disability Management and Workplace Integration: International Research Findings* (pp. 85–98). Farnham, UK: Gower.

Chartered Institute of Personnel and Development (CIPD) 2018. Health and well-being at work survey. Survey report. Available at: https://www.cipd.co.uk/Images/health-and-well-being-at-work_tcm18-40863.pdf [last accessed 25 August 2019].

Convention on the Rights of Persons with Disabilities (2007). Available at: https://www.un.org/disabilities/documents/convention/convoptprot-e.pdf [last accessed 8 January 2020].

The Council of the European Union (2000). Council Directive 2000/78/EC of 27 November 2000 establishing a general framework for equal treatment in employment and occupation. *Official Journal L, 303*, 2 December, 16–22. Available at: https://eur-lex.europa.eu/LexUriServ/LexUriServ.do?uri=CELEX:32000L0078: en:HTML [last accessed 8 January 2020].

Domzal, C., Houtenville, A. & Sharma, R. 2008. *Survey of Employer Perspectives on the Employment of People with Disabilities: Technical Report.* Prepared under contract to the Office of Disability and Employment Policy, US Department of Labor. McLean, VA: CESSI.

Eurostat 2011. Disability statistics – labour market access statistics explained. Available at: https://ec.europa.eu/eurostat/statistics-explained/pdfscache/34420.pdf [last accessed 15 March 2019].

Faragher, E.B., Cass, M. & Cooper, C.L. 2005. The relationship between job satisfaction and health: A meta-analysis. *Occupational and Environmental Medicine, 62*(2), 105–112.

Future of Work Institute 2012. The benefits of flexible working arrangements. A report prepared by the Future of Work Institute. Available at: http://www.citywomen.co.uk/wp-content/uploads/2014/04/The-Benefits-of-Flexible-Working-Arrangements-for-CEOs.pdf

Gewurtz, R. & Kirsh, B. 2009. Disruption, disbelief and resistance: A meta-synthesis of disability in the workplace. *Work: A Journal of Prevention, Assessment and Rehabilitation, 34*(1), 33–44.

Giardini, A. & Kabst, R. 2008. Effects of work-family human resource practices: A longitudinal perspective. *The International Journal of Human Resource Management, 19*(11), 2079–2094.

Giovanis, E. 2018. The relationship between flexible employment arrangements and workplace performance in Great Britain. *International Journal of Manpower, 39*(1), 51–70.

Giovanis, E. & Ozdamar, O. 2019. Accommodating employees with disabilities: The role of flexible employment schemes in Europe. Available at: https://papers.ssrn.com/sol3/papers.cfm?abstract_id=3441925

Greenhaus, J.H. & Powell, G.N. 2006. When work and family are allies: A theory of work-family enrichment. *Academy of Management Review, 31*(1), 72–92.

Greve, N. 2009. The labour market situation of disabled people in European countries and implementation of employment policies: A summary of evidence from country reports and research studies. Prepared for Academic Network of European Disability experts (ANED). Available at: http://includ-ed.eu/resource/labour-market-situation-disabled-people-european-countries-and-implementation-employment-po

Gröschl, S. 2013. Presumed incapable: Exploring the validity of negative judgments about persons with disabilities and their employability in hotel operations. *Cornell Hospitality Quarterly, 54*(2), 114–123.

Hale, T., Hayghe, H. & McNeil, J. 1998. Persons with disabilities: Labor market activity, 1994. *Monthly Labor Review, 121*(9), 1–12.

Hernandez, B. & McDonald, K. 2007. Exploring the bottom line: A study of the costs and benefits of workers with disabilities. Available at: http://bbi.syr.edu/_assets/staff_bio_publications/McDonald_Exploring_the_Bottom_Line_2007.pdf

Hernandez, B., McDonald, K., Divilbiss, M., Horin, E., Velcoff, J. & Donoso, O. 2008. Reflections from employers on the disabled workforce: Focus groups with healthcare, hospitality and retail administrators. *Employee Responsibilities and Rights Journal, 20*(3), 157–164.

Hernandez, G.M. & Peele, P.B. 2009. Workplace absenteeism risk model. US Patent Application 12/486,800, UPMC.

Hill, E.J., Miller, B.C., Weiner, S.P. & Colihan, J. 1998. Influences of the virtual office on aspects of work and work/life balance. *Personnel Psychology, 51*(3), 667–683.

Kaletta, J.P., Binks, D.J. & Robinson, R. 2012. Creating an inclusive workplace: Integrating employees with disabilities into a distribution center environment. *Professional Safety: Journal of the American Society of Safety Engineers, 57*(6), 62–71.

Kaye, H.S., Jans, L.H. & Jones, E.C. 2011. Why don't employers hire and retain workers with disabilities? *Journal of Occupational Rehabilitation, 21*(4), 526–536.

Kossek, E.E., Lautsch, B.A. & Eaton, S.C. 2006. Telecommuting, control, and boundary management: Correlates of policy use and practice, job control, and work–family effectiveness. *Journal of Vocational Behavior, 68*(2), 347–367.

Kulkarni, M. & Lengnick-Hall, M.L. 2011. Socialization of people with disabilities in the workplace. *Human Resource Management, 50*(4), 521–540.

Lambert, S. (2000). Added benefits: The link between work-life benefits and organizational citizenship behavior. *Academy of Management Journal, 43*(5), 801–815.

Leicester, M. 1999. *Disability Voice: Towards an Enabling Education.* London: Jessica Kingsley Publishers.

Lengnick-Hall, M.L., Gaunt, P.M. & Kulkarni, M. 2008. Overlooked and underutilized: People with disabilities are an untapped human resource. *Human Resource Management, 47*(2), 255–273.

Ljungqvist, L. & Sargent, T.J. 2008. Two questions about European unemployment. *Econometrica, 76*(1), 1–29.

Louis, M.R. 1980. Surprise and sense making: What newcomers experience entering unfamiliar organizational settings. *Administrative Science Quarterly, 25*(2), 226–251.

McAfee, J. & McNaughton, D. 1997. Transitional outcomes: Job satisfaction of workers with disabilities – Part two: Satisfaction with promotions, pay, co-workers, supervision, and work conditions. *Journal of Vocational Rehabilitation, 8*(3), 243–251.

McKay, P.F., Avery, D.R., Tonidandel, S., Morris, M.A., Hernandez, M. & Hebl, M.R. 2007. Racial differences in employee retention: Are diversity climate perceptions the key? *Personnel Psychology, 60*(1), 35–62.

Marsay, G. 2014. Success in the workplace: From the voice of (dis)abled to the voice of enabled. *African Journal of Disability, 3*(1), 99.

Martensen, A. & Grønholdt, L. 2006. Internal marketing: A study of employee loyalty, its determinants and consequences. *Innovative Marketing, 2*(4), 92–116.

Mor Barak, M.E., Cherin, D.A. & Berkman, S. 1998. Organizational and personal dimensions in diversity climate. *Journal of Applied Behavioral Science, 34*(1), 82–104.

Official Journal of EU 2003. Regulation (EU) No 1304/2013 of the European Parliament and of The Council, Article 8, 20 December. Available at: https://eur-lex.europa.eu/legal-content/EN/TXT/PDF/?uri=CELEX:32013R1304&from=EN

Pagán, R. & Malo, M.A. 2009. Job satisfaction and disability: Lower expectations about jobs or a matter of health? *Spanish Economic Review*, *11*(1), 51–74.

Perry, E.L., Hendricks, W. & Broadbent, E. 2000. An exploration of access and treatment discrimination and job satisfaction among college graduates with and without physical disabilities. *Human Relations*, *53*(7), 923–955.

Scharle, A. & Csillag, M. 2016. Disability and labour market integration. European Commission, Luxemburg. Available at: https://ec.europa.eu/social/BlobServlet?docId=16601&langId=en

Schur, L., Kruse, D., Blasi, J. & Blanck, P. 2009. Is disability disabling in all workplaces? Workplace disparities and corporate culture. *Industrial Relations*, *48*(3), 381–410.

Sousa-Poza, A. & Sousa-Poza, A.A. 2000. Well-being at work: A cross-national analysis of the levels and determinants of job satisfaction. *The Journal of Socio-Economics*, *29*(6), 517–538.

Stone, D.L. & Colella, A. 1996. A model of factors affecting the treatment of disabled individuals in organizations. *Academy of Management Review*, *21*(2), 352–401.

Thornton, P. & Lunt, N. 1997. *Employment Policies for Disabled People in Eighteen Countries: A Review.* GALDNET Collection, Social Policy Research Unit, York, UK: University of York.

Uppal, S. 2005. Disability, workplace characteristics and job satisfaction. *International Journal of Manpower*, *26*(4), 336–349.

VanWormer, J.J., Fyfe-Johnson, A.L., Boucher, J.L., Johnson, P.J., Britt, H.R., Thygeson, N.M. & Dusek, J.A. 2011. Stress and workplace productivity loss in the Heart of New Ulm project. *Journal of Occupational and Environmental Medicine*, *53*(10), 1106–1109.

Wooten, L.P. 2008. Guest editor's note: Breaking barriers in organizations for the purpose of inclusiveness. *Human Resource Management*, *47*(2), 191–197.

World Health Organization (WHO) (2011). World report on disability 2011. Geneva, Switzerland. Available at: https://www.who.int/disabilities/world_report/2011/report.pdf

14 Lone parents and blended families

Advocating flexible working to support families in transition

Anneke Schaefer, Caroline Gatrell, and Laura Radcliffe

Introduction

In this chapter, we examine how flexible working policies might be an important source of organisational support for families in transition. We give an overview of what we already know about families in transition and flexible working, the gendered nature of access to flexible working, and reasons why it is important to consider the impact of flexible working policies on such complex non-traditional families. Furthermore, this chapter will explore limitations in our knowledge and suggest a future research agenda laying out why flexible working policies need to be even more flexible than they currently are so as to fit with the transitory nature of today's families and the increasing need for flexibility that results from this.

In recent decades we have observed an increasing heterogeneity in family types (Valiquette-Tessier et al., 2018). Families tend to be less static than in the past with a rising number of lone-parent families, many of whom eventually re-partner and transition to blended families in which at least one partner has a child from a previous relationship (Letablier & Wall, 2018; Ganong & Coleman, 2018). To visualise this trend, the United Kingdom reports a higher than average proportion of lone parents of around 21 per cent compared to the EU average of 15 per cent (EUROSTAT, 2017) and by 2011, nearly 1 in 10 dependent children in the UK lived in a step-family (Office for National Statistics (ONS), 2014). However, this diversity of family types is not represented in work-family research and policy, which are still treating more traditional family types (i.e. heterosexual married parents with resident children) as their main point of reference (Gatrell et al., 2013).

The implications of this oversight became apparent when turning towards recent statistics; lone-parent families with dependent children make up 21 per cent of families with dependent children in the UK (ONS, 2017). The latest official statistics regarding the number of blended families in the UK are from 2011, claiming that 11 per cent of couple families with dependent children in England and Wales were blended families. In 85 per cent of those families the woman brought children from a previous relationship into the blended family, in 11 per cent it was the man, and in 4 per cent both partners had children from a previous relationship (ONS, 2014). However, this statistic does not take into account a range of other family arrangements such as blended families in which not all partners and their respective children live together. Despite this lack of more recent and complete statistics for blended families, it can be deduced that they make up a significant number of families with dependent children in the UK today (Gatrell et al., 2015). When adding the number of lone parent families to the number of blended families, it becomes apparent that at least around one third of families with dependent children in the UK do not fit with the dominant picture of family as two married parents living together with birth children.

As such, the boundaries of who and what constitute a family have become increasingly blurred as the patterns of family formation and dissolution become more dynamic and, according to some authors, transitional, a concept Beck-Gernsheim (2002) coins the 'post-familial family'. In such transitional families, family roles may be especially complex and demanding. Also, these roles can be subject to sudden major changes. For example, both lone parents and blended families might have to navigate highly volatile relationships with ex-partners, which impact custody arrangements and can mean that the level of parenting responsibility can vary significantly on a daily basis (Ganong & Coleman, 2017). This can have a significant impact on the work domain and might lead to different experiences of work-family conflict (WFC) for those types of families. Flexible working arrangements (FWAs) might prove a key source of organisational support for blended and lone-parent families to reduce their work-family conflict and support them in managing their numerous, often complex, work-family arrangements. However, flexible working arrangements often assume that people utilising such policies are married heterosexual couples living with birth children, referred to often as 'nuclear' families (Bernardes, 1999). Traditionally, it has further been assumed that for parents in those 'nuclear' families, mothers will act as primary caregivers and fathers as main breadwinners (Gatrell, 2005), which for so many parents is not the case; in 19 per cent of UK families with heterosexual parents, mothers are main income earners (Ford & Collinson, 2011). The potential of flexible working for families who do not fit with often out-dated assumptions about family composition has rarely been explored in the management literatures (see Ladge et al., 2015).

Family transitions and complex family arrangements

Lone parents in the workplace

A recent report by Gingerbread (a charity supporting lone parents) using the Labour Force Survey and Understanding Society datasets estimates that lone-parent families make up around one in four families with children in the UK and have done so for the past two decades (Rabindrakumar, 2018). However, the term 'lone' or 'single' parent hides a diverse array of family types, such as single mothers and fathers with resident children, single mothers and fathers whose children are not resident with them, mothers and fathers who are single parents by choice, and parents whose spouse has passed away or whose co-parent is not in the picture. So far, few studies make distinctions between different types of lone parents and tend to work with a narrow definition of the term, mostly restricting their samples to parents with resident children who do not live with a partner (e.g. Reimann et al., 2019). As policy echoes research, public policy defines lone parents as single adults who live with a dependent child (Rabindrakumar, 2018). However, making distinctions between different groups of lone parents both in research, and policy based on the outcomes of such research, is of vital importance. Different types of lone parents might experience considerably diverging degrees of family commitments depending on whether they have a co-parent, what their relationship with their co-parent is like, and how much childcare responsibilities they experience on a daily basis (Ganong & Coleman, 2017; Bakker & Karsten, 2013).

Childcare responsibilities are an especially vital issue to consider when it comes to lone parenthood given that there is evidence that lone parents tend to experience more childcare-related obstacles than coupled parents (Moilanen et al., 2016; Rabindrakumar, 2018). Nursery and school pick-up and drop-off times are often highly restricted, leading to challenges for all working parents to manage pick-ups and drop-offs. However, while coupled parents can shift parenting responsibilities between each other to manage childcare arrangements, this strategy is often inaccessible for lone parents (Rabindrakumar, 2018) as they might not have a co-parent or their co-parent is not available to offer childcare support. Hence, it is suggested that lone parents may often not be able to synchronise their work schedules with a partner as coupled parents tend to do, to manage daily childcare (Moilanen et al., 2016).

Furthermore, results from Germany demonstrate that lone parents experience more family-to-work conflict but not more work-to-family conflict than other parents (Reimann et al., 2019), contrasting results from the UK, which find that lone mothers experience more work-to-family conflict than other parents (Minnotte, 2012; Moilanen et al., 2019). Regarding their finding that lone parents experience more family-to-work conflict, Reimann et al. (2019) suggest that might be due to lone parents having to rely on formal childcare in absence of a co-parent. Those childcare facilities are often subject to strict drop-off and pick-up times and also require parents to pick fixed days of care that usually cannot be altered on a week-to-week basis (Bernardi & Mortelmans, 2018) as might be needed by lone parents whose residency arrangements differ from week to week. This exacerbates the time pressures that lone parents experience in the family domain, which then in turn impacts the work domain.

In one of the few studies differentiating between different types of lone parents, Bakker and Karsten (2013) find that Dutch lone mothers who live with their children full time experience more difficulties in managing their work and childcare demands than do lone mothers whose children live with them part time on a daily basis. The authors explain these differences between the two groups by arguing that lone mothers whose children live with them full time tend to work fewer hours, are not as highly educated, and have fewer resources than lone parents who have a co-parent to share care responsibilities with. Hence, research has shown that when lone parents' children reside with them full time, they are more constrained in how they combine work, childcare, and other life domains than parents who have a co-parent with whom their children stay part of the time (Bakker & Karsten, 2013). The implications of such childcare related obstacles can be far-reaching. For example, in the absence of a partner, lone mothers are forced to turn to more precarious forms of childcare, which are less reliable and flexible, making the arrangement of short-notice childcare a challenging endeavour (Moilanen et al., 2016). This leads to lone parents having lower incomes than coupled parents as they either have to reduce their work hours to handle their childcare demands or seek more flexible and at the same time more expensive forms of childcare (Rabindrakumar, 2018).

This also shows how lone parenthood can have a significant impact on the work domain. Although lone parenthood is often a temporary state in the life course of many people, it can permanently alter lone parents' career trajectories (Bernardi et al., 2018). Extant research has made evident some of the distinct challenges that lone-parent families face in the labour market. While the number of lone parents in the UK labour market is at a record high and 68 per cent of lone parents are engaged in paid work, they tend to have to deal with more precarious employment and are more likely to work in low-paid employment than other parents (Rabindrakumar, 2018). Similarly, results from Germany indicate that lone parents are more often employed on fixed-term contracts (Reimann et al., 2019). This high level of precariousness lone parents have to face when navigating employment might be one reason why studies comparing lone and coupled parents conclude that lone parents experience higher work-to-family conflict than coupled parents. Studies by Moilanen et al. (2019) and Minnotte (2012) exemplify this by demonstrating how lone mothers in the UK experience more work-to-family conflict than their coupled counterparts, i.e. they feel that their work role interferes with their desired family role more than coupled mothers do. Moilanen et al. (2019) speculate that this might be due to aforementioned obstacles surrounding childcare arrangements. However, there is a lack of in-depth research explaining why this is the case in terms of the daily experiences and challenges of working lone parents.

Blended families in the workplace

Lone parenthood is often a transitory state that lasts an average of five years for lone parents in the UK (Rabindrakumar, 2018). When a lone parent re-partners, a blended family is created (Letablier & Wall, 2018). However, despite the relatively large number of blended families, they are often considered an apparently undesirable family arrangement, while the nuclear family continues to represent the dominant cultural norm of an ideal family unit (Blyaert et al., 2016; Dupuis, 2010). This might be one reason why, similarly to the concept of lone parenthood, the 'blended family' remains a mystery in work-family research. Also known as step-families or patchwork families in the literature, definitions regarding the nature of this family type vary due to its complexity. The most encompassing definition construes a blended family as a type of family in which at least one partner in a cohabiting or married couple has a child from a previous relationship (Ganong & Coleman, 2018). However, blended families are highly heterogeneous, and an almost infinite variation of family structures exists within the given definition. For example, one or both partners in the couple may have children from a previous relationship, who may or may not live with them. They can also be of the opposite or the same sex. Moreover, either partner may be divorced, never married, or widowed before entering the current relationship. Furthermore, they may or may not have children together. Due to this complexity blended families are notoriously difficult to study, offering another explanation as to why they remain understudied (Weaver et al., 2001). We are not even sure about numbers and formations of blended families within the United Kingdom. According to the Office for National Statistics, step-families have declined by 14 per cent between 2001 and 2011. However, we do not have any official statistics post-2011 to see the development up to the present day and the ONS provides only speculation as to why the numbers decline, one of the suggestions is that couples might not formally live together.

As a consequence of this significant gap in the work-family literature, little is known about the distinct challenges that blended families might encounter in forming and maintaining the family unit, which may differ significantly from those faced by nuclear families, and the impact this might have on the work domain. These difficulties include the relationship with co-parents and partners from previous relationships, consolidating different parenting approaches with new partners, and building relationships with step-children (Kumar, 2017).

The transition to becoming a family can be an especially challenging time for couples in blended families. While the traditional transition to parenthood in which a man and a woman become first-time parents has been extensively studied, evidencing this as a challenging time in which new identities are emerging and existing identities are shifting (e.g. Greenberg et al., 2016; Singley & Hynes, 2005), we know very little about the impact of non-traditional transitions to parenthood on parents' work-life experiences and identities.

We know that one of the challenges blended families experience when forming are related to bringing together a number of unrelated adults and children, such as step-children, step-parents, and step-siblings into the newly formed family. Where couples in first-order relationships (i.e. couple relationships before either partner has children) form their relationship prior to becoming parents, couples in step-families have to navigate their new relationship with each other in addition to developing step-relationships with children and even ex-partners (Cartwright & Gibson, 2013).

Blended family systems are far more complex and diverse than nuclear family systems and the multiplicity of roles each family member can hold, and the lack of clarity of said roles, can result in distinct challenges. This is exacerbated by the fact that most blended family systems transcend the boundaries of a single household as co-parents, partners, and dependent biological children, and step-children can be located in multiple households (Braithwaite et al., 2003). Here, a major distinction between two types of blended families systems becomes clear, those formed post-bereavement and those formed post-divorce or separation (Gold, 2010). Blended families formed post-divorce or separation have replaced bereavement as the leading precursor to contemporary blended families and where blended families that formed post-bereavement often mimic the nuclear family system by substituting deceased biological parents, post-divorce blended families instead add parental figures (Coleman et al., 2000).

In addition to the difficulties in bringing together a number of unrelated adults and children to form a new family unit and handling ex-partners while doing so, negative connotations of blended families and lack of social support amongst other factors make blended families more fragile, unstable, and vulnerable to dissolution (Coleman et al., 2000; Kumar, 2017).

All these challenges blended families encounter may have a significant impact on the work domain, and flexible working arrangements could prove a major source of organisational support for blended families in the workplace.

However, before turning to the connection between families in transition and flexible working, we feel that it is paramount to first discuss gender relations. Flexible working arrangements are highly gendered and as a consequence have distinct drawbacks for both fathers and mothers using them or seeking to use them. In the following section, we show the consequences of this and argue that these drawbacks might be exacerbated for lone parents, re-partnered parents, and step-parents due to the complex nature of their family arrangements that do not fit within the gendered nature of flexible working arrangements.

Gender and the state of flexible working arrangements

In the context of this chapter we define flexible working as organisational policies and practices that are designed to offer workers greater control over when, where, how long, and how much they engage in work-related activities (Hill et al., 2008). Flexible working arrangements have been linked to employee satisfaction (Wheatley, 2017), employee engagement (Richman et al., 2008), and overall organisational performance (Beauregard & Henry, 2009), highlighting how FWAs might offer advantages for both employers and employees.

However, studies investigating the effectiveness and impact of flexible working arrangements on a variety of domains are usually constructed based on gendered assumptions, presuming an intact nuclear family with a male primary breadwinner and a female primary caregiver. Here, we can establish a direct link between the prevalence of the nuclear family in work-family research, and how organisational policy and practice is directly shaped by this focus. Organisational policies and practices in the Global North are the product of assumptions based on ideal worker norms (Lewis & Cooper, 2005). The 'ideal worker' is characterised by masculine working standards (and the implied notion that men are not usually closely involved in childcare). Workers conforming to ideal and masculine worker norms participate in full-time paid employment, are expected to be deeply committed to their work, and to be relatively free of non-work commitments such as family demands (Williams, 2000). However, family-friendly working policies, a classification that can be used for flexible working, are usually studied using samples that constitute supposedly 'ideal work-life balancer' norms. Ideal work-life balancers are those who are targeted by the policies and typically consist of heterosexual coupled, white, middle-class mothers of young children working in white-collar jobs (Özbilgin et al., 2011). The ideal worker norm for men coupled with the ideal work-life balancer norm for women remains gendered – still implying a family arrangement in which a heterosexual couple (even if they had not intended this prior to the birth of their first child) 'fall back into gender' (Miller, 2011), distributing paid and unpaid work between them in a neo-traditional way: i.e. the man has capacity to invest more time and commitment in his job than his female partner, because she takes on the majority of family-related tasks. As the number of women in the workforce has risen exponentially in the second half of the 20th century, a great deal of research has focused on gender equality and work-family conflict in nuclear families, with flexible working policies gradually introduced, often with the explicit aim to support mothers in the workplace (Gatrell et al., 2013; Lewis & Humbert, 2010). However, this focus has also had negative implications for gender equality as it reinforces gendered norms of work and parenting and hence upholds the status quo in which women are expected to be the main caregivers and men the main breadwinners. Organisational presumptions that mothers are usually secondary earners tend to support gendered line-manager views that work-life balance policies are aimed mainly at women and are less relevant for men (Gatrell & Cooper, 2016; see also Tracy & Rivera, 2010; Lewis & Cooper, 2005). Mothers may thus be regarded by line managers as having particular entitlements to access flexible working schemes (even if managers are not especially enthusiastic about facilitating such access) (Gatrell et al., 2014). Whatever the nature of their role, women who take up family-friendly policies (especially if working part-time) may be disadvantaged at work as a result of working fractionally or flexibly. Mothers are often assumed to be less work-orientated than fathers and may find themselves excluded from job enhancing opportunities (the 'mummy track'), regardless of their personal ambitions (Blair-Loy, 2003; Smithson & Stokoe, 2005).

Employed fathers, by contrast, might experience significant benefits as regards workplace prospects due to (often unsubstantiated and potentially incorrect) assumptions that they are unencumbered with childcare responsibilities, at least compared with mothers. Regardless of status however (i.e. whether lone or partnered), fathers may experience difficulties in accessing flexible and work-life policies. This is because, while such policies may appear on paper to embrace 'parental' needs, employers' assumptions about mothers being the primary users of work-family initiatives mean in practice that line-managers might treat fathers as less entitled than mothers to utilise offers of flexibility at work (Burnett et al., 2010; Tracy & Rivera, 2010). Flexibility may be thus, in theory, gender neutral and designed to support employed 'parents'. In practice, however, supervisor attitudes towards paternal entitlements remain often suffused with gendered visions of maternal responsibility for domestic care agendas (Burnett et al., 2010; Tracy & Rivera, 2010), meaning that fathers may find it harder than mothers to access such entitlements.

What Gatrell and Cooper (2016) term the 'Parsonian' image of heterosexual couple parenting (drawing upon the work of 1950s' sociologist Talcott Parsons, in which fathers are positioned as lead income earners, and mothers as principal child carers (see also Gatrell, 2005)), continues to influence the gendered approach to flexible working within many organisations. As Gatrell and Cooper (2016) observe, the 'Parsonian' family image may be increasingly irrelevant to men and women who are not parenting within intact heterosexual relationships but are single, divorced, living in blended families or in single sex relationships, and/or seeking to allocate responsibilities for paid work and domestic care according to criteria other than gendered lines. It may be equally irrelevant to couples parenting within intact relationships where the division of labour is fluid and may not emerge along gendered lines, despite continued social pressures on couples to fall back into gendered roles (Miller, 2011).

Yet still, the Parsonian image of supposedly work-oriented fathers and child-oriented mothers remains deeply ingrained within organisational cultures. Flexible working policies and entitlements to access these thus continue, often, to be constructed around out-dated and gendered notions of family stability and heterosexual two-parent families, which does not reflect the experience of the 21st-century workforce in the Western world (Gatrell & Cooper, 2016).

In conclusion, current FWAs are geared towards heterosexual coupled mothers of young children in first-order relationships, while other groups such as fathers suffer from restricted access to flexible working. Due to aforementioned ideal worker norms, work organisations may be either unconscious of men needing access to flexible working or reject outright the notion of men striving to be equal parents, requiring organisational support to achieve their desired work-family balance (Gatrell & Cooper, 2016). Due to these gendered organisational norms and expectations, FWAs are stigmatised in that men are more likely to feel as though they are disadvantaged by

204 *Anneke Schaefer et al.*

colleagues' flexible working, most of whom are mothers (Humberd et al., 2015; Gatrell et al., 2014). Women, on the other hand, are more likely to feel that their flexible working leads to negative career outcomes (Chung & Van der Horst, 2018).

Families in transition and flexible working

Lone mothers and fathers, blended families in which one or both partners have children from prior relationships, amongst other non-traditional family forms such as same-sex parents, have been mostly omitted from flexible working studies and hence policy. While there is a growing awareness that many family forms do not fit into the nuclear family model (Greenhaus & Powell, 2006), the lack of knowledge on how diverse family forms manage their work and family responsibilities remains a critical gap in work-family research (Parasuraman & Greenhaus, 2002; Casper et al., 2007), and can be linked to a lack in policies to support families who function differently. FWAs might be a key source of organisational support for non-traditional family types such as lone-parent-led families and blended families to enable them to successfully manage their work and family commitments, the nature of which might be very different from intact nuclear families.

It has been noted that non-traditional families may face unique work-family pressures while at the same time having less access to support (Parasuraman & Greenhaus, 2002). One issue that might cause work-family conflict for both lone parents and parents in blended families is that they are likely to experience more intensive and complex family demands than traditional families. Due to the nature of their parenting situation, lone parents usually experience heavier parenting responsibilities than coupled parents when they have to manage both work and family demands on their own (Reimann et al., 2019). While parents in blended families might be able to rely on their new partner to support them with childcare arrangements, research has shown that not all step-parents are necessarily highly involved in the upbringing of their step-children and often take on a more auxiliary role while the birth parent takes on the role as primary parent (Cartwright, 2010). While step-parents are often found to assist in activities such as transporting the children to and from school, their engagement in other, more intimate parenting activities such as providing discipline are often limited (ibid.). Hence, re-partnered parents cannot automatically rely on their new partner to become an equal co-parent to their children and are likely to experience heavier parenting duties than do coupled parents in first-order unions. On the other side of the equation, step-parents might struggle with their newfound parenting responsibilities, especially if they do not have children themselves. Research has found that step-parents, and especially step-mothers, experience more parenting-related stress than biological parents (Shapiro, 2014). Major obstacles that step-parents encounter and that might lead to increased stress levels are often related to the co-parenting relationship between their partner and their ex-partner (Cartwright & Gibson, 2013) and unrealistic expectations by all regarding the parenting role of the new step-parent (Cartwright, 2010).

Moreover, co-parenting relationships are a common challenge for both lone parents and blended families and can result in conflicts related to residency arrangements and lead to a lack of stability in childcare responsibilities (Ganong & Coleman, 2017). Research has shown how both lone parents and parents in blended families often have to navigate volatile relationships with their ex-partners, which can lead to serious obstacles in co-parenting with them. When a lone parent re-partners, co-parenting relationships have been observed to deteriorate, which can lead to increased stress and conflict for all family members (Cartwright & Gibson, 2013).

In connection to this, residency arrangements can be quite unstable as a result of ongoing custody battles (Cartwright & Gibson, 2013). Depending on how co-parents share physical residency of their children, childcare responsibilities for parents in blended families and lone-parent families might diverge significantly. For example, co-parents might agree for their children to live with either parent 50 per cent of the time in which case childcare responsibilities will often be different from week to week. As a seven-day week cannot be fairly divided between co-parents, novel residency arrangements are implemented by courts in which children might stay with one parent for four days and then with the other parent for four days, or alternatively one week with one and the next week with the other parent (McIntosh & Chisholm, 2008). Thus, it is difficult for both lone parents and parents in blended families to predict their childcare commitments and adapt their work schedules accordingly. Hence, flexible working arrangements designed for nuclear families are not likely to meet the needs of lone parents and blended families when considering their unique family practices (Gatrell & Cooper, 2016).

One FWA that might be particularly useful to support lone parents and blended families in navigating both their heavier family demands and workloads is work schedule flexibility. Work schedule flexibility, defined as a tool which offers employees control over their work hours within certain parameters (Jung Jang et al., 2012), might be a major tool to allow parents to meet strict nursery and school pick-up and drop-off times, which is especially important for lone parents who often cannot rely on a co-parent for childcare (Reimann et al., 2019) but might also be relevant for blended families in which partners do not live in the same household or in which step-parents take on a more auxiliary role and the main share of parenting responsibility falls on the birth parent (Cartwright, 2010).

This is supported by findings from previous research which has demonstrated that work schedule flexibility can help reduce stress and negative work-family spill over for lone parents and those with a higher family workload (Jung Jang et al., 2012), including parents in blended families as established earlier. Hence, for employees with heavier family demands, schedule flexibility may be an easily implemented and economical organisational work-family initiative to support such employees in managing their work and family responsibilities (Jung Jang et al., 2012).

The 'dark side' of flexible working

However, work organisations need to be careful implementing flexible working arrangements as research has shown the existence of a 'dark side' of flexible working. In some cases, flexible working can lead to overtime and increased work hours, and as such increased instead of decreased work-family conflict (Chung & Van der Horst, 2018). For example, Reimann et al. (2019) found that when lone parents utilise remote working or flexitime working it does not necessarily lead to enhanced benefits in comparison to other parents. Instead, remote working is found to increase WFC for both lone and coupled parents (Abendroth & Reimann, 2018).

Controls need to be in place ensuring that employees utilising flexible working policies such as flexitime and remote working are safeguarded against such adverse outcomes. Especially lone parents belong to a vulnerable group for which flexible working has the potential to create more pressure. Chung and Van der Horst (2018) demonstrated that if schedule control as a means of flexible working is implemented by organisations to increase employee performance, it leads to more unpaid overtime for men. As 75 per cent of lone fathers are estimated to be in full-time employment (Bernardi et al., 2018), they might be adversely affected, especially considering how they remain an invisible group in organisations (Gatrell et al., 2014). Hence, while work schedule flexibility might be a key resource for lone parents to negotiate timing conflicts between work and childcare, lone fathers are at risk to work more unpaid overtime using flexitime.

Lone fathers and flexible working

Studies on lone parenthood in the context of paid work tend to focus on lone mothers. Scholars justify this decision by arguing that first, lone parents are mainly women. Moreover, it is argued that for men relationship status seems to have less of an impact on the work domain as can be seen in the fact that lone fathers tend to exhibit more stable work patterns and are objectively more successful than lone mothers (Bernardi et al., 2018). This is supported by findings from a quantitative study of work-to-family conflict among lone and coupled parents by Minnotte (2012) who finds that lone fathers report less work-to-family conflict than lone mothers, coupled mothers, or coupled fathers. The author suggests that this might be because lone fathers have more resources available to them than lone mothers, which enables them to navigate work and family demands more successfully. However, even if this is the case, it does not explain why lone fathers experience less work-to-family conflict than coupled parents who have a partner they can share family responsibilities with.

Current estimates suggest that 90 per cent of lone parents in the UK are women (Gingerbread, 2019) and it has been suggested that the current focus of flexible working policies on supporting lone mothers promotes the marginalisation (instead of mainstreaming) of policies to support parents in balancing work and family commitments (Lewis, 2001). It has been suggested however, that statistics might underestimate the numbers of men who are lone fathers some of the time, for example when children are classified as 'officially' resident with mothers but with fathers providing care (and therefore acting as lone parents) where required (Gatrell et al., 2015). Lone fathers might be under even more pressure than lone mothers given their restricted access to flexible working policies, which are based on assumptions that those utilising them will be working mothers. Lone mothers can hence access flexible working relatively easily whereas lone fathers might feel discouraged from using such policies (Gatrell et al., 2014). This might exacerbate work-family conflict for lone fathers as organisational norms and policies continue to assume that fathers can rely on mothers to take on the main share of parenting work, which is not the case for lone fathers.

Hence, due to the gendered nature of flexible working arrangements, lone fathers, among other groups, experience a perceived restricted access to flexible working arrangements.

Conclusion and future research directions

In this chapter we argue that research and policy need to recognise and address shifts in attitudes and behaviours rather than assuming social stability (Wood et al., 2018). As the diversity of family in the UK increases, we need to recognise this diversity and give special consideration to the transitory nature of many family types such as lone parenthood. If it ever existed, the idealised 'Parsonian' image of the nuclear family and the gendered division of labour is no longer appropriate for today. As David Morgan (2011) suggests, such notions of nuclear families are out-dated. Research and policy need to take into consideration present fluidities in family formation and maintenance: what Morgan terms 'family practices'. The limited body of research on families in transition demonstrates that current flexible working policies do not meet the needs of these groups, as they were designed based on research drawing on samples representing traditional notions of family. Indeed they do not necessarily meet even the needs of parent couples where adult relationships may be intact, but divisions of labour in relation to paid work and domestic care agendas may not align with Parsonian ideals. Hence, for new policies that can effectively support non-traditional family types to be designed, research needs to be undertaken first to establish the needs of these diverse groups and make policy recommendations to meet those needs.

Also, distinctions need to be made between different types of lone-parent-led and blended families as their needs might differ vastly (Bakker & Karsten,

2013). These distinctions should not only be based on gender but also on other socio-demographic factors. One of the most important but so far overlooked factors might be residential status and co-parental relationships. It is only logical that work-family experiences, and needs, of lone parents who have to navigate a complex relationship with their former spouse and who might encounter child residency conflicts differ significantly from that of single parents by choice or lone parents whose spouse has passed away. Similarly, future research needs to carefully detangle relationships in blended family systems as experiences of families in which only one partner or both partners have children from a previous relationship or where not all family members live in the same household might differ vastly.

While this chapter only deals with non-traditional family types that are a result of relationship transitions, i.e. becoming a lone parent or re-partnering and parenting with a new partner, an abundance of other non-traditional family types requires further consideration. Among them, parents who identify as members of the Lesbian, Gay, Bisexual, Transgender, and Queer and/or Questioning (LGBTQ) community are in urgent need of scholarly attention. To design flexible working policies that address the needs of individuals that have so far been overlooked, studies should take an intersectional approach, taking into consideration non-traditional forms of family and recognising the diversity of current workforces (Özbilgin et al., 2011).

Recommendations

Perhaps the key problem facing policy makers is the paucity of extant research on diverse blended families, meaning there is a limited evidence base upon which to craft appropriate policy decisions. We lack, for example, understanding of how step-parents manage their responsibilities towards work and family. We have limited information regarding how new, blended families relate to each other within households, and how previous partners interact – as well as how childcare is shared between parents and step-parents. We lack sufficient statistical understanding of what is occurring within non-traditional families in the Global North, and this poses problems from the highest levels in government through to local and organisational level.

The ultimate priority must be to commission new research which embraces these non-stable family forms which characterise the 21st century, so that family policy may reflect what is happening in practice now, rather than what occurred in the past.

Once such research has established the needs of different types of lone parents and members of blended families, specific policy recommendations can be made. For now, we can only deduce from the body of research on lone parenthood and blended families that their family workload is likely heavier and more complex than that of members of intact nuclear families. Workplaces need to recognise this complexity and offer more flexible approaches to FWAs that do not assume that the employee utilising them has got another parent at home who is available for short-notice childcare arrangements. Workplaces need to recognise that families are not stable entities and that the requirements for flexible working arrangements may change over time, both on a day-to-day basis and over the long term when it comes to relationship transitions and more complex family arrangements.

References

Abendroth, A.-K. & Reimann, M. 2018. Chapter 15 Telework and work–family conflict across workplaces: Investigating the implications of work–family-supportive and high-demand workplace cultures. Bingley, UK: Emerald Publishing.

Bakker, W. & Karsten, L. 2013. Balancing paid work, care and leisure in post-separation households: A comparison of single parents with co-parents. *Acta Sociologica, 56*(2), 173–187.

Beauregard, T.A. & Henry, L.C. 2009. Making the link between work-life balance practices and organizational performance. *Human Resource Management Review, 19*(1), 9–22.

Beck-Gernsheim, E. 2002. *Reinventing the Family: In Search of New Lifestyles*. Maiden, MA: Polity Press.

Bernardes, J. 1999. We must not define 'the family'! *Marriage & Family Review, 28*(3–4), 21–41.

Bernardi, L. & Mortelmans, D. (eds) 2018. *Lone Parenthood in the Life Course*. Cham, Switzerland: Springer.

Bernardi, L., Mortelmans, D. & Larenza, O. 2018. Changing lone parents, changing life courses. In L. Bernardi & D. Mortelmans (eds), *Lone Parenthood in the Life Course*. Cham, Switzerland: Springer.

Blair-Loy, M. 2003. *Competing Devotions. Career and family among women executives*. Cambridge, MA and London: Harvard University Press.

Blyaert, L., Van Parys, H., De Mol, J., & Buysse, A. 2016. Like a parent and a friend, but not the father: A qualitative study of stepfathers' experiences in the stepfamily. *Australian and New Zealand Journal of Family Therapy, 37*(1), 119–132.

Braithwaite, D.O., Mcbride, M.C., & Schrodt, P. 2003. 'Parent teams' and the everyday interactions of co-parenting in stepfamilies. *Communication Reports, 16*, 93–111.

Burnett, S.B., Gatrell, C.J., Cooper, C.L., & Sparrow, P. 2010. Well-balanced families?: A gendered analysis of work-life balance policies and work family practices. *Gender in Management: An International Journal, 25*, 534–549.

Cartwright, C. 2010. An exploratory investigation of parenting practices in stepfamilies. *New Zealand Journal of Psychology (Online), 39*, 57.

Cartwright, P. & Gibson, K. 2013. The effects of co-parenting relationships with ex-spouses on couples in step-families. *Family Matters, 91*, 18–28.

Casper, W.J., Eby, L.T., Bordeaux, C., Lockwood, A., & Lambert, D. 2007. A review of research methods in IO/OB work-family research. *Journal of Applied Psychology, 92*, 28.

Chung, H. & Van der Horst, M. 2018. Flexible working and unpaid overtime in the UK: The role of gender, parental and occupational status. *Social Indicators Research*, 1–26.

Coleman, M., Ganong, L., & Fine, M. 2000. Reinvestigating remarriage: Another decade of progress. *Journal of Marriage and Family, 62*, 1288–1307.

Dupuis, S. 2010. Examining the blended family: The application of systems theory toward an understanding of the blended family system. *Journal of Couple & Relationship Therapy*, *9*, 239–251.

EUROSTAT. 2017. *Families with children in the EU* [Online]. Available at: https://ec. europa.eu/eurostat/web/products-eurostat-news/-/EDN-20170531-1 [last accessed 27 August 2019].

Ford, J. & Collinson, D. 2011. In search of the perfect manager? Work-life balance and managerial work. *Work, employment and society*, *25*, 257–273.

Ganong, L. & Coleman, M. 2018. Studying stepfamilies: Four eras of family scholarship. *Family Process*, *57*, 7–24.

Ganong, L.H. & Coleman, M. 2017. *Stepfamily Relationships – Development, Dynamics and Interventions*. New York: Springer.

Gatrell, C. 2005. *Hard Labour: The Sociology of Parenthood* [electronic book]. Maidenhead, UK: Open University Press.

Gatrell, C. & Cooper, C.L. 2016. A sense of entitlement? Fathers, mothers and organizational support for family and career. *Community, Work & Family*, *19*, 134–147.

Gatrell, C.J., Burnett, S.B., Cooper, C.L., & Sparrow, P. 2013. Work-life balance and parenthood: A comparative review of definitions, equity and enrichment. *International Journal of Management Reviews*, *15*, 300–316.

Gatrell, C.J., Burnett, S.B., Cooper, C.L., & Sparrow, P. 2014. Parents, perceptions and belonging: Exploring flexible working among UK fathers and mothers. *British Journal of Management*, *25*, 473–487.

Gatrell, C.J., Burnett, S.B., Cooper, C.L., & Sparrow, P. 2015. The price of love: The prioritisation of childcare and income earning among UK fathers. *Families, Relationships and Societies*, *4*(2), 225–238.

Gingerbread 2019. *Single Parents: Facts and Figures* [online]. Available at: https://www.gingerbread.org.uk/what-we-do/media-centre/single-parents-facts-figures [last accessed 20 June 2019].

Gold, J.M. 2010. Helping stepfathers 'step away' from the role of 'father': Directions for family intervention. *The Family Journal*, *18*, 208–214.

Greenberg, D.N., Clair, J.A., & Ladge, J. 2016. Identity and the transition to motherhood: Navigating existing, temporary, and anticipatory identities. In C. Spitzmueller & R. Matthews (eds), *Research Perspectives on Work and the Transition to Motherhood*. New York: Springer.

Greenhaus, J.H. & Powell, G.N. 2006. When work and family are allies: A theory of work-family enrichment. *Academy of Management Review*, *31*, 72–92.

Hill, E.J., Grzywacz, J.G., Allen, S., Blanchard, V.L., Matz-Costa, C., Shulkin, S., & Pitt-Catsouphes, M. 2008. Defining and conceptualizing workplace flexibility. *Community, Work & Family*, *11*, 149–163.

Humberd, B., Ladge, J.J., & Harrington, B. 2015. The 'new' dad: Navigating fathering identity within organizational contexts. *Journal of Business and Psychology*, *30*, 249–266.

Jung Jang, S., Zippay, A., & Park, R. 2012. Family roles as moderators of the relationship between schedule flexibility and stress. *Journal of Marriage and Family*, *74*, 897–912.

Kumar, K. 2017. The blended family life cycle. *Journal of Divorce & Remarriage*, *58*, 110–125.

Ladge, J.J., Humberd, B.K., Baskerville Watkins, M., & Harrington, B. 2015. Updating the organization man: An examination of involved fathering in the workplace. *Academy of Management Perspectives*, *29*, 152–171.

Letablier, M.-T. & Wall, K. 2018. Changing lone parenthood patterns: New challenges for policy and research. In L. Bernardi & D. Mortelmans (eds), *Lone Parenthood in the Life Course. Life Course Research and Social Policies* (Vol. 8). Cham, Switzerland: Springer, pp. 29–53.

Lewis, S. 2001. Restructuring workplace cultures: The ultimate work-family challenge? *Women in Management Review*, *16*, 21–29.

Lewis, S. & Cooper, C. 2005. *Work-life integration: Case studies of organisational change*. Wiley Online Library. Available at: https://onlinelibrary.wiley.com/doi/book/10.1002/9780470713433

Lewis, S. & Humbert, A.L. 2010. Discourse or reality?: 'Work-life balance', flexible working policies and the gendered organization. *Equality, Diversity and Inclusion: An International Journal*, *29*, 239–254.

McIntosh, J. & Chisholm, R. 2008. Cautionary notes on the shared care of children in conflicted parental separation. *Journal of Family Studies*, *14*, 37–52.

Miller, T. 2011. Falling back into gender? Men's narratives and practices around first-time fatherhood. *Sociology*, *45*, 1094–1109.

Minnotte, K.L. 2012. Family structure, gender, and the work–family interface: Work-to-family conflict among single and partnered parents. *Journal of Family and Economic Issues*, *33*, 95–107.

Moilanen, S., Aunola, K., May, V., Sevón, E., & Laakso, M.-L. 2019. Nonstandard work hours and single versus coupled mothers' work-to-family conflict. *Family Relations*, *68*, 213–231.

Moilanen, S., May, V., Räikkönen, E., Sevón, E., & Laakso, M.-L. 2016. Mothers' non-standard working and childcare-related challenges. *International Journal of Sociology and Social Policy*, *36*, 36–52.

Morgan, D.H.G. 2011. Locating 'Family Practices'. *Sociological Research Online*, *16*, 1–9.

Office for National Statistics (ONS) 2014. Stepfamilies in 2011. Available online: https://webarchive.nationalarchives.gov.uk/20151014015956/http://www.ons.gov.uk/ons/rel/family-demography/stepfamilies/2011/index.html

Office for National Statistics (ONS) 2017. Families and households: 2017. Available online:https://www.ons.gov.uk/peoplepopulationandcommunity/birthsdeathsandmarriages/families/bulletins/familiesandhouseholds/2017

Özbilgin, M.F., Beauregard, T.A., Tatli, A., & Bell, M.P. 2011. Work-life, diversity and intersectionality: A critical review and research agenda. *International Journal of Management Reviews*, *13*, 177–198.

Parasuraman, S. & Greenhaus, J.H. 2002. Toward reducing some critical gaps in work-family research. *Human Resource Management Review*, *12*(3), 299–312.

Rabindrakumar, S. 2018. *One in Four – A Profile of Single Parents in the UK*. London: Gingerbread.

Reimann, M., Marx, C.K., & Diewald, M. 2019. Work-to-family and family-to-work conflicts among employed single parents in Germany. *Equality, Diversity and Inclusion: An International Journal*.

Richman, A.L., Civian, J.T., Shannon, L.L., Jeffrey Hill, E., & Brennan, R.T. 2008. The relationship of perceived flexibility, supportive work–life policies, and use of formal flexible arrangements and occasional flexibility to employee engagement and expected retention. *Community, Work and Family*, *11*, 183–197.

Shapiro, D. 2014. Stepparents and parenting stress: The roles of gender, marital quality, and views about gender roles. *Family Process*, *53*, 97–108.

Singley, S.G. & Hynes, K. 2005. Transitions to parenthood: Work-family policies, gender, and the couple context. *Gender & Society*, *19*, 376–397.

Smithson, J. & Stokoe, E.H. 2005. Discourses of work-life balance: Negotiating 'genderblind' terms in organizations. *Gender, Work and Organization, 12,* 147–168.

Tracy, S.J. & Rivera, K.D. 2010. Endorsing equity and applauding stay-at-home moms: How male voices on work-life reveal aversive sexism and flickers of transformation. *Management Communication Quarterly, 24,* 3–43.

Valiquette-Tessier, S.-C., Gosselin, J., Young, M., & Thomassin, K. 2018. A literature review of cultural stereotypes associated with motherhood and fatherhood. *Marriage & Family Review,* 1–31.

Weaver, S.E., Umaña-Taylor, A.J., Hans, J.D., & Malia, S.E. 2001. Challenges family scholars may face in studying family diversity: A focus on Latino families, stepfamilies, and reproductive technology. *Journal of Family Issues, 22,* 922–939.

Wheatley, D. 2017. Employee satisfaction and use of flexible working arrangements. *Work, Employment and Society, 31,* 567–585.

Williams, J. 2000. *Unbending Gender: Why Work and Family Conflict and What to do About It.* New York: Oxford University Press.

Wood, G., Phan, P.H., & Wright, M. 2018. The problems with theory and new challenges in theorizing. *Academy of Management Perspectives, 32,* 405–411.

15 Employee FWA needs and employer provisions across diverse age groups

Bernice Kotey and Stuart Wark

Introduction

Employees constitute an important resource for organisational success (Guest, 2011; Jiang et al., 2012) because their tacit knowledge, abilities, skills and experiences are often inimitable and non-substitutable, making them valuable for competitive advantage (Wright & McMahan, 2011; Wright et al., 2001; Barney et al., 2011). Unlike physical resources, employers must design the work environment and employees' work to motivate and assist employees to higher performance. The human resource (HR) literature has focussed on identifying practices that help achieve this aim (Jiang et al., 2012). However, the literature points to a gap in alignment of HR practices with changing employee values, attitudes to work and personal situations (Kooij et al., 2013; Cogin, 2012).

Technological advancement, intense competition, globalisation, consumerism and multiculturalism (Lewis et al., 2007), in addition to increasing feminisation and ageing of the workforce (Stirpe et al., 2018), require a rethink of the factors that create conducive environments for employees and motivate them to perform. Establishing conditions that enable employees to achieve an effective balance between their work and non-work commitments and appeal to the diverse age groups in the workforce (Cogin, 2012) are at the forefront of HR practices that improve employee performance (Posthuma et al., 2013). The importance of work-life balance (WLB) to employee welfare and performance has seen some countries legislate a *'right to request'* flexible work arrangements (FWAs) for employees (for example, the Australian Fair Work Act 2009; the Flexible Working Legislation (UK) 2014. In response, organisations make a variety of FWAs available so employees can tailor FWA requests to their specific needs. These needs differ with employee characteristics, including gender and age (Atkinson & Hall, 2009; Armstrong-Stassen & Lee, 2009; Bal & de Lange, 2015). As such, the gender and age distribution of employees in an organisation should impact the volume of requests for specific FWAs. This situation poses a challenge to employers who must effectively negotiate FWA requests to ensure the organisation is not subsequently disadvantaged by the changes in work conditions.

In Australia, the legislation addresses this dilemma by allowing employers to refuse FWA requests on specific grounds such as excessive costs, significant loss of productivity, negative impact on customer service and lack of capacity to accommodate the request (Australian Fair Work Act 2009). Despite employers' rights to refuse FWA requests, Thevenon et al. (2016, p. 6) find that between 50% and 90% of employees in Europe benefit from some form of flexible work schedule. Nonetheless, the means of access (whether through pursuit of non-standard positions or FWA requests) are not so clear.

Limited attention has been paid to how age diversity in the workforce affects HR practices (Cogin, 2012; Twenge, 2010); although it is known that employee values, health, expectations and behaviours vary across age groups and that these affect their work performance (Glass, 2007; Cogin, 2012). The literature base is even more unclear on how age differences affect requests for and access to FWAs (Sweet et al., 2014). To motivate performance, organisations must tailor their HR practices, including FWAs, to the age groups within their workforce (Kooij et al., 2014; Cogin, 2012). Nonetheless, specific conditions within organisations may prevent accommodation of the flexible work needs of employees.

This chapter explores how employers address the flexible work needs of the diverse age groups within their workforce. It identifies employee age groups for which employers would explicitly negotiate FWAs and those whose FWA needs are likely to be met from employer numerical flexible practices. The latter are at risk of either not meeting their FWA needs or becoming under-employed. Numerical flexible practices involve alterations to the number of employees or their work hours to match available labour with labour required to meet demand of an organisation's goods or services (Valverde et al., 2000). This chapter makes recommendations for an effective balance between FWA needs and provisions for all age groups within an organisation's workforce.

Employer flexible workplace practices and FWA provision

Employers adopt various flexible workplace practices, each aimed at specific outcomes. Numerical flexibility refers to the ability of employers to alter the number of employees or work hours in response to fluctuating customer demand (Roca-Puig et al., 2008; Stavrou & Kilaniotis, 2010; Valverde et al., 2000). Employers may do this by engaging employees on part-time, casual or short-term contracts, on-call 'as needed' basis or on shift work. They may also take on temporary workers who are paid by labour hire firms. Employers may use these numerical flexible positions to meet employees' FWA needs (Whyman et al., 2015). Functional flexibility provides employees with job enrichment through job sharing, job rotation, participation in decision-making, training, long-term development and autonomy (Voudouris, 2007). In addition to motivating employees, functional flexibility allows development of a multi-skilled and innovative workforce. It ensures employees with relevant skills are available as needed and can generate new ideas to move the organisation forward as they broaden their skills and knowledge of operations (Whyman et al., 2015; Roca-Puig et al., 2008; Valverde et al., 2000). Employers also use various remuneration structures to match employee performance with organisational outcomes and motivate employees to high performance (Whyman et al., 2015). Numerical and functional flexibility practices are relevant to employee flexible work needs and are expanded below.

Drawing from Atkinson's (1984) work, Valverde et al. (2000) identify three groups of employees associated with numerical flexibility, based on permanency of their positions and level of employer commitment. The first group comprises employees on permanent and standard contracts, responsible for the core activities of the organisation, and to whom employers direct their high-performance work practices (HPWPs), including functional flexibility practices, and provide long-term commitment (Kalleberg, 2001; Osterman, 2000). This core group constitutes an important source of competitive advantage as their capabilities and competencies become aligned with employer needs over time (Voudouris, 2007; Barney et al., 2011), and employers seek to retain them.

The next group includes employees with non-standard contracts such as part-time, casual or short-term, apprentices and those job-sharing (Valverde et al., 2000). Although the organisation has administrative responsibility for this group (Kalleberg, 2001), their inability to participate fully in functional flexible activities due to their absences from the workplace may limit any long-term commitment to their development and motivation (Valverde et al., 2000). Nonetheless, organisations may draw from this group to meet vacancies in the core group. Moreover, in Australia casual employees have the right to request permanent employment if they work the same weekly hours consistently over a year (Skinner et al., 2016). A third group, engaged temporarily from labour hire firms or as contractors, are not considered employees of the organisation (Kalleberg, 2001) and are excluded from its HPWPs (Voudouris, 2007). Organisations use non-standard contracts for specific purposes such as to:

- Address fluctuations in customer demand,
- Reduce labour cost,
- Fill temporary vacancies in the core group, or
- For short-term projects.

Their use protects core employees from involuntary employee turnover and enhances their internal job mobility by limiting competition for higher positions within the organisation (Kalleberg, 2001).

Research indicates that employees on these non-standard contracts tend to be more productive than those on standard contracts, as they have capacity to work intensively within the relatively short hours available to them (Valverde et al., 2000). Non-standard contracts also allow employers to access skilled and experienced workers who may otherwise not be available to them, and the effective integration of skilled professional contractors with core employees facilitates innovation (Voudouris, 2007).

Despite the advantages, numerical flexibility may cause problems that require careful management of employees in the various groups. In particular, non-standard employees may respond to the limited development opportunities with disinterestedness, disaffection and less-than-optimal performance (Kleinknecht et al., 2006). Moreover, highly specialised contractors and short-term professionals may demand high pay, defeating the aim of reducing labour costs. Poor communication, conflict with core employees and inadequate attention to safety may also significantly increase the cost of employees on non-standard contracts (Kleinknecht et al., 2006). Organisations therefore, tend to allocate specialist functions to core employees to whom they direct their HPWPs (Osterman, 2000).

Available statistics indicate that non-standard employment is on the rise while full-time permanent positions are decreasing; a situation attributed to increasing feminisation and ageing of the workforce (Organisation for Economic Co-operation and Development (OECD), 2019a). Katz and Krueger (2019) also confirm a gradual rise in the share of workers in non-standard jobs in the United States since the early 2000s. The OECD 2019 Employment Outlook suggests that job stability has decreased over the past two decades, especially among the less-educated workforce (OECD, 2019a). It attributes this to employee mobility rather than to involuntary separation for countries such as Sweden, Germany, France, Great Britain and Hungary. However, for Italy, Australia, Denmark, Spain and Latvia, the excess of involuntary separations over job-to-job movements poses real risk and uncertainty to stable employment.

The above trends, together with increasing automation and polarisation of labour markets (with a declining share of middle-skilled positions) explain the decrease in full-time employees (OECD, 2019a) to whom employers direct HPWPs. Employers are likely to focus FWA provisions on these full-time, usually skilled employees (OECD, 2019a; Thevenon et al., 2016). The implications are that employers may overlook employees outside these demographics for FWA provisions, particularly FWAs such as job sharing that may add to labour costs.

Employees may seek part-time or temporary employment to manage their non-work commitments themselves, while employers may accommodate the flexible work needs of core employees in order to retain them. The literature is unclear as to whether and how employers use flexible workplace practices to manage employee flexible work needs and the extent to which employees avail themselves of numerical flexible positions to self-manage their flexible work needs. The various types of FWAs are explained next so they can be matched with the flexible work needs of employees in various age groups.

Types of flexible work arrangements requested by employees

In contrast to employer flexible practices, employees primarily initiate FWAs (Kelliher & Anderson, 2010; Russell et al., 2009), which may require specific structures and systems to administer. FWAs are important to social sustainability of employees and are key components of high-performance work systems (Wang et al., 2011; Posthuma et al., 2013). They take various forms and include flexible start and finish times, compressed work time, flexible leave entitlements, reduced work hours, job sharing and telecommuting or working from home (Fairwork Ombudsman, 2016).

Employees who work flexible hours are able to start or leave early/late or compress their work hours, i.e. work longer hours on specific days and take longer breaks on others. However, they must work the standard daily, weekly or monthly hours and be available for work during core periods (Fairwork Ombudsman, 2016). In general, these FWAs do not involve profound changes to work organisation and entail little or no cost to employers (Thevenon et al., 2016). Employers are therefore, often willing to accommodate flexible work hours and it is the most common form of FWA provision (OECD, 2019a). Employees can access similar flexibility by selecting shifts or roster times that suit their personal circumstances, trading off payment for overtime work on some days with reduced hours on other days, i.e. time off in lieu, or compressing their workweek into fewer days (Riedmann et al., 2006). Depleted energies from long hours of compressed work could impact performance negatively.

Employers may also allow flexible use, accrual or extension of leave entitlements with or without pay (Australian Fair Work Act 2009). For flexible leave to be effective, the timing must be discussed in advance to enable work of employees on leave to be covered (Kotey & Sharma, 2016). Flexible leave allows employees to allocate time to critical family and personal needs.

Employees can negotiate reduced work hours to care for a dependent child or relative, advance education, take up another job, or reduce personal stress. Employers may allocate employees who request shorter working hours to part-time positions or allow them to job-share with one or more co-workers. Job-sharing involves splitting work between two or more people, such as 2.5 days each or a 2:3-day split (Fairwork Ombudsman, 2016). To be effective, job-sharing must be well planned and organised; it must have the direct supervisor's support, the right partner and work divisions should be equitable and clearly communicated (Walton et al., 2011). The difficulty of finding suitable partners and organising work for seamless transition from one partner to another limits the use of job-sharing (Gallo, 2013). However, if well implemented, the additional intellectual capital, reduced stress, increased job satisfaction and motivation can generate productivity gains (Gallo, 2013). The evidence suggests that women with children tend to use part-time and other reduced work arrangements more than other employees (Eurofound, 2016;

Thevenon et al., 2016), although the number of male part-time workers is ris-ing (OECD, 2017). Re-organising work to accommodate employee requests for reduced hours may entail costs (Beauregard & Henry, 2009) and employ-ers may turn to flexible workplace positions to accommodate such requests.

Employees can negotiate to work from home, but tasks must be completed on schedule (Lee & Hong, 2011). Employers are often reluctant to allow work from home since family commitment may interfere with work (Thev-enon et al., 2016). Moreover, work from home is not feasible for employees in service industries that require direct contact with customers (Kotey & Sharma, 2016). Nonetheless, Bloom et al. (2015) note that this FWA has be-come widespread practice for professional staff, with about 50% of managers in the US, UK and Germany allowed to work from home occasionally dur-ing normal hours.

Researchers report positive associations between FWA availability or provi-sion and job satisfaction (Haar et al., 2014). Others note that FWAs encourage work commitment among employees (Maxwell et al., 2007; Chow & Keng-Howe, 2006). Kim and Wiggins (2011) and Wang et al. (2011) suggest that employee empowerment from FWA provisions reduces absenteeism and turn-over intentions, encourages commitment, improves job attitudes and reduces work-related stress. According to Posthuma et al. (2013), FWAs ultimately improve organisational learning, environmental adaptability and competi-tiveness. Grzywacz et al. (2008) conclude that FWAs contribute positively to productivity because they enhance employee health and reduce the rate of absenteeism and turnover. Kossek and Michel (2011) acknowledge that FWAs provide employees greater control over their work environments and there-fore, improve their wellbeing. Despite these positive assertions, the business case for FWAs remains unclear (de Menezes & Kelliher, 2011), with Beaure-gard and Henry (2009) arguing that the pathways from FWA provisions to reductions in work-life conflict for employees and enhancement in organisa-tional performance may not be strong. The next sections draw from life cycle theories to establish age groups and analyse their FWA needs. This assessment is important given aging of the population and employee FWA needs.

Employee age and life cycle theories

Loretto and Vickerstaff (2015) draw attention to the disjointed literature on the flexible work needs of employees in various age groups. They note the tendency for research to focus on younger employees with children, while the needs of the workforce aged over 50, who may have dual carer responsibilities and/or emerging personal health issues, have received limited attention.

Lifespan theories have emerged over time to explain the biological, psy-chological and social changes that occur as people age and how these alter their needs, preferences and work performance (Kooij et al., 2011). Cars-tensen's (2006) socioemotional selectivity theory identifies differences in mo-tivation and resource deployment between young and old people. It notes that young people's expansive perception of time and belief in a long and unknown future push them to pursue growth goals, particularly with respect to knowledge acquisition and career development. As a result, they are motivated by extrinsic rewards, such as challenging work, career advancement, recognition and compensation (Kooij et al., 2014). This is consistent with Fuchs' (1983, p. 76) description of the years between 25 and 44 as a 'sowing period'. In contrast, older people recognise time as limited and turn their attention to the present and to emotional aspirations, allocating resources to maintaining resilience.

According to Baltes' (1997) Selection, Optimisation and Compensation (SOC) model, people experience gains and losses in physical and mental capabilities as they age and endeavour to maximise gains and minimise losses by reducing the goals for which their diminishing resources are used. Other researchers have noted that older workers respond to intrinsic rewards such as interesting work, autonomy, accomplishment, opportunity to use their skills to mentor others and job security (Kooij et al., 2011; Kanfer & Ackerman, 2004). Old age is, therefore, a period of reaping rewards from earlier years of hard work and using the knowledge, skills and experiences gained over time to mentor younger employees (Fuchs 1983).

Overlaying the above age-related psychological and biological changes are social pursuits that impose responsibilities outside of work and affect work performance. These include marriage, starting a family, and caring responsibilities for children and/or ageing parents. Levinson (1978) identified these events as signalling a change in life cycle.

The average age of childbirth in 2016 for countries in the OECD was 30 years, ranging from 26 years in Bulgaria to 31.4 years in Korea (OECD, 2018). Over the following 10 to 20 years, parents have the responsibility of caring for their dependent children while simultaneously working to build assets and grow their careers. As teenage children become less dependent, their parents are able to pursue growth and career ambitions with less intensive family responsibilities. Even so, this freedom could be impacted if ageing parents, family members with lifelong disability and/or new grandchildren require care, all of which could adversely affect work options for employees (Haberkern et al., 2011). While the chapter focuses on these traditional life-changing events, increasingly people are choosing not to have children, to remain single, or to raise their children as sole parents or in same-sex families. It is acknowledged that this diversity and societal change has implications for flexible work needs (Bond, 2002; Parasuraman & Greenhaus, 2002; Bourke, 2004; O'Connell & Russell, 2005; Janasz et al., 2013; Khan & Agha, 2013; Bird, 2016); although these are not discussed in depth in this chapter.

Barrett et al. (2014) note that, concurrently with increasing life expectancy, informal family support networks are reducing, limiting the number of individuals able to share caregiving responsibilities for children and ageing parents. According to Kim et al. (2013), inadequate government support structures make it difficult for caregivers to maintain full-time work. To alleviate the resulting financial hardship from low wages in the short term and reduced retirement income in the longer term, there is growing recognition of the potential use of FWAs for older workers and those with carer responsibilities, as a mechanism to provide a conducive workplace (Goldman & Lewis, 2005). Atkinson and Sandiford (2016) report that older workers value FWAs and that the use of FWAs can assist to prolong their working lives. However, there is limited research that specifically compares employee request for FWAs among the age groups in the workforce against employer provisions.

Four age groups are delineated based on the life events described above. The first is young adults (15–24 years), then middle adults (25–44 years), mature workers (45–54 years) and lastly, senior workers (aged 55 years and older). There is general consensus that age-related changes in work motivation begin around the age of 45 (Bal & Dorenbosch, 2015; Kooij et al., 2011) and that 55 years is the age at which employees begin to consider retirement and work options (Soidre, 2005; Westerlund et al., 2010). Researchers often focus on the age groups before and after 45 years. However, OECD statistics consider employees aged 15–24 years as having different work profiles from the other age groups. Since retirement intentions affect employee behaviours, the work profiles of 55-year-olds and above should differ from those aged 45–54 years. Even so, Agarwal et al. (2018) identify the super-aged (65 years plus) as having different characteristics from those aged 55–64 years. They note that with increasing lifespan and decreasing birth rates, the super-aged represent an untapped source of competitive advantage for organisations. The super-aged are included in the 55 years plus group in the analyses of employment profiles and FWA needs of the age groups in the next section, which are summarised in Table 15.1 below.

Employment profiles and FWA needs and access among the age groups

The 'young adult' stage starts when children transition into adulthood and begin to exert their independence; working to earn income, starting a family and/or extending their knowledge, skills and experiences to shape their careers. With limited experience and bargaining positions, the employment rate is low among young adults (42.2% for first quarter of 2019; OECD, 2019b) who are pushed into available job openings. They are likely to access non-standard employment as part-time or temporary workers, which is conducive to studying or working multiple jobs. This position is consistent with data from the OECD (2019a) and the Ai Group (2018) for Australia, which show that young adults, particularly those without tertiary education, have low work hours and face high risk of under-employment. The Ai Group (2018) identifies studying as the main reason for part-time work among this age group. FWA needs of young adults are, therefore, likely to be met from non-standard employment and few would successfully negotiate FWAs as full-time employees.

Table 15.1 Employment profiles and FWA access for employee age groups in developed and emerging countries

Age group	Employment profiles	FWA access
15–24 years. Young adults – commencing careers.	Studying, limited family commitments, limited skills and experience, multiple jobs, part-time or temporary positions involving non-standard hours, high levels of unemployment and under-employment.	Flexible work needs met through non-standard positions. Weak negotiating capacity for FWAs.
25–44 years. Middle adults – pursuing career growth, starting families and building assets.	Employment status depends on skill, experience, education and gender. The highly educated and skilled can access standard employment and enjoy FWAs. Low- to middle-skilled workers without tertiary education, especially females with carer responsibilities, may access part-time or temporary positions.	Highly educated and skilled employees can negotiate FWAs, especially flexible work hours. Low- to middle-skilled workers without tertiary education, including females with carer responsibilities, may access flexibility through non-standard contracts.
45–54 years. Mature workers – consolidating work, seeking stability and recognition.	The highly skilled and experienced employees, with or without tertiary qualifications but sustained career growth could be at the peak of their careers, with positions as professionals or managers. Some outside this group would access non-standard positions comprising part-time, casual or short-term contracts or temporary employment. Under-employment and unemployment would be lowest in this group.	Those with standard employment can negotiate flexible hours and other FWAs, though some FWAs (e.g. compressed hours) may be less desirable. Those with carer responsibilities should be able to negotiate reduced work hours. Others would seek flexibility through non-standard employment.
55 years and above. Senior workers – with reduced energies, contemplating retirement.	Pursuit of social goals and any potential changes in health status could encourage older workers to seek non-standard contracts.	Many, especially from 60 years onwards, would negotiate reduced hours. They will avoid explicitly requesting compressed hours and overtime.

Source: Compiled by the authors from information in this chapter, which draws on research noted in the reference list. For example, see Agarwal et al., 2018; Atkinson & Sandiford, 2016; Bal & de Lange, 2015; Cogin, 2012; de Lange, Kooij & Van der Heijden, 2015; Glass, 2007; Goldman & Lewis, 2005; Kanfer & Ackerman, 2004; Kooij et al., 2014; Loretto & Vickerstaff, 2015; Riedmann et al., 2006; Twenge, 2010; Wang et al., 2011; and Whyman et al., 2015, amongst others. See References at the end of the chapter for further details.

Pursuit of growth and extrinsic rewards is prevalent among middle adults who are looking to raise families and establish careers (Baltes, 1997). Their employment status and FWA requirements depend on their gender, education and skill levels. Those with limited skills and without tertiary qualifications may access part-time, casual or short-term contracts or temporary positions or they may require flexible work hours if they are in full-time positions and have preschool-age children (OECD, 2019a). Middle adults include the large number of females who work part-time to meet flexible work needs (Eurofound, 2016; Ai Group, 2018). They are less likely to access the HPWPs available to core employees (Thevenon et al., 2016), including desired FWAs. On the contrary, highly educated and experienced middle adults are good candidates for permanent positions as core employees to whom organisations direct their HPWPs (Kooij et al., 2011). Employees in this group are likely to be successful at negotiating flexible work hours, telecommuting and other FWAs. FWAs for employees in this group often relate to meeting carer responsibilities (Ai Group, 2018). In general, the risk of under-employment is lower for middle adults than for young adults (OECD, 2019a).

Careers peak simultaneously with declining carer responsibilities for children for mature workers. Similar to middle adults, their education, skills and carer responsibilities would determine their employment status (OECD, 2019a). Those with tertiary education, established careers, stable work and limited carer responsibilities would be attracted to few FWAs, although in good bargaining positions to negotiate them. Mature workers would seek to consolidate their work achievements and pursue recognition for their accomplishments (Kooij et al., 2011; Fuchs, 1983). Those without carer responsibilities are likely to seek job security with flexible hours to attend to social commitments that meet their emotional needs, while those with carer responsibilities may negotiate other FWAs (e.g. reduced hours and working from home). Despite the long work hours associated with high-level positions, mature workers in these positions would avoid explicitly negotiating compressed work hours. Unemployment is usually low among mature workers (OECD, 2019b) and those who work non-standard hours do so by choice (Ai Group, 2018), although at the risk of under-employment if unable to secure their desired work hours.

Senior workers may experience a reduction in work performance due to potential changes in health status. However, other reports suggest that overall an age-diverse team can enhance profits and productivity since older workers bring experience, skills and better people skills to their job (Agarwal et al., 2018). Senior workers would, therefore, seek exemptions from compressed hours and overtime work. Moreover, social and emotional needs and care for older relatives or grandchildren may lead them to request flexible or reduced hours, part-time work, job sharing or even retirement (de Lange et al., 2015). Preference for reduced hours puts senior workers, particularly males, at risk of under-employment (OECD, 2019a). The indications are that senior workers are in a lesser position to negotiate suitable FWAs.

Summary and conclusions

Employees initiate FWAs, which may require different structures and systems from employer numerical flexibility practices to administer. However, employers consider their flexibility practices when negotiating FWAs. They focus their HPWPs, including FWAs, on motivating and retaining employees working standard hours in core positions. Employees on part-time or short-term contracts and temporary workers, all with non-standard work hours, complement those in the core group. In comparison to the core workers, absences from the workplace tend to limit long-term development of employees on non-standard contracts. Employees, particularly young adults and senior workers, as well as females with carer responsibilities may apply for non-standard positions to manage their flexible work needs or are allocated non-standard positions when they negotiate FWAs. These employees are most at risk of under-employment if unable to secure their desired work hours (OECD, 2019a). In contrast, highly skilled and experienced employees with tertiary qualifications, usually in the middle adult and mature worker groups, are the most likely to secure standard work and to negotiate FWAs successfully (Thevenon et al., 2016).

Young adults can reduce their risk of unemployment or under-employment over time through education and skill enhancement. However, middle adults and mature and senior workers in low- to middle-skill occupations face declining job quality when forced into lengthy non-standard positions to manage their flexible work needs. Inability to access the hours required to maintain effective work-life balance, job insecurity and poor working conditions could have negative short- and long-term consequences for these employees. Low income and inadequate retirement savings leave them at the risk of reduced standards of living. The ensuing recommendations follow from the above analyses.

Recommendations

With respect to developed and emerging countries to which this chapter applies, we recommend government intervention (at the national level) beyond legislation, to reduce the risk of under-employment and improve work-life balance for all employees. Our recommendations are based on the premise that the *right to request* legislation (Thevenon et al., 2016) cannot oblige employers to accommodate FWA requests at the expense of economic viability of their organisations. This means several employees are unlikely to have their FWA requests met. We therefore recommend that governments:

- Increase dependable care facilities so that employees can work in their desired positions and hours, knowing that their children and/or family members are well cared for.
- Encourage employers to engage older workers by supplementing any additional costs of their employment.
- Encourage upgrade in skills and tertiary qualifications to empower employees and enhance access to standard employment with FWA provisions.

Work-life balance issues have significant economic and social implications and should be among the priority areas of government agenda.

References

Agarwal, D.J.G., Schwartz, J. & Volini, E. 2018, 'The longevity dividend: Work in an era of 100-year lives', *2018 Global Human Capital Trends*. Available at: https://www2.deloitte.com/insights/us/en/focus/human-capital-trends/2018/advantages-implications-of-aging-workforce.html [last accessed 5 August 2019].

Ai Group 2018, 'Economics research: Casual work and part-time work in Australia in 2018'. Available at: www.aigroup.com.au/policy-and-research/economics [last accessed 19 July 2019].

Armstrong-Stassen, M. & Lee, S.H. 2009, 'The effect of relational age on older Canadian employees' perceptions of human resource practices and sense of worth to their organization', *International Journal of Human Resource Management*, 20(8), 1753–1769.

Atkinson, C. & Hall, L. 2009, 'The role of gender in varying forms of flexible working', *Gender Work and Organization*, 16(6), 650–666.

Atkinson, C. & Sandiford, P. 2016, 'An exploration of older worker flexible working arrangements in smaller firms', *Human Resource Management Journal*, 26(1), 12–28.

Atkinson, J. 1984, 'Manpower strategies for flexible organizations', *Personnel Management*, 15(8), 28–31.

Australian Fair Work Act 2009, 'Division 4: Request for flexible working arrangements'. Available at: https //wwwfwcgovau/documents/documents/legislation/fw_act/FW_Act-01htm#P1496_137337 [last accessed 3 November 2018].

Bal, P.M. & Dorenbosch, L. 2015, 'Age-related differences in the relations between individualised HRM and organisational performance: A large-scale employer survey', *Human Resources Management Journal*, 25(1), 41–61.

Bal, P.M. & de Lange, A.H. 2015, 'From flexibility human resource management to employee engagement and perceived job performance across the lifespan: A multi-sample study', *Journal of Occupational and Organisational Psychology*, 88(1), 126–154.

Baltes, P.B. 1997, 'On the incomplete architecture of human ontogeny selection, optimization and compensation as foundation of developmental theory', *American Psychologist*, 52(4), 366–380.

Barney, J.B., Ketchen Jr, D.J. & Wright, M. 2011, 'The future of resource-based theory: Revitalization or decline?', *Journal of Management*, 37(5), 1299–1315.

Barrett, P., Hale, B. & Butler, M. 2014, 'Caring for a family member with a lifelong disability'. In P. Barrett, B. Hale & M. Butler (eds), *Family Care and Social Capital: Transitions in Informal Care* (pp. 75–90). Dordrecht, Netherlands: Springer.

Beauregard, T.A. & Henry, L.C. 2009, 'Making the link between work-life balance practices and organizational performance', *Human Resource Management Review*, 19(1), 9–22.

Bird, R.C. 2016, 'Precarious work: The need for flexitime employment rights and proposals for reform', *Berkeley Journal of Employment and Labor Law*, 37(1), 1–42.

Bloom, N., Liang, J., Roberts, J. & Ying, Z.J. 2015, 'Does working from home work? Evidence from a Chinese experiment', *The Quarterly Journal of Economics*, 130(1), 165–218.

Bond, J.T., Thompson, C.A., Galinsky, E. & Prottas, D. 2002, *Highlights of the National Study of the Changing Workforce*. New York: Families and Work Institute.

Bourke, J. 2004, 'Using the law to support work/life issues: The Australian experience', *American University Journal of Gender, Social Policy & the Law*, 12(1), 19–68.

Carstensen, L.L. 2006, 'The influence of a sense of time on human development', *Science*, *312*(5782), 1913–1915.

Chow, I.H. & Keng-Howe, I.C. 2006, 'The effect of alternative work schedules on employee performance', *International Journal of Employment Studies*, *14*(1), 105–130.

Cogin, J. 2012, 'Are generational differences in work values factor or fiction? Multi-country evidence and implications', *International Journal of Human Resource Management*, *23*(11), 2268–2294.

Eurofound 2016, *Sixth European Working Conditions Survey: Overview Report*. Luxembourg: Publications Office of the European Union.

Fairwork Ombudsman 2016, 'Flexible working arrangements'. Available at: https://wwwfairworkgovau/employee-entitlements/flexibility-in-the-workplace/flexible-working-arrangements [last accessed 3 November 2018].

Flexible Working Legislation (UK) 2014 *Flexible Working Gov UK*, viewed 11 September 2019, http://www.legislation.gov.uk/uksi/2014/1398/pdfs/uksi_20141398_en.pdf

Fuchs, V.R. 1983, *How We Live*. Cambridge, MA: Harvard University Press.

Gallo, A. 2013, 'How to make a job sharing situation work', *Harvard Business Review*. Available at: https://hbr.org/2013/09/how-to-make-a-job-sharing-situation-work [last accessed 3 November 2018].

Glass, A. 2007, 'Understanding generational differences for competitive success', *Industrial and Commercial Training*, *39*(2), 98–103.

Goldman, L. & Lewis, J. 2005, 'Equality comes of age: Forthcoming regulations are set to make age discrimination a thing of the past', *Occupational Health*, *57*(10), 10–12.

Grzywacz, J.G., Carlson, D.S. & Shulkin, S. 2008, 'Schedule flexibility and stress: Linking formal flexible arrangements and perceived flexibility to employee health', *Community Work and Family*, *11*(2), 199–214.

Guest, D.E. 2011, 'Human resource management and performance: Still searching for some answers', *Human Resource Management Journal*, *21*(1), 3–13.

Haar, J.M., Russo, M., Sune, A. & Ollier-Malaterre, A. 2014, 'Outcomes of work–life balance on job satisfaction, life satisfaction and mental health: A study across seven cultures', *Journal of Vocational Behavior*, *85*(3), 361–373.

Haberkern, F.K., Schmid, T., Neuberger, F. & Grignon, M. 2011, 'The role of the elderly as providers and recipients of care', *The Future of Families to 2030* (pp. 189–257). Paris: OECD.

Janasz, S., Forret, M., Haack, D. & Jonsen, K. 2013, 'Family status and work attitudes', *British Journal of Management*, *24*(2), 191–210.

Jiang, K., Lepak, D.P., Hu, J. & Baer, J. 2012, 'How does human resource management influence organisational outcomes? A meta-analytic investigation of mediating mechanisms', *Academy of Management Journal*, *55*(6), 1264–1294.

Kalleberg, A.L. 2001, 'Organizing flexibility: The flexible firm in a new century', *British Journal of Industrial Relations*, *39*(4), 479–504.

Kanfer, R. & Ackerman, P.L. 2004, 'Aging, adult development and work motivation', *Academy of Management Review*, *29*(3), 440–458.

Katz, L.F. & Krueger, A.B. 2019, 'The rise and nature of alternative work arrangements in the United States, 1995–2015', *International and Labour Relations Review*, *72*(2), 382–416.

Kelliher, C. & Anderson, D. 2010, 'Doing more with less? Flexible working practices and the intensification of work', *Human Relations*, *63*(1), 83–106.

Khan, S. & Agha, K. 2013, 'Dynamics of the work life balance at the firm level: Issues and challenges', *Journal of Management Policy and Practice*, 14(4), 103–114.

Kim, J. & Wiggins, M.E. 2011, 'Family-friendly human resource policy: Is it still working in the Public sector?', *Public Administration Review*, 75(5), 728–739.

Kim, J., Ingersoll-Dayton, B. & Minyoung, K. 2013, 'Balancing eldercare and employment: The role of work interruptions and supportive employers', *Journal of Applied Gerontology*, 32(3), 347–369.

Kleinknecht, A., Oostendorp, R.M., Pradhan, M.P. & Naastepad, C.W.M. 2006, 'Flexible labour, firm performance and the Dutch job creation miracle', *International Review of Applied Economics*, 20(2), 171–187.

Kooij, D., Guest, D., Clinton, M., Knight, T., Jansen, P. & Dikkers, J. 2013, 'How the impact of HR practices on employee well-being and performance changes with age', *Human Resource Management Journal*, 23(1), 18–35.

Kooij, D., Jansen, P., Dikkers, J. & de Lange, A. 2014, 'Managing aging workers: A mixed methods study on bundles of HR practices for aging workers', *International Journal of Human Resource Management*, 25(15), 2192–2212.

Kooij, D., de Lange, A., Jansen, P., Kanfer, R. & Dikkers, J. 2011, 'Age and work-related motives: Results of a meta-analysis', *Journal of Organizational Behavior*, 32, 197–225.

Kossek, E. & Michel, J. 2011, 'APA handbook of industrial and organizational psychology'. In S. Zedeck (ed.), *Flexible Work Schedules* (pp. 535–572). Washington, DC: American Psychological Association.

Kotey, B. & Sharma, B. 2016, 'Predictors of flexible working arrangement provision in small and medium enterprises SMEs', *International Journal of Human Resource Management*, 27(22), 2753–2770.

de Lange, A.H., Kooij, D.T. & Van der Heijden, B.I. 2015, 'Human resource management and sustainability of work across the lifespan: An integrative perspective'. In L.M. Finkelstein, D.M. Truxillo, F. Fraccaroli & R. Kanfer (eds), *Facing the Challenges of a Multi-Age Workforce, a Use-Inspired Approach* (pp. 50–80). New York and London: Routledge.

Lee, S.Y. & Hong, J.H. 2011, 'Does fairly-friendly policy matter? Testing its impact on turnover and performance', *Public Administration Review*, 71(6), 870–879.

Levinson, D. 1978, *The Seasons of a Man's Life*. New York: Alfred A Knopf.

Lewis, S., Gambles, R. & Rapoport, R. 2007, 'The constraints of a work-life balance approach: An international perspective', *International Journal of Human Resource Management*, 18(3), 360–373.

Loretto, W. & Vickerstaff, S. 2015, 'Gender, age and flexible working in later life', *Work, Employment and Society*, 29(2), 233–249.

Maxwell, G., Rankine, L., Bell, S. & MacVicar, A. 2007, 'The incidence and impact of flexible working arrangements in smaller businesses', *Employee Relations*, 29(2), 138–161.

de Menezes, L.M. & Kelliher, C. 2011. 'Flexible working and performance: A systematic review of the evidence for a business case', *International Journal of Management Reviews*, 13(4), 452–474.

O'Connell, P.J. & Russell, H. 2005, *Equality at Work? Equality Policies, Flexible Working Arrangements and the Quality of Work*. Dublin, Ireland: Equality Authority Research Series.

Organisation for Economic Co-operation and Development (OECD) 2017, 'Chapter 18 Flexible working arrangements'. In *The Pursuit of Gender Equality: An Uphill Battle*.

OECD. Available at: https://read.oecd-ilibrary.org/social-issues-migration-health/the-pursuit-of-gender-equality/flexible-working-arrangements_9789264281318-21-en#page1 [last accessed 19 July 2019].

Organisation for Economic Co-operation and Development (OECD) 2018, *SF2.3: Age of Mothers at Childbirth and Age-Specific Fertility*. Paris: OECD, Social Policy Division, Directorate of Employment, Labour and Social Affairs.

Organisation for Economic Co-operation and Development (OECD) 2019a, *OECD 2019 Employment Outlook*. Paris: OECD.

Organisation for Economic Co-operation and Development (OECD) 2019b, *Employment Rate (Indicator)*. Available at: https://data.oecd.org/emp/employment-rate.htm [last accessed 19 July 2019].

Osterman, P. 2000, 'Work reorganization in an era of restructuring: Trends in diffusion and effects on employee welfare', *Industrial and Labor Relations Review*, *53*(2), 179–196.

Parasuraman, S. & Greenhaus, J.H. 2002, 'Toward reducing some critical gaps in work-family research', *Human Resource Management Review*, *12*(3), 299–312.

Posthuma, R.A., Campion, M.C., Masimova, M. & Campion, M.A. 2013, 'A high performance work practices taxonomy: Integrating the literature and directing future research', *Journal of Management*, *39*(5), 1184–1220.

Riedmann, A., Bielenski, H., Szczurowska, T. & Wagner, A. 2006, 'Working time and work-life balance in European companies', *European Foundation for the Improvement of Living and Working Conditions*. Luxembourg: Office for Official Publications of the European Communities.

Roca-Puig, V., Beltrán-Martín, I., Bou-Llusar, J. & Escrig-Tena, A. 2008, 'External and internal labour flexibility in Spain: A substitute or complementary effect on firm performance?', *The International Journal of Human Resource Management*, *19*(6), 1131–1151.

Russell, H., O'Connell, P.J. & McGinnity, F. 2009, 'The impact of flexible working arrangements on work-life conflict and work pressure in Ireland', *Gender Work and Organization*, *16*(1), 73–97.

Skinner, N., Cathcart, A. & Pocock, B. 2016, 'To ask or not to ask? Investigating workers' flexibility requests and the phenomenon of discontented non-requesters', *Labour & Industry: A Journal of the Social and Economic Relations of Work*, *26*(2), 103–119.

Soidre, T. 2005, 'Retirement-age preferences of women and men aged 55–64 years in Sweden', *Ageing & Society*, *25*(6), 943–963.

Stavrou, E. & Kilaniotis, I.C. 2010, 'Flexible working and turnover', *British Journal of Management*, *21*(2), 541–554.

Stirpe, L., Trullen, J. & Bonache, J. 2018, 'Retaining an ageing workforce: The effects of high-performance work systems and flexible work programmes', *Human Resource Management Journal*, *28*(4), 585–604.

Sweet, S., Pitt-Catsouphes, M., Besen, E. & Golden, L. 2014, 'Explaining organizational variation in flexible work arrangements: Why the pattern and scale of availability matter', *Community Work and Family*, *17*(2), 115–141.

Thevenon, O., Clarke, C. & Adema, W. 2016, *Be Flexible! Background Brief on How Flexibility can Help European Employees Balance Work and Family*. OECD Technical Report. Paris: OECD, Better Policies for Better Lives, Social Policy Division, Directorate for Employment, Labour and Social Affairs.

Twenge, G.M. 2010, 'A review of the empirical evidence on generational work attitudes', *Journal of Business Psychology*, *25*(2), 201–210.

Valverde, M., Tregaskis, O. & Brewster, C. 2000, 'Labour flexibility and firm performance', *International Advances in Economic Research*, 6(4), 649–661.

Voudouris, I. 2007, 'The co-evolution of functional and numerical flexibility: Do technology and networking matter?', *New Technology, Work and Employment*, 22(3), 224–245.

Walton, P., Gatrell, C. & Tomlinson, J. 2011, 'Job sharing: A literature review'. In L. Daniels (ed.), *Job Sharing at Senior Level: Making it Work* (pp. 46–56). Report prepared for Capability Jane, The New World of Work, UK.

Wang, S., Yi, X., Lawler, J. & Zhang, M. 2011, 'Efficacy of high performance work practices in Chinese companies', *International Journal of Human Resource Management*, 22(11), 2419–2441.

Westerlund, H., Vahtera, J., Ferrie, J.E., Singh-Manoux, A., Pentti, J., Melchior, M., Leineweber, C., Jokela, M., Siegriest, J., Goldberg, M., Zins, M. & Kivimäki, M. 2010, 'Effect of retirement on major chronic conditions and fatigue: French GAZEL occupational cohort study', *British Medical Journal*, 341, c6149.

Whyman, P.B., Baimbridge, M.J., Buraimo, B.A. & Petrescu, A.I. 2015, 'Workplace flexibility practices and corporate performance: Evidence from the British private sector', *British Journal of Management*, 26(3), 347–364.

Wright, P.M., Dunford, B.M. & Snell, S.A. 2001, 'Human resources and the resource-based view of the firm', *Journal of Management*, 27(6), 701–721.

Wright, P.M. & McMahan, D.C. 2011, 'Exploring human capital: Putting human back into strategic human resource management', *Human Resource Management Journal*, 21(2), 93–104.

16 Flexible working for older workers

Carol Atkinson

Introduction

Working populations across the Global North are ageing rapidly, meaning that human resource practices that address the needs of older workers are increasingly important. Definitions of what constitutes an older worker vary, but most suggest that those aged 50 or older fall into this category (Atkinson & Sandiford, 2016), albeit women are often considered to be 'older' at a younger age than men (Loretto et al., 2005). Another important factor is chronological versus subjective age (Nagy et al., 2019). The former is fixed from date of birth, the latter reflects how old someone actually feels – which can vary widely depending on a number of factors, such as health or individual perceptions. Perceptions of subjective age and other issues, such financial status, marital status and career stage, mean that the over-50s form a very diverse group and practices designed to meet their needs should reflect this in order to be effective (Bal & Jansen, 2015).

In the UK, the number of workers aged 50 or over already exceeds 10 million, an increase of 30% in just a decade. These numbers will only continue to grow (Centre for Ageing Better (CfAB), 2018) and the number of people aged over 65 is set to increase by more than 40% by 2040 (CfAB, 2019). The state pension age has been increased and the default retirement age, which required a worker to retire at a specific age, abolished (Cridland, 2017), and skill gaps are predicted as the younger generation shrinks (Chartered Institute of Personnel and Development (CIPD), 2019a). These patterns are reflected across developed economies and extending working lives is a focus for policy-makers internationally, as part of a discourse of active ageing. Zaidi et al.'s (2016) Active Ageing Index (AAI), for example, compares how countries differ on enabling active and healthy ageing and has 'supporting workers to remain in employment into older age' as the first domain of active ageing. Their analysis of European countries demonstrates that Scandinavian countries, the UK, Netherlands and Ireland fare best, many southern Europe countries form a middle group and Greece, together with many Central European countries, brings up the rear. Their analysis also evidences that women fare worse than men in their experiences of remaining in the labour market beyond 50. The UK's relative success in the AAI analysis may relate to long-standing policy initiatives, including Fuller [i.e. longer] Working Lives (Department for Work and Pensions (DWP), 2017), and similar types of initiative can be seen in countries beyond Europe, e.g. Australia (see, for example, Perera et al., 2015).

Note, however, our use of the term 'relative success'. For in the UK, despite initiatives such as Fuller Working Lives (DWP, 2017), more than a quarter of those aged over 50 and who are not eligible for the UK state pension until 65 or later are not in work (CfAB, 2018). Further, less than half of older workers are in employment by the date they eligible for their state pension (Thomson, 2018). Of these, 1 million are not working but would like to be, the so-called 'missing million' (Business in the Community, 2014). Older women particularly are in or seeking work, even though their economic activity rates remain below those of men of a similar age (Zaidi et al., 2016). While the reasons for this are complex, older workers face age discrimination, and women face both age *and* sex discrimination (Riach et al., 2015). Health and caring responsibilities also combine for some to create difficulty in remaining in employment. Despite the best efforts of policy-makers, many organisations seem oblivious to the ageing demographic and the fact that the older workforce is a reality, failing to take any action to support their recruitment and retention (CfAB, 2018). A change in organisational culture that supports older workers in remaining in employment is urgently needed and, without this, workers, organisations and wider society will suffer (CfAB, 2019).

Flexible working is one of the five strategies recommended by CfAB (2018) that supports extended employment for older workers. Other research supports this as well. The Taylor Review of Good Work (2017), for example, identified older workers as a key group that benefits from flexible working, and this is echoed by Thomson (2018). Indeed, benefits from flexibility for this group may exceed those for younger workers (Pitt-Catsouphes & Matz-Costa, 2008) because they are such a diverse group (Bal & Jansen, 2015). Despite this, as we discuss in this chapter, the offer of flexible work to older workers is limited (CIPD, 2019a).

We start this chapter by first defining flexible working and then we discuss formal flexible working arrangements (FWAs) that meet the needs of older workers. We then discuss how these arrangements need not be formal and policy-driven but can be arrived at both via personalised arrangements and informally. We next consider the offer and take-up of flexible working before concluding with some practical recommendations for accommodating older workers' needs for flexibility and for extending their working lives.

Flexible working practices

Flexible working can be hard to define and can take many forms. For example, the CIPD (2019a) recently argued that it is simply anything that is not a standard 9 am to5 pm, Monday to Friday working pattern. One common practice is part-time working, for which there is no standard definition but which usually comprises less than 30 working hours per week (Office for National Statistics (ONS), 2018). Other practices include: compressed working weeks, e.g. 37 hours across 4 days; or other forms of time compression, e.g. 9-day fortnights; term-time-only, where no work is scheduled in school holidays; job share, where 2 workers split a job role; and flexitime and annual hours, neither of which involve reduced working hours, but rather their flexible scheduling. These types of flexibility address hours of work; other types of flexibility address place of work, for example the ability to work remotely and/or from home. For more a detailed explanation of flexible working practices, see Torrington et al. (2020).

While other types of flexibility exist, they are not a focus of discussion in this chapter. Here we focus on flexibility that benefits workers and not that which is predominantly for employer benefit. Flexibility should be a contract of choice (Atkinson & Sandiford, 2016) and the negotiated work arrangements should be of mutual benefit (Smeaton & Parry, 2018). Good quality flexible work is important and we do not include practices such as zero-hours working, where no guaranteed hours of work are offered, as these often serve to undermine job quality (Taylor, 2017). It is nevertheless important to note that the over-65s form one of the largest groups on zero-hour contracts (CIPD, 2019a) and that these workers are often susceptible to job intensification, at the very time of their lives when they may wish to reduce the pressures upon them (Perera et al., 2015). Poor work-life balance can also reduce job quality (CIPD, 2019c) and so flexible working/good quality jobs go hand in hand. Recognition is emerging that the flexibility needs of older workers can be different to those of other workforce groups (CIPD, 2019a) and we discuss this in more detail in the next section. Here, we simply note that the over-50s indicate that the offer of flexible work would both encourage them to delay retirement and support those aged 50–64 who are out of the labour market, and who often struggle to re-enter it, to return (Thomson, 2018). Flexible working is thus important for the older workers themselves, organisations and wider society.

Formal flexible working arrangements for older workers

Definitions of flexible working arrangements usually comprise temporal flexibility, variations in time worked and spatial flexibility (variations in where the work is undertaken) (see e.g. Maxwell et al., 2007). Discussion of flexibility typically focuses on *formal* FWAs, that is, an offer is arrived at via use of organisational policy and leads to permanent rearrangement of working patterns. Formal FWAs are the focus of this section, although we note the increasing importance of *personalised* FWAs (arrived at by mutual agreement rather than policy) and *informal* FWAs (ad hoc or temporary arrangements) and consider these later. As noted above, FWAs are currently mainly designed to meet the needs of working parents rather than other groups such as older workers. There is much discussion, given demographic change, of the four generation (4G) workforce that includes workers aged from 18 to 80 plus and how to manage their diverse needs (Thomson, 2018). The notion that the needs and preferences of entire cohorts can be easily categorised is open to challenge (e.g. Smeaton & Parry, 2018) and we broadly agree that 4G is overly simplistic. That said, the flexible working needs of older workers can be very different to those of working parents (or of other groups, e.g. younger workers) (CIPD, 2019a). Here we consider FWAs that might particularly suit older workers, although that is not to say that they could not also benefit other workforce groups.

Buyens et al. (2009) carried out one of the most detailed studies of older workers and how their late career might be managed. They proposed several groups of practices (not all FWAs) that might support their retention in the workplace. We have grouped these as follows:

- *Adjustment in obligations related to contractual time*: removal of shift work or overtime; taking extra holidays.
- *Adjustment of role*: more/less demanding responsibilities; release from specific tasks; adjustments designed to improve efficiency and comfort in the working environment.
- *Adjustment in working hours*: more flexible patterns; reduced hours.
- *Focus on development*: extra training; career management support (neither discussed in this chapter).
- *Financial arrangements*: partial drawing of pension; retention bonus for remaining past a particular date (only the former is discussed in the chapter as it supports flexible working).
- *Bridge employment*: transfer to a different (often less demanding role) within the organisation; transfer to (a different often less demanding role in) another organisation.

What is immediately obvious is that Buyen et al.'s (2009) list, although including FWA arrangements that are temporal or spatial, goes beyond this to present different forms of flexibility. Of particular interest are adjustments of role and bridge employment, neither of which are typically present in current discussions of FWAs. Our own work supports their inclusion, with one of our projects, which explored the FWA needs of older workers, clearly highlighting their importance (Atkinson & Sandiford, 2016).

In Table 16.1, we present currently well-recognised FWAs relating to temporal and spatial adjustments. While these typical FWAs might suit older workers, we also indicate how they could be varied to better address their needs as many are usually designed to meet the (often different) needs of working parents. We also include adjustments of role and bridge employment and outline how these might be offered. We then discuss these FWAs in more detail in the rest of this section.

Table 16.1 FWAs for older workers

Type of flexibility	Typical practices	Practices addressing older worker needs
Temporal	Part-time	Removal of shift work/overtime
	Job share	Extra holiday (possibly in blocks)
	Term-time only	Elder care leave
	Compressed working weeks	Phased retirement
	Flexitime	Adjustments to accommodate
	Annual hours	health needs
Work role	N/A	Adjustment of role
		Bridge employment within organisation (downshifting) or to new employers
		Improving comfort/efficiency in the work environment
Spatial	Tele-/remote working	Adjustments to accommodate
	Working from home	health needs

Temporal flexibility

Temporal FWAs vary the number and timing of hours worked. As we note in Table 16.1, common practices here include part-time working, job share, term-time working, compressed working weeks, flexitime and annualised hours. In the working population as a whole, these types of FWAs tend to be taken up by women (Atkinson & Hall, 2009), particularly where they accommodate the *reduction of* rather than the *rearrangement* of hours. This reflects the UK's 'male breadwinner' model (Rubery & Hebson, 2018), where men tend to work (often long) full-time hours and women, especially those raising children, tend to work part-time (Healy et al., 2018). Men generally, including the over-50s, draw mainly on flexitime and annualised hours arrangements (CIPD, 2019a), where no time (and income) reduction is involved. Part-time work in the over-50s is still a largely female occurrence, perhaps because of ongoing caring responsibilities, e.g. for grandchildren or parents. As we note above, however, older workers might also benefit from additional temporal FWAs designed to meet their particular needs and this is now discussed.

Removal of shift work/overtime

Buyens et al. (2009) identified demand among older workers for flexibility around working patterns that might place additional burdens upon them. Central to this was the option to cease working shifts or overtime, perhaps because of the demands that these practices make. While not always easy to accommodate, this is an important matter to consider in designing work that is attractive to this demographic group.

Extra holiday

Buyens et al. (2009) similarly argued that older workers value the option to take extra holiday, often to accommodate family or health needs. In our work, we identified a demand for so-called 'Benidorm leave', which relates to a trend of older people spending the winter in warmer climes. Here workers were offered blocks of annual leave, up to three months in some cases, which they could use to spend winter in another country but for other reasons too (Atkinson & Sandiford, 2016). Our research demonstrated, for example, that older workers also used this FWA to fulfil their travel ambitions (travelling while still in relatively good health) or to visit children and grandchildren who lived overseas. Blocked leave can thus be either a regular annual event or organised on an occasional basis. Other forms of additional leave will also be valued by older workers.

Elder care leave

Elder care refers to looking after older dependants, often parents. For many, its demands are less predictable than childcare, with the potential for sudden health crises. While UK legislation does offer emergency leave for domestic responsibilities, this is often short term in nature and can be unpaid. More supportive policies that offer working-time flexibility to deal with health crises, together with blocks of leave for end-of-life care, were much appreciated by the older workers in our study, and prevented them from having to temporarily exit the labour market or indeed retire when dependants had health crises (Atkinson & Sandiford, 2016).

Phased retirement

Perera et al. (2015) demonstrated the importance of allowing flexibility around retirement itself. Older workers may not wish to adopt a 'cliff edge' approach of working one day and not the next. Part-time working can be important in a phased approach to retirement (see e.g. Smeaton & Parry, 2018), particularly where this is accompanied by a partial drawing of any pension (Buyens et al., 2009). Given the complexity of pensions, FWAs that specify how to approach and support the offer of phased retirement are important to older workers.

Adjustments to accommodate health needs

Older workers may need to manage chronic health conditions while in work and, for women, growing numbers are also working while in menopause transition (Atkinson et al., 2018). This is increasingly recognised as an issue of significant importance. While the menopause is a natural biological process, up to three-quarters of women experience troublesome symptoms and around a quarter have symptoms that have a substantially negative impact on their lives and well-being (CIPD, 2019b). While taking sick leave is an option, many seek to avoid this and well-designed FWAs can be of support. For example, the UK police service uses 'passports' for women in menopause transition (Brewis et al., 2017), whereby flexibility in working hours can be agreed on an 'as and when' needed basis and recorded on the passport. The woman then simply has to show the passport to their line manager/supervisor to access the required flexibility. Passports can also be effective for other chronic health conditions and avoid the need for repeated discussion of sensitive conditions, supporting older workers to continue to work while managing health conditions.

Work-role flexibility

As already noted, there is little current recognition of work-role flexibility as an FWA that supports older workers. We argue that it is an important form of flexibility for this group and we outline below some key practices, arguing that job crafting is vital to support this (Nagy et al., 2019).

Adjustment of role

Both our work (Atkinson & Sandiford, 2016) and that of Buyens et al. (2009) has demonstrated the importance of the adjustment of role, which involves adding, changing or removing tasks to/from the roles of older workers. One example from our study was an older car mechanic who no longer pushed cars into and out of the workshop, relying on team members to do that. He nevertheless brought huge knowledge and experience that was of substantial benefit to the team. Another worker no longer dealt with telephone calls as she found this difficult, but she was able to make a valuable contribution in face-to-face customer contact and data inputting. Recently, the concept of *job crafting* has come to prominence (Nagy et al., 2019), and we use that here as a mechanism to explain how and why older workers may seek to adapt the contents of their jobs.

Job crafting is a 'form of proactive work behaviour that is defined as the self-initiated changes regarding one's job which are aimed at optimizing the alignment of personal preferences, goals, and motives with one's job' (Tims et al., 2016, p. 45). Job crafting is often positioned as a way for workers to take on additional challenges, but it may also offer other ways of adapting the job to suit the needs of older workers (see e.g. Nagy et al., 2019). The key is the job/person fit, that is, the match between a worker's characteristics (e.g. knowledge, skills, abilities, needs) and the job's tasks (Kooij et al., 2017). Crafting (i.e. adjusting the tasks in the job) seeks to improve this fit and is important for older workers, as fit changes over time and as a result of their changing needs, preferences and abilities (Nagy et al., 2019). Tims et al. (2016) evidence the importance of improving the job-person fit in maintaining motivation and so job crafting supports older workers in having positive workplace experiences. Indeed, Kooij et al. (2017) have argued that older workers have better insights into their strengths and needs, and they are more likely to seek to influence their fit with a role; they are also more likely to be successful in this as they tend to be more confident. As we noted at the outset, there can be a difference between chronological and subjective age (Nagy et al., 2019), and so older workers can be a very varied workforce group, with their careers less fixed to rigid timeframes than those of other groups (Van der Heijden, 2015). Job crafting then becomes a very useful tool to offer the flexibility individual workers need at particular points in their later working lives.

Job crafting can be challenging at a policy level, however, as its very responsiveness to individual needs makes it difficult to provide universally. Nevertheless, organisations need to find innovative approaches to role design (Thomson, 2018) and policy can be explicit in offering older workers the opportunity to have discussions about job crafting and in encouraging line managers to be responsive to this. The kinds of i-deals we discuss later also provide an effective mechanism to support job crafting.

Bridge employment

Bridge employment differs from adjustment of role discussed above in that it involves a complete change in role. When these job moves are not on a traditional linear career trajectory, they are often referred to as downshifting when in the same organisation, or as bridge employment when moving to a different organisation (Atkinson & Sandiford, 2016). Perera et al. (2015) explored the exit decisions of older workers and evidenced many of these types of job moves, and that exit decisions are more complex than remain or retire. Yet policies are needed to support workers in accessing this type of FWA. Downshifting is countercultural, as most organisations have embedded expectations that job moves will be upwards or, at the very least, sideways. Downward moves can thus be met with resistance, amid fears of overqualification or demotivation. Opportunities to move to less demanding roles should be made explicitly available via policy, and line managers and colleagues encouraged to see the benefits of this. There were a small number of examples of this in our research project and they were generally successful, a team supervisor moving to an administrative role for instance, but these were unusual and downward moves were often not well accommodated (Atkinson & Sandiford, 2016).

Similarly, policy should provide for recruitment of those who have worked at a more senior level elsewhere into a different organisation, that is, bridge employment, and again address barriers created by employer concerns about overqualification. It is often very difficult for older workers to access bridge employment, literally a bridge between a more demanding and a less demanding stage of their career and retirement. Nevertheless, our research demonstrated that this could be successful. In one instance, the former area manager of a national car parking firm joined a small firm to run its two car parks; in another, a former RAC engineer worked as a mechanic (Atkinson & Sandiford, 2016). Both made substantial contributions to the organisation they joined. Organisational policy should be explicit in providing for bridge employment as an effective mechanism to extend the working lives of older workers.

Improving comfort/efficiency in the work environment

Buyens et al. (2009) propose improving comfort/efficiency but give little detail about what this might involve. It is likely to include FWAs that accommodate workers' changing physical abilities. In our study, for example, work was rearranged so that an older worker who had had a hip replacement did not have to use the stairs for an agreed period of time (Atkinson & Sandiford, 2016). Other adjustments might include offering reading aids or chairs and other equipment that supports any physical requirements.

Spatial flexibility

Spatial flexibility refers to where hours are worked, and usually includes working remotely (sometimes at home) or working at varied office bases. Here the needs of older workers appear to be largely similar to those of other workforce groups, although the use of passports to support health needs, which we discussed above, can be used to authorise spatial flexibility. Use of technology can also support in adapting job roles to the needs of older workers and make it easier for them to work remotely (Thomson, 2018).

Personalised approaches to flexibility

So far, we have focused on formal FWAs, the offer of which is provided for by organisational policy. There is, however, a growing trend to adopt more personalised approaches to agreeing employment terms and conditions, and this includes flexibility (Bal & Jansen, 2015). These personalised approaches are referred to as 'i-deals' (Bayazit & Bayazit, 2019) and describe FWAs that are formally offered but as a result of individual negotiation not policy. In our study, this happened because we investigated small firms that often did not have formal policies (Atkinson & Sandiford, 2016). It is becoming more common, however, for these agreements to happen in larger firms as a recruitment and retention mechanism: there is no policy that provides for a particular FWA, but a potential or current employee negotiates as it as part of their idiosyncratic (individualised) deal (Rousseau et al., 2006). This is a very powerful mechanism for accommodating the needs of the heterogeneous older worker group (Perera et al., 2015) and can include any of the FWAs discussed in the previous section. It is extremely effective in meeting wide-ranging and often changing individual needs and allowing the organisation to be highly responsive (CfAB, 2018). It does, however, require careful management to avoid perceptions of, or the realities of, favouritism, unfairness or indeed discrimination (see Rousseau et al. (2006) for further discussion of this).

Informal approaches to flexibility

So far, we have discussed formal FWAs, arrived at by either application of policy or negotiated via an i-deal. There is also growing recognition of the importance of an additional form of flexibility, informal flexibility (de Menzes & Kelliher, 2017). Here, FWAs are not permanently embedded in contracts of employment. Rather they are ad hoc arrangements that are often temporary and are negotiated between a manager and employee to meet their particular circumstances. CfAB (2018) gives the example of a carer who was allowed to keep their phone on their desk in an environment where this was usually prohibited, in case their dependant needed to make contact. In our research, older workers appreciated informal flexibility to deal with unexpected caring or health situations, or sometimes simply to meet one-off commitments (Atkinson & Sandiford, 2016). CfAB (2018) argues that informal flexibility can be as beneficial in particular situations as contractual FWAs. In one of the few studies of this, there was greater uptake of informal than formal FWAs (de Menzes & Kelliher, 2017). Their use is perhaps underreported, and hence undervalued, as there tends to be little measurement or visibility of their usage (CIPD, 2019a). Yet they may better meet workers' needs and thus drive the positive attitudes discussed below (de Menzes & Kelliher, 2017). Skilling managers to support and offer informal flexibility is an important organisational priority.

Offer of flexible working for older workers

In the UK, workers have the legislative right to request flexible working. For older workers, this is a relatively recent development, as it was only extended to include them (other than if they had caring responsibilities) in 2014. Rather than legislation, policy more typically relies upon a business case to promote the offer of FWAs. In the case of older workers, it argues that their skills, knowledge and experience make them an important labour market group and that their recruitment and retention is vital to organisational success. This is reflected in initiatives such as Fuller Working Lives (DWP, 2017), the government-/CIPD-led Taskforce on Flexible Working that started in 2018 and the Women and Equalities Commission 'Older People and Employment Inquiry' that also published its findings in 2018. These initiatives have, however, generally presented somewhat disappointing findings on FWAs, evidencing that its overall offer has stalled in the past ten years (CIPD, 2019a). While the reasons for this levelling off are somewhat unclear, it may be that it is seen as an unaffordable luxury in times of austerity (Lewis et al., 2017).

Also, management attitudes that outside commitments are an individual responsibility seem to persist stubbornly (van Wanrooy et al., 2013). The offer of flexibility to older workers is also limited, despite being highly valued (Marvell & Cox, 2018). Buyens et al. (2009) investigated the offer of formal FWAs to older workers already in employment and did indeed find that their use was not widespread. No single practice was offered by more than 25% of organisations, and for those offered by more than 20% the figures are: taking additional holidays, 24%; more flexible working hours, 20%; phased retirement, 24%; and improving comfort and efficiency, 25%. This would appear to be very short-sighted given the strength of the business case outlined below for offering FWAs to older workers and the missed opportunity to build a reputation as an employer of choice for this important workforce group (Smeaton & Parry, 2018).

The business case for offering FWAs to older workers rests on three pillars: ease of recruitment, the creation of positive attitudes that enhance their performance, and improved retention. Taking first recruitment, there is evidence that the offer of FWAs attracts older workers and thus widens an organisation's potential pool of labour (Perera et al., 2015). Despite this, it is rarely used. Figures vary, but the Women and Equalities Committee (2016) suggests that only around 6% of vacancies are advertised offering FWAs to older workers, while CfAB (2018) found that only around 10% use it in recruitment for this group. Whatever the exact figure, it is clearly very small. Second, FWAs have been widely demonstrated to create positive worker attitudes, including job satisfaction (Wheatley, 2017), increased goodwill and improved productivity (Clarke & Holdsworth, 2017), and better employee engagement (Pitt-Catsouphes & Matz-Costa, 2008). For older workers particularly, they offer support in fulfilling their potential at work (Marvell & Cox, 2018). FWAs do need, however, to be well managed, otherwise they can create perceptions of unfairness and stress (Smeaton & Parry, 2018). Finally, FWAs have been demonstrated to aid in the retention of older workers, particularly where role redesign enhances job quality (Perera et al., 2015), and their individualised offer is important to this retention (Pitt-Catsouphes & Matz-Costa, 2008). This helps to address the concerns of around a quarter of UK workers, one-third of lower-skilled workers, who fear that they may not be able to continue in their job beyond the age of 60 (Thomson, 2018). They are of particular benefit to those with health difficulties or caring responsibilities (CfAB, 2018). Smeaton and Parry (2018) do, however, sound a note of caution that they can perhaps trap workers, citing a Timewise Foundation study in 2013 that found that around two-thirds of older workers with FWAs would not move employers due to concerns around not being able to find alternative FWAs. The overwhelming evidence, however, supports a clear business case for offering FWAs to older workers: they create labour market advantages in recruitment, they underpin positive attitudes that lead to improved performance and they help to retain an (often) skilled and experienced labour market group.

Uptake of flexible working by older workers

Despite the positive business case outlined above, the offer of FWAs remains relatively limited and their uptake has also stalled in past ten years (CIPD, 2019a). Using Labour Force Survey data, Smeaton and Parry (2018) demonstrated that around only 25% of men aged 50-plus have some form of FWA, mainly flexitime, annualised hours and zero-hours, and we have above noted concerns about the extent to which zero-hours actually benefits workers. For women aged 50-plus, around 30% have some form of FWA, mainly part-time and flexitime. This limited uptake would appear to be a missed opportunity, and in what follows we discuss the likely reasons for this, including line manager attitudes and structural and cultural resistance.

Line manager attitudes

Line manager attitudes can both promote and create a barrier to the uptake of flexible working. To effectively support its uptake, they need information on policy and practice and training on how to design flexible jobs and support flexible working processes (Smeaton & Parry, 2018). They also need information and training on how to support informal FWAs (CfAB, 2018). A good understanding of the business case is also important in encouraging a supportive response from them. Further, they need to create awareness/ knowledge about the FWAs on offer, whether via policy, i-deal or informal means, as a lack of visibility often leads to a lack of uptake (Atkinson & Hall, 2009). A lack of skills and confidence often leads managers to resist offering FWAs. Both CIPD (2019a) and CfAB (2018) also argue that the uptake of FWAs at a senior level is needed to create positive role models for others to emulate. In our research, however, we found that older workers at senior levels who wished to work flexibly also met with resistance to their requests (Atkinson & Sandiford, 2016). Influencing line managers and supporting their own desire to access FWAs is fundamental to encouraging the wider uptake of flexibility.

Structural and cultural resistance

There is a widespread resistance to FWAs in many organisations. This is particularly so in cultures where long hours are worked, where there is a lack of willingness to explore what flexibility might look like, together with a view that the rearrangement of work to accommodate it is not possible. In our own work with the police service, for example, concerns about offering flexibility to those coping with symptoms of menopause transition were expressed, amid fears that it would be 'opening the floodgates' to requests that could not be accommodated (Atkinson et al., 2018). Older workers have also expressed concerns that they will be seen as less motivated and committed, and thus more vulnerable to redundancy and dismissal as an older workforce group (Smeaton & Parry, 2018). There can also be a lack of understanding on how to accommodate their needs for flexibility, given how different these can be for groups such as working parents, and a resistance to different ways of working (CfAB, 2018). Older workers are also overrepresented in the SME sector, where sophisticated human resource practice is often lacking and concerns over resource constraints create barriers to uptake (Smeaton & Parry, 2018). Our own work in small firms, however, demonstrates that an informal approach to FWAs can be very successful (Atkinson & Sandiford, 2016).

More training, information and supportive attitudes are essential if the uptake of FWAs among older workers is to increase.

Recommendations

Drawing our discussions together, we present here some practical steps for organisations that will support the design, offer and uptake of FWAs for older workers and allow both them and the organisations to reap the benefits.

Build a business case for FWAs

It is important to demonstrate the organisational benefits of FWAs, which re-quires collection of data on their offer and uptake. For example, with formal FWA requests, how many there have been and whether they have been ap-proved; with informal FWAs, what is their prevalence and usage (Smeaton & Parry, 2018). Benefits in terms of recruitment, attitudes and retention should also be measured through, for example, opinion surveys, exit interviews and focus groups.

Offer FWAs that address older worker needs

Organisations should provide a range of FWAs that are tailored to the needs of older workers (Bal & Jansen, 2015; Smeaton & Parry, 2018). This is not to say that they should only be offered to this group, indeed their wider offer may more generally improve diversity and inclusion, but job redesign and flexibility that goes beyond the needs of working parents is essential. Trials of FWAs may also be effective in building confidence in the feasibility of their offer.

Create role models and champions

Effective communication and creating awareness of available FWAs is im-portant, as is demonstrating that it is culturally acceptable to work flexibly. Ensuring the visibility of role models and appointing champions to promote FWAs will support this (CfAB, 2018)

Support flexible recruitment

Recruitment processes that embed the the offer of flexbility are essential. This might be either through formal FWA policy (Smeaton & Parry, 2018) and/or via i-deals that attract older workers into the organisation (Atkinson & Sandiford; 2016; Bal & Jansen, 2015).

Offer training

Training for both older workers and line managers on how to navigate policy or work with informal FWAs is essential to developing the awareness, capability and attitudes that will create flexibility.

Conduct mid-life reviews

Mid-career/life reviews, or mid-life 'MOTs', were a key recommendation of the Cridland Review (2017). These should be holistic and incorporate considerations of health, finance and working preferences to inform choices that support sustainable working lives. They should be in place around the time workers reach the age of 50, facilitating employment into their 60s, rather than waiting until a later stage when it may not be possible to make necessary adaptations.

Organisations adopting some or all of these recommendations are likely to benefit from recruiting and retaining a skilled and experienced workforce group who can make an important contribution.

References

Atkinson, C., Carmichael, F. & Duberley, J. 2018. The menopause taboo and work: The impact of menopause on the working lives of women in the police force. *Work, Employment and Society Conference*. Belfast.

Atkinson, C. & Hall, L. 2009. The role of gender in various forms of flexible working. *Gender, Work and Organisation*, *16*(6), 650–666.

Atkinson, C. & Sandiford, P. 2016. An exploration of older worker flexible working arrangements in smaller firms. *Human Resource Management Journal*, *26*(1), 12–28.

Bal, P. & Jansen, P. 2015. Idiosyncratic deals for older workers: Increased heterogeneity among older workers enhance the need for i-deals. In P. Bal, D. Kooij & D. Rousseau (eds), *Aging Workers and the Employee-Employer Relationship*. New York: Springer.

Bayazit, Z. & Bayazit, M. 2019. How do flexible work arrangements alleviate work-family-conflict? The roles of flexibility i-deals and familysupportive cultures. *International Journal of Human Resource Management*, *30*(3), 405–435. DOI:10.1080/09585192.2017.1278615

Brewis, J., Beck, V., Davies, A. & Mattheson, J. 2017. The effects of menopause transition on women's economic participation in the UK. In Government Social Research (ed.), *Research Report*. London: Department for Education (DfE).

Business in the Community 2014. *The Missing Million: Illuminating the Employment Challenges of the Over 50s.* London: Business in the Community.

Buyens, D., Van Dijk, H., Dewilde, T. & De Vos, A. 2009. The aging workforce: Perceptions of career ending. *Journal of Managerial Psychology, 24*(2), 102–117.

Centre for Ageing Better (CfAB) 2018. *Becoming an Age-Friendly Employer.* London: Centre for Ageing Better.

Centre for Ageing Better (CfAB) 2019. *The State of Ageing in 2019: Adding Life to Our Years.* London: Centre for Ageing Better.

Chartered Institute of Personnel and Development (CIPD) 2019a. *Megatrends: Flexible Working.* London: CIPD.

Chartered Institute of Personnel and Development (CIPD) 2019b. *Menopause at Work.* London: CIPD.

Chartered Institute of Personnel and Development (CIPD) 2019c. *UK Working Lives.* London: CIPD.

Clarke, S. & Holdsworth, L. 2017. *Flexibility in the Workplace: Implications of Flexible Work for Individuals, Teams and Organisations.* London: Acas.

Cridland, J. 2017. State pension age independent review: Final report [online], https://www.gov.uk/government/publications/state-pension-age-independent-review-final-report

Department for Work and Pensions (DWP) 2017. *Fuller Working Lives: A Partnership Approach.* London: DWP.

Healy, G., Tatli, A., Ipek, G., Ozturk, M., Seierstad, C. & Wright, T. 2018. In the steps of Joan Acker: A journey in researching inequality regimes and intersectional inequalities. *Gender, Work and Organisation*, DOI:10.1111/gwao.12252.

Kooij, D., van Woerkom, M., Wilkenloh, J., Dorenbosch, L. & Denissen, J. 2017. Job crafting towards strengths and interests: The effects of a job crafting intervention on person–job fit and the role of age. *Journal of Applied Psychology, 102*(6), 71–981.

Lewis, S., Anderson, D. & Wood, S. 2017. Public sector austerity cuts in Britain and the changing discourse of work–life balance. *Work Employment and Society, 31*(4), 586–604.

Loretto, W., Vickerstaff, S. & White, P. 2005. *Older Workers and Options for Flexible Work.* Manchester: EOC.

Marvell, R. & Cox, A. 2018. *Fulfilling Work: What Do Older Workers Value About Work and Why?* London: IES/CfAB.

Maxwell, G., Rankine, L., Bell, S. & MacVicar, A. 2007. The incidence and impact of flexible working arrangements in smaller businesses. *Employee Relations, 29*(2), 138–161.

de Menzes, L. & Kelliher, C. 2017. Flexible working, individual performance and employee attitudes: Comparing formal and informal arrangements. *Human Resource Management, 56*(6), 1051–1070.

Nagy, N., Johnston, C. & Hirschi, A. 2019. Do we act as old as we feel? An examination of subjective age and job crafting behaviour of late career employees. *European Journal of Work and Organizational Psychology, 28*(3), 373–383.

Office for National Statistics (ONS) 2018. *Employment and Labour Market: People in Work* [ONS online], https://www.ons.gov.uk/employmentandlabourmarket/peopleinwork/employmentandemployeetypes/timeseries/lf2v/lms [last accessed 4 February 2018].

Perera, S., Sardeshmukh, S. & Kulik, C. 2015. In or out: Job exits of older workers. *Asia Pacific Journal of Human Resources, 53*(1), 4–21.

Pitt-Catsouphes, M. & Matz-Costa, C. 2008. The multi-generational workforce: Workplace flexibility and engagement. *Community, Work and Family, 11*(2), 215–229.

Riach, K., Loretto, W. & Krekula, C. 2015. Gendered ageing in the new economy: Introduction to special issue. *Gender, Work and Organization, 22*(5), 437–444.

Rousseau, D., Ho, V. & Greenberg, J. 2006. I-deals: Idiosyncratic terms in employment relationships. *Academy of Management Review, 31*(4), 977–994.

Rubery, J. & Hebson, G. 2018. Applying a gender lens to employment relations: Revitalisation, resistance and risks. *Journal of Industrial Relations, 60*(3), 414–436.

Smeaton, D. & Parry, D. 2018. Becoming an age-friendly employer: Evidence report. London: Centre for Better Ageing.

Taylor, M. 2017. *Good Work: The Taylor Review of Modern Working Practices*. London: Department for Business, Energy and Industrial Strategy.

Thomson, P. 2018. *A Silver Lining for the UK Economy? The Intergenerational Case for Supporting Longer Working Lives*. London: Centre for Ageing Better.

Tims, M., Derks, D. & Bakker, A. 2016. Job crafting and its relationships with person–job fit and meaningfulness: A three-wave study. *Journal of Vocational Behavior, 92*(1), 44–53.

Torrington, D., Hall, L., Taylor, S. & Atkinson, C. 2020. *Human Resource Management* (11th ed.). Harlow, UK: Pearson.

Van der Heijden, B. 2015. Sustainable careers: Introductory chapter. In B. Van der Heijden & A. De Vos (eds), *Handbook of Research on Sustainable Careers*. Cheltenham, UK: Edward Elgar.

van Wanrooy, B., Bewley, H., Bryson, A., Forth, J., Freeth, S., Stokes, L. & Wood, S. 2013. *The 2011 Workplace Employment Relations Study: First Findings*. London: BIS.

Wheatley, D. 2017. Employee satisfaction and use of flexible working arrangements. *Work Employment and Society, 31*(4), 567–585.

Women and Equalities Committee 2018. Older People and Employment Inquiry [online], https://www.parliament.uk/business/committees/committees-a-z/commons-select/women-and-equalities-committee/inquiries/parliament-2017/older-people-and-employment-17-19/publications

Women and Equalities Committee 2016. *Gender Pay Gap: Second Report of Session 2015–16* (HC 584). London: House of Commons.

Zaidi, A., Gasior, K., Zolyomi, E., Schmidt, A., Rodrigues, R. & Marin, B. 2016. Measuring active and healthy ageing in Europe. *Journal of European Social Policy*, DOI:10.1177/0958928716676550

Index

Note: **Bold** page numbers refer to tables and *italic* page numbers refer to figures.

For Product Safety Concerns and Information please contact our EU
representative GPSR@taylorandfrancis.com
Taylor & Francis Verlag GmbH, Kaufingerstraße 24, 80331 München, Germany

www.ingramcontent.com/pod-product-compliance
Lightning Source LLC
Chambersburg PA
CBHW070355270326
41926CB00014B/2557